MORALITY AND RELIGION IN LIBERAL DEMOCRATIC SOCIETIES

World Social Systems

Morton A. Kaplan
General Editor

LIBERAL DEMOCRATIC SOCIETIES

Roger Michener and Edward Shils, Editors

THE SOVIET UNION AND THE CHALLENGE OF THE FUTURE

Alexander Shtromas and Morton A. Kaplan, Editors

CHINA IN A NEW ERA

Ilpyong J. Kim, Series Editor

Professors World Peace Academy Books

MORALITY AND RELIGION IN LIBERAL DEMOCRATIC SOCIETIES

Edited by
Gordon L. Anderson
and
Morton A. Kaplan

A PWPA Book

PARAGON HOUSE
New York

Published in the United States by
Professors World Peace Academy
4 West 43 Street
New York, New York 10036

Distributed by Paragon House Publishers
90 Fifth Avenue
New York, New York 10011

A Professors World Peace Academy Book

The Professors World Peace Academy (PWPA) is an international association of
professors, scholars and academics from diverse backgrounds, devoted to issues
concerning world peace. PWPA sustains a program of conferences and publica-
tions on topics in peace studies, area and cultural studies, national and international development, education, economics and international relations.

Library of Congress Cataloging-in-Publication Data

Morality and religion in liberal democratic societies / edited by Gordon L.
Anderson and Morton A. Kaplan.
    372 p.
    "A PWPA Book."
    Includes index.
    ISBN 0-943852-96-X (hard). — ISBN 0-943852-97-8 (pbk.)
    1. Democracy — Religious aspects. 2. Democracy — Moral and ethical aspects.
3. Religious pluralism. 4. Cultural relativism. 5. Religion and state. I. Anderson,
Gordon L. (Gordon Louis), 1947- II. Kaplan, Morton A.
BL65.P7M67   1991
322'.1 — dc20   91-11309
                                                                        CIP

TABLE OF CONTENTS

SERIES EDITORS' FOREWORD

Liberal democratic societies, as patterns of political, economic and social arrangements, would seem to be vindicated against their detractors. Until recently Marxism in its various forms and other proponents of single party states and centrally planned economies appeared to offer realistic and allegedly beneficial alternatives to liberal democracy. Events in China, the Soviet Union, Eastern Europe, and the Third World have so reduced the persuasiveness of these arguments that there are no readily apparent alternatives to liberal democratic societies.

Nevertheless, the discomfitures and embarrassments of single party states should not be regarded as a justification for complacency. We should be appreciative of the merits of liberal democratic societies, but we should be aware of their shortcomings, in light of their own ideals, and of the dangers to which they are liable.

The purpose of the present series of books is to take stock of and to assess, in a historical perspective, the most central achievements and shortcomings of liberal democratic societies, and to encourage thought on their maintenance and improvement.

Not only do we seek to delineate some of these main lines of historical development of the variant forms of liberal democracy, but we also seek to discern certain fundamental postulates that are common to these institutions and processes. In this way, we hope to define more clearly the liberal democratic ideal and its limits. We wish to learn where the practice falls short of the ideal or deforms it. We wish to form an estimate of the destructive forces within the liberal democratic ideal itself and of their potentialities for causing its deteriorization or its collapse. We wish above all to learn how these destructive potentialities may be averted.

MORALITY AND RELIGION

This series insists on the bond between liberalism and democracy. Liberalism and democracy are two distinguishable components of present day liberal democratic societies. Their combination into a particular form of society is a great achievement but it is also a source of difficult problems. For instance, can these societies reconcile the fundamental conflict between minimizing governmental authority and intrusiveness and the democratic demand for more governmental activities and greater governmental provision of welfare services? What are the consequences of some of the institutions of liberal democratic society for the daily life of the individual in his or her private sphere? These questions and others like them constitute a continuing challenge for the present and successor generations. These books are devised to assist in the understanding of that challenge.

In addition to those who contributed chapters to this volume, we recognize the valuable role played by Father Thomas M. Gannon of Loyola University in Chicago and Professor Roger Scruton of the University of London in assisting us in securing the papers herein.

Roger Michener
Edward Shils

INTRODUCTION

Gordon L. Anderson and *Morton A. Kaplan*

This book is designed to explore the relationships between religion and morals on one hand and liberal democracy on the other. With the decline of communism in Eastern Europe, democracy has become highly popular. Yet its continued success is far from assured.

Cultural and religious pluralism are both the glory and the possible bane of democracy. Throughout most of human history people have been acculturated through rituals that could not easily be questioned. Through them, tribes distinguished themselves from others, whom they considered barbarian or evil. In more recent times, divisive religious, cultural, national, or ideological values were taught. In this century, national socialist, fascist, and communist totalitarian value systems were enforced by the power of the state.

Yet in modern liberal democracies, a plurality of cultural and ethnic traditions are able to coexist. There is a strong desire within liberal political theory to prevent the oppression of one group of people by another. However, the current overemphasis on individual desires at the expense of the public good has helped promote rampant problems that threaten the fabric of liberal democracy.

How can we preserve liberal democracy? Several authors of chapters in this book maintain that individualism unguided by tradition and religion will likely give rise to terrorism parallel to that of the French Revolution. Such a juxtaposition equates rationality with rationalism.

However, unlike the French, the British never succumbed to such rationalism. Even Hobbes, whose philosophy was quite similar to French Enlightenment views, took a position that favored public security over individual rights. Was British rationality a product of religion and tradition? Or was it, as Morton Kaplan believes, due to differences in intellectual temperament between the English and the French?

The essays in this book predominantly focus on Judeo-Christian traditions. Historically, these were the two major religions of western Europe and the United States up until the end of World War II. Afterwards, with the increasing mobilization of virtually every ethnic population worldwide, this religious balance began to change substantially, introducing a whole new array of issues within pluralistic societies.

The first part of this book examines liberal democratic political theory and the role of morality and religion within a liberal democracy. Robert Grant begins by looking at the concept of liberty, as perceived by major liberal philosophers. He discusses the natural political, economic, mental, and moral constraints put upon freedom. He points to the contradiction within liberalism between its purported goal of achieving maturity of the individual and its theory that an individual is the best judge of his or her own interests. Grant points out that freedom depends upon the use of one's autonomy. One is not 'unfree' because one has moral inhibitions against certain forms of behavior. He points out that, with the exception of Immanuel Kant, who spoke of obligations, most liberal thinkers base their ethics on rights, which Grant views as implicitly selfish.

Kaplan agrees with the general theses of Grant but uses concepts somewhat differently. Morality is a constraint, but it is also a condition for character. Every freedom depends upon a constraint. The real problem is to determine which freedoms are important. This view is not original. Aristotle made perhaps the original case from the standpoint of eudaemonism. Kaplan's argument is made from the standpoint of the problem of self-identity and the relationship of the self to society. But he acknowledges that it would be too great a charge to expect an intellectual argument alone to preserve liberal democracy. Ecumenical religion and some degree of traditionalism are likely to be more effective guarantors, a view propounded by the founding fathers of the American experiment.

David Levy notes that former supporters of socialism, once convinced of the benefits of rational state control, now attack this position in traditionally liberal terms. In a brief discussion of the liberal positions developed by David Hume, Thomas Hobbes, and Friedrich Hayek, Levy notes that amid the antipolitical sentiment of the time, there is an Aristotelian revival and neo-Hegelian strain that argues the primacy of politics in human self-realization. Given our large ethnically diverse cities and pluralized discourse, Levy views as naive those Aristotelian concepts of a like-minded *polis*. He maintains that we may have to accept a reality in which state and civil societies are differentiated.

Michael Perry, a legal theorist, explains that it is impossibly idealistic to expect pluralistic societies to be morally neutral or impartial. In a discussion of the theories of Bruce Ackerman and Thomas Nagel, Perry shows that their own positions are neither neutral nor impartial toward the convictions of many Americans. Even John Rawls, whose ideas Perry finds more plausible, had to change his conception of justice from 'right prior to good' to a 'good prior to right.' However, Perry contends that because of modern society's vast diversity, it is not feasible for Rawls to develop an 'overlapping consensus' on human good. Rather, Perry believes that pluralism allows for healthy contests over concepts of human good, an 'ecumenical politics,' that will lead to an eventual convergence of our concepts of human good.

Morton Kaplan finds both practical and moral reasons to support the liberal democratic form of government. He begins with a discussion of the development of the contemporary world view and the role of language. Like Perry, Kaplan does not find an adequate foundation for government in a theory of rights. He makes a case for political obligations based on objective morals.

Part II of this volume examines the religious practices and institutions that nurtured the concepts of human nature and goodness espoused by the architects of American liberal democracy. The traditional views of Judaism, Roman Catholicism, and Protestantism on church-state relations are described by Gershon Weiler of Tel Aviv University, Battista Mondin of the Urban Pontifical Institute, and Dean M. Kelley of the National Council of Churches in the United States. They point to the problems that each tradition faces in modern liberal democracies.

Weiler argues that after the fall of the Temple, the church-state problem ceased to be relevant to Judaism. It premised the supremacy of the temple under Davidic rule but not under the latter run of Jewish Kings. Spinoza argued that Jewish law was municipal law only and, therefore, not binding in the Diaspora. However, Moses Mendelssohn later argued that Jewish law still guided behavior among Jews, but not beliefs. However, as Weiler points out, Mendelssohn leaves unanswered the question why the law should be followed if it is not supported by belief.

Although current day Israel was initially founded as a secular state, the conflict between church and state has re-emerged. The religious courts, which alone can perform marriages or grant divorces, supposedly operate under the terms of secular law. Yet the state has never secured the chief rabbi's submission to Israel's Supreme Court. The religious community and the rabbinate in Israel refuse to recognize the legitimacy of non-observing Jews. There is a constant struggle to impose Jewish law on the non-religious.

Weiler concludes that it is not possible for the *Torah* to function as the municipal law of a modern liberal democracy. The only alternatives that remain are assimilation as individuals, secular nationalism, self-ghettoization, or religious fundamentalism. Any solution to the church-state problem, he argues, would turn Judaism into a different religion.

Mondin examines religion and politics from a European Catholic perspective. He starts with the categories of culture, society, and politics in descending order of inclusiveness. Mondin concurs with Tillich's thesis that culture is the form of religion and religion is the substance of culture. However, Mondin rejects the Enlightenment view of religion as the enemy of culture. The death of God, Mondin says, leads to the death of man.

Catholic writing has changed considerably over the centuries, according to Mondin. Augustine believed that the city of man begins with the rebellious angels and Cain's murder of Abel. Hence it was necessary to recreate the City of God. By the time of Boniface VIII, the state was subordinate to the church in matters of faith. According to Aquinas, however, both state and church were perfect societies. Each had its proper end, although there was an implied subordination of state to church.

Mondin notes that although democracy became the dominant political ideal by the nineteenth century, it was not until Vatican II that the church became an advocate of democracy. Then, the Vatican saw freedom of religion as a means for its own protection.

On the other hand, the close connection between the church and the Christian Democratic Party in Italy hastened the secularization of their government, leading to a stifling of religion by the secular culture.

According to Mondin, this was the catalyst for a shift in attitude concerning the function of religion in politics. He supports the position that religious interventions in politics should be restricted to critical problems. This may be satisfactory in western Europe which is democratic and economically developed. However, the conditions in Latin America led to the development of liberation theology and the decision to use Marxist means to revolutionize society.

Although the pope approved the option for the poor, he objected to the class warfare analysis of Marxism. Mondin states that beyond the pope's objection, it is not merely the class analysis but the economic bankruptcy of Marxism that is dangerous. Although many South and Central American societies do require revolutionary change for humanitarian reasons, a move toward real market economies is needed to accomplish this.

Dean M. Kelley of the National Council of Churches had the difficult task of portraying the Protestant approach to church and state, which, because of the profusion of Protestant religions, does not fall into a simple pattern. He accepts Laski's argument that Calvinism is the modern source of Protestant support for liberal democracy. But he finds the origins of Protestantism and its orientation to democratic representation in the Conciliar movement of the late Middle Ages. He finds its inspiration in Gelasius I's percept of the two swords. Kelley has charted the spectrum of Protestant positions which runs from theocracy on the extreme right to secular separationists on the left.

Although Christian faiths often have supported non-democratic governments, Kelley believes they all share beliefs that are congenial to democracy: the dualism of church and state, the sovereignty of God, and the (at least) partly evil character of the state. The Anabaptists felt most strongly about the evil elements of the state and were among the prime movers to work toward the separation of church and state. The United States Supreme Court decision in 1941 against prayers in school, although supported by other religious groups, received its strongest support from Protestant faiths that shared these aspects of the Anabaptist position. However, today there is a strong evangelical movement within Christianity working to reverse this decision.

There is a strong case to be made that prayers in public schools run the risk either of being invidious to some faiths or belief systems—Jews, Moslems, Buddhists, or atheists—or so denatured that they promote the view of a secular religion that is largely ceremonial. On the other hand, there is also the possibility that an absolute wall between state and religion is harmful. Many have ventured that the areligious stance propagated in the schools is rapidly becoming antireligious. One possible solution, the editors suggest, might be to have clerics of different faiths and perhaps even a secular humanist give inspirational sermons at voluntary assemblies. This might help to cultivate a religious spirit without denaturing it or imposing on the beliefs of some.

The third section of this book is an analysis of the antinomies existing between religion and culture and Western liberal democratic governments.

Besançon argues that in the twentieth century, the church blundered by supporting insupportable regimes. It mistook the current totalitarian systems for more traditional authoritarian regimes. In condemning Naziism and communism, the church failed to recognize their truly radical nature. It treated them as equivalents of contemporary Italian, Spanish, and Portuguese authoritarianism.

Besançon points out that in addition to mistaking the true character of political systems, the church also mistook the character of economic systems. Thus, it equated Leninism with socialism. By adopting such inapt views, the church condemned both liberalism and socialism impartially. It viewed capitalism or market economies as exploitative and credited socialism for striving toward justice. Communism was not condemned in principle by Vatican II. Both capitalism and Marxism were condemned as materialistic. This false neutrality between the opposing systems led to a dialogue between Christianity and Marxism that was doomed to failure. This parallel condemnation, coupled with the church's inherent underestimation of Marxism's radical nature, seriously compromised human freedom.

In his essay on religion and American democracy, A. James Reichley states that organized religious institutions are playing a more public political role than ever before. However, Reichley sees this as evidence of a decline in their influence. He presents the rise in public activity as a response to the closure of a former and greater private access. Reichley maintains that this trend is indicative of a decline in religious influence on society. Social values today, both moral and cultural, tend to be secular despite widespread church attendance. This secular trend tends to devalue religion.

Despite contemporary rulings of the United States Supreme Court, Reichley says, the founders of the American Constitution expected religion to play a more significant role in the Republic. Even those founders who were skeptics considered religion a necessity for the majority of Americans. The First Amendment was intended to prevent the federal government from establishing a particular faith as the state religion. Yet Massachusetts had an official state religion as late as 1833. It was not until 1940 that the United States Supreme Court barred the establishment of state religions through its interpretation of the 14th Amendment. Further court decisions eventually led to establishing a wall between religion and the state.

Reichley argues that American democracy is permeated by Judeo-Christian values. Reichley also notes that the Moslem religion and Oriental religious philosophies are consistent with a social orientation that submerges the individual for the greater good of the whole. He asserts that humanism can function only so long as it is permeated by Judeo-Christian values. Minus those values, humanism eventually digresses into endless self-gratification.

Reichley points out the dilemmas faced by religions as they attempt to influence the political process. He believes that churches should influence government only when the most important human values are at stake. As a warning, he cites the failure of the German churches under Hitler. He contends that the Catholic bishops' letter on nuclear arms was an example of appropriate moral leadership, but argues that the Catholic stance on economics was ill-conceived.

There are endless dilemmas regarding the issue of church involvement in politics. Some believe that the formal political role of churches should be restricted only to the most important human values. Others contend that the church should make its views known in every aspect of human endeavor. There is no clear-cut answer on this issue.

Surprisingly to some, George Weigel views the Catholic church as a strong supporter of political democracy. Weigel cites what he considers valid reasons for its hostility toward democracy in modern times. The first reason stemmed from the terrorism generated by the French Revolution on its path to democracy. The second reason stemmed from the newly centralized authority of the pope and the church's reliance upon monarchies for support. The third reason stemmed from the challenge to faith that the church perceived in Darwinism. The final argument stemmed from the fear that religious liberty would produce religious indifference.

An important factor in changing the above attitudes stemmed from the church's experience in America. Religious liberty did not lead to religious indifference. The impact of antidemocratic movements on the church was unfavorable and their impact on society was frequently immoral. Furthermore, the existence of Christian democratic parties in Europe and the decline in anticlericalism provided an added impetus for change.

Most important, according to Weigel, was the principle of subsidiarity of Leo XIII. There were six elements to the principle of subsidiarity. The first stated that the individual was the source and end of society. The second stated that society was an essential requirement for the existence of humanity. The third maintained that the individual should be considered responsible for his or her own choices save under exceptional circumstances. The fourth held that there was a hierarchy of communities, the relative independence of which required respect. The fifth was that each person should encourage the autonomy of other persons. And the last was that the individual should not be deprived of the opportunity to act and choose for himself.

The church's transition favoring democracy culminated in Vatican II. The prominent American Catholic theologian, John Courtney Murray, had long supported this position. Murray based his position on Pope Gelasius I's (494 C.E.) concept of religious liberty in a confessionally neutral state.

According to Weigel, liberation theology, with its politicization of the Gospels, breaks with this tradition of neutrality. Unfortunately, Weigel says, liberation theology found widespread representation within the Catholic church's institutions. Weigel has aptly sketched the broader changes in the position of the Roman Catholic church. However, there have always been countercurrents that transferred the authoritarian character of church government to civil society.

During the fascist period, the Jesuits were strong supporters of fascism and corporatism. After a period of moderation following World War II, many Jesuits, and especially the Maryknoll Order provided strong support to leftist totalitarian movements, particularly in Central America. Unfortunately, as Reichley noted in his essay, they have been joined by some of the professionals within mainline Protestant denominations, who, like the Jesuits and Maryknolls, have ceased to represent the laity.

In the past, the Jesuits were the educated professionals of the Roman Catholic church. Mainline professionals are now more highly educated than ever. One wonders whether there is something within the educational process that produces an antipathy to society and a desire for perfection, even if it must be imposed. From this perspective, the principle of subsidiarity, clearly connected to the concept of a God-given free will, seems to be a strong, and perhaps essential, support for political democracy. From such a religious perspective, the Rousseauian totalitarianism of the religious left, seems to represent nothing less than a rebellion of 'fallen angels' pitting themselves against a God whom perhaps they consider dead.

John Carroll examines the contribution of liberalism to political democracy. He defines liberalism as a philosophy that places essential weight on the rational autonomous individual's exercise of free will. The concept of the autonomous rational individual incorporates essential elements of the Catholic principle of subsidiarity (discussed by Weigel) and free will as a Judeo-Christian principle.

Kaplan argues that the world view of the seventeenth century was one of complete determinism. According to some of the French philosophes, God could predict the future only inasmuch as he knew the initial location and momentum of each atom. Such a philosophy gave rise to rationalism—the deduction of the world from a small set of premises—and a 'mirror image' theory of knowledge in which our ideas reflect an external world. Furthermore, it gave rise to a utilitarianism that treated minds as if they were calculating machines that could arrive at decisions mathematically. That dehumanizing combination helped produce the terror of the French Revolution.

However, this distorted world view is not that of contemporary science. A world view appropriate to contemporary science is not deterministic. It does not accept a copy theory of knowledge. It is loosely rather than strongly ordered. And, as shown in Kaplan's essay, human thinking relies as much upon rules as it does upon flexible calculations to achieve well-being. Such a world view is inconsistent with the rationalism of the French Revolution but is consistent with rationality. Thus Kaplan states individualism by itself would not give rise to the terror of the French Revolution.

However, Kaplan's position is admittedly sophisticated and difficult to understand. Carroll's stance is correct in practice when he states that respect for tradition and religion are the underpinnings of the parliamentary political democratic process.

Part IV of this volume looks at some particularly sensitive and complicated moral issues that have arisen in modern democracy and which have emotionally charged public debates.

Roger Scruton regards the liberal, contractual position on politics as inherently faulty. In the first place, he says, there can be no such thing as a neutral state. This seems eminently correct. Until the United States Supreme Court erected a wall between religion and the state, the American polity was clearly pro-religious. After the wall was built, the state became at least partly antagonistic to religion. A similar problem arose with respect to morality, according to Scruton. Either there is such a thing as a correct morality, in which case the state ought to impose it, or it is a matter of individual choice, in which case there is no barrier to any form or degree of corruption that does not directly harm others. In his essay on liberal democracy, Kaplan takes a position inconsistent with the form in which Scruton states the dilemma. The moral world may be as loosely ordered as the physical world, in which case the state may have an obligation to place limits on behavior but not to impose any strict conception of morals.

Scruton argues that most moral standards come from religion, although Aristotle found a defense of virtue from the standpoint of the individual's happiness. Scruton also argues that it is likely that evolution bonded into humans a receptivity to moral training and virtuous behavior, although that may be negated by conditioning. The moral permissiveness found in contemporary society is likely to undermine those moral sentiments that make for a cohesive and functional society. Scruton then makes the argument that open and legitimized homosexuality is a threat to intergenerational sentiments.

Like Scruton, Geoffrey Partington points out that Protestant fundamentalists were satisfied with the public schools as long as these schools inculcated standard social moral values, which were largely Protestant. However, the Catholics objected on religious grounds. However, by 1970 when 'value-free' education had become quite common, a defensive reaction set in by parents who felt that their children were being indoctrinated with a morally relativistic point of view radically opposed to theirs. Even some parents who were neither Catholics nor fundamentalists began to send their children to private religious schools in preference to the public schools.

According to Partington, parents objected because schools began to teach that there were no bad or inferior students except those who were made that way by society. The schools further digressed to expound all forms of sex as normal. Schools began to propagate radical feminist, homosexual, and other value systems. They even employed encounter groups as a way of transforming the consciousness of young children.

This book also looks at the liberal democracies in eastern Europe and the formation of global democratic culture.

Milowit Kuninski, a Pole, looks at the effect of communism on the moral and cultural values of the societies it dominated. He argues that laws and morals are mutually dependent. Both are necessary for freedom and social order. Both the eastern and western systems have disconnected their governments from the consciences of the citizens. The communists attempted to impose alien legislation through party control, but liberal societies have attempted to substitute legislation for culturally validated law, separating it from its moral justification. In fact, politicians have passed laws based on the weaker part of human nature: lack of discipline, selfishness, and hedonistic passions. Where communist systems are being reformed from above, Kuninski argues that western democracies will have to be reformed from below.

The Catholic church in Poland, the main bastion of moral resistance to the communist system, found itself in a difficult situation
in 1991. Pluralism had re-emerged in Poland and the Catholic
church was one, albeit the strongest, among many voices speaking
out in Poland. The moral basis of the post-communist society must
expand beyond the private sphere and enter the public arena.
This will take time and will be a challenge to both the politicians
and the clergy.

Gordon Anderson looks at the possibility of a global democratic
culture developing values grounded in both scientific and religious tradition. Anderson argues that science can provide a new
understanding of 'natural law' by giving general values and limits
to human behavior through explaining the nature of human life
and physical existence. In his discussions of the 'naturalistic fallacy'
he agrees with Kaplan's analogy of the bridge: one cannot derive a
design for a bridge from the laws of physics, yet a bridge will not
function unless the constraints of those laws are taken into
account. What constitutes 'the good life' is ultimately different in
the mind of each individual. Any attempt to legislate it externally
would be felt as oppression. Anderson argues that each person is
obligated to pursue 'the good life' publicly and to transmit an
image or an example of goodness to inspire others. In the contemporary situation of pluralism, he argues that the doctrine of separation of church and state has been used as a cloak to avoid
teaching difficult and controversial moral positions in public
schools. This produces graduates of public schools who are unable
to make sound value judgments. He argues that it would be far
more productive, in the absence of value agreement, to expose students to a wide array of religious value systems so that they can
make their own choices on the basis of the most complete presen-
tation of possible alternative views.

ONE

FREEDOM FOR WHAT?

R. A. D. Grant

The ground I propose to work has already been so well-tilled that I have no expectation of increasing what seems to be its so far meager yield. Nevertheless, I shall proceed in hope of turning up the odd *trouvaille*.

Let us follow Mill, Berlin, Hayek and others in ruling out as irrelevant any considerations concerning so-called metaphysical liberty or free will. What we are concerned with is political or psychological liberty: we may as well call it distinctively 'human' freedom, by analogy with the usual translation of Dilthey's *Geisteswissenschaften* as the "human sciences." The human sciences, like the conception of liberty I am concerned with, treat choice as being for all practical purposes real, no matter how illusory it may seem, or actually be, in the light of our natural-scientific conceptions.

To begin with as broad and uncontentious a definition as possible, freedom (a term I shall use interchangeably with liberty) consists in the ability to do what you want to do.[1] (Let us postpone the distinction between being able, and being permitted, to do a thing, and the still more important question as to what constitutes a genuine "want.") Like democracy, freedom is a thing which even those suspicious of it in its widest construction nevertheless profess to support in some more qualified sense.

Thus the conservative, for whom the *summum bonum* is "order" of one kind or another, maintains that his conception of order is really "true" liberty, or at least that it distils from the abstract conception of liberty whatever of genuine value it contains. The socialist will do the same for "equality." Liberalism, however, is

13

innocent of such apparent equivocations. For the pure or classical liberal, liberty is the central, explicit goal of political endeavor, and political arrangements the world over, irrespective of the cultures from which they emerge, and over which they notionally preside, are to be judged according to the extent to which they do, or do not, realize it.

To regard liberty as the *summum bonum* is obviously to make it indefeasible under pressure from any rival or superior good (there being none, by definition). Nevertheless, there is an important strand in liberalism which regards liberty less as an end in itself than as an absolutely indispensable means to a yet higher end, viz. fulfillment, self-realization, or individuality. This is to treat not freedom but its consequences, for both individuals and societies, as the good. However, being thus indispensable, liberty will naturally attract to itself all the teleological properties of the good it subserves. Although I believe the idea of self-realization to be the most valuable contribution that liberalism has made to our political self-understanding, as we shall see it also harbors an insight which, if we accept its implications, makes a simple, unqualified liberal conception of freedom impossible to endorse.

So far, the following observations seem to be in order:

1. The definition of liberty as being able to do what you want to do subsumes so-called "positive" and "negative" liberty under a single head. I am not free *to* do a thing (positive liberty) unless I am also free *from* obstacles—of whatever kind—to my doing it (negative liberty).

2. Unlike liberalism—with which it is nevertheless compatible—this definition does not yet accord any value to liberty. The value of liberty may depend on whether what I want to be free to do is itself right, good, or otherwise valuable. Unlike Mill in his *Utilitarianism*, it will not do to equate the desirable or the valuable simply with what people happen to desire or value. Apart from his logical error, Mill is confuted by his own earlier argument to the effect that some desires are qualitatively superior to others. But it is not unreasonable for the liberal to claim that *aggregate* good may be increased by an increase in liberty, despite the fact that what some individuals desire, and are thereby left free to attain, may not necessarily be good. That is an empirical question, to be settled either by experience or (possibly) by cost-benefit analysis.

3. Our formula can be expressed mathematically. To say that freedom consists in the ability to do what you want to do is to say that freedom varies directly with capacity, and inversely with desire (i.e. $F = C/D$). Freedom is increased either by an increase in one's capacity to satisfy one's desires, or by a scaling-down of one's desires to match one's capacity to satisfy them. Conversely, freedom is diminished by any reduction in one's capacity to satisfy one's desires, or by any increase in one's desires relative to one's capacity to satisfy them. It follows that if I have persuaded myself to want nothing at all, I am in a sense totally free, as free as if my most boundless desire were immediately outstripped by my capacity to satisfy it. Each of these extreme cases deserves a passing comment.

In the first, I might be a Buddhist or a Stoic.[2] I have conquered all desire, even the desire to live. The question then arises whether, if I want nothing, I have not also abolished value. Valuation, after all, is a special, personally disinterested case of desire.[3] Moreover, I have not really abolished desire, since I "desire" to remain free of it.

There is, I believe, a certain covert egotism in all doctrines of absolute self-renunciation, which may account for their moral repugnance.[4] The Stoic who can genuinely contemplate the massacre of innocents, or of his nearest and dearest, with equanimity or *apatheia* deserves no one's admiration. It is one thing to be indifferent to one's own sufferings, but another thing altogether to be indifferent to those of others. Somewhat like the pacifist, the Stoic solves life's problems by washing his hands of them or sweeping them under the carpet. Overall, if I am to stay human and not simply sink into insensibility, there are certain things I should continue to want, and some desires from which I ought never to be free.

In the second case, the instantaneous satisfaction of a desire might as well be regarded as its absence or abolition, for a desire is not felt as such until it is constrained. A lotus-eater, like a slug with a lifetime's supply of lettuce, might be thought contented in some very banal sense. But his life could hardly be called satisfying, let alone fulfilling, since in the absence of any obstacles, of any conscious desire, it would lack the dimension of achievement. Neither could it be called "free," since it would not, according to our formula, involve doing anything.[5]

A further case is that of one who enjoys the consciousness of a capacity to satisfy his desires in excess of what they actually are. This, depending on the capacities and desires involved, may be either a virtue or a vice. I may refrain from a crime which I nevertheless know I can commit with impunity. A man endowed with power over others who, in those others' interests, forbears to exercise it may be possessed of magnanimity or self-mastery. On the other hand, he may have sought them solely in order to plume himself on his restraint in not employing them. It is characteristic of Nietzsche, for example, that though he frequently hinted at this distinction, he was generally reluctant to make it. For all his brilliance, there is a certain muscle-bound narcissism about Nietzsche's ethics. They are, if you like, the spiritual equivalent of bodybuilding.

4. Finally, if freedom varies directly with capacity, then it also varies inversely with external constraint, or negative capacity. (The same is not true of internal, or at least of moral, constraints, since those are both self-imposed and revocable in principle, and involve the exercise of other capacities of the subject.) This has the interesting consequence of putting desire (with which freedom also varies inversely) implicitly in the same category as at least some constraints. Much traditional moral thought views desire—or at least, some desires—as a kind of compulsion from which human beings require deliverance. This intuition is not as paradoxical as it seems, nor is it as reprehensible as the example of Stoic *apatheia* appears to suggest.

It will be convenient to discuss capacities and desires separately, and to begin from capacities in their negative aspect, viz., as incapacities, impediments, or constraints.

Constraints upon one's ability to do what one wants are broadly of two kinds, external and internal. The external kind may be further split into natural and political, with economic constraints perhaps constituting an ambiguous or intermediate case. Some natural constraints are common to all human beings. Neither I nor anyone else is "free," in Helvétius' phrase, to fly like an eagle or swim like a whale, should we so desire.[6] Other constraints are specific to individuals: however great my personal ambition to be a professor of mathematics, I shall never achieve it, unless perhaps, like Stan Laurel in the film *A Chump at Oxford,* I receive a fortunate blow to the skull.

Two things deserve notice about natural incapacities. First, the unfreedom I suffer as a result of natural incapacities may be abated by my accepting those incapacities, and moderating my desire accordingly. There is a sense in which, if I continue to chafe against my unfreedom, then I myself am the author of it. Furthermore, whatever helps me to recognize my desire as unreasonable and thus to extinguish it—a moral education, for example—may quite rightly be regarded as setting me free, even though it too may involve constraints. The second point is that many natural incapacities can be overcome. The orator Demosthenes cured his stammer by speaking with pebbles in his mouth. Perhaps we have an obligation wherever possible to provide similar services for each other, if necessary through the mechanism of the state, which, readers of Bosanquet will recall, can be "a hindrance to a hindrance."[7] Up to a point, therefore, natural incapacities are amenable to non-natural remedies, whether those involve the moderation of desire or the increase of the capacity to satisfy it.

Political constraints involve deliberate human obstacles, in the shape of public power or authority, to my doing what I want (or might want) to do. (We may rank private coercion alongside them since coercion of any kind, private or public, is a political matter.) They may be called just if they prevent me from doing what I want but ought not to want, unjust if they prevent me from doing what I ought to want (or from doing what is unobjectionable). They are also unjust if they force me to do what I know I ought not, and for that reason do not want, to do. Here again my freedom depends on the nature of my desires and the nature of the obstruction to their fulfillment.

Whatever Rousseau may say about his being "forced to be free,"[8] a criminal is certainly made less free in our sense by having to conform to just constraints, or by the penalties he suffers for nonconformity. His unfreedom, however, lies less at the door of the authority which restrains or condemns him, than at his own. For it is open to him as a rational being to recognize those constraints as just, and hence to identify himself with them and in so doing to moderate, or extinguish, his desire to flout them. So far as he does not, he is as much a slave to himself as is the victim of irremediable natural constraints.

What I am suggesting is that as long as I genuinely wish to obey laws or accept other constraints, I am not externally constrained, since I have aligned my desires with them. At least in the simple sense, to be constrained is to feel constrained. Law is a constraint not on the law-abiding person, but on the criminal. Liberals have long been accustomed to make merry over the Hegelian notion that freedom consists in obedience to the law. But they are wrong. It is freedom, but only so long as (a) the law is just, and (b) the subject's subscription to it is wholehearted, i.e., moral rather than merely prudential; in other words, so long as the subject obeys from motives of law-abidingness rather than from fear of punishment.

Space forbids my saying much about justice, but I have said enough to indicate that, though it demands support from the political order, it is not determined by it. If it were, then someone (e.g., a brainwashed person, or simply a natural zombie) who wholeheartedly submitted to tyranny, like Winston Smith when he finally comes to love Big Brother, could be described as free, and such a tyranny (along with its laws, if any) as just. But the contrary is true. A political order is legitimate to the extent that it conforms to justice.

This, however, is not to locate justice entirely outside the social order. Justice of course varies, or appears to vary, from place to place. But for us to condemn a given political order as unjust and unworthy of obedience, we do not have to measure it directly against some cosmopolitan or transcendental standard. We need only point to a general awareness of its injustice among those subject to it. "If any ask me," said Burke, "what a free government is, I answer, that for any practical purpose it is what the people think so; and that they, not I, are the natural, lawful and competent judges of this matter."[9] For Burke's "free," of course, we could as easily read the word "just." It is probably a mere quirk of language that "injustice," which is morally negative, should also be cast in grammatically negative form, unlike the words "bad" or "evil." This leads us off on a wild-goose chase after the ideal positive it negates. In fact, we probably do justice no indignity if, on reflection, we find it to consist of little more than the perceived absence of injustice.

Economic constraints on freedom are, as stated before, ambiguous as between political and natural constraints. So long as desires in general multiply beyond the technological possibility of satisfying them, so long will economic constraints—i.e., scarcity—be natural. On the other hand, so far as specific economic arrangements are the outcome of human choices and maintained by political arrangements, so far does it becomes plausible to see scarcity, and in particular unequally distributed scarcity, as political. I shall say little about this except to observe that the aggregate outcome of free individual choices—in this case, economic inequality—may well be something that no one, in so choosing, has deliberately sought to bring about. In which case, however undesirable in egalitarian eyes, it is morally blameless (as it might also be even if deliberate, e.g., when I decide to pay more than the going rate for, or to, a good worker). And as Nozick has pointed out, to "rectify" the end-state may involve injustice, if the individual transactions out of which it has emerged were just.

I do not wish to underrate the importance of economic constraints on freedom. Like most people, I should quite like to be rich. However, my not being so is of little consequence beside the absolute deprivation I should have suffered had I not received— what everyone should receive—educational opportunities in line with my capacities and inclinations. Indeed, my education has had two effects: in enabling me to do things I have discovered I prefer doing, it has unfitted me for the pursuits which might have made me rich. At the same time it has more than reconciled me to that fact and the ensuing financial loss.

These reflections lead us now to consider the "internal" constraints on freedom, which we may call "mental" and "moral." A word or two about them will lead us into the second part of our discussion, concerning wants or desires. It is here also that the ambiguity in the word "want" begins to show itself. For, suppose my wants conflict with my needs: if my wants are ignored or suppressed in favor of my needs, am I more, or less, free than if my wants should be gratified to the detriment of my needs? Is a need a deeper or superior kind of want? If it is, does all depend on whether I agree, or am able to perceive, that it is?

A moral constraint exists when I want to do something but know I should not, and to that extent also want not to. Whichever way the conflict is resolved, I may still be the subject of conflicting desires. In other words, all desire is not in a single mode. So far as

I accept a moral constraint, even if my desire to defy it persists, it may be doubted whether I am really constrained except (in what can only be a manner of speaking) by myself. It would be truer to say that each of my desires is a constraint on the other, for a moral impulse is no less a desire than the impulse it constrains. If I feel constrained by moral considerations, it is simply because I have not ordered or harmonized my desires. Morality involves the perception of a hierarchy of desires, ranged not primarily on a quantitative scale (that is, in respect of their strength), but rather on a qualitative scale (in respect of their worth).

What, for lack of a better word, I have called "mental" constraints bear more directly on questions of external authority. A mental constraint is one that I can perceive only with hindsight, that is, once I am no longer subject to it. Good examples might be ignorance, immaturity, or narrow-mindedness: in other words, the things education in its various forms sets out to rectify. These are constraints, not on my actual desires—since as things stand I am perfectly satisfied with myself—but on my future or potential desires. Those desires are not merely different, but are qualitatively superior, more rational, more harmonious, and so on. If I do not here and now experience my ignorance as a constraint, how can it be one? Yet how can it not be a constraint if, once it has been removed, I recognize it as such and would resist any attempt to re-impose it supposing such a thing were possible?[10]

In practice, and to use the language of Bradley and Bosanquet, no one much worries about the right of parents and educators to override their charges' "actual" will in the interests of their future, putative "real" will. Counterconstraints, imposed now, are generally recognized to be justified insomuch as they lead to autonomy later. But it is only the imputed interests of the recipient that make such counterconstraints just. Furthermore, those interests have to be more than merely egoistic. I may, for example, have an egoistic interest in following my immediate pleasure, as I may have equally in obeying a tyrant's orders. I escape frustration in the first case, and punishment in the second. But neither escape conduces to my autonomy. Indeed, genuine autonomy is incompatible with egoism, for the egoist is "determined," as he is enslaved, by his desires. (And these will lead him equally to enslave or sacrifice others.) But in desiring the good, I cease to be an egoist, for it is not just *my* good, but *the* good, to which, if need be, I must sacrifice myself.[11]

Mental constraints, as I have called them, illustrate a contradiction at the heart of liberalism: the fact that its goal of self-realization or autonomy may conflict with its central claim that the individual is the best, or at any rate the most appropriate, judge of his own interests. So he is, of course, but only upon achieving maturity. What the claim really amounts to is that the individual has a unique, immediate, Cartesian knowledge of his own desires. He is the best judge of his interests only in the sense that he knows better than anyone else what he *takes* them to be.) The autonomy rightly prized by the liberal is not given, but is learned or acquired. It cannot be acquired without the exercise of authority. A genuinely educational authority is justified in that it aims at its subject's independence, and in so doing aims also at its own supersession. These features, indeed, are what distinguish education from indoctrination.[12]

Let us move on to wants or desires. "I am a degenerate modern semi-intellectual," wrote George Orwell in *The Road to Wigan Pier*:

who would die if I did not get my early morning cup of tea and my *New Statesman* every Friday. Clearly I do not, in a sense, "want" to return to a simpler, harder, probably agricultural way of life. In the same sense I don't "want" to cut down my drinking, to pay my debts, to take enough exercise, to be faithful to my wife, etc., etc. But in another and more permanent sense I do want these things, and perhaps in the same sense I want a civilization in which "progress" is not definable as making the world safe for little fat men.

Ignore Orwell's particular likes and dislikes and his tendentious language. What concerns us is his distinction between selfish, irresponsible, hedonistic wants and, to use his word, more "permanent" desires. These depend for their satisfaction precisely on our repudiating or suppressing wants of the first kind. Few would deny that this is a real conflict, and that it lies at the heart of the moral life. The great weakness of liberalism, however, is that it fails to recognize either the distinction or the conflict. In part this is due to its according so much authority to the individual's express will, so that whatever I very much "want" must be assumed to be a value *for me*. Another way of putting it is to say that, contrary to what I have suggested is "normal" morality, liberalism tends to value desire quantitatively, according to its intensity. (A thing intensely desired may, of course, be objectively valuable, and something objectively valuable will certainly be intensely desired by those who perceive it as such. But a value that is a value for me alone is no value at all, but a preference.)

At the same time liberalism adopts a neutral, almost behavioristic stance in its indifference to the precise content or quality of the indvidual's desire. What it gives with one hand it takes away with the other. Desires qualify for consideration only as proceeding from the sovereign individual. But from this perspective all desires, and all individuals, must be generically equal. ("Each is to count for one," said Bentham, "and none for more than one.") This means that because all desires are, in a purely technical sense, egocentric, all must be treated as though they were so in a moral sense.

This assumption is of course false. However, on a quasi-democratic utilitarian view such as Bentham's, or that of Mill's conservative opponent, Fitzjames Stephen, its falsity might be of no practical consequence. For public opinion—which Mill more or less identified with the so-called "tyranny of the majority"— might, in the long run, chance to favor genuine, and hence non-egoistic, values (i.e., Rousseau's General Will, or the communal "real will" of the Idealists).

But suppose this were not the case, and that a liberal-democratic order were sustained solely by the desire of each to indulge as much of his egoism as should be compatible with others' similarly doing so. In other words, imagine a society based purely on selfishness, on its guarantee to each subscriber of a self-limiting, but nevertheless inviolable, quota of egoistic satisfaction. (The sort of society, in short, that Hobbes thought most people, as opposed to himself and his friends, would find logically deserving of allegiance.)

I do not, of course, mean to imply that all purely private satisfactions or utilities are narrowly egoistic. The most agreeable feature of liberal societies is the way in which private individual satisfactions seem spontaneously to proliferate without substantially trespassing on each other, either in intention or in effect. Many, perhaps most, private utilities are what the economist Wicksteed called non-tuistic.[13] That is, they are neither selfish, in the sense of requiring others' unwilling cooperation, nor positively altruistic: they are simply neutral, unobjectionable preferences. Other private utilities *will* be altruistic. Their intentional object, however, will not be the community as a whole, but merely those (e.g., family and friends) for whom the agent feels an immediate personal responsibility, of an intimate kind which he recognizes that the community as a whole, while it must care about them in a general way or as members of itself, cannot be expected to shoulder.

Any liberal society, of course, must permit altruism (as it permits everything to some degree). But by treating all desire as implicitly egoistic, and as no less just for being so, such a society effectively disprivileges altruism and puts itself in danger. A society whose official ideology is selfishness, or something structurally indistinguishable from selfishness, engages no individual's disposition to defend it beyond the point at which it ceases to deliver that individual's goods. Bound by interest rather than loyalty, it is like a cartel, perpetually at the mercy of those of its members most disposed to cut and run as opportunity dictates. Once a society goes soft—i.e., selfish—there is no saving it from tyranny, which is always amply supplied with the only currency selfishness understands, sticks and carrots.

Kant excepted, liberal thinkers couch their ethics almost entirely in the language of rights. (Duties consist merely of the legal obligation not to infringe others' rights.) And rights, it must be said, are implicitly selfish, since those I am most likely to care about are my own. (Agitation on behalf of others' rights usually exhibits a quality of vicarious selfishness, whereas a real care for their welfare, while properly indignant at whatever genuine injustices they suffer, recognizes that their selfishness deserves no more consideration than one's own.) The cultural consequences can be seen in the United States, whose law courts and legislature are a ceaseless, unedifying babble of competing claims to entitlement. From the liberal standpoint, right is an advantage and duty a burden. The idea that one's fulfillment might lie in doing one's duty is on the whole foreign to liberalism. In other words, and paradoxically, the liberal ethos is at odds with the ethos of liberality.

A simple way to make the distinction is to say that liberality is "noble," while liberalism is all too often "base." Liberality begins from duty, or the just man's disposition to give others their due, and more than their due.[14] Liberalism begins from right, or the disposition to exploit others' duties toward oneself, to claim one's pound of flesh. Liberality waives its rights, and performs its duty willingly and in overplus; liberalism sees duty as the tax paid by selfishness for its guaranteed enjoyments, and will calculate its payment to the last penny. Liberality presumes that there must be something wrong—a lack of generosity—in a society where rights need constantly to be claimed, and duties to be enforced. Liberalism's tacit presumption, on the other hand, because rights are always claimed against someone, is of a constant potential hostility between subjects, or between subjects and the state. If socialism, as some say, is the politics of envy, liberalism is the politics of jealousy. Neither seems a good basis for morality. Unselfishness is forced to eke out an existence as best it can, unsupported by public recognition.

This brings us finally to the question of value. Can there be genuine values in a liberal society? How can freedom be a value irrespective of what is done with it? And how can I value myself and my projects—that is, attribute objective worth to them—when I see that the public order outside me attributes worth to nothing except an unqualified, subjective "freedom"?

This much may be said in answer to the first question. As we have seen in the case of justice, values exist wherever there is a cultural consensus. But when a cultural consensus lacks positive support from the political order, and exists merely as everything exists that is not forbidden, it sees itself cast into relativity and its values treated as mere preferences. It then either evaporates, like the established church, or retreats, like British Islam, into self-defensive bigotry and intolerance. There is, I beleive, a limit to the amount, or perhaps rather to the depth, of cultural pluralism possible within a single political order. Pushed beyond that limit, society dissolves either into sectarian violence, or into materialistic anomie and despair.

Second, the value of freedom in the sense of toleration does depend on what is done with it. In other words, freedom is a means, not an end. There will always be some who will abuse it, and it is only tolerable, or valuable, to the extent that its benefits outweigh its costs. Extend it too far, and all subordinate values are relativized. Freedom becomes the sole value or the standard of value (that is, becomes an end). It thus culminates in the abolition of value as commonly understood, and few, accordingly, will be anxious to preserve it. What people require of politics is something more than mere toleration of their personal preferences (though they usually, and not unreasonably, want that too). What they want is the kind of freedom for their cultural values which can come only from those values' being recognized as authoritative, i.e., as continuous with, and recognized by, the political order which demands their allegiance.

That continuity, in fact, is the source of obedience and hence of civil peace. Multicultural societies are perfectly viable, even entertaining, so long as the main fabric of each subordinate culture consists, and is admitted by its members to consist, of mere collective options, tastes, and idiosyncrasies—of preferences, in short— such as exist even within a single culture. But when such differences are imbued with value, when they are the coordinates of a person's identity, and especially of his religion—above all when, as cultural values proper, they not merely differ, but actually conflict—then the overall consensus necessary for peaceable government becomes hard to find. Societies so plural as to lack any basis whatever for consent are either ungovernable, or (what is substantially the same thing) can be governed only by force.

The third question, I believe, has answered itself. I can attribute value to myself or to any of my projects only in relation to a culture, for it is my culture which provides me with the instruments of valuation. It is the objective mirror of my existence and achievement. Freed entirely from culture's more exigent imperatives, as liberalism offers to free me from them by refusing its support, I am freed also from any sense of my own necessity, and excluded from the possibilities of fulfillment which lie in my measuring up to them. In short, I need to have duties, to have moral demands made upon me, to know that others will value me if I do right (and despise me if I do wrong). I need to be obliged, to feel wanted, to belong. Redundancy is generally reckoned a great misfortune in the sphere of employment; it is not less so in the existential spheres of culture and morality. From this fate, liberalism, no less than any other politics, had better learn to protect us, if it wishes to survive. For though, when directly under its sway, the world is an unsettled, discontented place, a world in which no liberalism existed would be a good deal worse. Liberalism is at its best and most needful in its traditional composite role: that of adversary, pedant, critic, sleeping partner, friend, and gadfly.

NOTES

1. Cf. Voltaire: Quand je peux faire ce que je veux, voilà ma liberté (quoted F.A. Hayek, *The Constitution of Liberty*, RKP 1963, 423). See also Roger Scruton, 'Freedom and Custom,' in A. Phillips Griffiths, ed., *On Liberty*, CUP 1983, 181.

2. A possibility approached from a somewhat different angle by Isaiah Berlin, 'Two Concepts of Liberty,' III (*Four Essays on Liberty*, OUP 1975, 135f.)

3. Cf. Michael Oakeshott, *Experience and its Modes*, CUP 1933, Ch. V ('Practical Experience'), 247f.

4. A subtle analysis of the self-renunciative impulse and its tragic potential is to be found in L.H. Myers's portrait of the Buddhist ruler, Rajah Amar, in his novel *The Root and the Flower*, Cape 1935 (repr. Secker and Warburg 1984.)

5. Baudelaire's 'roi d'un pays pluvieux,' in the second of his 'Spleen' poems, is a person in this position, "riche, mais impuissant":

   > Rien ne peut l'égayer, ni gibier, ni faucon,
   > Ni son peuple mourant en face du balcon.

6. Quoted Berlin, cit., 122.

7. *The Philosophical Theory of the State* (1899), Macmillan 1965, 18f.

8. *Du Contrat Social*, I, vii; IV, ii (note on the galley slaves of Genoa).

9. *Letter to the Sheriffs of Bristol*, 1777.

10. Willy Russell's film *Educating Rita* (1984) is an interesting case in point, particularly since Rita, as a mature student, volunteers for the university education which, though she does not realize it at the outset, will make it impossible for her ever to return to being a hairdresser. Critics of a leftist disposition found the film excruciatingly patronizing, though in fact it registered only a simple, sober truth.

11. 'Patočka [Czech philosopher, pupil of Husserl, d. 1977 after police interrogation in connection with the Charter '77 movement of which he was a founder] once wrote that a life not willing to sacrifice itself to what makes it meaningful is not worth living' (Václav Havel, in *Václav Havel, or Living in Truth*, ed. J. Vladislav, Faber 1987, 150.)

12. As can be seen from the very similar authority figure of Prospero in Shakespeare's *Tempest* and Sarastro in Mozart's *Magic Flute*, who both renounce their power when their educational mission is accomplished. For a dissentient voice, however, see Berlin, cit., 145f. ('The Temple of Sarastro').

13. P.H. Wicksteed, *The Common Sense of Political Economy*, 1910.

14. On giving others their due, cf. Ulpian's famous definition of justice: 'constans ac perpetua voluntas suum cuique tribuere.' On giving them more than their due, see Enobarbus in *Antony and Cleopatra*:

   > O Antony,
   > Thou mine of bounty, how wouldst thou have rewarded
   > My better service, when my turpitude
   > Thou dost so crown with gold!

TWO

LIBERALISM, POLITICS AND ANTI-POLITICS: ON THE POLITICAL ETHIC OF LIBERAL DEMOCRACY

David I. Levy

As the twentieth century enters its final decade the political culture of liberalism, and the political theory or theories that seek to justify it, find themselves in a paradoxical situation. The great mid-century crisis—the *furor ideologicus*—which once seemed to threaten the very survival of liberal, constitutional order, even in its Western, European and North American heartland, has passed. The radically anti-liberal, messianic political creeds, which once enchanted the intellectuals and activated the masses in a destructive fury directed against the institutional heritage of nineteenth century constitutionalism and individualism, have lost much though not yet all of their appeal. The burden of the historical legacy of murder and destruction has proved too much for fascist and now, it would seem, for communist faith. Western socialists, once sold on the supposed benefits of 'rational' state control of economy and society, now define their critical positions in what are, historically speaking, typically liberal terms. They talk of the need to defend 'civil society' against the encroachments of the state; they expound the sacredness of individual rights, the dangers of revolutionary change, and the need constantly to improve the human condition by what John Gray calls "the judicious exercise of critical reason."[1]

Alongside these political and ideological factors we must set the overwhelming fact of twentieth century economic history: the fact that the mechanism of the competitive market (embodying primarily if not exclusively the principle of private ownership of the means of production) has alone proved capable of providing mass populations with a reasonable and, generally speaking, improving standard of living—whether measured in terms of productive innovation, wealth creation or general economic well-being. It is far from the irrational obstacle to the furtherance of economic advance that Marxists supposed it to be. In view of the apparent historical affinity between liberal, constitutional politics (based on the priority of the value of individual liberty) and capitalist economics (founded in the privileged status accorded to private enterprise) the achievements of the competitive market also serve the supporters of a liberal political order—even if the association between economic success and political liberalism is by no means as invariable as the neo-conservative, *de jure* liberal, advocates of the benefits of 'global democracy' would like us to suppose.

The widespread invocation of the name and work of F.A. Hayek, a theorist whose combined contributions to liberal constitutional thought and market oriented economics are original and unique, testifies to the unaccustomed spirit of confidence with which the public spokesmen of liberal political order now face the future. Yet here we should take pause: for Hayek himself seems by no means to share the historical optimism of those who most commonly invoke his name. The advocate of spontaneous order seems to have little faith in the spontaneous self-correction of the historical process of modernity. The new Marx of the bourgeoisie is no representative of what the Tory editor of London's *Sunday Telegraph* has termed 'bourgeois triumphalism'. In the contemporary world, Hayek is the pre-eminent author of a liberal rather than a socialist account of the theoretical, but not spontaneously practical, identity between the ethically desirable and the economically necessary in the order of what he calls the 'Great Society.' But he is certainly no advocate of the 'let rip' credo of the global democrats, still less the stateless fantasies of the anarcho-capitalists.

Instead, he advocates the installation of a complex system of authoritative institutions—a machinery of state, and a rationally constructed one at that—designed not to facilitate but to curb the consuming dynamic of democratic desire.

Then again, consider the state of liberal political theory. Without entering territory I cannot hope to cover in the space of this essay, I refer to the recent and, I assume, regretful analysis of the incoherence of classical liberal theory offered by John Gray.[2] Gray characterizes what he calls a 'post-liberal political theory'— we now need a theory capable of legitimating continuing liberal practice without recourse to untenable beliefs about the nature of man and the dangerously libertarian programs they engender—in terms of an arranged marriage between a modified version of the Hobbesian imperative of coercion and the Humean doctrine of the authority of convention.

Thus an influential theorist who was, until recently, rightly regarded as the most judicious of contemporary liberal political philosophers now seeks the security of a maximally free political order not in a doctrine of freedom like his liberal mentors, but in the anthropologically necessary restraints of sovereign power advocated by Hobbes and customary cultural practice advocated by Hume. If nothing else, this line of argument testifies to the tension that now subsists between the established political order of the free world and the libertarian, quasi-anarchist rhetoric with which many of its less thoughtful supporters still urge its claims upon our allegiance.

In the pages that follow I want to examine certain aspects of this tension as it affects liberal political theories and the polities they seek to inform. In doing this I shall orient myself primarily to the work of Hayek and to a recent work, *The Self, the Individual and the Community*, whose author, Brian Lee Crowley, seeks to show that there are surprising affinities between the anthropological assumptions of the liberal Hayek and the early twentieth century British socialists, Beatrice and Sidney Webb.[3]

However, before proceeding further it is worth considering a little more deeply the nature of Gray's 'post-liberal' turn and its relationship to Hayek's grand theoretical enterprise. For at the center of Crowley's provocative thesis is an argument concerning the inadequacy of the concept of man which he finds embedded equally in the apparently opposed practical philosophies of the liberal individualist Hayek and the utilitarian collectivists, Sidney and Beatrice Webb. For all the differences in the outcome of their thought, it is Crowley's claim that both Hayek and the Webbs start from the inadequate anthropological premises which he identifies with a typically liberal view of man, knowledge and society. Reference to Gray's post-liberalism will help us to understand both the force of Crowley's criticism of Hayek and what he regards more broadly as the 'anti-political' nature of liberal thought, as well as the limits of Crowley's own modern, neo-Aristotelian alternative.

In posing the problem in terms of the relationship between politics and anthropology, I mean to draw attention to the continuing significance of Aristotle's definition of man as an essentially political animal. That is, the view that the human being is a form of life destined by his biologically given nature to live and find ⁻fulfillment only in a politically constituted society in which economic activity is only one, and by no means the most important, dimension. Crowley turned to Aristotle—an Aristotle significantly modified in a humanitarian and democratic direction by such 'moderns' as Hannah Arendt and Ronald Beiner—and Gray invoked Hume and, more particularly, Hobbes. Underlying both is a shared recognition that the classical liberal image of man, as we find it in both Hayek and the Webbs, privileges one dimension of human activity, the economic, without allowing due emphasis to the sustaining political and cultural conditions which render ordered economic activity, as well as every other element of the good life, possible.

A viable polity is not only an economy, as both Crowley and Hayek clearly recognize. But, I shall claim, neither Hayek's emphasis on the significance of the authority of legal order and the rule of law nor Crowley's supplementary account of community as a sphere of discussion and persuasion oriented toward the achievement of the common good, fully embraces the problem of political order. Each is important, but, as Gray reminds us in his reference to Hobbes—even a Hobbes "freed from the crudities of Hobbes's (own) anthropology and psychology"[4]—the field of politics is, whatever else it may be, also a field of power and force. It is a domain of ever potential violence in which—to use terms borrowed with some misgivings from Carl Schmitt—the 'normal' state of political affairs, characterized by debate and respect for legality, is always open to "the challenge of exception."[5] Where debate and law cease to be respected—not such an exceptional occurrence—only the decisive exercise of sovereign power can renew their sway. As we know all too well, such power can never be trusted to restore normal political life, but in the state of exception we have no recourse other than the decisions of an effective sovereign prepared, where necessary, to authorize the use of force.

Gray links Humean conventionalism with the Hobbesian vision of politics as a humanly founded order forced on us and more or less willingly accepted, in consequence of the murderous disorder of an anthropologically primordial 'state of nature'. Gray's suggested form of 'post-liberal theorizing' resumes at a stroke the hard insight of Weberian and Schmittian political anthropology: that while debate is to politics as contract is to economics—the normal medium of beneficial communication—neither is self-grounding. The foundation of each rests in the possibility of enforcing the norm by recourse to ab-normal but perennially necessary physical power. That is a fact of life which no modern sentimentalizing of the Aristotelian ideal of political community can ultimately avoid. The citizen of the *polis*, whom modern Aristotelians like to picture as primarily a partner in unconstrained yet orderly debate, was also a soldier, who could be summoned to arms to repress internal disorder as readily as to repel a foreign enemy from the borders of his state.

This unfashionable point needs making—but not, I stress, to the exclusion of the other, Humean, element in Gray's position. For the lesson of Humean conventionalism and its implied respect for traditional ways is that the deeper such respect is embedded and ingrained in the culture of a society the less likely the need for recourse to physical force. This is something that Hayek—a traditionalist even if, in his own terms, no conservative—well recognizes. At the same time, Hayek's over-juridical conception of sovereign order as embodied in law (which without force is no more than a body of words), leads him to overestimate the efficacy of the formal institutions of justice and underplay the decisive way that covert but widely spread perceptions of legitimacy translate the formal judgments of the law into the practical life of society.

This, as Crowley might say, is in part a function of Hayek's politically deficient anthropology, his failure to recognize the beneficent function of sentiments of community, and his rejection of the notion of the common good. It also, in my view, reflects his historical background as an Austrian, the child of a multinational empire which united the national political institutions of a dynastic state in a decisively non-communitarian way, both juridically and administratively.

HAYEK THE AUSTRIAN

This question of Hayek's background—his formative identity as an Austrian, by which I mean much more than that he is an economist in the Austrian tradition of Menger and von Mises— bears further consideration. It is, I think, not only a point too much neglected in discussions of Hayek's work but one which goes far to explain the reasons why his political anthropology takes the form it does. What Crowley regards as a neglect of the issue of community in Hayek's liberal, *Rechtstaatlich* vision of economy, state and society is based not on an underestimation of the political significance of community, *Gemeinschaft*, but on a conscious rejection of what it seems, or seemed at least in Hayek's youth, to imply.

When Hayek, in his characterization of the 'Great Society', goes out of his way to emphasize its origins in the overcoming of primitive community sentiment by the individualist ethos of self-seeking enterprise, his argument must be understood in the historical context of the ideological debate set in motion by the publication of Ferdinand Tönnies's celebrated work *Gemeinschaft und Gesellschaft* (*Community and Society*) in 1887. Whatever may have been Tönnies's original intention, his typology of social forms in terms of the contrast between traditional *Gemeinschaft*, based on communitarian ties of kinship and locality, and the modern *Gesellschaft*, based on mobility, competition and self-interest, provided a powerful ideological symbol for the next generation of Germans and German-Austrians in the notion of *Gemeinschaft* itself. The call for the renewal of *gemeinschaftlich*, communitarian values became a rallying point for all who felt uneasy with what they saw as the dehumanizing effects of the development of industrial, capitalist society. *Gemeinschaft*, or community, provided a watchword for all those who opposed and sought to overcome through the recreation of community, the liberal capitalist state which was, from the beginning, Hayek's ideal.

In the specific context of the multinational Habsburg Empire, the call to renewed community meant, for most of its advocates, the community of a self-consciously distinct nation, a *Volksgemeinschaft*, and thus the disruption of an imperial, supranational state which, at least in theory, ruled its subjects in a spirit of obedience to a legal order that paid no regard to nation, race or creed. Emptied of its historically accidental features as the inherited territories of a particular dynasty, this monarchical state, Austria in its older sense, provides, in many ways, the constitutional model for Hayek's preferred form of polity: a *Rechstaat* which generally confines itself to matters of law, order and defense guaranteeing, through the enforcement of law the framework in which a free economy can operate effectively. While claiming the allegiance of its subjects, such a state emphatically disavows the ambition to express or incarnate the communal spirit, real or imagined, of the nation or any fraction of it.

In the old Austria of Hayek's youth, the politics of community were thus perceived as being decisively opposed to the politics of universal law and of individual (in contrast to national or communal), liberty. The anthropology of community, whether conceived in nationalist or socialist terms, defined itself in opposition to the politically liberal, Hayekian anthropology of the self-dependent individual who is what he is by reason of individual achievement rather than birth or ascription. The appeal to community—which signifies to Crowley, as to so many of our contemporaries, merely the limitation of the effects of individualism and the market the mitigation of the harsher consequences of liberalism by care— meant for the young Hayek (as much as for his anti-liberal contemporaries) not the qualification of the liberal and capitalist order but its destruction.

THE CROWLEY THESIS

Without subscribing to the historicist myth that a man's political vision is determined by his historical situation, it is astonishing, I think, how far the differences between Crowley's vision and that of Hayek can be elucidated by reference to the historical factor. The Austria of the early 1900s is sufficiently different from the London

School of Economics in the 1980s (where Crowley's critique of Hayekian liberalism originated as a doctoral thesis), to explain to a great extent, the nature of the criticisms advanced in the work. What seemed an impossibility in the context in which Hayek's thought originates, Crowley (like so many of our generous-hearted contemporaries) takes most profoundly for granted: the compatibility of a liberal economic order with a renewal of communitarian, participatory politics.

What Crowley at one point astutely terms the 'authoritarian nature' of Hayek's dedication to liberty—embodied in his simultaneous endorsement of the free market and his advocacy of a state whose fundamental political and legal institutions are taken to be beyond the effective scope of mass-democratic debate—is a function of the historical position described above. Hayek's combination of what is, covertly at least, a legally limited political authoritarianism with a form of economic and social libertarianism—so puzzling to many of his current admirers—is no mystery when set against the background situation of Austria-Hungary, where what his great contemporary Eric Voegelin termed political 'like-mindedness,' *homonoia*, was notable by its absence. For the life of debate and ordered dispute, which is central to Crowley's neo-Aristotelian image of political life, can be a recipe for order rather than chaos only when there exists beneath the surface of argument a fundamental consensus as to what constitutes both the real, politically relevant community and the good life. Where *homonoia* is absent the *de facto* authoritarian state is, like it or not, the necessary correlate of the maintenance of economic freedom and individual liberties alike.

The starting point for Crowley's argument is what he takes to be a significant identity of view underlying the apparently opposed political theories of Hayek and the Webbs. Both Hayek and the Webbs "see the justification of society and politics as lying solely in the direction of society as an engine of material want satisfaction."[6] Compared with this, the distinction between the Webbs' endorsement of 'rational' socialist planning and Hayek's advocacy of the universal competence of the market is a secondary matter. While differing on the means of achieving the desired goal, the two—or rather three—are in full agreement on the purpose of politics.

Crowley attributes this identity to a shared intellectual inheritance, an abstract, ahistorical view of man or, as I would put it, an anthropology which he identifies as that of liberalism. According to this view, liberalism at its core presents us with a significantly depoliticized vision of man. In liberal thought, the Aristotelian conception of man as an essentially political being, one destined to achieve his proper ends through participation in the ordering activities of public life and in active citizenship, is displaced by a 'shallow' notion of the human person. One aspect of this shallowness is to be found in the liberal's overidentification of the human good with economic well-being (which for Aristotle is merely a precondition for the good life). But another, more significant dimension of the shallowness of liberal anthropology is to be found in its diminution of the scope of political reasoning—its reduction of reasoning about the ends of human existence—to a mere matter of instrumental calculation concerning an already-known good, material well-being.

This, in turn, is connected with the liberal's over-individualized view of man. The liberal tends to abstract what is supposed to be the essence of the human person, the core of his humanity, from the particular historical and cultural frameworks in which the historically real individual always finds himself, and then seeks to present the bloodless residue that remains as the essence of man as such. Against this, Crowley urges that we need a richer view of the human self—one which recognizes the apparently paradoxical truth that it is precisely the accidental, historical and cultural features of a man's being that make him what essentially he is.[7]

I cannot, in the space of this essay, enter further into the details of Crowley's generally astute and well-expressed analyses of the politics, or rather anti-politics, either of Hayek or of the Webbs. It is, however, important to note that, while recognizing the deep affinities between them, at least at the anthropological level, Crowley is quite clear that in juxtaposing the two visions we are not comparing like with like in qualitative terms. He well recognizes not only that Hayek is much the greater, more subtle and imaginative, thinker in every relevant sense but also that, despite the inadequacy of its theory of politics, the social vision or ideal of Hayekian liberalism is infinitely preferable to that of the Webbs' managerial socialism.

With neither judgment do I disagree, even though, as already suggested, I feel that Crowley would have understood the logic of Hayek's position rather better, and even shown it a bit more sympathy, if he had taken account of the historical background against which it first took shape. When all is said and done, there is nothing arbitrary or irrational about Hayek's resistance to the siren call of the apostles of community. That said, I turn to Crowley's alternative neo-Aristotelian political vision. For there we will find a rather different aspect of the tension between contemporary, *bien-pensant*, political thought and the nature of contemporary political reality. That is, the continuing tension between the fashionable concept of politics as purely a matter of debate and discourse, and the enduring political requirement, both within states and between them, of potential recourse to physical force or at least the credible threat of such action when circumstances so demand.

ANARCHO-ARISTOTELIANISM

As indicated above, the spirit of Crowley's work places him full square in the line of the current Aristotelian revival. I think that the recent renewal of interest in the Aristotelian conception of politics, conceived above all as politics centered on the concept of active, participatory citizenship must be understood in large part as simply a reaction to the failure of the ultimately anti-political ideologies of liberalism and socialism to provide, either in theory or in practice, satisfactory answers to the problem of the triadic relationship of man, state and society.

In describing these ideologies as 'anti-political' I mean that each aims, in the last resort, to make politics in the traditional sense redundant by so ordering society that men are freed both from the challenge of substantive political choice and from the burden of rulership by anything, or anyone, but the self-directing, yet somehow convergent, dictates of individual calculation and desire.

Thus, in the utopias of socialism and liberalism alike men are conceived as living non-conflictually alongside each other, each freely pursuing his well-being, yet, by virtue of the prevailing social, but primarily economic arrangements, without prejudice to the well-being of others. Where the liberal and the socialist visions differ is not in their endorsement of this ideal of an essentially nonpolitical, or historically post-political, existence but in their judgment of the sort of socio-economic arrangements that would make the ideal attainable—for the one a rationally planned system of socialized production and distribution, for the other the more or less spontaneous play and interplay of the market.

Crowley's critique of the antipolitical anthropology of liberalism, in terms of its exaltation of the significance of the economic over other aspects of man's being, certainly brings to light some of the sources of this shared vision. And it is, I agree, a vision whose ultimately dehumanizing aspect is well diagnosed in a passage by J.G.A. Pocock which serves as an epigraph to Crowley's second chapter. "The paradigm of commerce," Pocock observes, "presented the movement of history as being toward the indefinite multiplication of goods and brought the whole progress of material, cultural and moral civilization under this head. But so long as it did not contain any equivalent to the concept of *zoon politikon*, of the individual as an autonomous, morally and politically choosing being, progress must appear to move away from something essential to human personality. And this corruption was self-generating; society as an engine for the production and multiplication of goods was inherently hostile to society as the moral foundation of the personality."

The reference here to the *zoon politikon*, the animal that is political by nature, is crucial. For contemporary Aristotelianism, like the equivalent revival of interest in the Hegelian notion of "Civil Society" that has occurred in sections of the political Left, is motivated above all by the sensed need to recover an appreciation of the essentially political, as opposed to the economic, facet of human life—to revive the sense of politics as a creative dimension of human self-realization, the art of life *par excellence*, rather than as a more or less dispensable obstacle to the human good, as it appears in most traditional forms of liberal and social theory.

I say 'most' because, *pace* Crowley's blanket condemnation of the liberal tradition as inherently anti-political, there is, in the so-called 'New Liberalism' of certain late nineteenth century thinkers, notably Bernard Bosanquet, a profound appreciation of the positive human significance of politics and, with it, of the State as a center of authoritative power.[8] Indeed in its neo-Hegelian emphasis on the positive role of the State as a focus of allegiance and an ordering principle in the life of all but the smallest societies, a theory such as Bosanquet's may prove a valuable counterweight to a purported vindication of politics which, like Crowley's, recalls Aristotle's *polis* but somehow, like the new enthusiasts for Civil Society, forgets the place of Hegel's State in the political universe of modernity.

What I am getting at here is what I take to be a significant shortcoming in the project of renewing our sense of the human significance of politics as this is currently being pursued by neo-Aristotelians and neo-Hegelians alike. In opposition to the anti-politics of classical liberalism and socialism, both schools aim to restore to political activity its central role in the constitution of the good life. But at the same time, they both tend to fight shy of facing the problem of rulership. They both tend systematically to underestimate the enduring significance of the dimension of coercive power—the political function of a form of direction which is necessarily more than self-direction—that is, just as much as the determination of political policy by informed debate, an inevitable aspect of the political as such. The question here is whether such an evasion does not testify, alongside the legacy of what Crowley terms liberalism, to only another variety of anti-politics—a variety which, in the present context, we might justly term 'anarcho-Aristotelian.' By this I mean a position which, in the name of vindicating the value of politics as a form of creative human activity, more or less subtly defines out of the political field its other fundamental features as the domain of institutionalized force and power.

POLIS AND STATE

Let me explain my point further by reference to two of the terms already juxtaposed above, Aristotle's *polis* and Hegel's State.

Both *polis* and *Staat*, polity and state, belong to the vocabulary of what most people would recognize as authentically political visions of the human condition. And both are terms that refer to what may be called the essential element of governance, of authoritative but reasonable political direction in the conduct of social life. However, while recognizing this common element in the overlapping concepts of polity (Aristotle's *polis*) and state (Hegel's *Staat*), it is important to note that they do not refer to this element in precisely the same way. For, while the Aristotelian concept of the *polis* evokes the undifferentiated image of a polity of self-governing citizens in which, almost by definition, there is no distinction between rulers and ruled—truly a "government of the people, by the people, for the people," to recall a celebrated but none-the-less obfuscating modern formulation of the ideal—the Hegelian notion of the State suggests an institutional form in which rule and self-rule neither are nor can be identical.

Indeed Hegel's argument for the central role of the state as a source of rational political direction in the modern world is couched precisely in terms of the impossibility, in Aristotle's own terms, of maintaining the undifferentiated order of the classical *polis* in the historical and demographic conditions of modernity.

In contrast, Crowley's recourse to what claims to be a more purely Aristotelian vision of politics is, like that of many other contemporary neo-Aristotelians, based on the conviction that the principle of political rule as the unconstrained self-rule of a free citizenry is as applicable in the conditions of the present day as it was, however briefly, in ancient Athens. While recognizing that the matter of population size, if nothing else, renders impractical the revival of the forms of direct participation that characterized the classical *polis*, modern Aristotelians tend to believe that the contemporary, post-Burkean principle of representation is capable of making good the deficiency. On both points, however, I think that Aristotle, let alone Hegel, would have had considerable doubts.

Here we should recall that, while Aristotle may be read as positing the *polis* as a universal ideal, in the sense that it is and remains the anthropologically most desirable form of political life, he neither believed that it was everywhere attainable nor even thought that every type of man was capable of achieving or maintaining it. The universality of the ideal and its undoubted continuing attractiveness should not blind us to the very particular pre-political conditions (including demographic conditions concerning both the size and the composition of the population) which Aristotle, no less than Hegel, considered essential to its actualization. Whether these conditions can ever be met in the conditions of modernity is highly questionable. Where they are not met, it is doubtful how far the theory of the *polis*—conceived as a model of participatory citizenship and not, as the Greek city-state also was, one among other historically given forms of ultimately coercive rule—can provide us with an adequate understanding of what is at stake in political life.

In modern Cosmopolis, where the Greek ideal of the political identity between *ethnos* and *ethos*—between a single self-consciously distinct people and its self-constitutive way of being in the world—is notable by its absence both from our teeming cities and from the pluralist discourse of polite liberal or post-liberal society, the appeal to community can hardly be expected to produce the sort of like-mindedness presupposed by the model of the *polis*. If this is so, we are fated to inhabit a world in which the polity is, in Hegelian terms, differentiated into the mutually sustaining realms of State and Civil Society; and where something rather like Hayek's strict institutional separation between the two may, despite its anthropological shortcomings, be the best we can hope to achieve.

NOTES

1. John Gray, "Mill's and Other Liberalisms," *Critical Review* 1:3 & 3 (date).
2. *Ibid.*
3. Brian Lee Crowley, *The Self, the Individual and the Community; Liberalism in the Political Thought of F.A. Hayek and Sidney Webb* (London: Oxford University Press, 1987).
4. Gray, *op. cit.*
5. Carl Schmitt, *Political Theology: Four Chapters on the Concept of Sovereignty*, translated by George Schwab, (Boston: MIT Press, 1985).
6. Crowley, *The Self, the Individual and the Community*, 13.
7. See on this David J. Levy, "The Politics of the Self," originally published in the *Salisbury Review*, reprinted in *Conservative Thoughts*, edited by Roger Scruton (London: Claridge Press, 1988), 81-90.
8. Gerland F. Gauss, *The Modern Liberal Theory of Man* (London: Croom Helm, 1983).

THREE

THE IMPOSSIBILITY OF NEUTRAL POLITICS

Michael J. Perry

The United States, like many other societies, is morally pluralistic. No single set of beliefs about how it is good or fitting for human beings to live their lives prevails in American society. The morally pluralistic character of American society, however, unlike that of other societies, is congenital: "As it arose in America, the problem of pluralism was unique in the modern world, chiefly because pluralism was the native condition of American society. It was not, as in Europe and England, the result of a disruption or decay of a previously existent religious unity."[1] Although some quite general beliefs about human good are widely shared in American society, many beliefs about human good are widely, deeply, and persistently disputed. This state of affairs gives rise to a fundamental inquiry about the proper relation of morality to politics. In American society (or in any similarly pluralistic society) should disputed beliefs about human good play any role in public deliberations about, or in public justifications of, contested political choices? For example, is it ever appropriate, in American society, for a citizen to (seek to) justify to fellow citizens,[2] on the basis of one or more of his or her beliefs about human good, a political choice he or she has made or supports, if some to whom he or she is justifying the choice do not share the beliefs?

In the book on which this essay is based I deal with such questions at length—and with particular reference to religious beliefs about human good. In this essay I comment critically on several prominent arguments about the proper relation of morality to politics.[3]

I

Bruce Ackerman has recently contended for 'neutral' politics,[4] in this sense: A citizen should (seek to) justify a political choice to fellow citizens only on the basis of moral premises shared with all to whom he or she is justifying the choice. As Ackerman explains, "My principle of conversational restraint does not apply to the questions citizens may ask, but to the answers they may legitimately give to each others' questions: whenever one citizen is confronted by another's question, he cannot suppress the questioner, nor can he respond by appealing to (his understanding of) the moral truth; he must instead be prepared, in principle, to engage in a restrained dialogic effort to locate normative premises both sides find reasonable."[5]

A basic problem with Ackerman's shared-premises restraint on political justification is that in a society as morally pluralistic as the United States, there may often be no relevant normative premises shared among those engaged in political argument. Ackerman is not unmindful of the problem: "I have not ... tried to establish ... that the path of conversational restraint will not finally lead liberals to a dead end. As you and I discover that we disagree about more and more things, perhaps we will find that the exercise of conversational restraint leaves us nothing to say to one another about our basic problems of coexistence. This seems especially likely since the typical Western society contains many [different moral communities]."[6] Moreover, even when relevant normative premises are shared, or come to be shared in the course of the argument, the premises, and reasoning therefrom, may often be indeterminate. They may often fall far short of resolving the argument. (Resolution of the controversy would then require one or more other premises not to be shared.) It seems, then, that Ackerman's version of neutral politics is often impossible.

An even deeper problem infects Ackerman's 'path of conversational restraint,' a problem that remains even when there are relevant, determinate shared premises. By confining justification in any political conversation to normative premises shared among the participants in the conversation, Ackerman is obviously privileging particular premises or beliefs. Justification on the basis of shared and thereby privileged beliefs is what counts. Justification on the basis of other beliefs—beliefs accepted by some but not by all the participants—is beside the point. Consider what this approach means in practice. If Ackerman and I were participants in a two-party political conversation, I suspect that the proportion of Ackerman's relevant beliefs that I would share would be larger, perhaps much larger, than the proportion of mine he would share. (My relevant beliefs—relevant to most fundamental political-moral issues—include religious convictions about human good. My guess is that Ackerman's do not).[7] Consequently, the proportion of his relevant beliefs that would be privileged would be larger, perhaps much larger, than the proportion of mine that would be privileged. That state of affairs would leave me at a serious disadvantage. Ackerman might be able to rely on all or most of his relevant beliefs, including his most important relevant beliefs, while I would be able to rely only on some of my relevant beliefs, excluding my most important ones: my religious convictions about human good. In that sense Ackerman might get to rely on much of the relevant part of his web of beliefs[8] while I would get to rely only on strands of my web, strands approved, i.e., 'shared'—by Ackerman. I fail to see what is 'neutral' about such a practice of political justification,[9] even though particular arguments yielded by the practice are neutral in the special sense of presupposing the authority only of shared normative premises. (I have already explained why natural arguments in that sense are often inconclusive.)

II

Thomas Nagel contends for a practice of political justification not unlike Ackerman's. But whereas Ackerman's preferred term is 'natural,' Nagel's is 'impartial.' Nagel's effort to explicate the concept of 'impartial' political justification is addressed to "the ... issue of political legitimacy." It is an "attempt to discover a way of justifying coercively imposed political and social institutions and policies to the people who have to live under them, and at the same time to discover what those institutions and policies must be like if such justification is to be possible."[10] Nagel's point of departure, then, is the problem of the legitimacy of political coercion. A condition of such legitimacy, in Nagel's view, is satisfaction of "an especially stringent requirement of objectivity in justification."[11] For Nagel, political justification satisfies this requirement if it is 'impartial.'

What is Nagel's conception or interpretation of 'impartial' political justification?[12] Nagel posits "a highest-order framework of moral reasoning which takes us outside ourselves to a standpoint that is independent of who we are. It cannot derive its basic premises from aspects of our particular and contingent starting points within the world.[13] The epistemological standpoint of morality," insofar as political justification is concerned, must be 'impersonal.'[14] For Nagel, read 'impartial.' 'Impersonal' doesn't get us very far, as Nagel recognizes: "The real difficulty is to make sense of this idea [impartial/impersonal justification]. The idea is that when we look at certain of our convictions from outside, however justified they may be from within, the appeal to their truth must be seen merely as an appeal to our beliefs, and should be treated as such unless those beliefs can be shown to be justifiable from a more impersonal standpoint. If not, they have to remain, for the purposes of a certain kind of moral argument, features of a personal perspective—to be respected as such but no more than that.

This does not mean that we have to stop believing them—that is believing them to be true. Considered as individual beliefs they may be adequately grounded, or at least not unreasonable: The standards of individual rationality are different from the standards of epistemological ethics. It means only that from the perspective of political argument we may have to regard certain of our beliefs, whether moral or religious or even historical or scientific, simply as someone's beliefs, rather than as truths—unless they can be given the kind of impersonal justification appropriate to [the perspective of political argument], in which case they may be appealed to as truths without qualification.[15]

Thus Nagel continues, "When can I regard the grounds for a belief as objective in a way that permits me to appeal to it in political argument, and to rely on it even though others do not in fact accept it and even though they may not be unreasonable not to accept it? What kind of grounds must those be, if I am not to be guilty of appealing simply to my belief, rather than to a common ground of justification?"[16] Nagel's answer is in the form of a specification of the conditions political justification must satisfy if it is to be 'impartial' (and, in that sense, objective). According to Nagel's specification there are two requirements—two epistemological criteria—that "public justification in a context of actual disagreement" must satisfy. Nagel's first requirement governs one's offer of justificatory reasons, while his second requirement governs one's rejection of such reasons offered by others. The heart of the requirements, taken together, is that in political-justificatory discourse one should neither offer nor reject reasons except on the basis of what Nagel calls "the exercise of a common critical rationality" and of "consideration of evidence that can be shared."[17]

Is the practice of impartial political justification, as Nagel conceives it, truly impartial? What is 'evidence that can be shared'? Falsifiable empirical claims? Anything else? One's experience that an activity—drug use, for example—is destructive of the individual's well-being (not to mention the well-being of others—family members, for example—affected by the drug user's addiction)? Such experience can be personal/direct—I may be or have been a drug user—but it can also be vicarious/indirect—my spouse may be or have been a drug user, or I may have read a novel, or seen a movie, about drug use.[18] Does a community's experience (comprising many individuals' experiences, some of which are personal, some of which are vicarious) that an activity—say, homosexual sex—can be constitutive of well-being count as 'evidence that can be shared'? Can the experience of a historically extended community—of a 'tradition'— be evidence that a particular way of life is truly human? Consider, in that regard, James Burtchaell's comment that, "The Catholic tradition embraces a long effort to uncover the truth about human behavior and experience. Our judgments of good and evil focus on whether a certain course of action will make a human being grow and mature and flourish, or whether it will make a person withered, estranged and indifferent. In making our evaluations, we have little to draw on except our own and our forebearers' experience, and whatever wisdom we can wring from our debate with others."[19] If it rules out reliance on such experience, Nagel's 'evidence that can be shared' requirement is implausibly restrictive. Indeed, Joseph Raz has argued that the requirement "is so stringent that it rules out reliance on common everyday observations of fact, as well as much scientific knowledge. We often rely on sense perception and on memory as important reasons for our beliefs. Similarly, we rely on our situation (right next to the accident, in the bright light of day, and so on) as reason to trust our sense perceptions or our memories."[20]

Let's put aside problems with Nagel's implausibly restrictive 'evidence that can be shared' requirement, because more troubling ones await. What does Nagel mean by "the exercise of a common critical rationality?"[21] The implicit basic test for determining what beliefs or claims (propositions, etc.) it makes sense for a person to accept, reject, or be neutral on—what beliefs or claims it is 'rational' or 'reasonable' for her or him to accept, reject, (or neither)—is coherence with whatever else she or he happens to believe. It is coherent with beliefs presently authoritative for her or him. Confining political justification to "the exercise of a common critical rationality" seems to mean, then, in effect, confining it to reasons or premises that cohere with, that can be supported on the basis of, whatever beliefs are universally or near-universally accepted by all or almost all persons in our morally pluralistic society. If, as it certainly seems, that is what Nagel's rationality requirement finally comes to, then, in effect, Nagel has followed Ackerman's strategy of imposing something very like a shared-premises requirement on political justification.[22] Notice, however, that in Ackerman's hands the shared-premises restraint encounters an insurmountable difficulty it does not encounter in Nagel's hands. Ackerman, unlike Nagel, does not begin with a presumption against political coercion. Nor does he begin with a presumption for it. A decision not to pursue a coercive political strategy must be justified no less than a decision to pursue the strategy.[23] The fact that there may be no neutral justification for pursuing a coercive strategy does not mean that those against the strategy prevail, because there may be no neutral justification for not pursuing the strategy. For Ackerman, then, the fact that there are often no relevant shared premises among the interlocutors, or that the shared premises are often indeterminate, entails that there is often no neutral resolution of political conflict. Unlike Ackerman, Nagel begins with a presumption against political coercion. A decision not to pursue a coercive strategy need not be justified. Thus, for Nagel, the fact that there may be no relevant shared premises, or that the shared premises may be indeterminate, does not entail irresolution: If there is no impartial justification for pursuing a coercive strategy, those against the strategy prevail.[24]

Nagel's point of departure—his presumption against political coercion—is deeply problematic. It is, in effect, a question begging presumption in favor of the social and economic status quo.[25] Political coercion, after all, is a principal way of reforming the status quo. Ackerman's point of departure, by contrast, is neutral as to political coercion. But because it is neutral, his shared premises requirement encounters an insurmountable difficulty. Nagel's shared-premises restraint avoids the difficulty, but only because Nagel embraces a presumption, against political coercion, that is clearly not impartial. The politics partly constituted by the presumption is therefore not impartial. If Nagel were to correct his position by letting go his embrace of the presumption, he would then encounter the same difficulty Ackerman encounters: There would often be no impartial resolution of political conflict. Nagel's impartial politics, like Ackerman's neutral politics, would often be impossible.

But there is an even more basic problem with Nagel's approach, a problem that would remain even if Nagel did not embrace the presumption against political coercion, and even when there are relevant, determinate shared premises. It is a problem that, as indicated earlier, infects Ackerman's approach as well, and my criticism of Ackerman's approach can be adapted to Nagel, whose approach is similar. By confining political justification to "the exercise of a common critical rationality," Nagel is simply privileging particular beliefs accepted by all, or almost all, persons in our pluralistic society. Coherence with privileged (shared) beliefs is to be the sole touchstone of rational acceptability, insofar as political justification is concerned. Coherence with other beliefs—beliefs accepted by some but not by all persons in our society—is beside the point. I suspect that the proportion of Nagel's moral, including political-moral, beliefs that are privileged under Nagel's approach is much larger than the proportion of mine that are privileged. (For example, whereas I have what Nagel calls 'personal religious convictions,' apparently Nagel does not.[26] My 'personal religious convictions' are not privileged.)[27] That state of affairs leaves me and many others at a serious disadvantage *vis à vis* Nagel and other devoutly secular intellectuals. In many political arguments Nagel might get to rely on all or most of his relevant beliefs, including his most important relevant beliefs, while I would get to rely only on some of my relevant beliefs, not including the most important ones: my religious convictions about human good. Nagel might get to rely on much of the relevant part of his web of beliefs while others of us would get to rely only on strands of our webs, strands that are rationally acceptable in terms of, that cohere with, privileged beliefs. Therefore, just as Ackerman's practice of 'neutral' political justification is, in the end, not neutral, Nagel's practice of 'impartial' political justification is not impartial,[28] even though particular arguments yielded by the practice are impartial in the special sense of presupposing the authority only of widely accepted beliefs.

The only truly impartial practice of political justification is one that lets everyone rely on their relevant convictions. (Such a practice, however, does not often yield particular arguments that are neutral; it yields, instead, arguments that presuppose the authority of disputed convictions.) As my discussion of Ackerman's and Nagel's positions indicates, a practice of political justification that tolerates only neutral arguments is not itself impartial. The practice of political justification (and political deliberation) I elaborated and defended, like the practices defended by Ackerman and Nagel, is not neutral. A truly neutral practice of political justification is inappropriate in American society. Not every kind of reliance on every kind of conviction is appropriate in a liberal society as pluralistic as the United States. But unlike Ackerman's and Nagel's practices, the dialogic practice defended here does not exclude all but impartial arguments. A practice that includes only impartial arguments is, as Ackerman's and Nagel's practices illustrate, impossibly restrictive. The practice defended includes some, but not all, arguments that are not neutral. In particular, this practice makes room for some (but not all) kinds of reliance on disputed convictions. (This practice includes any political argument a secular liberal like Ackerman or Nagel would probably want to make, though their practices seem to exclude some arguments others would want to make. The particular way in which Ackerman's and Nagel's justificatory practices are partial, rather than neutral/impartial, is just what one might have expected, given

Nagel's and Ackerman's earnestly skeptical attitudes toward religious sensibilities and convictions.)[29]

III

Let us now consider relevant aspects of John Rawls' position on the central issue of political justification, which, while more promising than the positions of Ackerman and Nagel, is still not satisfactory. Rawls' early efforts were [30] aimed at justifying his principles of justice in a way that did not privilege—i.e., that did not presuppose the superiority of any conception of human good relative to any other conception. In that sense, Rawls' efforts were aimed at achieving a 'Right-prior-to-Good' (RpG) justification of his principles of justice. The principles could then serve as the neutral basis for the justification, or for the critique, of political institutions, practices, and policies. In that way political arguments could be appropriately impartial among all competing conceptions of human good.[31] The problem with Rawls' early strategy is that there are no such principles of justice, no principles that can be justified in an RpG way. At least, as I have explained in detail elsewhere, Rawls did not provide such a justification, and it is difficult to imagine an RpG justification of principles of justice.[32] Significantly, as Rawls' recent efforts illustrate, even Rawls does not consider now, if he ever did, that principles of justice can be justified in a way that does not privilege one or more conceptions of human good. That strategy for achieving neutral politics has been discredited and abandoned.

Rawls' recent efforts differ in a crucial respect from his early efforts. Whereas his early efforts were aimed at achieving an RpG justification of his principles of justice, his recent efforts are aimed at explicating and achieving a justification of a different sort: in effect, a 'Good-prior-to-Right' (GpR) justification, in the sense of a justification that presupposes the authority either of a certain conception or of a certain range of conceptions of human good.[33] As Joseph Raz, comparing the two kinds of justification, has explained, in a GpR justification, "different ideals of the good, far from being excluded from the argument for the doctrine of justice, will form the starting points of this argument.... As a result, supporters of different conceptions of the good will follow different routes in arguing for the doctrine of justice. There will be a unanimity in

the conclusion but (given the different starting points) not unanimity on the route to it."[34] Although Rawls' justification of his
'theory of justice'[35] had commonly been understood to be of the
RpG sort, in an essay published in 1985 Rawls makes a number of
statements indicating, in effect, that the justification at which he
(now) aims is of the GpR sort. For example: "We hope that this
political conception of justice may at least be supported by what
we may call an 'overlapping consensus,' that is, by a consensus that
includes all the opposing philosophical and religious doctrines
likely to persist and to gain adherents in a more or less just constitutional democratic society."[36] For Rawls, the relevant range of
opposing doctrines—the range privileged by, the range and
authority of which is presupposed by, his (GpR) justification—is
that of the conceptions included in the 'overlapping consensus.'

As of 1985, Rawls allows that for anyone who adheres to a comprehensive philosophical, religious, or moral doctrine—in effect, to
a conception of human good[37]—included in the overlapping consensus, his or her acceptance of Rawls' principles of justice, of his
"political conception of justice" depends on, is 'supported by,' the
doctrine or conception of human good to which he or she adheres.
In that sense, one's conception of human good plays an essential,
justificatory role in one's acceptance of the principles of justice.

> In such a consensus each of the comprehensive philosophical, religious,
> and moral doctrines accepts justice as fairness in its own way; that is, each
> comprehensive doctrine, from within its own point of view, is led to accept
> the public reasons of justice specified by justice as fairness. We might say
> that they recognize its concepts, principles, and virtues as theorems, as it
> were, at which their several views coincide.... In general, these concepts,
> principles, and virtues are accepted by each as belonging to a more compre-
> hensive philosophical, religious, or moral doctrine.[38]

In a 1987 essay elaborating on "The Idea of an Overlapping
Consensus," Rawls amplifies the point: "Despite the fact that there
are opposing [conceptions of human good] affirmed in society,
there is no difficulty as to how an overlapping consensus may exist.
Since different premises may lead to the same conclusions, we may
simply suppose that the essential elements of the political conception [of justice], its principles, standards and ideals, are theorems,
as it were, at which the [conceptions of human good] in the consensus intersect or converge."[39] By 1985, Rawls' efforts were aimed

at explicating and achieving a justification of the GpR sort. Yet, in 1988, Rawls published an essay contending for 'the priority of right.' "The idea of the priority of right is an essential element in what I have called political liberalism, and it has a central role in justice as fairness [i.e., in Rawls' theory of justice] as a form of that view."[40] The apparent thrust of this passage, and of the essay in which it appears, notwithstanding, Rawls did not change course again in 1988. Rawls defends the priority of right in his 1988 essay. If a priority at all, is a weak version of it—so much so as to be consistent with the priority of good. Recall the strong version of the priority of right: A justification is of the Right-prior-to-Good sort if it does not privilege any conception or range of conceptions of human good. Compare Rawls' version of the priority of right:

> I begin by stating a distinction basic for my discussion—namely, the distinction between a political conception of justice and a comprehensive religious, philosophical, or moral doctrine [i.e. a "conception of the good."] The distinguishing features of a political conception of justice are ... [*inter alia*] that accepting the political conception does not presuppose accepting any particular comprehensive religious, philosophical, or moral doctrine....
>
> A political conception must draw upon various ideas of the good. The question is: subject to what restriction may political liberalism do so? The main restriction would seem to be this: the ideas included must be political ideas. That is, they must belong to a reasonable political conception of justice so that we may assume [*inter alia*] ... that they do not presuppose any particular fully (or partially) comprehensive doctrine.[41]

Rawls' version of 'the priority of right' is consistent with the priority of good. To say that "accepting the political conception does not presuppose accepting any particular comprehensive religious, philosophical, or moral doctrine" is not to say that accepting the political conception does not presuppose the authority of a particular range of such doctrines. Clearly, the sort of justification Rawls began explicating in 1985 does privilege a particular range of such 'comprehensive doctrines,' namely, the doctrines included in Rawls' 'overlapping consensus.' The justification Rawls now wants to achieve for his own political conception of justice is, therefore, a justification of the Good-prior-to-Right sort—even though Rawls insists that "the priority of right is an essential element in ... political liberalism, and it has a central role in justice as fairness as a form of that view." In particular, it is a justification that privileges a certain range of conceptions of human good.[42]

As stated above, Rawls' position on the central issue of political justification is more promising than the positions of Ackerman and Nagel. Unlike Ackerman and Nagel, Rawls does not impose on the practice of political justification any impossibly restrictive conditions.

Nonetheless, Rawls' position on political justification is not satisfactory. Our practice of political justification will somehow have to proceed without the benefit of a political conception of justice supported by an overlapping consensus. As Rawls himself acknowledges, "An overlapping consensus is [not] always possible, given the doctrines currently existing in any democratic society. It is often obvious that it is not, not at least until firmly held beliefs change in fundamental ways."[43] It is doubtful that a political conception of justice supported by an overlapping consensus, whether Rawls' own conception ('justice as fairness') or some other, will ever emerge in a society as morally pluralistic as the United States. (Rawls acknowledges the "likelihood that more than one political conception may be worked up from the fund of shared political ideas; indeed, this is desirable, as these rival conceptions will then compete for citizens' allegiance and be gradually modified and deepened by the contest between them.")[44] As Raz suggests, "Rawls' route seems barren in pluralistic societies, like ours. The degree of existing diversity is just too great."[45] Raz continues: "Furthermore, ... there seems to be little reason to reject valid or true principles, the implementation of which may actually be of benefit to all, just because a small sector of the population cannot be convinced of this fact."[46] Even if a political conception of justice supported by an overlapping consensus is possible in American society, there is at present no such conception in the United States.

Are there at least some political-moral premises supported by an overlapping consensus, even if the premises are not sufficiently integrated to constitute a systematic political conception of justice? Some constitutional norms are political-moral premises. Do such norms, or some of them, enjoy the support of an overlapping consensus? Which ones? Norms pertaining to religious liberty? To racial discrimination? To the extent some political-moral premises enjoy consensual support, given our pluralism, they are likely to be rather abstract or general premises and thus rather indeterminate with respect to the actual political conflicts that beset us. To the extent some concrete or particular and therefore relatively deter-minate political-moral premises enjoy some support in our society, given our pluralism the support is likely to be narrow rather than broad and therefore hardly consensual. The conception of the proper role of beliefs, including religious beliefs, about human good in political deliberation and justification has some affinity with a Rawlsian strategy of identifying normative materials, con-cerning political morality, supported by a wide consensus. But the hope that there is on the horizon a full blown political conception of justice that, when it arrives, will enjoy the support of an overlap-ping consensus, seems wistful. For the foreseeable future, at least, it seems that our pluralistic politics must proceed without benefit of such a conception.

But proceed how? As I've explained, Rawls has given up the quest for a neutral politics in the sense of a politics in which the principles of justice that are to serve as the basis of political justification are themselves justified in an RpG way. Is there some other conception, some realizable conception, of a politics—of a practice of political justification—neutral/impartial in a strong sense?[47] Will some theorist succeed where Ackerman and Nagel, among others, have so far failed? As Ackerman has himself forthrightly acknowledged, "The history of liberal thought gives substance to [skepticism about the possibility of a practice of neutral political justification]. Although many have sought to blaze a path to neutrality, the goal has proven disturbingly elusive.[48] If Ackerman, Nagel, or others want to persist in the quest for a neu-tral/impartial politics, so be it. Understandably, others of us believe that the quest for the Holy Grail of neutral/impartial polit-ical justification is spent and that it is past time to take a different, more promising path.

IV

At the beginning of this essay it was asked whether disputed beliefs about human good should play any role in public delibera-tions about, or public justifications of, contested political choices. Arguments like those developed by Bruce Ackerman and Thomas Nagel are largely to the effect that disputed beliefs about human good should play no or at most a marginal role in political justification. The basic problem with that position is that a practice of political justification from which disputed beliefs about human good are excluded (because, as in Ackerman's argument, they are not shared or because, as in Nagel's, they fail certain epistemological criteria) is impossibly restrictive. Such a politics is bereft of the normative resources required for addressing, much less resolving, the most fundamental political-moral issues that engage and divide us. Only a politics in which beliefs about human good, including disputed beliefs, have a central place is capable of addressing our most basic political questions. Specifically, it can be argued that politics from which disputed beliefs about human good are excluded cannot address a political-moral question that, at the close of the twentieth century, is indisputably and appropriately at the very heart of domestic and international politics: Are there human rights and, if so, what are they?[49]

The claim that a right exists—any right, whether a moral right or a legal right, a human right or some other kind of right—may be either descriptive or prescriptive in character (or both). The descriptive claim that a right exists is the claim that the right is conferred by some specified entity or entities (a person, a family, a church, a state, etc.). The prescriptive claim that a right exists is the claim that the right ought to be conferred by some specified entity(ies).[50] There are different kinds of prescriptive rights claims; for example, prescriptive legal-rights-claims: claims that, given certain authoritative legal norms, such-and-such a (legal) right ought to be conferred (by the courts on behalf of the state, for example). I am interested here in prescriptive moral-rights-claims: claims that, given certain authoritative moral norms, such-and-such a (moral) right ought to be conferred. In particular, I am interested in prescriptive moral-rights-claims of a certain sort: claims that such-and-such a (moral) right ought to be conferred on all (or virtually all) human beings. Let us call claims of that sort "human-rights-claims."[51] How can such claims—claims that some specified entity(ies) ought, as a moral matter, to confer such-and-such a right on (virtually) all human beings, that conferral of the right is morally required—be justified, if at all? Can such claims be justified without reliance on further claims, sometimes disputed, about human good?[52]

The fundamental challenge to any and all human-rights-claims—claims about what rights ought to be conferred on all human beings—is this:

> Why should we [those who, according to the claim, ought to confer the right in question] take seriously the project of protecting the well-being of all human beings; in particular, why should we care about protecting such well-being to the degree it would be protected were we to confer the right in question? Why, indeed, should we give a damn about the well-being of all human beings, as distinct from the well-being of some human beings, for example, the members of our family/tribe/race/religion/etc.?

Let us consider four distinct responses to that challenge.

The "Moral" Response

One response to the challenge is, in effect, little more than a definitional stratagem, according to which giving a damn about the well-being of all human beings is what it means to be 'moral.' Indeed, according to a common version of the stratagem, being concerned about the well-being of all human beings no less than one is concerned about one's own well-being ('equal concern'), respecting the well-being of all human beings no less than one respects one's own well-being (equal respect), is what it means to be 'moral.' To be 'moral' is to be 'impartial' in that sense. 'The moral point of view' is 'the impartial (or universal) point of view.' One ought to give a damn about the well-being of all human beings because it is the 'moral' thing to do.[53] That response is unavailing because it avoids the real challenge, which can be expressed this way in response to the definitional stratagem:

> You claim that morally we ought to do X. We ask why we ought to do X. You say that doing X is what it means to act morally. That response is a wasted gambit. For the sake of argument we'll stipulate your definition of 'moral' in the stipulated sense. Why ought we to give a damn about being 'moral' or doing the 'moral' thing? As a practical matter we're back where we started: Why ought we to do X? What reasons—what real-world, flesh-and-blood reasons—can you give us for doing X? (Your definitional reason is hardly such a reason.)

The fundamental challenge to human-rights-claims is a demand for reasons. James Nickel has distinguished between two different interpretations of the demand: one according to which it is "a demand for prudential reasons" and another according to which it is "a request for moral [as distinct from merely 'prudential'] reasons."[54] (The distinction between 'prudential' and 'moral' is deeply problematic, at least for anyone with an Aristotelian understanding of morality.[55] But let us move on.) The second interpretation, Nickel suggests, "assumes that one's audience has transcended egoism and is prepared to accept arguments that appeal directly to what is reasonable from the moral point of view, whether or not it can be shown that adopting this perspective is likely to promote the long-term interests of the individual."[56] But the problem is larger, much larger, than 'egoism': One may favor, not oneself, or even one's family, but one's tribe, or race, or religion, or country. The assumption that those to whom human-rights-claims are addressed have 'transcended' such favoritism is wildly implausible. The fundamental challenge to human-rights-claims is a real world challenge: Many to whom such claims are addressed have conspicuously not adopted anything like "the moral (impartial, universal) point of view." "The moral point of view" is not a justificatory basis for human-rights-claims, at least, not a fundamental basis. "The moral point of view" is itself in dire need of justification, especially in a world, our world, the real world, that is often fiercely partial/local rather than impartial/universal.

The question remains: What reasons can be given to the addressees of human-rights-claims for giving a damn about the well-being of all human beings (and thus for adopting the moral point of view)? Charles Taylor, commenting critically on moral theories that are variations on the definitional stratagem, in particular theories that exclude discourse about human good, has put the point this way: "[Such theories] leave us with nothing to say to someone who asks why he should be moral.... But this could be misleading, if we seemed to be asking how we could convince someone who saw none of the point of our moral beliefs. There is nothing we can do to 'prove' we are right to such a person. But imagine him to be asking another question: he could be asking us to make plain the point of our moral code, in articulating what's uniquely valuable in cleaving to these injunctions [e.g., act 'impartially']. Then the implication of these theories is that we have nothing to say which can impart insight. We can wax rhetorical and propagandize, but we can't say what's good or valuable about [the injunctions], or why they command assent."[57]

The "Rational" Response

A second response to the challenge relies on an approach to the justification of rights according to which no person (or group) can 'rationally' reject their conferral on at least some—if not all—human beings, their conferral (and respect) of which somehow satisfies (maximizes satisfaction of) preferences the person has. The problem with that approach is that given a realistic view of the preferences many persons have, the approach may succeed in justifying conferral of only a few rights constituting in effect "a mere nonaggression treaty."[58] Further, it may succeed in justifying such rights not as human rights—rights possessed by (virtually) all human beings—but only as rights possessed by persons who are in, or who realistically may arrive at, a position to do one another harm.[59] Given the preferences many persons have, it is difficult to see how the approach could begin to justify the range of rights that in the period since the end of World War II many have urged be established as human rights in international law, or even the range of rights that have actually been established as human rights in international law in the postwar period: rights concerning *inter alia*, religious and political freedom, nondiscrimination based on race and sex, fairness in the enforcement of criminal laws, and material ('economic') well-being.[60] It is even difficult to see how the approach in question could justify the range of rights established as human rights in our own domestic legal system, in particular the human rights established under the Constitution. (Many constitutional rights are human rights: the rights, not merely of citizens, but of all persons.)[61] The justification of human-rights-claims of the sort with which we are familiar in the world today, and the evaluation of such claims, clearly require more substantial grounding—and, alas, more controversial grounding—than premises about what no person can "rationally" reject.

The "Neutral" Response

A third response relies on a practice of (putatively) 'neutral' political justification like the practices recommended by political theorists such as Ackerman and Nagel. The relevant problem with that response, however—a problem highlighted earlier in this essay—is that such a practice is impossibly restrictive: The justifications yielded by such a practice often underdetermine resolution of political arguments, including arguments about human-rights-claims. The approach to the justification of rights discussed in the preceding paragraph can be understood as a variation on 'neutral' political justification, because it is a justification to a person based on nothing more controversial than the good of maximizing satisfaction of her own preferences. But, like 'neutral' political justification generally, such an approach cannot begin to justify a significant range of rights, much less justify them as human rights.

The "Religious" Response

A fourth response to the fundamental challenge relies squarely on convictions about human good by arguing that giving a damn about the well-being of all human beings is a sensibility and a practice partly constitutive of 'the good life' for everyone. According to a response of this sort, the life that is profoundly good or fitting for everyone to live, the meaningful life for each and every human being, the life that is, in that sense, 'truly, fully' human,[62] includes concern and respect for the well-being of all human beings and not just for the well-being of oneself or one's family or tribe or race or religion, etc. Consider, for example, the moral image central to what Hilary Putnam has called "the Jerusalem-based religions": an image that "stresses equality and also fraternity, as in the metaphor of the whole human race as One Family, or all women and men as sisters and brothers."[63] For Christians the basic shape of the good life is indicated by the instruction given by Jesus at a Passover Seder on the eve of his execution: "I give you a new commandment: love one another; you must love one another just as I have loved you."[64] Such a sensibility is not confined to the Semitic spiritualities; it is an aspect of Indic spiritualities, too. For Buddhists, for example, 'the good life' centrally involves compassion for all sentient creatures and therefore for all human beings.

Why should we "love one another as I have loved you?" The answer, in the vision of the Jerusalem-based religions—rooted in the lived experience of the Jerusalem-based religious communities—is that the Other, too, including the outsider, the stranger, the alien, is a 'child' of the one creator, God[65] and therefore 'brother'/'sister'. The Other, too, no less than oneself, is therefore

of intrinsic and inestimable worth. As it has been put in the introduction to a recent selection of writings from *The Talmud*:

> From this conception of man's place in the universe comes the sense of
> the supreme sanctity of all human life. "He who destroys one person has
> dealt a blow at the entire universe, and he who sustains or saves one person
> has sustained the whole world."
>
> The sanctity of life is not a function of national origin, religious affilia-
> tion, or social status. In the sight of God, the humble citizen is the equal of
> the person who occupies the highest office. As one Talmudist put it:
> "Heaven and earth I call to witness, whether it be an Israelite or pagan, man
> or woman, slave or maidservant, according to the work of every human
> being doth the Holy Spirit rest upon him."... As the rabbis put it: "We are
> obligated to free non-Jews residing among us even as we free Jews; we are
> obligated to visit their sick even as we visit the Jewish sick; we are obligated
> to attend to the burial of their dead even as we attend to the burial of the
> Jewish dead."[66]

Such a response to the fundamental challenge to human-rights-
claims consists mainly of a conception of human good, in particular of convictions about what it means to be 'truly, fully' human,
about the meaningfulness of life, about what is of real and
ultimate value in life. ("To find out what our nature is seems to be
one and the same thing as to find out what we deeply believe to be
most important and indispensable [in a human life].")[67] It is far
from clear if there is any response to the challenge not rooted ultimately in such convictions.[68] The obvious and great problem with
any response that appeals to particular convictions about human
good, especially religious convictions about the meaningfulness of
life, is that in a pluralistic society like our own, and even more so
in our pluralistic world, there are competing convictions, both secular and religious, about human good. It is difficult to see how
grounding human-rights-claims on premises about the good or
fitting or meaningful way for human beings to live their lives can
serve to justify the claims to those for whom the premises are not
authoritative.[69]

But, in the course of arguing for the possibility of ecumenical
politics in our religiously and morally pluralistic domestic context,
there is good reason to believe that significant premises about
human good, significant standards of political-moral judgment, are
authoritative for many (though not for all) persons and groups in
American society. Indeed, basic premises about human good are

widely authoritative not just in American society, but international-ly. Consider the post-World War II phenomenon of international discourse about human rights, which has grown larger[70] and more vigorous with the passage of time. The existence and indeed vitality of this international human-rights discourse is not surprising: The great religious traditions, Indic as well as Semitic, are principal par-ticipants in the discourse. They are tending to converge with one another, and with Marxism, in holding that an essential part of what it means to be fully human, an essential requirement of the meaningful life for everyone, is to take some responsibility for the well-being of the Other (the outsider, the stranger, the alien). A growing literature documents and discusses that emergent conver-gence.[71] Just as religious pluralism has not been an impediment to, but rather an occasion of, a stimulus to, the emergence of ecu-menical theology,[72] religious and moral pluralism need not be an impediment to, but instead may be an occasion of, the emergence of ecumenical politics. International discourse about human rights, which illustrates the possibility of ecumenical politics even in an international context, certainly suggests the possibility of ecu-menical politics in a religiously/morally pluralistic domestic con-text such as our own. If ecumenical political discourse is possible internationally, then it is certainly possible domestically.

Becoming 'Human'

It is not surprising that in many societies, especially modern societies, conceptions of human authenticity—of what it means to be 'truly, fully' human—and interpretations of human needs are disputed. Nor is it surprising that such disputes are often contest-ed, sometimes obliquely, in politics. Nor, finally, is it surprising that in some societies, especially pre-modern societies, a particular con-ception/interpretation of the human—a particular "ideology," if you will—has sometimes achieved a hegemonic status, with the consequences that contests over the human have become repressed. What is surprising is the effort to imagine a neutral poli-tics from which such contests are to be excluded or, at least, in which they are to be marginalized. Contests over human good have been and remain central to politics, not marginal (however repressed such contests may sometimes be). Moreover, the ques-tions at issue in such contests—regarding human good, including the question of what it means to live a truly, fully human life—include questions that are indisputably political: questions about the authentically human way to live the collective life, the life in common. It seems fanciful to suppose that contests over human good could ever be anything but central to politics. The main point, however, is that a practice of political justification from which disputed beliefs about human good are excluded lacks the normative resources required for addressing our most fundamental political-moral questions, like questions about human rights. Only a politics in which beliefs about human good, including disputed beliefs, has a central place is capable of addressing such questions.

NOTES

*This essay is based on Michael J. Perry, *Love and Power: The Role of Religion and Morality in American Politics*, (Oxford University Press, 1991), 1, 2. Professor Perry holds the Howard J. Trienens Chair in Law at the Northwestern University School of Law.

1. J. Murray, We Hold These Truths 27 (1960). Murray added: "This fact created the possibility of a new solution; indeed, it created a demand for a new solution. The possibility was exploited and the demand was met by the American Constitution." Id.

2. I use "citizen" here and throughout the essay in a nontechnical sense. A person may reside in the United States, may intend to do so for the rest of his or her life, and may habitually and even prominently participate in arguments about issues that engage American politics, without being an American citizen, even without intending to become one, in the technical, legal sense.

3. For a complementary discussion, see M. Perry, *Morality, Politics, and Law*, chs. 3 & 4 (1988).

4. Bruce Ackerman, *Social Justice in the Liberal State* (1980) Ackerman uses the term 'neutral'; Ackerman, "What is Neutral About Neutrality?." (Ethics, Jan. 1983), 372. (So do kindred political theorists like Ronald Dworkin and Charles Larmore. See Dworkin, "Liberalism," in S. Hampshire, ed., Public and Private Morality, 113 [1978]; Dworkin, "What Liberalism Isn't," New York Rev., Jan. 20, 1983, 47; C. Larmore, Patterns of Moral Complexity [1987]; Larmore, "Political Liberalism," Political Theory [forthcoming]. I have commented elsewhere on Ackerman's basic position in *Social Justice in the Liberal State*, M. Perry, note 3, at 63-66; Perry, "Neutral Politics?," 51 Rev. Politics 479, 480-81 (1989). I comment here on a recent essay by Ackerman. See note 5.

5. Ackerman, "Why Dialogue?," 86 J. Philosophy 5, 17-18 (1989).

6. Ackerman, note 5, at 22. See note 18 (quoting Thomas Nagel: requirement that

"the premises be actually accepted" is an "impossibly restrictive condition on [the exercise of] political power.") When is a normative premise "shared"? What counts as evidence that a premise is shared? Reading Ackerman's *Social Justice in Liberal State* (note 4) retrospectively through the lens of his later essay "Why Dialogue?" (note 5), we may fairly interpret Ackerman to be suggesting that a distribution-of-scarce-resources-according-to-worth principle (see M. Perry, note 3, at 65) is shared across American society. But is it? People mean such different things by "worth": worth-in-God's-eyes, worth-according-to-the-laws-of-nature, and so on. Superficial sharing may conceal deep disagreement. See id., 155-56.

7. See note 29.
8. See W. Quine & J. Ulian, *The Web of Belief* (2nd ed. 1978).
9. See Smith, "Separation and the 'Secular': Reconstructing the Disestablishment Decision," 67 Texas L. Rev. 955, 1010 (1989); "[T]he common denominator argument [is] fraudulent. Suppose Dad and Daughter are discussing what to have for dinner. Daughter proposes: "Let's just have dessert."' Dad suggests that it would be better to have a full meal, with salad, meat, fruit, cooked vegetables, and then dessert. Daughter responds: "Obviously, Dad, we disagree about a lot of things. But there is one thing we agree on; we both want dessert." Although he might admire Daughter's cleverness, Dad is not likely to be taken in by this common denominator ploy. The argument that secular public discourse provides a common denominator that all citizens share is comparably clever—and equally unpersuasive."
10. Nagel, "Moral Conflict and Political Legitimacy," 16 Philosophy and Public Affairs 215, 218 (1987). Nagel emphasizes that by "justification" he does not mean "persuasion": "'Justification' ... is a normative concept: arguments that justify may fail to persuade, if addressed to an unreasonable audience; and arguments that persuade may fail to justify. Nevertheless, justification hopes to persuade the reasonable ..." Id.
11. Id. at 223. Nagel explains: "This would be implied, on one reading, by the second formulation of Kant's categorical imperative—that one should treat humanity never merely as a means, but always also as an end. If you force someone to serve an end that he cannot share, you are treating him as a mere means—even if the end is his own good, as you see it ..." Id. at 223 n. 8.
12. Cf. id. at 223: "If liberalism is to be defended as a higher-order theory rather than just another sectarian doctrine, it must be shown to result from an interpretation of impartiality itself, rather than from a particular conception of the good that is to be made impartially available. Of course any interpretation of impartiality will be morally controversial—it is not a question of rising to a vantage point above all moral disputes—but the controversy will be at a different level."
13. Id. at 229.
14. Id. at 230.
15. See id. at 230 (emphasis added & deleted)
16. Id. at 231, 232. Nagel goes on to emphasize that "by a common ground I do not mean submerged agreement on a set of premises by which the claim could in principle be settled in a way that all parties would recognize as correct." Id. See id., 231-32:

[Impartial justification involves] neither an appeal to my own beliefs nor an appeal to beliefs that we all share. It cannot be the latter because it is intended precisely to justify the forcible imposition in some cases of measures that are not universally accepted. We need a distinction between two kinds of disagreement—one whose grounds make it alright for the majority to use political power in the service of their opinion, and another whose grounds are such that it would be wrong for the majority to do so.

For this purpose we cannot appeal directly to the distinction between reasonable and unreasonable beliefs. It would be an impossibly restrictive condition on political power to say that its exercise may be justified only by appeal to premises that others could not reasonably reject (though less restrictive than the condition that the premises be actually accepted by all) ...

Reasonable persons can disagree not only over religious doctrines and ultimate conceptions of the good life, but over levels of public provision of education and health care, social security, defense policy, environmental preservation, and a host of other things that liberal societies determine by legislative action. What distinguishes those disagreements from the ones where liberalism rejects majority rule?

17. See id. 232:

Public justification in a context of actual disagreement requires, first, preparedness to submit one's reasons to the criticism of others, and to find that the exercise of a common critical rationality and consideration of evidence that can be shared will reveal that one is mistaken. This means that it must be possible to present to others the basis of your beliefs, so that once you have done so, they have what you have, and can arrive at a judgment on the same basis ...

Public justification requires, second, an expectation that if others who do not share your belief are wrong, there is probably an explanation of their error which is not circular. That is, the explanation should not come down to the mere assertion that they do not believe the truth (what you believe), but should explain their false belief in terms of errors in their evidence, or identifiable errors in drawing conclusions from it, or in argument, judgment, and so forth. One may not always have the information necessary to give such an account, but one must believe there is one, and that the justifiability of one's own belief would survive a full examination of the reasons behind theirs. These two points may be combined in the idea that a disagreement which falls on objective common ground must be open-ended in the possibility of its investigation and pursuit, and not come down finally to a bare confrontation between incompatible personal points of view.

18. Cf. Lovin, "Empiricism and Christian Social Thought," Annual of Society of Christian Ethics 25, 41 (1982); "[M]oral reality...[is] about an interaction between persons and the world which can only be known from the reports of

those who experience that interaction."

19. See Burtchaell, "The Sources of Conscience," 13 Notre Dame Mag. 20, 20 (Winter 1984-85). See also Ladd, "Politics and Religion in America: The Enigma of Pluralism," in J. Pennock & J. Chapman, eds., *Religion, Morality and the Law* 263, 279 (1988) (commenting on and recommending "the pragmatic attitude that ... most people in America take toward particular religions [and particular religious doctrines]," in which they are understood not as absolutist, dogmatic, authoritarian systems but simply as "experiments in living with other people in a shared world of suffering and hope.") Cf. Battaglia, "'Sect' or 'Denomination'?" The Place of Religious Ethics in a Post-Churchly Culture," 16 J. Religious Ethics 128, 137 (1988): "[David] Tracy's aim is to reintroduce into public life a reasonable discussion of the possibilities of human life. His great accomplishment is to make comprehensible to both believers and outsiders his willingness to let the public explanation of Christianity stand on that basis—as a profound and challenging disclosure of what it means to be human."

20. Raz, "Facing Diversity: The Case of Epistemic Abstinence," 19 Philosophy & Public Affairs 3, 40 (1990). See id., 43:

> We are left in a frustrating position. We know that the test of "sharing all the evidence" must be relaxed. But nothing in the rest of Nagel's discussion suggests how to relax it. I suspect that the principle of impartiality, when relaxed to admit all acceptable reasons, fails in the task that Nagel assigns it ... It can rule out only blatantly irrational beliefs. It does not rule out as grounds for coercive political action any beliefs that individuals are justified in holding to be true. No one is justified in holding beliefs that are not based on acceptable reasons. But the heart and soul of Nagel's argument is for epistemic restraint in appealing to truth, for the contention [is] that some truths which individuals are justified in believing, they are not justified in relying on politically. This seems an impossible task, given that to be personally justified in believing a proposition one must accept that one's belief is in principle subject to impersonal, impartial standards of correctness. Those who comply with this condition do subject their beliefs to valid impersonal tests. It may be that others do not see it that way, and deny the validity of those tests. But given that the tests are both valid and publicly, objectively, and impartially available, it seems impossible that others can reasonably deny the validity of those tests, unless they lack information. And that lack can be remedied, and so cannot serve as the basis for Nagel's theory. Ultimately Nagel's principle is bound to fail because it depends on driving a wedge between appeal to truth and acceptance of objective standards of justification; and that wedge comes unstuck.

21. Surely he means much more than the exercise of common logic. That would be a trivially weak requirement. Cf. A. MacIntyre, Whose Justice? Which Rationality? 351 (1988): "It is not then that competing traditions do not share some standards. All the traditions with which we have been concerned agree in according a certain authority to logic both in their theory and in their practice. Were it not so, their adherents would be unable to disagree in the way in which

they do. But that upon which they agree is insufficient to resolve the disagreements." Does "the exercise of a common critical rationality" partly involve, in Nagel's view, "consideration [only] of evidence that can be shared," so that the evidence-that-can-be-shared requirement is simply an aspect of the common-critical-rationality requirement?

22. Not that Nagel has done so wittingly. Cf. note 16 (quoting Nagel: requirement that "the premises be actually accepted" is an "impossibly restrictive condition on [the exercise of] political power.")

23. See Ackerman, note 5.

24. See Nagel, note 10, at 231-34.

25. For a critical comment on such question-begging moves in political theory, see Ackerman, note 5.

26. See note 29.

27. See Nagel, note 10, at 232-33.

Nagel struggles but, in my view, ultimately fails to specify, much less administer, a distinction, which he acknowledges to be "vague" and problematic, between (1) moral disagreements, including religious-moral disagreements, that "come down finally to a pure confrontation between personal [religious or] moral convictions" and (2) a "perceptibly different" kind of disagreement: "disagreement[s] in judgment over the preponderant weight of reasons bearing on an issue" (id. at 233). See id. at 233 et seq. "Perceptibly different" to whom? To Nagel? Certainly not to me. But then perhaps my perceptual apparatus isn't up to snuff. In any event, by the second kind of disagreement Nagel cannot mean either disagreements merely about the facts or even disagreements in reasoning from shared premises. Nagel specifically disclaims to be addressing political conflicts in which there is "submerged agreement on a set of premises by which the claim could in principle be settled in a way that all parties would recognize as correct." Id. at 232. See note 16.

28. See note 9. Cf. The Williamsburg Charter: A National Celebration and Reaffirmation of the First Amendment Religious Liberty Clauses 21 (1988) ("The Framers' intention is indisputably ignored when public policy debates can appeal to the theses of Adam Smith and Karl Marx, or Charles Darwin and Sigmund Freud but not to the Western religious tradition in general and the Hebrew and Christian scriptures in particular.")

In a letter to me, dated March 20, 1990, Thomas Nagel wrote that "I don't know whether it will please or disappoint you to learn that I have decided, since publishing the essay you criticize, that the attempt fails." (This is not to say that Nagel agrees that the goal of impartial political justification is impossible. In his letter Nagel expresses the hope that he can reinterpret and vindicate the notion of such justification.) I criticize Nagel's important essay not to beat a dead horse, but because I think Nagel's failure is instructive.

29. See T. Nagel, What Does It All Mean? ch. 10 (1987) (discussing "The Meaning of Life"). Cf. Nagel, "Agreeing in Principle," Times Literary Suppl., July 8-14, 1988, at 747 (reviewing A. MacIntyre, *Whose Justice? Which Rationality?* [1988]. See also B. Ackerman, note 4, 368: "There is no meaning in the bowels of the universe." Cf. R. Neuhaus, *The Naked Public Square: Religion and Democracy in America* 86 (1984): "In the minds of some secularists the naked public square

[i.e. neutral/impartial political discourse] is a desirable goal. They subscribe to the dogma of the secular Enlightenment that, as people become more enlightened (educated), religion will wither away; or, if it does not wither away, it can be safely sealed off from public consideration, reduced to a private eccentricity." For examples of a rather different attitude in contemporary Anglo-American philosophy, see D. Braine, *The Reality of Time and the Existence of God* (1988); S. Clark, *From Athens to Jerusalem: the Love of Wisdom and the Love of God* (1984). See also L. Kolakowski, *Metaphysical Horror* (1988).

30. Rawls has argued that the following interpretation of his early effort is mistaken. See Rawls, "Justice as Fairness: Political, Not Metaphysical," 14 Philosophy & Public Affairs 223 (1985). But see Ackerman, note 5, at 15 n. 7: "Despite Rawls's subsequent disavowal of this interpretation ... I do not believe critics were simply engaged in tea leaf reading in finding this theme (uneasily co-existing with many others) in Rawls's major works."

31. See M. Perry, note 3, 60-62.

32. See id., 59-63. See also Ackerman, note 5, 15-16.

33. On the distinction between GpR theories and RpG theories, see Taylor, "Hegel's Ambiguous Legacy for Modern Liberalism," 10 Cardozo L. Rev. 857, 857-58 (1989).

34. Raz, "Liberalism, Autonomy, and the Politics of Neutral Concern," 7 Midwest Studies in Philosophy 89, 105 (1982). See id.: "[T]he common feature of most routes will be the reliance on a rational reconstruction of a process of bargaining by which the common overriding goal to reach an agreement leads the parties to compromise by accepting a less than perfect doctrine as the optimally realizable second best."

35. See J. Rawls, *A Theory of Justice* (1971).

36. Rawls, "Justice as Fairness: Political Not Metaphysical," 14 *Philosophy & Public Affairs* 223, 225-26 (1985).

37. Although Rawls sometimes distinguishes loosely between "comprehensive doctrines" and "conceptions of the good," the distinction is unimportant for present purposes. See Rawls, "The Idea of an Overlapping Consensus," 7 Oxford J. Legal Studies 1, 4 (1987): "[A workable conception of justice] must allow for a diversity of general and comprehensive doctrines, and for the plurality of conflicting, and indeed incommensurable, conceptions of the meaning, value and purpose of human life (or what I shall call for short 'conceptions of the good') affirmed by the citizens of democratic societies." See also Rawls, "The Priority of Right and Ideas of the Good," 17 Philosophy & Public Affairs 251, 252-53 (1988): "[A moral conception (as distinct from a political conception of justice)] is said to be general when it applies to a wide range of subjects (in the limit to all subjects); it is comprehensive when it includes conceptions of what is of value in human life, ideals of personal virtue and character, and the like ... There is a tendency for religious and philosophical conceptions to be general and fully comprehensive ..."

38. Rawls, note 37, 247.

39. Rawls, "The Idea of an Overlapping Consensus," 7 Oxford J. Legal Studies, 1, 19 (1987).

40. Rawls, "The Priority of Right and Ideas of the Good," 17 Philosophy & Public Affairs 252, 251 (1988).

41. Id. 252, 253. "A doctrine is fully comprehensive when it covers all recognized values and virtues within one rather precisely articulated scheme of thought, whereas a doctrine is only partially comprehensive when it comprises certain (but not all) non-political values and virtues and is rather loosely articulated." Id., 253.

42. I have addressed only the first sense, a weak sense, in which the priority of right is a feature of Rawls' political liberalism: The justification at which Rawls aims does not privilege any particular conception of the good (though it does privilege a particular range of such conceptions). The priority of right is a feature of Rawls' political liberalism in a second sense as well. But the second sense is even weaker than the first. Rawls writes that in his theory of justice "the priority of right implies that the principles of (political) justice set limits to permissible ways of life; hence the claims citizens make to pursue ends that transgress those limits have no weight (as judged by that political conception)." Id., 251. See also id., 252, 253. However, this is just to make the tautologous point that principles of political justice trump other moral principles if political justice is the aim. Charles Taylor has recently discussed "three separate theses which are advanced at different times under the slogan of the priority of the right over the good." See C. Taylor, *Sources of the Self: The Making of the Modern Identity* 532-33 (1989).

Given the turn in Rawls' thinking, as marked in particular by his 1985 essay (note 36), it is not surprising that Richard Rorty has revised his earlier characterization of Rawls as a Kantian and now sees him as more Deweyan than Kantian. See Rorty, "The Priority of Democracy To Philosophy," in M. Peterson & R. Vaughan, eds., The Virginia Statute of Religious Freedom 257, 264-5 (1987). However, the fact that Rawls' theory is fundamentally of the Good-prior-to-Right sort has implications that Rorty, in his recent discussion of Rawls, seems not to understand. Such a theory implicitly claims that, contrary to what Rorty maintains, there is a need, sometimes, for "a religious or a philosophical preface to politics" (see id. at 264), especially in circumstances like our own, in which there is no political conception of justice supported by an overlapping consensus and there are only few determinate shared political-moral premises. Rawls seems to understand this—e.g., see Rawls, note 39, at 14 ("in affirming a political conception of justice we may eventually have to assert at least certain aspects of our own comprehensive ... religious or philosophical doctrine")—even if Rorty does not. For an excellent critical commentary on Rawls' recent writings and, in particular, an argument that political philosophy must be "metaphysical," see Hampton, "Should Political Philosophy Be Done Without Metaphysics?" 99 Ethics 791 (1989). See also K. Greenawalt, *Religious Convictions and Political Choice* (1988); M. Perry, note 3, at 87 & 102-104. Cf. J. Murray, note 1, at ix-x: "[For a Catholic] the principles of Catholic faith and morality stand superior to, and in control of, the whole order of civil life. The question is sometimes raised, whether Catholicism is compatible with American democracy. The question is invalid as well as impertinent; for the manner of its position inverts the order of values. It must, of course, be turned round to read, whether American democracy is compatible with Catholicism." (Murray went on to say that "[a]n affirmative answer to [the question] ... is one of the truths I hold." Id.)

43. Rawls, note 39, at 5.

44. Id., at 7.

45. Raz, note 20, at 45. For an interesting argument that "a Christian affirmation of [Rawls' political conception of justice] is impossible," see Jackson, "To Bedlam and Part Way Back: John Rawls and Christian Justice" (forthcoming). Compare Beckley, "A Christian Affirmation of Rawls's Idea of Justice as Fairness: Part I," 13 J. Religious Ethics 212 (1985); Beckley, "A Christian Affirmation of Rawls's Idea of Justice as Fairness: Part II," 14 J.

46. Raz, note 20.

47. In his 1988 essay on "the priority of right" Rawls distinguishes among (1) "procedural neutrality," (2) three kinds of "neutrality of aim," and (3) "neutrality of effect or influence." See Rawls, note 40, at 260-64. He acknowledges that his political conception of justice is neither procedurally neutral nor neutral in effect or influence. He acknowledges, too, that his conception is neutral in aim only in the weak sense that "the state is to secure equal opportunity to advance any permissible conception [of the good, i.e., any conception not ruled out by the political conception; and the social, political, and economic]...institutions are not intended to favor any [one of the permissible conceptions of the good]." Id., 262. This is a weak sense of neutrality, because the political conception of justice tolerates only some, not all, conceptions of the good; not every conception of the good is "permissible." See Macedo, "The Politics of Justification," 18 Political Theory 280, 289 (1990): "What does a liberal say about a range of religious beliefs that include ecumenical Catholicism, fundamentalist Protestantism, and sects that require holy war against non- believers? There are, says Rawls, 'no resources within the political view to judge those conflicting conceptions. They are equally permissible provided they respect the limits imposed by the principles of political justice.' Underline 'provided': All religions compatible with liberalism will be.

48. Ackerman, note 5, 12-13.

49. It's not that Ackerman doesn't advance positions on issues of human rights. See B. Ackerman, Social Justice in the Liberal State (1980). It's just that his doing so is inconsistent with his idea of neutral political justification. See, in addition to section I of this essay, M. Perry, note 3, at 63-66.

In the period since the end of the Second World War discourse about human rights has been rich and important. See R. Drinan, *Cry of the Oppressed: The History and Hope of the Human Rights Revolution* (1987); J. Nickel, *Making Sense of Human Rights: Philosophical Reflections on the Universal Declaration of Human Rights* (1987); J. Donnelly, *Universal Human Rights in Theory and Practice* (1989).

Like feminist critical-theorist Nancy Fraser, and "unlike some communitarian, socialist, and feminist critics, I do not believe that rights talk is inherently individualistic, bourgeois-liberal, and androcentric—rights talk takes on those properties only when societies establish the wrong rights, for example, when the (putative) right to private property is permitted to trump other social rights." N. Fraser, *Unruly Practices: Power, Discourse, and Gender in Contemporary Social Theory* *1983* (1989).

50. To claim that a right ought to be conferred by some specified entity is not necessarily to claim that the entity (or anyone else) ought always to respect the right, that is, ought never to violate the right. Not all rights that ought to be conferred are "absolute" rights.

51. A prescriptive legal-rights-claim, too, many concern a human right: The claim may be that such-and-such a (legal) right ought to be conferred on (virtually) all human beings. Even a descriptive rights-claim may concern a human right: For example, the United States confers some human rights by means of the U.S. Constitution. But I'm interested here in human-rights-claims as a species of prescriptive moral-rights-claims. For useful analyses of "rights", see L. Sumner, *The Moral Foundation of Rights*, ch. 2 (1987); J. Nickel, note 49, ch. 2.

52. Some rights-theorists argue that the basic point of conferring rights on human beings (and of respecting rights that have been conferred (cf. note 49) is to protect the well-being of the human beings on whom the rights are or should be conferred. Other rights theorists contend that the basic point is to protect, not well-being, but autonomy. Yet others argue—sensibly, in my view—that the basic point of conferring rights on human beings, whether some human beings or all human beings, is sometimes to protect well-being and sometimes to protect autonomy and sometimes to do both. See J. Nickel, note 49, 23-24. Compare L. Sumner, note 53, at 203-05. Indeed, if autonomy is a particular, and particularly important, constituent of human well-being (on the relation of well-being and autonomy, see Raz, "Liberalism, Skepticism, and Democracy," 74 Iowa L. Rev. 761, 779-86 [1989]), then protecting human well-being in its entirety requires protecting autonomy. Let's assume that the basic point of conferring rights on (some or all) human beings is to protect human well-being, including autonomy.

53. In commenting on "that sort of impartiality that constitutes the moral point of view," James Griffin has written that "[w]e all agree that to look at things morally is to look at them, in some sense or other, impartially, granting every person some sort of equal status. Of course, we should have to make this notion of equal status more determinate—say through one interpretation or other of the Ideal Observer or Ideal Contractor. In any case, principles of equality can be principles of impartiality in this sense: they can express the spirit with which one will, if one is moral, consider the facts of the matter." J. Griffin, Well-Being 239 (1987).

54. J. Nickel, note 49, at 91.

55. See Scott, "Motive and Justification," 85. J. Philosophy 479, 499 (1988): "When he was deliberating about how to live, St. Augustine asked, 'What does anything matter, if it does not have to do with happiness?' His question requires explanation, because he is not advising selfishness nor the reduction of other people to utilities, and even qualification, because other things can have some weight. All the same, the answer he expects is obviously right: only a happily led life matters conclusively. If I had a clear view of it, I could have no motive to decline it, I could regret nothing by accepting it, I would have nothing about which to deliberate further." Cf. Taylor, "Ancient Wisdom and Modern Folly," *13 Midwest Studies in Philosophy* 54, 57, 58 (1988): "The Greek *eudaimonia* is always translated 'happiness' which is unfortunate, for the meaning we attach to the word happiness is thin indeed compared to what the ancients meant by *eudaimonia*. Fulfillment might be a better term, though this, too, fails

to capture the richness of the original term.... The concept of happiness in modern philosophy, as well as in popular thinking, is superficial indeed in comparison." For an extended discussion of the "Why be moral?" problem from a neo-Aristotelian perspective, see R. Bittner, *What Reason Demands* (1983; Eng. tr. 1989).

56. J. Nickel, note 49, at 91.

57. C. Taylor, note 42, at 87.

58. See B. Williams, *Ethics and the Limits of Philosophy* 103-04 (1985).

59. For my earlier reflections on such an approach, see M. Perry, note 3, at 82-90.

60. See, e.g., J. Nickel, note 49. For a compilation of human-rights documents, transnational (e.g., European, African, Central American, etc.) as well as international, see R. Lillich, ed., International Human Rights Instruments (1986).

61. For example, section 1 of the Fourteenth Amendment to the United States Constitution provides, in relevant part: "[N]or shall any State deprive any person of life, liberty, or property, without due process of law; nor deny to any person within its jurisdiction the equal protection of the laws."

62. See King, "What is True Religion?: Toward An Ecumenical Criteriology," in L. Swidler, ed., *Toward a Universal Theology of Religion* 231, 239-43 (1987); Steinfels, "The Search for an Alternative," Commonweal, Nov. 30, 1981, 660, 661 (commenting on the importance of the distinction "between the human and the 'truly human'"); Nussbaum, "Aristotle on Human Nature and the Foundations of Ethics" (forthcoming) (discussing the difference, for the Greeks, between, on the one hand, the life of a beat-ly anthropomorph, like the Cyclops, or of a godly anthropomorph, like Zeus, and, on the other, the truly human life).

63. H. Putnam, The Many Faces of Realism 60-61 (1987).

64. John 13:34. See also John 15:12.

65. In the Bible God—Ultimate Reality—is often imaged as "parent," sometimes as "father," sometimes as "mother." See R. Ruether, *Sexism and God-Talk: Toward a Feminist Theology* (1983).

66. Bokser and Bokser, "Introduction: The Spirituality of the Talmud," in *The Talmud: Selected Writings* 7, 30-31 (1989) (selected and translated by B. Bokser) (footnotes omitted).

67. Nussbaum, note 62.

68. Cf. Tinder, "Can We be Good without God: The Political Meaning of Christianity," Atlantic, Dec., 1989, at 69, 80 (passages rearranged and emphasis added):

> Nietzsche's stature is owing to the courage and profundity that enabled him to make all this unmistakably clear. He delineated with overpowering eloquence the consequences of giving up Christianity, and every like view of the universe and humanity. His approval of those consequences and his hatred of Christianity give force to his argument. Many would like to think that there are no consequences—that we can continue treasuring the life and welfare, the civil rights and political authority, of every person without believing in a God who renders such attitudes and conduct compelling. Nietzsche shows that we cannot. We cannot give up the Christian God—and the transcendence given other

names in other faiths—and go on as before. We must give up Christian morality too. If the God-man is nothing more than an illusion, the same thing is true of the idea that every individual possesses incalculable worth. The standard of agape collapses. It becomes explicable only on Nietzsche's terms: as a device by which the weak and failing exact from the strong and distinguished a deference they do not deserve. Thus the spiritual center of Western politics fades and vanishes. If the principle of personal dignity disappears, the kind of political order we are used to— one structured by standards such as liberty for all human beings and equality under the law—becomes indefensible.

69. Difficult to see, that is, given the coherentist conception of justification (which I discuss in the book from which this essay is drawn.)
70. See, e.g., An-Na'im, "Human Rights in the Muslim World: Socio-Political Conditions and Scriptural Imperatives," 3 Harvard Human Rights L.J. 13 (1990); Nhlapo, "International Protection of Human Rights and the Family: African Variations on a Common Theme," 3 Int'l J.L. & Family 1 (1989).
71. See L. Rouner, ed., Human Rights and the World's Religions (1988); A. Swidler, ed., Human Rights in Religious Traditions (1988); H. King & J. Moltmann, eds., The Ethics "Buddhist Affirmations of Human Rights," 8, Buddhist-Christian Studies 13 (1988); Rossi "Moral Community, Imagination, and Human Rights: Philosophical Considerations on Uniting Traditions," in A. Hennelly & J. Langan, eds., *Human Rights in the Americas: The Struggle for Consensus* 167, 173 (1982) (noting convergence between Marxism and Catholicism).
72. See generally L. Swidler, ed., *Toward a Universal Theology of Religion* (1987); J. Cobb & C. Ives, eds., *The Emptying God: A Buddhist-Jewish-Christian Conversation* (1990). Cf. J. Dunne, *The Way of All the Earth: Experiments in Truth and Religion* (1972).

FOUR

THE PHILOSOPHICAL PRECONDITIONS OF DEMOCRATIC THEORY

Morton A. Kaplan

The modern conception of democracy—liberal democracy—finds support from both practical and moral points of view. However, most attempts to provide this support fail significantly to distinguish between the seventeenth century world view that gave birth to liberal democracy and a world view that is consistent with contemporary science. This failure merely replicates the more general failure of contemporary philosophy to provide an integrating world view.

Although standard philosophical approaches have much to teach us, they tend to suffer from a significant defect. They more often than not attempt to investigate ethical and moral problems in isolation from those developments in the realm of knowledge that provide an appropriate interpretive context. This tends to be the case whether we are dealing with more traditional philosophers who come from the natural law school (although these do pay attention to prudential considerations concerning society) or with those who adhere to formalistic neo-Kantian or utilitarian approaches, who usually ignore most contextual concerns.

The great classic philosphers who wrote on ethics and justice were systematic philosophers. Their moral positions were consistent with, although not determined by, their world views. Those who carry on their tradition, perhaps through some variation of natural law, often fail to ask, however, whether that tradition needs to be modified by the contemporary understanding of the world. Are unmodified views of natural law epistemologically viable? Do they accord with a reasonable understanding of how signs mediate between concepts and referents? Is there anything in the contemporary understanding of the nature of the physical universe that works against them?

Many contemporary philosophers deliberately avoid discussion of the nature of the good. They seem unaware, or even to doubt, that moral and ethical concerns are related to the dispositional nature of humankind and the nature of the world. Until recently John Rawls believed that one could choose the rules for governing society behind a veil of ignorance without knowing whether in fact one would emerge as Attila among the Huns or as a bourgeois clerk in contemporary society.

Rawls argued that someone who believed in a true religion (including, e.g., the Ayatolla Khomeini?) should accept tolerance in his actual world. He would opt for tolerance from behind a veil of ignorance, Rawls said, because, behind that veil, he could not know whether he could protect his religion in its absence. Thus, even though he knows he can impose his religion in the actual world, he is bound ethically, Rawls said, by the decision he would have made behind the veil. This shows only that Rawls does not know what a believer means by 'true religion.'

Allan Gewirth, for instance, believed that one's character as an agent and desire for freedom to accomplish one's desires logically entailed the recognition of the freedom of others for the same purposes. Thus, Gewirth argued that one could not claim a right in principle without recognizing that other agents could claim similar rights. This, he argued, would give rise to a regime of liberty. However, the 'agent' about whom Gewirth reasoned is a completely abstract agent who lacks real contextually-bound existence. He failed to perceive that if one were a deceitful agent who wished to enslave others, this would entail only the formal (and not necessarily public) requirement to understand that other agents have a similar formal claim to deceive or constrain us.

Moreover, even this purely formal constraint would depend upon the absence of relevant differentiation between us, for if we are different in respects that can be related to potential rights or obligations, symmetry is not logically entailed. For instance, if ninety percent of adults were of subnormal intelligence, it is unlikely that we would accept formal voting equality.

The meaning imputed to the sign 'agent' cannot be determined in the absence of contextual analysis. 'Agent' as a universal is abstract. Actual agents, that is, the referents of the concept and sign, will be either more or less than what Gewirth calls agents. These types of mistakes can be avoided by reference to an adequate contemporary world view.

ALL KNOWLEDGE INVOLVES INTERPRETATION

It is a commonplace today—as contrasted with a mere generation earlier—that our knowledge of the world is interpretational. Knowledge invokes an active transaction between a mind and the external world. The human mind, unlike Locke's *tabula rasa*, knows the world only because it can interpret incoming signals and organize them. For instance, we see a table as a stationary object. Because the pupil of a normal eye is in almost constant motion, some function of the brain must interpret the rapidly shifting signals from the table to the eye as a representation of a nonmoving object.

Although we might argue that the prior account is validated experimentally, the conditions of this or any experiment themselves draw on prior interpretations. They rest on a host of data and assumptions that are part of our common world. But our common world is different from that of prior generations; and the interpretations that govern the experiences we have are also different. We do not understand nature or human nature as our predecessors did. We could not do so, for many of the things that we 'know' are fundamentally different from what they 'knew.'

We do not believe with Aristotle that there are slaves by nature. We reject the divine origins of government. We know that objects do not rise because they are light and we acknowledge their capture by gravity. We know that names do not capture the essence of things, and that we cannot control things by manipulating formulas verbally. We do not believe that the shape of the head determines character or intelligence. Hence, what we perceive when we see a head differs from what the believer in head shapes perceives. We believe we know, although recent plasma theories of the universe challenge this, that the world began with a big bang billions of years ago and that the stars are vastly distant suns and not tiny dots of light or angelic beings. The things that we know constitute a framework that influences how we perceive, how we reason about, how we conceive hypotheses about, and when we look for evidence concerning the events both of every-day life and of the more highly disciplined world of science. Our experiences, thus, are the evolving products of our transactions with a world external to us and not merely passive copies of 'something out there.'

It may help to understand the implications of these differences if we start with a simplified view of some alternative natural worlds as they were understood in their time and then move to an account of our contemporary world. Aristotle's world was a world of perfect forms and final causes. Thus a tree already was con-tained in the seed as a final cause. A final cause produced the indi-vidual human from its fetus in a natural process unless some abnormal circumstance intervened. Every thing in the Aristotelian scheme had a nature that fit into a definite place in a world that was hierarchically ordered according to a unified scheme of final causes.

Theories were believed to be true not because of true predic-tions to which they gave rise but because their premises, which the mind had a natural capacity to know, were necessarily true. It was self-evidently true that space was Euclidean. Although politics and ethics were not theoretical subjects—and hence could not be reduced to axiomatic structure—still it was possible to know what the good was and to place men and their virtues in a natural order. One could then assess empirically how particular political orders contributed to a polity in which human nature could find its best expression.

Descartes and Hobbes helped to formulate the 'modern' scien-tific world view. Descartes undermined a view of language in which language resembled things and replaced it with the thesis that lan-guage permitted the ordering and representation of phenomena. However, once stipulated, the relationship between language and things was invariant. Hobbes accepted Aristotle's concept of theo-ry, but applied it to governance as well as to physics. Motion was the key term. Life and politics were variants of motion.

Descartes' concept of language played a key role in the development of modern physics. Instead of investigating the natural ordering of things, one would investigate the quantitative ordering of the qualities of things and of the relationships between these qualities, for instance, force, mass, and acceleration.

Some of the French philosophes, La Place and Condorcet, for instance, developed the concept of a hierarchically organized and fully determinate world in which God could predict every future state of the universe provided only that he knew the initial conditions of the atoms. Both humankind and the world were predictable machines. (*L'Homme Machine* was the title of one of de la Mettrie's books.) This was the best of all possible worlds because it was the only possible one. However, many of its unhappy features were produced by an ignorance that had removed humans from their happy conditions in the state of nature.

Although closer analysis would have revealed a problem in their deduction of this conclusion from these premises, they believed that it was possible for science to determine how to make men free, even if they had to be forced to be free, by structuring a perfect society. This general philosophy gave rise to a conception of the rights of man and of nations that was believed to be derived from the nature of the world. Deism—a philosophy which ascribed the creation of the world to God and then removed him from the scene—was the chief theological concept.

The Scottish philosophers Hutchinson and Hume were sceptical of this much determinism. Kant, who was "wakened from [his] dogmatic slumber" by Hume, distinguished between pure and practical reason. Hegel's great knowledge of Eastern philosophy led to a frontal attack on this type of positivistic science with its completely knowable and completely deterministic existential world, although he maintained a deterministic view with respect to the 'Absolute' (as Marx did with respect to the 'Totality'). But nothing really shook determinism deeply until the discovery of non-Euclidean geometry in the last quarter of the nineteenth century.

THE CONTEMPORARY WORLD VIEW

The classical and early modern view of the world as a strongly ordered hierarchy that the mind had a natural capacity to understand began to break down with the discovery of non-Euclidean geometry, for what could be more self-evidently true than the Euclidean character of space? However, it was the fact that the special theory of relativity established non-Euclidean geometry as the geometry of actual space that shattered the earlier paradigm.

We inferred from the evidence that supported relativity theory that our local space seemed Euclidean because the local deviations from non-Euclidean space were too small to be noticed visually. This led many to reason that if the mind did not have a natural capacity to recognize fundamental truths, then truth could lie only in experimental validation. (This was the apparent basis on which the logical positivists rested their doctrine even though it was inconsistent with an appropriate reading of relativity theory and especially of quantum theory.)

But matters became even more disruptive in terms of what had been natural understanding. If space was non-Euclidean, still it might be independently real. However, time, the fourth dimension, was paradoxical from the viewpoint of natural understanding. If two independent inertial systems were in motion with respect to each other, an observer on each would assert correctly that time was going more slowly on the other. But how could time simultaneously be going more slowly on each system? (Einstein was later to state that the concept of simultaneity was an error). Only if time is not an essence—a thing in itself—but relational would this be possible.

Worse shocks were in store for the then current world views. The statistical mechanics of Ludwig Boltzmann and Josiah Gibbs already had made the concept of a less than deterministic world somewhat familiar. But this perhaps was merely a measurement problem. Only with quantum mechanics did it appear possible that the laws of quanta were themselves probabilistic. Einstein thought that God would be playing dice with the universe if this were the case, and he refused to believe it. With Podolsky and Rosen, he devised a thought experiment designed to show how absurd such a world would be because local realism would not hold in it. (The most recent experiments indicate that what Einstein thought to be absurd is likely the case and that photons, for instance, can 'coordinate' their positions without communication.)

Niels Bohr attempted to provide a philosophical foundation for quantum mechanics with his Copenhagen thesis. Many things in the world are in a condition of complementarity, he said. For instance, the position and momentum of a quantum do not exist as such but only as transactional products in the context of experimental apparatuses. And these apparatuses cannot be used at the same time. Hence, to ask where the position was when momentum was being measured was to reify the concept of position. Similarly, he argued, it was a mistake to ask whether a quantum is a wave or a particle unless one asked in what respects and in what contexts.

Bohr's principle of complementarity solves what had been a perennial problem: How did mind evolve in a material universe? If information and matter/energy are in a relationship of complementarity, then information is present in the world even in the absence of minds. Given sufficient complexity in the organization of matter/energy—namely, the development of neurological networks—then information may complement neurological systems in the form of awareness. Eventually, as self-reflexive neurological networks evolved, self-awareness would emerge.

Hence, one need not ask what state of the neurological system produced a thought, for the two modes of analysis—of neurological and of mental states—are pursued by incompatible, but not contradictory, means. Brains and thoughts no more fit into a deterministic, hierarchically patterned universe than do the positions and momenta of quanta. But they are different and legitimate subjects of study that do not contradict each other, that complement each other, and that can be fitted into a world view that accords with the contemporary state of knowledge.

It is possible that more finely-grained determinations would reduce the weakness of prediction from particular individual frameworks of reference. However, if complementarity is a feature of the universe, it excludes the possibility of a strongly-ordered world that fits together in a neat package. If one accepts the Copenhagen thesis of Bohr—that is, of the ultimately probabilistic character of the laws of quantum theory—then there is an irreducible element of weakness in accounts of the world that is only somewhat, but not completely, reduced by the large scale character of macrophysical phenomena.

THE ROLE OF LANGUAGE

The understanding of language also must be adjusted to the contemporary world view. Words do not naturally indicate their objects as they would in an Aristotelian universe. Nor are they linked arbitrarily but univocally to different referents as they would be in a Cartesian universe. Instead words, that is, signs, link concepts to referents in ways that depend on the entire economy of concepts. 'True' does not mean the same thing in a syllogism that it does in an empirical attribution, a fact that undermines the Kripke/Putnam concept of necessary truths. The analytical 'true' is a stipulated concept that governs logical inferences. The empirical 'true' is a judgment that in some circumstances can be treated as if identical with the analytical 'true.' Its meaning shifts with context. 'Green' does not mean the same thing to a man and a tiger. The optic apparatus that produces colors is different and so is the framework of interpretation.

The same green object will be perceived differently even by a single individual depending on the colors with which it is surrounded, the lighting system, and the state of the optic apparatus with which it is viewed. The corresponding concepts and the linguistic signs (or language elements) that are linked to these greens also vary contextually.

This view of language fits with chaos theory. A scientific theory is a set of signs linking a set of concepts with external reality from a frame of reference. It does not exhaust the referent because other possible frameworks of reference also apply to it, although they define and circumscribe it differently. For instance, the two-body laws governing the path of heavenly bodies do not account for effects that over time might destabilize planetary paths. Every regularity is likely to break down at some extreme limit when the lack of fit—that results from processes accounted for by other frames of reference—between the equilibrium model (theory, system, set of signs) and the underlying real system that is the referent of the model becomes major.

The language games approach of Wittgenstein, although illuminating in certain respects, also misrepresents the character of language. Aristotle knew that if horses are animals, the heads of horses are the heads of animals. However, this conclusion could not be reached syllogistically. Modern propositional logic does permit this deduction. Modern logic could be formulated because logicians knew of truths that could not be proved in syllogistic language and were able to formulate a language that permitted their proof.

When we formulate a new language 'game,' we use knowledge we already possess to move beyond the confines of older langauge 'games' and to generate new knowledge. Languages are not encapsulated and insulated truth systems. They always can be critiqued from some other linguistic position. Hence, it does not follow, as Wittgenstein seemed to think, that the oracle and the scientist are on a comparable footing.

THEORY AND ASSESSMENT

Philosophy of science ought to be responsive to the procedures of science that are fruitful just as language 'games' should be developed to express what we know in ways that can generate new knowledge. Science proceeds not merely by theory and deduction but also by reference to the 'fit' between theories or logics and other elements of knowledge, including other theories and logics. This is a process of assessment, not of proof or deduction. There had been no disproofs of Newtonian theory by the time of Einstein and multiple confirmations. But Maxwellian physics, Lorentz equations, non-Euclidean geometries, and the constancy of the speed of light (although Einstein apparently was unaware of the Michelson-Morley experiment) were establishing a weaker fit between the theory and the current state of knowledge than had been the case.

This weak fit between Newtonian theory and the state of knowledge left room for Einstein's revolutionary theory. And, despite its apparent paradoxes and its violation of ordinary understanding, physicists were inclined to accept relativity theory, even though the early experimental validations were within the range of experimental error, because it fit the state of knowledge more closely than did Newton's theory.

The discussion of complementarity given above showed that there is no such thing as a 'correct' picture of the world—although there can be better and better accounts of it. This account of assessment reinforces that conclusion.

The realm of knowledge consists of partly independent and partly interdependent part systems. Some part systems of the realm of knowledge are used in reaching judgments about other part systems of the realm of knowledge. Sometimes these tentatively accepted external criteria are used in determining whether the elements of a proof are valid and sometimes they are used in global comparative assessments of theory.

For instance, the determinations of some red shifts in the light from stars are based on two-dimensional photographic film. Should new instrumentation show these determinations to be invalid, then some of the physical hypotheses that relied on them may fail. Yet all physical readings depend on instrumentation, which must be accepted as valid, even if only tentatively. On the other hand, new instruments that give different readings will be distrusted until and unless they are supported by evidence from other areas of inquiry or are useful in producing new theories for the particular area that are not subject to the anomalies of the former theory. In short, science is a process in which changes in any portion of the realm of knowledge, including observations, instrumentation, and theories, may be used to subvert other portions of the realm of knowledge. The reasoning used in reaching such judgments is an assessment of the complex realm of knowledge and is not based on anything so simple as a confirmation or falsification of a theory.

In the physical sciences, falsifications are likely to be the most economical method of choosing hypotheses because most investigations are carried out in a realm within which the connections between hypotheses tend to be close and relatively strong. Thus, a single instance of a large lead ball that rose in the air in the absence of an internal engine or external assistance would surely call the laws of gravitation into question. However, the discovery of a political system in which the candidate with the least votes won the office would not likely call into question theories of politics. We are not unlikely to decide that this was a different type of system to which the rules of the other system do not apply. In a sense something of the same sort occurred in physics with the development of quantum theory. But this is an unusual case in physics whereas it is the usual case in social science. Thus, although falsifications are still very useful, particularly with respect to well demarcated systems, in social science the balance between the two techniques is different. The connections between the elements of reality are weaker and, therefore, seemingly negative results are less likely to carry over from one experimental situation to another.

The prior discussion is prolegomena designed to set the stage for a discussion of morality and liberal democracy. There is no better place to start the discussion than with contract theory, for, philosophically speaking, the origins of liberal democracy and contractarian theory (and its offshoot, natural rights) seem to be symbiotically interwoven. It will be my task to disentangle them.

CONTRACT THEORY

It is generally believed that the concept of liberal democracy rests on contract theory. When the belief in divine authority for government broke down, philosophers could find no basis other than consent.

Contract theory, however, misrepresents the intellectual problem of obligation. It is misled by its state of nature assumptions. As a hypothetical device, Hobbes' state of nature is without support. Most animals, and all primates, are social animals. There have been controlled experiments in which monkeys have been raised with mothers, with broomsticks, and without even broomsticks. The monkeys raised with mothers became normal monkeys. The monkeys raised with broomsticks were able to learn to socialize, although with difficulty and without great success. The monkeys that did not even have broomsticks for support became not merely asocial but dysfunctional as well.

Hobbes, moreover, was misled, as more recently Nozick was, by the analogy between physics and society. Newton could rest his axioms on action in a vacuum because his equations could take into account gravitation or friction. Hobbes, and later Nozick, had no way to make adjustments within the frameworks of their theories for factors of altruism or human cohesion. Hence, their counterfactuals were vicious rather than fruitful.

Given a seventeenth century world view that included a deterministic nominalism that made of the individual an isolated atom, it is possible to understand Hobbes' assumptions. But a contemporary world view would not produce such ideas, and specific ethnological and anthropological evidence is strongly inconsistent with them. Although a contemporary position is inconsistent with obligation based on contract and the concept of universalized natural rights, those concepts can be controverted without resort to it. Hobbes reached his conclusions only by a sleight of hand. No contract is binding in the absence of a moral duty or a physical need. Because Hobbes provided no moral ground for the observance of the contract that established the state, he placed the requirement in the sovereign's power to punish. Still, he knew that the sovereign, unlike God, could be neither omnipresent nor omniscient. So he changed his definition of liberty. In the state, he said, we did not have liberty to oppose the sovereign because of the threat of punishment. In the state of nature, however, we were free unless physically constrained. That was the trick.

Leo Strauss believed that Hobbes' logic was sound. Because failure to keep the covenant would return men to the brutal war against all of the state of nature, it was a natural law that keeping the covenant was mandated. However, Hobbes' logic was flawed with respect to making and keeping the covenant. Because men were equal in the state of nature, no specific person was singled out by nature as ruler. Thus, only combat could decide this issue. But engaging in combat for this purpose would be more dangerous than remaining in the state of nature, for it would be fiercer. Hence, none would seek to lead unless they desired rulership even more than they feared death. Yet Hobbes disallowed this choice. And, if such combat began, one was more likely to survive if one remained neutral or joined only when the issue appeared settled. On the other hand, if the state was in existence, breaking the covenant would not be dangerous if one were not caught. Even staging a coup would not return men to the state of nature, for many coups historically had been successful and had merely changed rulership. Thus, Hobbes' deduction of a law of nature that mandated keeping the covenant was flawed. His starting conditions were not sufficiently constrained to necessitate his conclusions. This perhaps was an excusable error on Hobbes' part, for he wrote before game theoretic analysis had been discovered. More likely, because Hobbes feared civil war, he made a deliberate error because he wanted men to believe it.

Contract theory will not sustain the legitimacy of government in any form, let alone liberal democracy. Two grounds need to be prepared for a defense of liberal democratic government. One would lie in its efficiency in achieving or avoiding certain ends in the conditions for which it has been proposed. For instance, few would argue for a democratic vote among citizens on how to proceed with a heart transplant operation. The other defense would lie in the values promoted by democracy. Few would want a successful heart transplant operation on an Adolf Hitler. And many would reject a democratic government if it produced a majoritarian tyranny.

THE GOOD AND JUSTICE

To make a case for political obligation, we must first make the case for objective morals. The argument has already been prefigured in the discussion of colors and relativity theory.

Both relativity and quantum theory provide contextual reasons for believing that objectively true phenomena are true not as such but only relative to some framework of reference. This position was foreshadowed philosophically by Peircean pragmatics, which itself was responding to the problems bequeathed by the Hegelian legacy. This understanding is inconsistent with the concept of objectivity in all natural law theories and also with the concept of objectivity involved in Toulmin's 'Reason in Ethics,' which led him to dismiss the notion of the objectivity of the good.

Toulmin argued that unlike the taste of sweetness, which might vary among individuals, green was green, apart from defective vision, and hence objective. If one denied this, one was simply using words differently. What is good, however, cannot be distinguished in this fashion. Hence, according to Toulmin, it could not be objective.

Toulmin failed to note that dogs see colors differently from us and that there are angstrom wave patterns we are incapable of perceiving. Color is a product of a transaction between us and an external world. Moreover, although he referred to the scientific basis of colors, there are no colors in physics, only angstrom waves, which themselves are the products of transactions. The angstrom wave form we see as green may not be green under different lighting, including that of some other star. Hence, it is variable also, although, from our normal frame of reference, it is less variable than sweetness. Toulmin's notion of the objectivity of color—that is, of a quality that is independent of transactions with others—was similar to that of the natural law theorist's concept of the objectivity of natural law. This casts additional doubt on most theories of natural law.

The discussion thus far also entails conclusions with respect to language. Language does not match an internal concept with an external object either as a copy or as a universal correspondent. Green things, except as potentialities, are not out there independently of how we engage in transactions with them. Instead language uses signs to mediate between a concept (and its environment) and a referent (and its environment) to produce meaning. The greenness of external objects is dependent on conceptual coding as part of a transactional process. Because this is so, concepts are not such as such but only from a frame of reference. This fits with chaos theory. Laws are sets of signs that link sets of concepts with external reality from a frame of reference and that do not exhaust that external reality. Hence, every regularity is likely to break down at some limit.

To understand the role of morality in political obligation, it is necessary to move away from universalistic world views that do not take context into account in reaching conclusions. Let us lead into a contextual account of morality by returning to the simpler problem of color perception. We cannot perceive greens or solids in the absence of a framework of coding. So too we cannot perceive something as good in the absence of a relevant coding system. This does not mean that the infant has a sophisticated coding system that would be responsive to what adults recognize as moral qualities. The infant's coding system for good things may be something very simple. For instance, the sight of the mother's breast may be interpreted (non-linguistically) as the availability of a particular kind of good: food.

Moral understanding develops through acculturation and with experience. Our moral universe has its origins in primitive codings for good things, things perhaps as simple as the 'goodness' of the breast and its milk. Much as our knowledge of colors becomes sophisticated after much simpler beginnings, the criteria and reasoning applied to the conception of good things develops out of experience with relatively simple phenomena. Judgments related to such discriminations are shaped by their fit with other elements of experience. Thus, contrary to what Kant stated, we know that there are circumstances in which lying is moral. The greater our experience, the more likely we are to be able to make satisfactory, and more finely shaded, moral discriminations.

It is important to understand the difference between definitional and dispositional referents if one is to understand the differences between goods and some other types of things. Trees, for instance, are definitional objects. They are recognized for what they are, although they also have dispositional aspects. Goods are recognized by what they do. They are dispositional. Dispositional referents also exist in physics. For instance, the term 'electric charge' means, among other things, that if one body is placed near another body and is attracted by that second body, then it possesses an electric charge. The ensuing electric current can be inferred from the heat produced in a conductor, the deviation of a magnetic needle, the quantity of a substance separated from an electrolyte, and so forth.

Thus, the concept of an electric current cannot be reduced to any one set of terms nor can it be measured simply by measuring a temperature. This is characteristically the case with goods. There are criteria that determine whether something is good, and these depend on dispositional relationships that are analyzed from some frame of reference and not on definitional accounts of particular goods.

The reason this process is difficult to recognize as objective is that we have become used to the myth that we prove or disprove theories only by the results of tests. Thus, we assume a relatively simple test which many statements concerning the good cannot meet. But in fact many determinations in physics cannot meet this test either. We ignore many experimental results that do not accord with accepted theories because we assume that they are mistaken or that they will be accounted for by further knowledge. When conflicting theories contest with each other and the experimental data are insufficient, we prefer one theory over another if it fits the current framework of knowledge better. Indeed, the experimental evidence itself depends for its coding upon assessments that are employed within a wider realm of knowledge. It is this kind of assessment that is the paradigmatic case with respect to goods.

Because some philosophers misunderstand this process, they believe that objectivity has been undermined. They then retreat to different concepts such as that of uncoerced discourse in the case of Jurgen Habermas and that of conversation in the case of Richard Rorty, who even dismisses the concept of truth. It is certainly true that we cannot know objective truth in the absence of minds and that such truths cannot be communicated in the absence of discourse of one sort or another. This, however, is as true in physics as in politics.

It may be the case that on the average it is easier to find truth if inquiry is uncoerced. But that is not always true. Try reasoning with a sadistic psychopath or someone who refuses to look at evidence unless forced to. And sometimes the evidence would be so misleading that ordinary people, who do not share a background that would place the evidence in proper context, would be able to accept the truth only if evidence that they would misinterpret is withheld from them. The determination of when it is better for inquiry to be free cannot be made in the absence of other criteria. It may be true that political decisions, particularly in contemporary modern societies, are accorded greater legitimacy when all affected interests are consulted. But the criteria that determine application of this rule are not in turn determined by it.

Rorty challenged the concept of truth. If by truth he had meant essence, he would have had a case. The table on which my word processor rests is solid. It is also empty, as any gamma particle could attest if it were capable of attesting. Both of these statements are empirically true even though that judgment cannot be established with absolute certitude. However, Rorty's emphasis on conversation is misleading because the criteria for acceptance of a judgment of truth and not conversation itself are the determining factors. They also determine judgments concerning the good.

Let us move from a discussion of the objectivity of the good to the objectivity of justice. Justice—in a simplified and preliminary sense—involves giving everyone his due. What this due is will differ from society to society. The same process of assessment that enables us to critique conceptions of the good also permits us to critique conceptions of justice. I discuss this elsewhere under the rubric of the 'test in principle.'

THE MATRIX OF KNOWLEDGE

Languages, logics, beliefs concerning science and the philosophy of science, and our notions of good things and justice all develop out of an historically conditioned matrix. The idea of pure reason, which lay behind the French Revolution, always was nonsense. Any attempt to jettison entirely the received store of knowledge can lead only to chaos.

Traditions are important buttresses for the assimilation of enfunctional change in society. And because the web of interrelationships is densely connected, the weight of tradition is not to be jettisoned easily or quickly. In the absence of catastrophic necessity it is important to change slowly to provide time for assimilation and understanding.

Morality and ethics are not disembodied abstract subjects. Their subject matter is concrete. They apply to particular kinds of beings in particular kinds of environments and with particular historical experiences and understandings. Marx's concrete universal 'man' is an aberration that is detached from every quality that makes him concretely human. Marxian man has no history, no ancestry, no individual human wishes, no particular physical characteristics or personality. He is a myth who can never have real existence, for he exists only as a denatured concept in the mind of Marx. The humans of Rawls, Nozick, and Gewirth are equally denatured.

HUMAN NATURE AND MORAL INQUIRY

What does it mean to argue, as I do, that moral inquiry must be related to a conception of human nature? It does not mean that we can derive a prescription for a good society from knowledge of human nature. But then we cannot derive a prescription for a good bridge from the laws of physics even though, unlike human nature, the nature of macrophysics is only peripherally dispositional. It does mean that the approaches of philosophers such as John Rawls and Robert Nozick, who devise schemes of ethics that are unrelated to either more general or more specific and dispositional accounts of human nature, are doomed to irrelevance except in highly special circumstances. But then we cannot build a theory of physics unless we have some conception of the character of the forces we are dealing with.

There is a thesis that nature is selfish and disposed to self-reproduction. That is an oversimplification that reifies particular boundary conditions. It treats gene pools in virtually the same non-contextual way that was criticized earlier in the discussion of colors and goods. The gene pool will vary with the ecological niche and chance factors. Moreover, one could as easily argue that mutational evolution, which involves changes in the gene pool, is natural and, hence, that there are altruistic tendencies toward evolution inherent in every gene pool. All gene pools are in process. They are dispositional and shift under changing conditions. The task of analysis is to make sense of this complex natural process. It is obvious on purely evolutionary grounds that early social systems could not have survived if the individual members never placed the survival of the group over that of the individual. Therefore, some degree of group bonding, particularly within the family, must have played a role in selection. The great advantage of decentralized decision making most likely would have inhibited the selection of individuals who always subordinated the individual to the group. In fact, this does not occur in so-called primitive systems but usually requires a large society in which centralized control over a monopolized energy source is possible.

Thus, although unusual circumstances could make either authoritarian control or virtually anarchic behavior temporarily advantageous, societies would be well-advised in most cases to avoid either extreme. Even during the period of absolute monarchy in Great Britain, the commercial and industrial orders were left substantially free of regulation. That did not occur in France, and industrial development in France suffered greatly because of this.

Our knowledge of sociobiology, as contrasted with that of physics, is so limited that speaking about the constraints nature places on political, social and moral systems has authority only in extremely limited ways. Most responsive behavior is overdetermined by contextual historical factors. We know that we need the assurance of relatively unconditional support in some areas of life and yet the freedom to explore and differ. Probably much of our myth and fantasy life—and our receptivity to it—responds to a generalized preconscious coding. But this puts very few constraints on evaluation until we are in a position to judge the 'fit' between our needs more narrowly expressed and a variety of institutional modifications.

We know that there are different somatotypes and that these somatotypes tend to produce individuals of different dispositions. One of the advantages of modern society, along with concomitant disadvantages, is the complexity that provides opportunities for those of different psychological dispositions. I have watched a litter of cats from birth and observed traits in the exit from the womb that persisted through life.

Although humans may differ in the strength of their competitive behaviors because of genetic differences, there is no such thing as an inherent store of aggressive instinct. There are instead predispositions that are activated under a variety of circumstances and dampened under others. Life circumstances, experience, social arrangements, including the roles particular individuals play, and culture have crucial roles in arousing various forms of active and passive behavior. Thus, no deductions can be made from relatively unstructured social behavior to activities invoked by complex social structures.

The difficulty of speaking with authority on the relationships between nature, human nature, and society does not rule out reasoned speculation about some serious contemporary controversies. We know that humans have great adaptability and that they may differ in their predispositions to respond to certain kinds of situations. Yet, great plasticity does not mean infinite malleability. Humans have a great capacity for autonomy, and this is supportive of liberal democracy. Yet many contemporary individuals have made the mistake of divorcing the concept of autonomy from that of transstable character and of identifying it with the pursuit of transient pleasures to the detriment of character and a sense of identity. Our minds, as in the case of the compulsive loser, may lead us into dangerous bypaths, particularly if we resort to abstract thinking, whether individualistic or collectivistic.

DEMOCRACY AND CONTEMPORARY SOCIETY

If we wish to inquire into the appropriateness of democratic institutions in contemporary society, we need to inquire into those characteristics of individuals and society both in general and in particular that make democracy an appropriate solution to the problems that we face. If there were genuine and vast biological differences in the intelligence of individuals, democratic government would be questionable, although not necessarily ruled out. Even if the differences in intelligence were the consequences of differences in life chances, similar conclusions might follow. I do not think differences in biological intelligence are a key factor in actuality. There are individuals with astronomical IQs whose practical judgment I would not trust for a moment. There are others with modest IQs whose judgmental ability is outstanding. On the other hand, the decline in practical intelligence, and even more in knowledge, which is resulting from contemporary schooling, could become inconsistent with democracy, particularly as we head into an age in which skills become much more important than they are even now in jobholding and in political judgment. It is perhaps ironic, although not surprising, that the decline in educational standards has coincided with its most egalitarian, and thus democratic, extension. The highly skilled teachers who were available for the elite in a relatively primitive economy have not been reproduced in a mass educational system and an industrial economy.

Democracy depends upon the relative equality of skills and judgment in individuals, for, in its absence, it will not work; and, in its presence, nothing else will be accepted failing the myth of selection by God or control of a scientific theory of history. Democracy is supported by the potential for autonomy of individuals, by the great efficiency of decentralized decision making, and by the ability of people to 'throw the rascals out' when they are judged to have failed. The historical development of empathy from tribe to ethnic group to nation supports the extension of democracy to previously excluded groups who reside within the state, and perhaps beyond it.

THE MARKET

In an age in which the superiority of the market over planned economies and the relationship of a decentralized economic system to political democracy is generally accepted, it still would be a mistake to regard market decisions as invariably desirable. F.A. Von Hayek and Anthony de Jasay have made a powerful, but overstated, case for market methods.

For instance, I disagree with the evolutionary case von Hayek makes in *The Fatal Conceit: The Errors of Socialism* for what he calls the extended order, the market. I do not agree that the distinction between 'mine' and 'thine' is entirely an externally imposed constraint that is foreign to animals. My dog may beg from my plate, but he will not take from it. However, if I take something from his plate, he jumps at me and takes it back. The well-known phenomenon of territoriality is one aspect of animal recognition of the difference between mine and thine.

The forms within which self-centered and other-centered activities occur are learned—and they do evolve over time—but the distinction has been built into our nature by evolution. Although the infant has no clear recognition of self and others, it is as predispositionally disposed to learn these distinctions during maturation as it is to learn how to walk. Furthermore, every successful culture must satisfy the need for both the *gemeinschaft* and *gesellschaft* aspects of human nature.

Von Hayek is so impressed by the productive power of the market that he believes conceptions of justice are destructive. But we would not want laws that made it easy to convict innocent people, to evade taxes, or to cause starvation among the poor. A society so radically unfair would lose its legitimacy.

Although an effort generally to pay people according to non-market evaluations of their worth would undermine productivity, it does not follow that no considerations of justice or aesthetics should ever be applied. Italy's subsidization of the opera is not indefensible. Private and public donations to universities may produce an amount of human capital that improves society as well as individual lives when other mechanisms to produce similar results at this early stage of life are absent.

The market does not really maximize, or even optimize, goods because it is constrained by the mechanisms of choice. An individual who would otherwise play his high fidelity equipment loudly may still prefer an ordinance that forbids this. Perhaps Gresham's law applies to atomized tastes. The state of television might be used to support the conclusion that bad taste drives out good taste. If so, carefully considered support for countervailing tendencies would make good sense. The fact that legislatures and award committees sometimes make us regret these choices does not mean that we should never make them. I also differ with von Hayek on the subject of planning. If by planning he means rationality of the type sponsored by the French philosophes—which attempts to plan an entire society on the basis of a few definitions and axioms—then of course it will fail. If, however, we think of rational planning as assessment, as I use that term, then it can work, although any particular plan may fail. Although the danger may have been exaggerated, society needs a plan to prevent ecological disaster. The recent report of the National Academy of Sciences (April 1991) on global warming is germane. Furthermore, European planning of urban growth and mass transit has produced cleaner, more liveable and more accessible cities than in the United States.

De Jasay has shown brilliantly how vacuous the concept of freedom is when it is discussed in its generality rather than in terms of specific freedoms and the trade-offs they involve. However, his defense of unimpeded contract suffers from the fact that he treats the concepts of justice and social goods as abstractly as others treat the concept of freedom.

If contract continues to produce an underclass that is uneducable by current techniques, then I would not want to live in a society that did not raise tax money in an effort to correct this. If individual contract produces a plenitude of highly visible porno shops and movies in the heart of New York City and Washington D.C., then I want government to do something about it. If freedom of contract has produced a decadent atmosphere in our national capitals, it has deprived me of the freedom to walk with pride in the center of those cities.

I do not apologize for being prepared to limit the freedom of those who turn the national capital into a pigsty. Even if we knew how to add freedoms and to calculate them—and there is no way to do this—and even if counterfactually there were no trade-offs among them, the qualitative determination of which freedoms to facilitate would take precedence over an abstract analysis of the problem of freedom.

New York recently passed a law outlawing the use of midgets as bowling balls. The columnist Mike Royko took the position that if midgets, who had to eat like the rest of us, liked earning $2,000 a week by impersonating bowling balls, they should have the right to do so. This is not an unreasonable argument. If we could know that this would occur only in a few cases in remote areas, I perhaps would agree. But widespread activity of this kind would run the risk of desensitizing us to the rights of all humans, including even deformed and crippled humans.

There is no doctrinaire solution to this problem. Some might try to outlaw ethnic jokes or irreverent remarks. Both the absence of limits and an abundance of limits can be dangerous to liberal democracy and human autonomy. There is no neutral framework and no substitute for good sense. My own preference would be to err on the side of liberality. But I would not raise this to high principle. De Jasay suggests that we have to choose between the socialist principle that society distributes goods and the market or contractual mode of distribution. That also is too general. We can choose between the areas in which we want the market to operate and the areas in which we want some other principle to predominate. Food stamps or the distribution of surplus goods to the poor may be quite defensible choices.

We do not have to choose between a level playing field for individuals and that which the market produces, as de Jasay states, because society can decide to restructure the field when imbalances produced by the market begin to offend our sense of what is just, of what is politically feasible, or of what is socially desirable. In any event, the actual playing field is highly imperfect and never entirely neutral. The belief that previous defects will repeat themselves is overstated although new defects may be expected. It is not unreasonable to expect the political system to compensate periodically for the imperfections and biases of the playing field. On the other hand, it is important to exercise great care in deciding how to accomplish this. And de Jasay, of course, is correct when he warns against extending socialist principles to the process of the production of material goods.

Unlike Rawls, I do not object to the benefits that stem from luck, whether it is a matter of genes or land of birth. It is part of our human heritage, part of our concrete reality. And it is up to us whether we make use of it. On the other hand, I am collecting rent from those who came before me and from Dame Fortune. I do not have to choose between keeping all the benefits provided by good fortune or giving all of them up. Decency requires that I recognize a moral obligation to others, including those who follow. If I am unwilling voluntarily to respond to this obligation, and if too many others join me in this refusal, then others have the moral right, even the moral duty, legislatively to compel us.

Thus, although I also am fearful of those who too easily invoke concepts of social redistribution and am aware of many of their deadly results, I fail to see that all redistributions are undesirable. A purely contractual society, whatever its other defects, would so deprive us of the deep need for membership in collectivities that it would be as self-destructive as a socialist society. Moreover, the discontent the acute perception of injustice would foster would provide ambit for demagogy.

THE WEAKNESSES OF DEMOCRACY

Democracy has its weaknesses. It is slow to respond to crises. Often it requires violence before great injustices are responded to. The racial question in the United States was an example of this. Policies are often determined by veto groups at great expense for the polity. Fortunately for the defense of democracy, Leninist regimes are not good at this either. Not only did Gorbachev experience great difficulty in imposing *perestroika* in the Soviet economy but it took a severe crisis—the threat that the Soviet Union's economy would degenerate to a 'third world' level—belatedly to produce a Gorbachev. And his efforts hit a dead end before the coup.

Democracy appears to be a failure culturally in the United States. It does not take extensive inquiry into TV, the movies, newspapers, novels, or even contemporary social science to document this conclusion. On the other hand, we may be in a developmental trough. American food, for instance, became homogenized in the postwar era as a consequence of economic efficiencies. However, we are now seeing a recrudesence of specialty stores as the efficiencies that made food and other products cheap produced the wealth that creates demand for better products. One may hope that a similar process will occur with respect to the more serious features of life where higher standards are required for democratic systems to work well.

LIBERAL DEMOCRACY

Liberal democracy in the older, and more legitimate, sense of liberal, implies a form of majority rule constrained by the values of liberty or freedom. The older English and Scottish philosophers were inclined to think of freedom negatively, that is, as absence of external constraint. This had some justification, for Rousseauian concepts of forcing people to be free raised the specter of authoritarian government. Yet the distinction between positive and negative freedoms depends entirely on frame of reference. Because we do not possess wings, we are not free to float like butterflies. If we are born without legs, or if they are bound, we are not free to walk. If we are abandoned at birth to the care of animals we are not free to talk or even to think in ways that require certain kinds of concepts. And every facilitation that permits certain kinds of freedoms, inhibits others. The feathered wings that permit a bird to fly make it difficult, and perhaps impossible, for some birds to swim.

Negative and positive concepts of freedom are bound together in an inextricable symbiosis. It is dangerous to apply either abstractly rather than in historical and comparative context. One is not free to make rational decisions if under the influence of drugs. One is not free to be a concert violinist except under conditions of strenuous study and practice. One is not free to behave morally unless there are internalized constraints on the pursuit of individual wants. One is not free to live at peace unless the police constrain criminals.

Both concepts of freedom are dangerous when treated abstractly. Freedom can be used to destroy freedom even when external constraints are not imposed on individuals. One of the possible dangers in the legalization of hard drugs is that the legitimation of drug taking may erode the cultural constraints that limit it. The concept of those things that injure others and those that do not, taken abstractly, is dangerously misleading, for it fails to recognize the consequences of social legitimation and example.

The abstract rejoinder that we should be independent enough to make our own decisions—apart from its failure to understand that impressionable children are also members of society—responds to a real problem with an ideal type that few, if any, individuals match. It ignores the process of socialization and of how the concept of the self is formed. And it substitutes for the complex self—a self that is not a simple or fixed process, let alone a thing—a doctrinaire and abstract concept.

Every proper concept of freedom develops in a historical matrix that limits its application through cultural standards that constrain what is meant by freedom and also what is meant by 'human.' Surely a future in which we would be linked voluntarily to pleasure machines that constantly entertained us, stimulated our pleasure centers, and fed us would not now be regarded as human. The freedom I want is the freedom to be human.

It is the rapid extension of the concept of freedom that threatens freedom by threatening the matrix within which it has appropriate meaning. And it could be the 'slippery slope' extension of the concept that could take us to the point of cultural 'no return.'

This is why it is desirable in the American system of democracy that the courts be strong in constraining legislative infringements of recognized freedoms, that is, freedoms that have endured or that now attain predominant and sustained support, and extremely hesitant about inventing 'rights' that lack historically sustained and dominant public support.

Our founders wisely devised a system of government that was slow to change and in which various elements of government were balanced with each other. The Bill of Rights was intended to defend established rights against the federal legislature and it was expected that the Court would restrain the Congress from infringing upon those rights. The Court does have the right to adapt the Constitution to changed conditions (as also do the legislature and the executive), but it was neither intended nor expected that this would be done in the service of some abstract theory or conception of liberty.

The amendment process was made difficult deliberately and it is reasonable to believe that changed interpretations of rights or duties should be equally difficult. The legislature, the democratic element in the system, undoubtedly was the one intended to make these interpretations and the Court was expected to restrain it when it went too far and too fast. Certainly a Court that was appointed for life was not expected to be the agent for radical change unless fidelity to the entire institutional system required this.

Thus, although the Court properly can enshrine and protect against the legislature changed conceptions that have not merely majority but predominant support and that have retained them over a reasonable passage of time, it should not enshrine them merely because they have majority support even if that appears wise or just.

There is no absolute guarantee against villainies. Past civilizations did not regard newborn infants as human. There is no abstract principle that will prevent us from reaching that conclusion again if it attains predominant and sustained popular support. But a conservative philosophy by the Court could prevent a temporary predominance of opinion from attaining that result and provide time for reconsideration. In the meantime, it might be possible to allow the states, depending on the issues, to follow different rules in an effort to become familiar with the consequences and to allow time for reconsideration.

It may be the case, although I do not believe so, that a society in which there are homosexual marriages and adult sex with children—positions now defended openly by small but substantial groups—would be a happier and healthier society than ours. Surely, however, it is wise not to enshrine such liberties until such time as opinion has shifted predominantly and enduringly. Yet some of the dicta of the Court in other somewhat similar cases could be read to accept such practices if more substantial minorities were to defend them. This would be the kind of abstract libertarianism to which the French and Russian revolutions responded. And it is very dangerous, for it threatens to shatter that web of definitions and meanings within which alone liberty—which depends for its existence upon relevant constraints—can survive.

No constitutional system is immune to subversion. Predominant and sustained majorities have the power to destroy democracy. In the American system, however, both the division and the separation of powers slow down the process of subversion and provide time for temperate reconsideration of radical changes. Restraint by all three branches of the government, except under highly necessitous circumstances, supports the democratic system the founders installed.

THE ENDS OF SOCIETY AND POLITY

Every political system, and every society, ought to be evaluated according to the types of human beings who are sustained by it. Slaves and members of a permanent underclass are, or are turned into, inferior human beings and the types of polities and societies that increase their incidence are unjustifiable if alternatives exist. Greek and Roman society at least encouraged the education and manumission of slaves whereas the American underclass seems to be self-reinforcing. Perhaps smallness of human spirit, the pursuit of transient pleasures to the neglect of enduring character, bureaucratic self-protectiveness, dishonesty, and neglect of wider human interests are an inevitable byproduct of any social organization, but their incidence in contemporary American society and politics is deplorable.

The degree of intelligence, moral understanding, and human sensitivity that a society fosters are among the most important factors in judging it. Economic productivity, although essential, is only a means to these ends. The degree of selfishness, dishonesty, and addiction to drugs and transient pleasures in American society today stands strongly against it as a long-term exemplar despite its clear advantages over contemporary alternative types of government and society. It cannot be true that with the resources available to us we cannot do better than this. The belief that history has ended, that the superiority of our present system is self-evident, is dangerously wrong. Even apart from the problems that technology will present to us—and that I shall discuss shortly—satisfaction with American society and politics is uncalled for, however much we may applaud the demonstrated inferiority of totalitarian, authoritarian, and centrally-planned alternatives.

LEGITIMACY AND DEMOCRACY

Legitimacy is a key concept for political systems, and it has not been well served by the definitions of Max Weber and David Easton. To say that the political system possesses a monopoly of legitimate force or that it authoritatively allocates values at best is truistic because the key terms 'legitimate' and 'authoritatively,' which themselves are undefined, contain the essential material. The political system, that is, the political subsystem in society, is the government. The scope of its authority depends upon its legitimacy in various circumstances. It has authority to the extent that its prescriptions will be obeyed. It has legitimacy, either in general or in particular, to the extent that such obedience is regarded as rightful.

The key to understanding the political is to understand legitimation. There are three levels at which this subject can be understood. The first is that of the mythical observer from Mars. If he looks at the actual behavior of people and if they obey established authorities, he might assert a concordance between the actual behavior of people and the legitimacy of government that, at least at this level, makes clear what is meant by a monopoly of legitimate force or an authoritative allocation of values.

But this would miss important elements of legitimacy. It is also necessary to investigate the mental states of people, for this gives a clue to what they might do under different conditions. If they see the authority structure as effective in maintaining control, as governing in accordance with reasonable rules of justice, as coping reasonably well with disturbing influences in the environment, and as not grossly inconsistent with their interests, they will tend to view it as legitimate. What will be regarded as such, however, depends on the backgrounds of those making the judgments. For instance, few doubted the divine right of kings at the time of Louis XIV, but many of the French doubted it at the time of Louis XVI.

If we left the discussion there, it would lack an important dimension. One would be left in a relativist or historicist position in which all judgments are made in light of a parochial setting. There is, however, a reflexive process of thought—the 'test in principle'—that can be applied to the subject of legitimacy which takes into account comparative knowledge of both the system under analysis and the broad sweep of human history. This range of knowledge can include human nature, social science, judgments about environmental possibilities, procedures, justice, and so on. If the political system is adequately responsive within the framework of such an examination, it retains its legitimacy and citizens have an obligation to support it because of their interest in good ends. Even when it fails this test to some extent, it may call upon obligatory, if limited, support if it can be replaced only at great cost.

The thesis that history has ended with the current forms of polity and society fails at this third level of analysis. Although contemporary American society and polity warrant unselfish support against external threats under contemporary forms of organization, this support should not exclude an active search for superior conditions. Although the society and polity toward which we move may retain important elements of pluralism and market, their context likely will be substantially different. This third level of legitimacy invokes one of the key concepts of liberal democracy: individual autonomy. One of the most important functions of liberal democracy is to assure the autonomy of the individual in making political and moral choices. It is the possibility of autonomy that makes freedom valuable.

However, one of the crucial and sad defects of contemporary democracy lies in the identification of autonomy with the pursuit of transient desires rather than with the type of transstable character that makes moral and political judgments reflexively with appropriate consideration of responsibility toward others. It is this type of responsible behavior to which Aristotle referred when he spoke of the pursuit of happiness, which he did not identify with transient pleasures.

Please note that nothing has been said about the political system's embodying the will of the people. Its legitimacy stems from its achieving reasonably good ends by reasonably good means and from its accountability in democracies if it fails to do so. The intellectual puzzle posed by the Arrow paradox of the agenda order is of interest only if one believes both that political decisions should express in some maximal way the will of the people and that preference orders are transitive both for groups and individuals.

The first proposition is uninteresting except to mathematical economists, who are more interested in intellectual puzzles than in real-world problems. No one could engage in the calculations required to determine what the maximal will of the people is with respect to a particular legislative proposition and it could be formulated in so many different ways that no determination could be made with respect to maximal consequences, even apart from wills. The second is incorrect.

Even for individuals, let alone for groups, preferences are too context-dependent for transitivity to hold. Ross Ashby provided an amusing illustration of this. An Englishman went on vacation without his wife. He went to the post office to send her a cheap telegram. The clerk said there were two choices: "Having a wonderful time" and "Wish you were here." The man said, "Send 'Wish you were here.'" The clerk then remembered a third choice: "Please join me at once." The man said, "Send 'Having a wonderful time.'"

Moreover, Arrow's way of stating the problem invokes a group dominance that may be inconsistent with the actual identifications of humans. It fails frame of reference analysis.

If one took seriously the assumptions underlying Arrow's analysis, it would follow that any law that maximized collective preferences should be obeyed. Why, however, should an American Indian who desires a tribal life take obligation to the American polity seriously apart from the penalty that might be invoked? The right of the American Indian to vote and to take part in the political process in ways fully equal to all other members of society may be entirely beside the point if the Indian identifies with tribal society and not with American society. To use as a metaphor the clock paradox of relativity theory, these Indians and ordinary Americans may be on different inertial paths.

If this is so, it follows neither that the Indian has an obligation to recognize the legitimacy of the American government nor that the government has an obligation to recognize his right to rebellion. I am not arguing that moral individuals will fail to search for some acceptable compromise if different legitimate considerations are at stake but only that sometimes war is the only solution to otherwise insoluble problems.

There are multiple identifications in contemporary society. One identifies with oneself, one's family, one's ethnic or religious group, one's nation, humankind, the animal kingdom, and so forth. Which of these identifications takes primacy cannot be determined in the abstract. Such examinations can be agonizing and often, because of the looseness of the web of considerations, inconclusive.

There is a huge potential for tragedy in such conflicts. If justice were purely abstract—if it were a system for ghostly humans without particular characteristics and histories—if the world were only strongly ordered, then there would be an identical answer for all questions and only bad, evil, ignorant, or stupid people would fail to accept it.

Humans working through history grind these tragedies out of existence or submerge them by superior force. Tribal society cannot be restored meaningfully for the Indians, for the tribe within the United States, and the life and culture within it, are poor and dysfunctional substitutes for what tribal life was before Europeans occupied the land. Few of us would be willing to agree to end the existence of the United States even while empathizing with the tragedy of the Indian and regretting the inability or unwillingness of many Indians to assimilate. But the democratic procedures of American society are neither a solvent nor, from the Indian frame of reference, a justification.

THE FUTURE AND DEMOCRACY

The current democratic systems and their social, cultural, and technological environments are the matrix out of which future political systems will arise. Their unfolding surely will create tragedies for some individuals and groups—tragedies that cannot be justified from their frame of reference—and perhaps tragedies for all if we fail to apprehend and respond to some of the unfortunate, or perhaps even evil, potentialities that are present in the contemporary matrix.

It is not difficult to project a desperate future if some tendencies in contemporary society continue to grow. The functional illiteracy of vast numbers of Americans and their inability to perform at the simplest levels of skills is frightening. The decline of Americans with skills in mathematics, the sciences, and engineering raises serious questions with respect to the continued health of the American economic system. The growth of crime and dishonesty at all levels of American society is extremely troubling. These problems could give rise to waves of discontent that could be exploited by demagogues. The low level of discourse in the last presidential campaign provides a slight hint of how far we can decline.

Let us examine a few of the technological developments likely to emerge in the first third or half of the next century and briefly examine how they can affect the prospects of our value system and also of democratic government. Manufacturing will be largely automated and robotic. There will be few workers in factories and these will be highly skilled technicians, professional people, and managers. The molecular basis of materials will be understood and materials will be produced to order. Power—solar or perhaps fusion—will provide cheap energy. The genome will be fully mapped and microsurgery will permit the elimination of unwanted and the substitution of wanted characteristics. Chemical enhancement of learning will be achieved. (It is important to understand that this will have only marginal value in the absence of sustaining cultural and social conditions.) The chemical and electronic control of behavior will become possible.

Universal surveillance will be easy. Both visual and auditory means will be light years more efficient than any devices now available. The major problem that has always impeded intelligence organizations—the massiveness of the data bank—will be overcome by cheap supercomputers that utilize enormously efficient scanning programs that select out key terms from the stream of information in which they are embodied and that interpret them.

It should be clear even from this brief selection of items that the means will be at hand to produce a relative utopia or a 'Brave New World.' It is fortunate indeed that the Soviet system entered its crisis in the contemporary world rather than in this world. But it does not follow that either we or they will escape the disastrous possibilities that are pregnant in the contemporary matrix.

How many in Washington, let alone in Beijing, could be trusted to solve these problems in a humane way if they had the opportunity to solve them in ways that perpetuated their rule and their perquisites? Are the values placed on the sanctity of human life, values beyond the state (God for many), respect, concern and empathy for others, honesty, humility so strong in contemporary society that the survival of democratic institutions is assured?

I am an optimist despite the weight of evidence to the contrary, but surely it is time to anticipate these developments. The institutions that should be in the forefront of these examinations, the universities, are particularly deficient in their attention to them. They are caught up in the race of specialization. The linkage between realms of knowledge that makes for civilized discourse and understanding is neglected and devalued.

Even apart from these problems, how will humans convince themselves of their value sufficiently to preserve decency, let alone democracy? As computers begin to mimic reason more successfully, the distinctions between humans and machines may seem smaller. Substitute parts for the body will be manufactured, again diminishing our sense of uniqueness. Some will argue for genetic adaptation to different environments, the sea, for instance. Once we start, where will we stop? Will we begin to adapt humans to particular tasks?

What will individuals do with their lives to make them fulfilling? Most work, both blue and white collar, will be done by machines. How much service work will be left? How many can write novels, paint pictures, or compose music? (And perhaps the computers will do many of these things also.) What vocation will give life its value?

If computers begin to mimic intelligence, if individuals are adapted to different environments, if they are improved by prosthetic devices, if robots begin to perform more skilled tasks, how will this affect the self-conception and identification of humans? Will it undermine their sense of uniqueness and the humane qualities of life that are essential to liberal democracy? Or will it lead to greater sensitivity? We have the myth that if only we can solve life's material problems—if only we can abolish hunger, sickness, and inadequate living conditions—we can create a utopia. But that may create only worse problems. Men used to get satisfaction from unskilled jobs because that provided for the family. Women received satisfaction from the important task of raising the children. Both men and women seem less satisfied and more alienated in contemporary society.

Ambition will not vanish. It may get more intense primarily because the number of avenues through which it can be fulfilled are diminished. To what psychological dysfunctions will this give rise? To what political perversions?

Perhaps the reader may feel that I have vastly overstated the case. My optimistic side is inclined to agree with this evaluation. If there is an excuse for this exercise, it is to indicate that we should not be complacent in our defense of democracy.

Still, the future of liberal democracy is not secure. It is important to understand that liberal (in an older sense of the term) democratic institutions which, for the first time in human history, make dignity a possibility for all humans, need an intelligent defense if they are to survive and flourish into the next century.

There are many contemporary problems urgently in need of solution. The educational problem and that of moral values surely are among the most important. But other problems that could be even more serious may emerge before we become aware of them. It is good that contemporary society has set up committees of experts to discuss the ethical issues in such matters as gene splicing. We need to go beyond this, however. We need to examine how possible future developments may affect the solutions we institutionalize today. And we need to ask how these solutions today and in the future will affect the larger sets of values and institutions of society.

Many of these speculations will be incorrect. Surely surprises will be in store for us. Even so, I would argue that the comparative evaluations provided by speculation about the future, even if wrong, will open up ethical evaluation to a wider and more desirable range of considerations.

NOTE

More systematic discussions of Rawls, Toulmin, Nozick, and political obligation are presented in *Justice, Human Nature, and Political Obligation*, The Free Press, New York, 1976. My epistemology, philosophy of science, theory of language, moral theories, and the test in principle are treated at length in *Science, Language, and the Human Condition*, Revised Edition, Paragon House Publishers, 1989. Transstable character, identity, authenticity and alienation are defined and discussed in *Alienation and Identification*, The Free Press, New York, 1976. A philosophy of science similar to mine is presented brilliantly in Richard H. Schlegel, *Contextual Realism*, Paragon House Publishers, 1986.

FIVE

THE JEWISH PERSPECTIVE ON THE INTERRELATIONSHIP OF CHURCH AND STATE

Gershon Weiler

The title of this paper is deeply paradoxical. While on the theoretical, theologico-political level nothing could be more inappropriate than to think of Judaism in terms of church and state yet, on the practical, sociological-political level, church-state conflict seems an accurate description of much of what is occurring in Israel today. It is the purpose of this essay to illuminate this paradox.

The designation of certain conflicts of political supremacy as 'church-state' has roots in the history of Christendom where both church and state have their own specialized domains of legitimacy. The reason is simple enough. It could never be disputed that, historically, the newcomer on the scene was the church. The 'Empire' was there before the 'Coming.' Thus, no matter how passionate the struggle between secular and religious authority, there has never been a suggestion by either side that the other was not legitimate.

In perhaps the earliest document of this struggle for power, the admonition of Pope Gelasius to Emperor Anastasius I, in the year

494, the Pope opens his argument by recognizing the legitimacy of his adversary:

> There are indeed two powers ... by which this world is ruled: the sacred authority of the popes and the royal power.

The point of conflict is determining the right relationship between these two authorities. (*Duo quippe sunt ... quibus principaliter mundus hic regitur*). Recognizing the legitimacy of secular power is never absent from clerical polemics, not even from the *Unam Sanctam* of Boniface VIII. A late champion of church supremacy, the Spanish Jesuit Ludovico Molina (1535-1600), in his *De justitia et jure*, argues for subordination of secular power to the church. These two powers *non sunt duae diversae respublicae ... sed sunt invicem subordinatae*. In order to be subordinate, secular power must be, of course, in a meaningful way different. This difference is, for Molina, that while the secular political power has the task of securing the temporal common good (*bonum commune temporale*), the church is entrusted with safeguarding the far superior interest, the spiritual common good (*bonum commune spirituale*). This division of labor was not disputed until the rise of radical political secularism which denied that the church could be any good from a political point of view. Thus Hobbes, the greatest representative of secular politics, is consistent when he rejects the assumption, common to both adversaries in the preceding age, that politics is part of theology. At the opening of Chapter XI of *Leviathan*, this point is made perfectly clear:

> For there is no such Finis ultimus, (utmost ayme) nor Summum Bonum, (greatest good,) as is spoken of in the books of old moral philosophers.... Felicity is a continual progress of the desire, from one object to another; the attaining of the former, being still but the way to the latter.

Judaism too rejects the principle of a Christian division of labor but on grounds entirely different from those advocated by Hobbes. As Josephus Flavius explained, in the context of introducing the term *theocracy*, what is unique in Judaism is that "Moses did not make religion a part of virtue but ... ordained other virtues to be parts of religion."[1] For Marxists everything is politics and for Judaism, as Flavius perceptively puts it, everything is religion.

Flavius wrote at a time when not much beyond religion remained of the Hebrew past. The collapse of political independence, first under the assault of the Babylonians and then as a consequence of defeat by the Romans, created an anti-political mood under the impact of which the political national past underwent an *ex post facto* religious metamorphosis. As Wellhausen put it: "The Mosaic theocracy, the residuum of a ruined state, is itself not a state at all, but an unpolitical artificial product...."[2] It is this, post-political artificial product which has become known in the last two millennia as the Jewish religion or Judaism. It is no wonder that it does not know and has no room for the conflict between church and state. There was at that time no state against which the institutions of Judaism could play the role of a church. That role was predicated on the presence of a potentially antagonistic and yet undoubtedly legitimate concentration of secular power. Judaism became the religion of a dispersed and politically subject community. Politics came to mean for Jews the active presence of Gentile powers, i.e. oppression. They had no politics of their own, since they exercised no power, neither over themselves nor over others. It is this *ethos* of powerlessness which has become known, together with its distinctive system of norms, as historical or normative Judaism. It became an anti-political religion and yet, in the deeper recesses of Jewish self-awareness nurtured by holy books which recorded their national history (*sacra historia* for others), the political past has never been forgotten and, more importantly, never been deprived of its legitimacy.

Since the political past could not be delegitimated, it had to be integrated into the later religious conceptions. The Empire existed before Christianity and hence it was legitimate. In the Jewish context, great importance was attached to Deuteronomy 27:9, "Listen and hear Israel, today you have become a people for Yahve your God." This verse was interpreted in the constitutive mood: before that day you were not a people but, to use a phrase much made of by Sir Robert Filmer, merely a 'headless multitude'. As for the day indicated by the verse, it referred to the day on which the portable religion of the Torah was given to Israel, and not to any significant day for the national political past. In the same spirit, the Talmud restructured the history of legitimacy when, in Aboth I.1, it records that "Moses received the Torah at Sinai, handed it over to Joshua, who transmitted it to the elders, who handed it over to the prophets and they to the Men of the Great Assembly ..." after which there follow only rabbinic authorities. It is not denied explicitly that kings had any authority; they are merely passed over in silence.

Judaism, as the religion of a politically powerless community, faced the problem of state and religion only in the age of emancipation and enlightenment. The leading figure of this age, Moses Mendelssohn (1729-1786), is the author of the major theoretical treatment of the topic. His *Jerusalem oder Uber religiose Macht und Judenthum*[3] is an attempt to come to terms with the modern age, with its equality of rights, and with its freedom of thought while safeguarding the interests of Judaism *qua* religion. Significantly, this work contains a criticism of Hobbes, which tells us that Mendelssohn is not a secularist who holds, like Hobbes, that human happiness consists in getting what one wants. His view is that Judaism, while manifestly not secular, is not a religion in the strict sense either. He holds that Moses revealed to his people, in a supernatural way, such laws as are necessary for happiness in this world and in the one to come (*um zur zeitlichen und ewigen Gluckseligkeit zu gelangen*), yet he did not teach any doctrines (*keine Lehrmeinungen, keine Heilswahrheiten, keine allgemeine Vernunftsatze*).[4] The general idea of Mendelssohn is that Judaism is not revealed religion (*geoffenbarte* religion) but revealed legislation (*geoffenbarte Gesetzgebung*).[5] Hence, the great advantage of Judaism over other religions is that it commands no beliefs, only actions. It never says what one should believe, only what one should or should not do.[6] A further plank in Mendelssohn's platform is that Gentile society should be tolerant about Jews observing their own laws; such tolerance is prescribed by the principle of freedom of conscience. Thus, addressing his fellow Jews Mendelssohn adopts a rigorously fundamentalist position: they are duty-bound to obey the Divine Law, the Torah, to the letter. In addressing Gentiles he advocates tolerance. Freedom of conscience for the individual will make it possible for Jews, as a group, to obey their own laws. The inconsistencies of Mendelssohn have not gone unnoticed.[7] Let it suffice to note that no one today believes that these views can be defended and that revealed law is in truth less oppressive than revealed doctrine and therefore, is more in line with the autonomy of modern man. If Judaism is indeed ideologically neutral, it remains a serious question why the individual Jew should obey the law of Moses.

For unless it has an underpinning stronger than mere individual commitment, then such commitment cannot be demanded or exacted as if it were a duty. The position of Mendelssohn, because of its manifest inconsistencies, is a faithful mirror of the Jewish predicament in the modern Exile. It is intellectually strained to demand and to support freedom in society at large and to deny the same freedom within the community, while urging that normative obligation overrides private conviction.

Mendelssohn's doctrine shows something else also. It is perfectly reasonable to argue that his theory is valid only under the constraints of Exile where the possibility of observing Mosaic law is conditional upon outside toleration. However, should these constraints be removed, then Mosaic law becomes law again in the full sense of the word, no longer depending for its observance on outside tolerance and individual commitment from within, but on enforcement, as all law does. I began this essay by sketching the process by which Judaism avoided a division of authority, such as exists between church and state. All Jewish authority became religious; there was no state. Now, by the simple dialectic of history, this very same proposition explains that once Israel the state was established, there was no avoiding the confrontations which are typical of church-state conflicts. For if all authority is united, the crucial question becomes in whose hands these authorities and powers should be concentrated, or as Alice said on that memorable occasion: "The question is who is to be boss, that is all."

In the Jewish context this conflict cannot be, and is not, about anything less than the legitimacy of the secular state, i.e., Israel. It was the central argument of Spinoza in his *Tractatus-Theologico-Politicus,* insofar as Judaism was concerned, that the Torah was municipal law, or as he put it *lex patriae,* and that, therefore, once the Hebrew state ceased to exist, the Torah could no longer be obligatory. We have seen, in outline, how this defunct *lex patriae* survived into Exile. Now that the *patria* is sovereign once more, the question arose, with full force, how far is *lex* obligatory, and to what extent it is obligatory on those who govern to make it obligatory for others. Democracy and moral autonomy are precarious concepts in the context of *geoffenbarte Gesetzgebung.* The real life background to current controversies in Israel is that, despite the claims for supreme authority, the adherents of normative Judaism constitute an *ecclesia*. To explain how this occurred is our next task.

As before, it facilitates our task if we make a short detour through Christendom. As long as both *sacerdotium* and *regnum* were regarded as impeccably legitimate, each in its own right, possessing the authority appropriate to the performance of its special tasks, viz., securing spiritual and temporal benefit respectively, there could never be a question, before the advent of the modern age, of delegitimating the church *qua* an authority which is universally binding.

However, once nationalism came onto the scene, all changed. The German emperors were no match for the church in the struggle for supremacy, for they had no tradition to support their claims to legitimate supremacy. But when the King of France confronted Boniface VIII, national feelings were sufficiently aroused for the church's claims of supremacy to lose their plausibility.[8] Indeed, considering the panorama of two millennia of European history, one must concede that only the national idea, as an identity-constituting factor, was ever a match for the church. "I am a Christian" gave way only once, when it met "I am an Englishman" and the like. Pio Nono clashed with Italian nationalists and nationalism was defined, for a while at least, as a Catholic heresy. For that is indeed what it was. By opting for the nation, a person is choosing a self-description incompatible with the primacy of the Catholic church. By identifying with the nation, the individual is declaring that he belongs to a natural body which takes precedence over all competitors. Rousseau's general will, actualized in history as the national will *qua* a natural elemental force, is hardly compatible with the idea that *anima naturaliter Christiana*.

Mutatis mutandis, a similar course was traversed by the Jewish people. We saw how Judaism became the non-territorial, yet exclusively supreme, normative framework for Jews. According to Maimonides, the difference between the Torah and the *nomoi* of the Gentiles is that while the latter have concern only for the welfare of the body, the Torah, by contrast, caters to the welfare of both soul and body.[9] (Remember: *bonum temporale/spirituale*.) This claim strictly entails that any competitor who would care for soul and/or body, would inevitably be in conflict with the Torah. If some agency claimed to cater to the soul, it would conflict with the Torah in the narrowly religious sense. However, even the agency suggesting remedies for the ailments of material existence would also be in conflict, for it is implicit in the claim of Maimonides that there is no remedy for the body outside the norms of the Torah, or as it came to be called, the *halakha*. This situation was perceived by the rabbis who understood how the ideas of modernity came to effect their flock, from the early nineteenth century onward. On the whole they tended to oppose emancipation which removed from the individual Jew the constraints of obedience to their authority. On equally good grounds, most of the rabbis also opposed the Jewish national movement, i.e., Zionism. The history of this movement, from its inception, is one long effort to come to terms with, and to overcome, rabbinic authority. This struggle between the secular national movement and its child, the state of Israel, is an ongoing process from the first Zionist Congress in Basle, in 1897, to this day.[10] This struggle for primacy is the substance of state-church controversies in Israel.

However, before I address directly some current issues in Israeli political life, let me provide the theological background. Much effort has been invested into showing that Jewish nationalism was not contrary to the Torah. Indeed, it was not difficult to argue this, for submerged under the layer of Exilic ideology, there was the record of a national past of political existence. It could be argued, on perfectly orthodox grounds, that Zionism was legitimate. Let me give one illustration. In the Babylonian Talmud there is a passage[11] the substance of which is that God made Israel swear that they will not willfully throw off the yoke of the Gentiles, that they will not return to the land of Israel as an organized body. The passage also says that at the same time God made the Gentile nations swear that they will not oppress Jews with exceptional harshness. Now, there have been many learned disquisitions about whether Zionism is a transgression of this prohibition or whether, because of the exceptional harshness of recent Gentile behavior, Jews are now free to seek their own earthly benefits by their own collective efforts.

It would be easy to dismiss such controversies as typical of Talmudic minds with nothing better to occupy them. However, this would be a grave mistake. It is time to recall that the conceptual framework of Mendelssohn, despite its inconsistencies, lost nothing, to this day, of its practical importance. In other words, if the confession and practice of Judaism were confined to the territory of the State of Israel, then the controversy about supremacy within those municipal boundaries, could properly be regarded as a local political controversy of interest to outsiders only in an academic or diplomatic mood. But this is not the case. Not only does the Jewish Diaspora continue its existence, and not only is there a steady stream of emigration from Israel into that most attractive of Diasporas, the U.S., but all concerned agree that the Jewish people constitute one entity and that their religion, Judaism, is valid and binding uniformly, without regard to place. Hence, whatever Israel may wish to enact, *qua* municipal law, in this regard, has consequences for Jews elsewhere and, naturally, they claim their right of say. It should be emphasized that this is a genuinely two-way street. Some of the leading rabbis whose rulings are regarded as obligatory by people who live in Israel themselves reside in the U.S. The *religious* legitimacy of the Diaspora is, so far, challenged by only a small minority.

Let me illustrate this briefly. Is there a religious duty to reside in the 'Land of Israel'? I put it this way, because the 'Land of Israel' is a normative concept within the system of the *halakha*, while the state of Israel is not. Thus, many commandments, such as the tithe, are obligatory in the land, but not abroad. Is there a duty to live in the land? There is a famed controversy on the subject between Maimonides (1135-1204) and Nachmanides (1194-1270). All agree that the Torah consists of 613 commandments, but there is extensive debate about the exact details of this list. Maimonides produced a complete list of the 613 commandments and Nachmanides subjected this list to extensive criticism.[12] Among other things, he faulted Maimonides for having omitted from his list of positive commandments the duty to take possession of the 'Land of Israel.' It is not an accident perhaps that Maimonides resided by choice in Egypt, where he served as a court physician. Nachmanides made his way to Israel. It is still a matter of great importance how one answers, within the bounds of Judaism, the question whether to take possession of the ancestral land is a religious duty, commanded directly by God, or whether it is merely an option, or even perhaps altogether forbidden, as would follow from a Diasporic interpretation of the *dicta* in *Ketuboth* adduced above.

Thus emerges one of the most ubiquitous features of the inter-relationship between state and church in Judaism: that relation-ship varies with place. Jewish attitudes outside Israel bear, on the whole, the stamp of Mendelssohn. Maximization of individual rights improves the chances of specifically Jewish self-expression, whatever it may be. Of course, such freedoms also increase the chances of heteropraxy, but, it seems, time is finally gone for lamenting the demise of feudalism, of all regimes the most suit-able for communalistic Diaspora existence. Thus, we have to dis-tinguish, as clearly as possible, between the attitudes of Jewish communities or individuals on the one hand, and the normative position of Judaism on the other hand. The desired distinction is hard to come by, for as we have seen in the Maimonides-Nachmanides controversy regarding the religious significance of 'the Land,' real-life needs are apt to affect normative rulings. In a Diaspora condition, the state is always the Gentile state, which is but a physical given and does not raise the question of the church-state relationship within Judaism. The Diaspora community is not a church because it has no state to confront and so the relation-ship is not a real one. This question arises with a vengeance in Israel.

As I initially stated, we are dealing with a paradox. The norma-tive system of historic, mostly Exilic, Judaism is based on the assumption that no church-state division of authority exists within its conceptual boundaries. However, certain questions of govern-ment remained proper subjects of *halakhic* study but they had no application. Thus, once history subtracted the element of politics and of political power from the ideas related to government, all that remained was the rules pertaining to the management of the affairs of the subject community. History played a strange trick on this normative system: it restored politics and political rulership to the Jewish people in 1948. So, a whole layer of norms, dormant during the long hibernation of the Diaspora, suddenly became full of practical meaning. The rules were there all the time, only they had no application. With the existence of a Jewish state, the ques-tion could not be avoided how and in what manner these ancient rules were applicable to the new political statehood. This circum-stance, in itself, would not have generated a church-state problem in Israel. It is thinkable in theory, if not with any degree of reality, that the Jewish people could have arrived at statehood in a socio-logically traditional manner. That is, it is possible that they could have established their state under the leadership of the rabbis. Even though the same practical questions of applicability would have then arisen, these by definition, would not have created a church-state conflict. The question then would have been how to apply rules to a new situation since, *ex hypothesi*, no one would have disputed the appropriate authoritative rulings. Nothing would have changed in the ongoing practice of *halakhic* case-law. The only difference would have been the content of the rulings. In the new situation many of these rulings would have had a political content. But, as we know, this is not what in fact happened.

Israel was established in 1948 as a secular state. The Declaration of Independence, although invoking the ambiguous 'Rock of Israel,' opens with a recital of 'natural and historic rights' which the Jewish people have to their land, and these concepts of natu-ral and historic rights are taken from the secular vocabulary of politics, especially from the arsenal of nationalist argumentation. That Israel came into being and is to this day a secular state is the most fundamental fact about it. This fact also determined that organized religion should function in Israel as a church, thus cre-ating a real life state-church controversy in that country. This assertion is generally disputed. It is normally argued, on the basis of legal-theological background that the idea of a church is alien to Judaism. I do not dispute that. Indeed, it has been the burden of my arguments so far to show why this has been so. What I am saying now is that Israel created an entirely new situation in the context of which it is meaningful to speak, perhaps for the first time in Jewish history, of a church-state confrontation. I qualify my assertion by saying 'perhaps.' There have been conflicts between the kings of Israel and religious personalities, such as prophets and rabbis. These conflicts left their traces in legal literature and these literary remains inform the present conflict. However, those ancient conflicts could not be described simply as state-church conflicts. It is the liberal-democratic structure of modern Israel which makes it possible for a church-like institution to arise. There are now religious political parties in parliament, the *Knesset*, whose main aim is to advance the cause of what is called 'religious legislation,' i.e., to put on the statute-book as much religious law as possible. To outsiders, these aspects of Israeli political life seem exceptionally confusing. Let me attempt to clarify them.

It is quite usual in democratic countries for pressure groups, including religious ones, to use their electoral power to advance their cause. This is clerical politics and the organizations which promote such measures are properly called churches. These latter are institutions of the secular state and in this sense sociologists refer to their religion as secularized religion. This means that they function as the structure of the secular state prescribes. In a sense, the same thing happens in Israel. Judaism in Israel, because of its participation in the political game, is to a large extent secularized. Yet there is a difference. From the point of view of the religious segment, the state and its organs, like all individual Jewish citizens, are duty-bound to observe rabbinic rulings.

Religious legislation is perhaps nowhere more significant, and for the nonreligious more oppressive, than in the impositions of ecclesiastic courts on the citizenry. The *Rabbinic Courts Jurisdiction* (Marriages and Divorces) Act-1953 decrees that marriages and divorces, between Israelis who are deemed Jewish by *halakhic* standards, are under the sole jurisdiction of rabbinic courts.

This act may seem to many a violation of the principle of freedom of conscience, because it subjects citizens, independently of their religious convictions, to the authority of ecclesiastic courts. The abolition of the duty to submit to the jurisdiction of such courts is counted among the many achievements of the English Revolution. Yet, it could be argued, the situation is not all bad. These religious courts do operate by the power of the secular legislator and under the constraints imposed by it. It is a kind of 'sub-letting' of the performance of Jewish marriages and divorces to a subsidiary agency. Indeed, this is how Israeli jurisprudence perceives the situation. It has been reiterated many times by the High Court that the Kelsenian basic norm of the country is the will of the *Knesset*, as it is expressed in legislative acts. However, this is not how rabbinic courts see themselves. In their view, their own authority is more ancient than that of the state and it does not depend for its validity on any act by the secular legislator. This view has been partially adopted by statute. For example, the law governing the appointment of judges who sit in rabbinic courts does not prescribe that these judges, in their oath of office, undertake to observe the laws of the state. The fine point is that the ecclesiastic judge, when he sits on the bench, is subject only to his own law but not to that of the state.

It is an established fact that since the establishment of the state, no chief rabbi has ever appeared before the High Court to account for his actions under Act 1953. They have been served *sub poena* more than once, but there has always been some political way out of a final confrontation. The point at issue goes to the heart of the matter. Judaism in Israel functions like a church, insofar as it pursues clerical politics, but at the same time, it retains its claims to supremacy. Thus, the division of powers between secular and religious authorities is not a kind of mixed government which, in the tradition of political philosophy, made for stability. It is rather that kind of built-in conflict over supremacy to which Spinoza in his *Tractatus Theologico-Politicus* attributed the collapse of the Jewish state and against which the philosophy of Hobbes is an eloquent warning.

This fundamental irreconcilability between the two competing systems of law is often obscured by religious apologists who advocate that 'Hebrew Law' should be adopted by, or introduced into, secular legislation. This approach promotes the idea that *halakha* could be made the law of the land through the will of the secular legislator. Among those who advocate this line, the most notable are the late Justice Moshe Silberg[13] and Professor Menachem Elon who is, at present, also a judge of the Israeli Supreme Court. Elon's monumental work *Jewish Law: History, Sources, Principles*[14] is, in all probability, the last word on this program for many years to come. What these theories fail to explain is how the conflicting sources of validity, divine versus human, are to be reconciled. Like compromises often do, this approach too, leaves the parties bitter and frustrated. Israel is in the throes of a church-state conflict.

It is sometimes suggested that *halakha* has the conceptual ability to deal with the modern state and especially with the emergencies which make up the life of politics. It is suggested that Talmudic legislation, especially as codified by Maimonides in his *Laws Concerning Kings and Wars*[15] is able to cope with any emergency. The substance of this argument is that Talmudic legislation already recognized a division of power, between the king and the *Sanhedrin*, the supreme legislative-judicial body. In terms of this, the king is empowered to do all he must do in an emergency.[16] As an illustration, take III.9 of Maimonides' laws:

> If a person kills another and there is no clear evidence, or if no warning has been given him, or there is only one witness, or if one kills accidentally a person whom he hated, the king may, if the exigency of the hours demands it, put him to death in order to insure the stability of the social order.[17]

In a murder case, under *halakha*, to secure conviction, not only must there be clear evidence, but it is necessary for the murderer to have been warned before the act that what he is about to do is a crime. There should be clear evidence that he understood the warning and that despite the warning he persisted in the execution of his murderous design, and there should be two witnesses to the deed, etc. Historically, of course, this codification is much later than the actual political conditions in which it was meant to be operational. However, this *ex post facto* legislation about the king's powers to deal with emergencies, not only murderers, came into being since it was realized, even theoretically, that the constraints of *halakhic* legality render impossible not only the conviction of murderers but also orderly government as such. Such a situation is socially insupportable and so, after the demise of the kings (and also on the basis of the experience of the conflicts of the Second Temple period), the Talmudic sages sanctioned the so-called Law of the King. The general idea is that the king is a stopgap, who steps in whenever *halakha* becomes ineffective. Now the crucial question is simple enough—who decides whether a situation is an emergency and what needs to be done? Maimonides is silent on this question. What he has to say about the justiciability of the king's actions, in III.7 of the *Laws of Kings and Wars*, only confuses matters.

> ... the kings of the House of David may be judged and testified against. But with respect to the kings of Israel, the rabbis enacted that they neither judge nor be judged, neither testify nor be testified against, because they are arrogant, and (if they be treated as commoners) the cause of religion would suffer.[18]

It needs no lengthy argument to establish that neither arrangement is satisfactory. It is the simple yet profound message of Justice Marshall, in Marbury v. Madison, that if someone possesses a right then there must be a procedure available in the law which secures the enjoyment of that right for him. How would the law formulated by Maimonides fare under both kinds of kings, in practice? Clearly, Davidic kings would be subordinate to the *Sanhedrin*. They would not enjoy executive privilege and their acts would be fully justiciable thus making government ineffective. Israelite kings, on the other hand, took executive privilege and were, Maimonides describes in so many words, lawless rulers who did as they pleased. Obviously, theirs is not an example to follow. They are lawless, *legibus soluti*, and their deeds are in the category of *rechtloser Hochheitsakt*. Only the Davidic, not the Israelite, kings can offer a blueprint for the proper arrangement of authority between the rabbinic legislator-judge and the politician whose job is execution. This is not what is meant by a state where the people are sovereign. Indeed, Israel has no constitution to this day because the religious parties could not accept the idea that the people of Israel give themselves a constitution. From the religious point of view, they already have an eternally valid constitution, the Torah, and to opt for another is to rebel against God.

Thus the church-state conflict in Israel has no resolution in principle and the best that can be attained is in the nature of pragmatic adjustments. On principle, the Israeli church party acts as a party of legitimists, as representatives of a legitimate regime which has been driven from power. It is forced to make compromises with usurpers but it will not surrender its title and its claim to legitimacy. Consequently, the burden of tolerance is shifted to the shoulders of the other party. The secularists are expected to 'understand' the limitation that religion places on its followers, while the religious are not expected to recognize that another lifestyle can be equally legitimate within the context of a free society. From the church party's point of view, the nonreligious, i.e., the nonobservant, are transgressors whose proper place is before a religious court of law. They are wrongdoers and only the circumstances of the times allow them to get away with their iniquities. Looking at the world from such a normative point of view, the devout views as criminals the secular other such as those who uphold the values of personal freedom in matters of religion and conscience. The religious sector must deal with secular people but cannot recognize that it is right that such people exist. This disagreement about the basis of the conflict makes state-church relations in Israel unique and singularly bitter. Nevertheless, the religious establishment in Israel functions as *sacerdotium* of sorts; it provides 'religious services' to the population and satisfies their 'religious needs.' The quoted terms are taken from standard Israeli parlance. The majority of the population in Israel, although it follows an entirely irreligious lifestyle, regularly engages religious functionaries who perform the ceremonies appropriate to major events like circumcision, *bar mitzvah*,[19] weddings, and funerals. The rare exceptions to this are only a small minority of militant secularists. It is an Italian sort of arrangement: rabbis are mostly mere celebrants. Thus the Torah, which originally was the law of a nation (and later an exilic community), is reduced in the sociological sense, to church regulations consulted only for ceremonies. The religious functionaries came to be called 'holy tools' (*klei kodesh*). Anyone who has seen an overworked, and probably underpaid, religious functionary, making his rounds in a large public cemetery, with timetable and lists of names of dead in his hand, chanting over corpses once every twenty minutes or so, knows how far this is from the self-understanding of *halakha* and how near to the secularized church.

This situation is well understood by the religious part of the population. Hence their understandable frustration: they realize that no matter how much political power they accumulate and no matter how often they provide their specialized services, they are still catering to an essentially secular population. Given their claims to legitimacy, they compensate for their frustration by extensive, and ideologically aggressive, missionary activity. The purpose of these activities is to 're-convert' Jews to their religion, to persuade them to 'return.'[20] Missions are, of course, typical of churches. The inherent difficulty in these missionary undertakings is that their final aim is unclear. Like all missions, the Judaistic ones address themselves to individuals whom they exhort to change their way of life, to become, as it were, 'reborn' Jews. However, it is not clear, nor is there a consensus among the groups engaged in these missionary projects, what message they have for society as a whole. This would not matter, were it not for the fact that Judaism was fashioned for a people who have no political responsibilities. Thus, should the whole population of Israel become observant, it is probable that this would leave society bereft of those motivations characteristic of and necessary for the existence of an active citizenry. Only a small and extreme minority has the brazen consistency to demand openly that Israel become a clerical dictatorship in which the Torah would be made municipal law. Most of the religious populace would be satisfied with less, where 'less' is conceptually accommodated within this or that definition of a better and stronger religious life. Their aims are typical of churches which seek more influence.

This is my explanation of the paradox with which I began. It seems that in following its current direction, Judaism is merely following the course prescribed, for the last two centuries, by the predicaments of modernity. It is impossible for the Torah to function, under these new conditions, as the municipal law of a modern nation, which respects the values of democracy, liberalism and moral autonomy. Thus, there remain only the familiar nineteenth century alternatives of assimilation as individuals, secular nationalism and self-ghettoization, or its latter-day Israeli version, reactionary nationalist-religious fundamentalism. None of these is satisfactory or without controversy from the point of view of the historic Torah, made for conditions of pre-modernity. The same dissatisfaction attaches, with added force, to movements of Reform and Conservatism; neither of these has succeeded in attaining religious legitimacy.

Herein lies the predicament of Judaism at the present time. Should it ever successfully adopt modernity by accommodating moral autonomy and the basic ideas and institutions of liberal democracy, it will have largely solved the church-state problem. But that will be another religion.[21]

NOTES

1. Josephus Flavius, *Against Apion*, Book II.17.
2. Julius Wellhausen, *Prolegomena to the History of Ancient Israel*, (Cleveland & New York, 1957) 422.
3. Moses Mendelssohn, *Phadon Jerusalem oder Uber religiose Macht und Judenthum*. Ed. Arnold Bodek, (Leipzig, 1869). *Jerusalem and other Jewish Writings*, translated and edited by Alfred Jospe, (New York, 1969).
4. Mendelssohn, op. cit. 166.
5. Op. cit. 173.
6. Op. cit. 175.
7. Eliezer Schweid, *A History of Jewish Thought in Modern Times*, (Jerusalem, 1977) 142, 144-145. Also in the introduction of A. Jospe to his translation, see note 3 above.
8. Ernest Barker, *Church, State and Study*, (London, 1930), chapter I.
9. Maimonides, *Guide to the Perplexed* II.39. See also L. Strauss, "Maimonides Statement of Political Science," *Proc. of the American Academy for Jewish Research*. Vol. XXII (1953), 124ff.
10. For a detailed account of these events, see S.Z. Abramov, *Perpetual Dilemma; Jewish Religion in the Jewish State* (Rutherford, Madison & Teaneck, 1976), 62ff.
11. *Ketuboth* 111a.
12. Maimonides, *Sefer Hamitsvoth* (Kuk Inst. ed.), 244-5.
13. Moshe Silberg, *Talmudic Law and the Modern State* (New York, 1973).
14. Menachem Elon, *Jewish Law; History, Sources, Principles* (Jerusalem, 1988), 3 vols. 3rd ed.
15. 'Laws Concerning Kings and Wars,' *The Code of Maimonides, Book Fourteen, The Book of Judges*, Yale Judaica series, vol. III. (New Haven & London, 1949), 205-243.
16. See my *Jewish Theocracy*, (Leiden, 1988), chapter 8, esp. 159ff.
17. 'Laws Concerning Kings and Wars,' 214.
18. Op. cit. 213.
19. A *rite de passage* marking the thirteenth birthday of a male, which makes him an adult member of the community.
20. Some of the groups engaged in these activities, such as Lubovitch sect, under the leadership of Rabbi M. Schnevrson, who resides in New York, are known outside the confines of Jewish communities.
21. It is tempting, when revising this paper for print, to depart from theory and to refer to the escalation of the *Religionstreit* in Israel in 1990, in the course of which a few octogenerian rabbis emerged as the black eminences of Israeli politics. However, in my view, these events should come as surprise to no one who pondered the predicaments discussed here.

SIX

RELIGION AND POLITICS FROM A ROMAN CATHOLIC PERSPECTIVE

Battista Mondin

CHRISTIANITY AND POLITICS: A HISTORICAL SURVEY

It is generally agreed that the New Testament does not present any specific doctrine on political institutions and on social life. Yet in the teachings of Jesus we find several elements that concern directly the organization of society and the political duties of its members, which may provide some solid grounds for a Christian understanding of politics. The evangelical texts which refer more explicitly to politics are twofold: the words of Jesus to Peter and the other apostles, "Give back to Caesar what is Caesar's, and to God what is God's" (Mt. 22:21); and Jesus' words addressed to Pilate, "Thou wouldst not have any power over me at all, if it had not been given thee from above" (Jn. 19:11). In this text, two principles are clearly stated: The existence of two powers—the power of state and of earthly kingdoms, and the power of God and of the spiritual community (the church); the nature of these two powers is essentially different and also their ends are different—welfare and happiness in this world is the end of the state; eternal happiness is the goal of the spiritual community. But it must also be noted that the power of the political society comes from above: "*Omnis auctoritas a Deo.*" In this way, Jesus proclaims that the earthly power does not find its justification in itself but in God. This implies that the earthly power and the state have something in common with the spiritual community, since both have a common origin and in some way point to the same final end: God.

In his behavior, Jesus remained faithful to these two principles. Due to the spiritual character of his mission and in his quality as founder of the spiritual community, he always refrained from intervening in the political affairs of his country although he well knew that this would have caused great disappointment among his people who were full of messianic hopes. He never condemned evil systems such as slavery nor promoted any form of rebellion against the Roman domination. This does not mean that Jesus was indifferent to politics. On the contrary, he was very critical of those who exercised political power with violence and greed: "You know that, among the Gentiles, those who claim to bear rule, lord it over them, and those who are great among them make the most of the power they have. With you it must be otherwise; whoever has a mind to be great among you, must be your servant, and whoever has a mind to be first among you, must be your slave" (Mk. 10:42-43). All this is perfectly coherent with the two principles stated above. The priority of the supernatural order over the temporal one provides Jesus with the authority of judging the behavior of those who exercise the political power. But, actually, Jesus shows no interest in the detailed application of the two principles; he left responsibility of doing this to his followers, who in the course of history, came out with many different solutions.

In the Middle Ages, the main views on the relationship between Christianity and politics (and between church and state) are represented by St. Augustine of Hippo and St. Thomas Aquinas.

St. Augustine, being aware of the deep hostility of the Roman empire against the church, has a very negative concept of the state. According to the Doctor of Hippo, the end of the state is not only different from that of the church but is essentially contrary to that of the church. In his famous *The City of God*, Augustine presents the history of mankind as a history of two cities, the city of God (the church) and the city of man (the state);

the two cities are in perennial conflict with each other. "Accordingly, two cities have been formed by two loves, the earthly by the love of self, even to the contempt of God, and the celestial by the love of God even to the contempt of self."[1] The former, in a word, glories in itself, the latter in the Lord. For the one seeks glory from men; but the greatest glory of the other is God, the witness of conscience. The one lifts up its head in its own glory, the other says to its God, "Thou art my glory, and a lifter up of mine head" (Ps. 3:3). In the one, the princes and the nations it subdues are ruled by the love of ruling, in the other the princes and the subjects serve one another in love, the latter obeying, while the former take thought for all. The one delights in its own strength, represented in the person of its rulers, the other says to its God, "I will love Thee, O Lord, my strength: (Ps. 18:1).

St. Augustine's purpose in *The City of God* was to find a consistent explanation for history. He believed that the dualistic theory of the Manicheans that he had discarded for metaphysics, could be useful for history. So he sees the entire course of history as governed by two main spiritual forces: the force of good (which coincides with love, obedience, humility, faith, hope and charity) and the force of evil (which coincides with selfishness, pride, avarice, cupidity, and lust). Those who are guided by the force of good belong to the city of God and those who are guided by the force of evil belong to the city of man. But, according to Augustine, the history of the two cities does not start on earth but in heaven, with the split of the angels in two groups, the group of those who remained faithful to God and the group of those who rebelled against Him. The city of God begins with good angels, the city of man (or Babylon) begins with the rebellious angels.

On earth, Augustine places the origin of the two cities in the symbolic figures of Abel and Cain. Abel is the prototype and the founder of the city of God, whereas Cain is the prototype and the founder of the city of man. "What happened between Cain and Abel shows the enmity that exists between the two cities, the city of God and the city of man" (*quod autem inter Cain et Abel, inter duas ipsas civitates, Dei et hominum, inimicitias demonstravit*).[2]

Through several stages Augustine narrates the history of the city of God from Abel down to the birth of the 'new Abel,' Jesus Christ, the foundation of the church. Augustine traces the descent of the city of man from Cain to the rise of the Roman empire, and shows that the hostility between the two cities touches here its highest peak.

The very negative view that Augustine has of the state does not prevent him from recognizing that civil institutions fulfill some positive functions even for the members of the church. But in general, he believes absolutely impossible any sort of dialogue and cooperation between the spiritual community, the church, and the temporal community, the state.

St. Augustine's theory of the two cities contributed to shape the views of many theologians on politics during the Middle Ages. Yet, already towards the end of the patristic period, after the fall of the Roman empire and the foundation of the Christian empire of the East (Byzance), Augustine's pessimistic view on the state begins to decline, and a new more positive theory, directly inspired by the evangelical principle of the two powers, takes shape. The new vision finds its first clear expression in a letter of Pope Gelasius I to the Emperor Anastasius. In 494, the pope, in writing to the emperor, affirms the distinction of the two spheres, spiritual and temporal, and at the same time the bond that exists between the two, since both derive directly from Christ: "Two are indeed the authorities on which this world is principally grounded, the holy authority of the pontiffs and the royal authority of the kings. Of these two the responsibility of the priests is heavier inasmuch as they must render account also of the souls of the kings. Since you know, dear emperor, that although you are superior to all men in dignity, in religious matters you are supposed to bow down your head before the priest in order to receive from him the means necessary for eternal life. Consequently, towards the priest you owe obedience rather than command, and must accept his decision rather than to subdue him to your power. If in the temporal matters priests, being aware of the fact the power that you have has been granted to you by divine disposition, obey to you, the more so is required from you in the administration of divine ministries."[3]

The importance of this text was so great that in 858 Pope Nicholas I cited it word for word in a letter to the emperor Michael III and later it was included in the famous decree of Gratianus.

According to the evangelical doctrine, Gelasius states that the spiritual power has universal jurisdiction on believers and that the clergy has a right to autonomy in the exercise of its functions. To the state, which in turn has a divine origin, belongs the government of temporal affairs and the care of the common good. Both authorities must contribute and cooperate for the supreme good of the souls. However, the priestly order as such has a greater dignity since its end is higher than that of the *regalis majestas.*

To the doctrine of Gelasius, St. Thomas Aquinas in his *De regimen principium* provided a more accurate and solid formulation, with his theory of the *subordinatio indirecta* of the state to the church.

St. Thomas was the first to introduce the principle of secularization, which proclaims the autonomy of human activities (free will, science, philosophy, politics, etc.) with respect to Christian faith. On the ground of his principle he shows that the church and the state are two perfect societies, each one with its proper end: The spiritual good of the souls is the domain of the church and the common good of society is the responsibility of the state. But, according to St. Thomas, though church and state are distinct, they cannot be separated since the same human beings are at the same time members of both the church and state. But there is more than this, since the common good to be really such should contribute to the achievement of the supernatural good (*bonum supernaturale*). Here St. Thomas applies the theory of indirect subordination (*subordinatio indirecta*). Such subordination is required by the fact that the end of the church, the supernatural good, is superior to the end of the state, the common good.

St. Thomas' solution represents the *via media* between the two theories, which were the cause of so many disputes during the fourteenth and fifteenth centuries. The theory of direct subordination of the state to the church was taught by Pope Boniface VIII, and the opposite theory of the subordination of the church to the state was supported by Marsilius of Padua. Boniface's theory corresponds to the needs of the *Respublica Christiana* but it became quickly outdated with the decline of the political power of the church and with the collapse of the same Christian republic at the end of the Middle Ages. Consequently Marsilius' view received larger and larger consensus and was generally espoused by the political philosophers of the modern ages, starting with Machiavelli, Locke, and Montesquieu. Compared against these political philosophers, Roman Catholic philosophers and theologians (Rosmini, Gioberti, Sturzo, Maritain, Congar etc.) found St. Thomas' theory of the two perfect societies and of the indirect subordination of the state to the church quite valuable and tried to make it fit to the new political situation with new arguments.

CATHOLICISM AND DEMOCRACY

St. Augustine, Gelasius, St. Thomas, and Boniface VIII elaborated their theories of the relationship between church and state in the light of what, following Plato and Aristotle, they considered the best form of government, namely monarchy. For this reason, they viewed it as primarily a question of the relationship between the pope and the emperor. They did not take into consideration democracy, which in their views was a bad form of government. Even after the end of the Middle Ages it has taken a long time for Catholic thinkers to revise their negative evaluation of democracy.

Democracy, as we all know, is a big conquest of modern civilization, which little by little created the necessary conditions to transform what was believed to be a utopia into a concrete institution. Democracy first developed in the English and French parliaments as a *praxis*, while at the same time it was provided with a solid theoretical basis by Locke and Montesquieu. The French and the American revolutions, which were inspired by the democratic ideals of freedom, equality and fraternity, were the decisive factors for the spread of democracy in Europe and in the United States of America. The nineteenth century is marked by the triumph of democratic ideals and institutions in many countries of the Old and the New World. In no case, however, were the principles of democracy fully realized. Even today in many so-called democratic countries we notice deep disparities and discriminations among citizens regarding access to power and in the application of civil rights. But notwithstanding such failures it is commonly agreed that democracy remains the best form of government and that its social, political and personal value cannot be disputed.

Within the Roman Catholic church, the acceptance and recognition of democracy as a good political institution were rather slow. Up to Leo XIII, official documents of the magisterium again and again disapprove of democracy. Pope Leo XIII held a position of indifference toward democracy. In his encyclical *Libertas*, Leo XIII declared that "the Church does not condemn any form of government provided they are apt to ensure the welfare of the citizens." The final approval of democracy came only with Vatican II and the Popes Paul VI and John Paul II. However, an implicit approval of democracy is contained in some documents of Pius XI (cf. encyclicals "Mit brennender Sorge" and "Divini redemptoris") and Pius XII (cf. Christmas message of 1944). These documents take a stance against fascism, communism, nazism, and other forms of totalitarianism.

Vatican II devotes an important chapter of the pastoral constitution *Gaudium et spes* to 'the life of the political community'. There the Council shows that the political institution is not a conventional but a natural institution. It is the insufficiency in the matters of establishing a fully human condition that leads individuals and families to set up the political community in its manifold expressions:

> Hence the political community exists for the common good in which the community finds its full justification and meaning, and from which it derives its pristine and proper right. Now the common good embraces the sum of those conditions of social life by which individuals, families and groups can achieve their own fulfillment in a relatively thorough and ready way. It is therefore obvious that the political community and public authority are based on human nature and hence belong to an order of things divinely foreordained. At the same time the choice of government and the method of selecting leaders is left to the free will of citizens (GB 74).

Gaudium et spes goes on to approve and to encourage the specific elements of democracy, namely political participation and the division of governmental roles:

> It is in full accord with human nature that juridical-political structure should, with ever better success and without any discrimination, afford all their citizens the chance to participate freely and actively in establishing the constitutional bases of a political community, governing the state, determining the scope and purpose of various institutions, and choosing leaders. Hence let all citizens be mindful of their simultaneous right and duty to vote freely in the interest of advancing the common good. The Church regards as worthy of praise and consideration the work of those who, as a service to others, dedicate themselves to the welfare of the state and undertake the burdens of this task.
>
> If conscientious cooperation between citizens is to achieve its happy effect in the normal course of public affairs, a positive system of law is

required. In it should be established a division of governmental roles and institutions and, at the same time, an effective and independent system for the protection of rights. Let the rights of all persons, families, and associations, along with the exercise of those rights, be recognized, honored and fostered. The same holds for those duties which bind the citizens. Among the latter should be remembered that of furnishing the commonwealth with the material and spiritual services required for the common good (G 75).

A more accurate and detailed concept of democracy is offered by Pope Paul VI in *Octogesima adveniens*. Paul VI first recalls the motivation that binds every Christian conscience to directly engage in political life in order to ensure the creation of a truly participated democracy. Then he stresses not to divide one's own political action from that of other individuals or groups that work for the cause of justice and peace. Moreover, Paul VI recommends that Christians avoid false and arrogant cloistering and recognize legitimate pluralism in political choices:

> In the concrete situation it is necessary to recognize a legitimate variety of political options. The same Christian faith may lead to distinct engagements. To the Christians that at first sight may seem to be divided and to clash with one another because of different options, the church asks to make an effort of reciprocal understanding for the positions and motivations of the other side; the examination of one's behavior and of its righteousness will suggest to everybody an attitude of charity that, without ignoring the differences, believes in the possibility of convergence and unity, since what unites the believers is much stronger than what divides them.

John Paul II is a strong advocate of democracy. Democracy is praised and recommended in many of his speeches and documents. To him democracy means first of all freedom and solidarity. John Paul II repeatedly claims freedom of religion and of the Catholic church from those countries where such freedoms are neither guaranteed nor safeguarded. On the other hand he is very critical of those liberal democracies of the West that are extremely permissive and consent to a use of freedom that makes a mess of moral values, fosters discriminations and injustice and does not acknowledge the dignity of every human being.

In the encyclical *Sollicitudo rei socialis* John Paul II strongly supports the practice of truly democratic procedures, built on solidarity and participation, not only for the inner life but also for international relations. Consequently he vigorously condemns the politics of both communist states and liberal democracies. John Paul II splits the world into two areas of economic, political, and ideological influence: the area of liberal capitalism and the area of Marxist collectivism. Such division, according to the pope, does not help the cause of justice and peace but contributes to deepen the trench that separates the rich from the poor countries, the developed from the underdeveloped nations:

> The developing countries, instead of becoming *'autonomous nations'* concerned with their own progress toward a just sharing in the goods and services meant for all, becomes part of a machine, cogs in a gigantic wheel. This is often true also in the field of social communication which, being run by centers mostly in the northern hemisphere, do not always give due consideration to the priorities and problems of such countries or respect their cultural makeup. They frequently impose a distorted view of life and man and thus fail to respond to the demands of true development.
>
> Each of the two blocs harbors in its own way a tendency towards imperialism, as it is usually called, or towards forms of new colonialism, an easy temptation to which they frequently succumb, as history, including recent history, teaches. It is this abnormal situation, the result of a war and of an unacceptably exaggerated concern for security, which deadens the impulse toward united cooperation by all for the common good of the human race, to the detriment especially of peaceful peoples who are impeded from their rightful access to the goods meant for all. Seen in this way the present division of the world is the direct obstacle to the real transformation of the conditions of underdevelopment in the developing and less advanced countries.

The most significant practical consequence of the teaching of the popes on democracy and of the participation of Catholics in political life was the constitution of Christian democratic parties in Europe.

The idea of creating a Christian democratic party, in some Catholic countries (France, Belgium, Austria, Italy) goes back to the papacy of Leo XIII. His famous social encyclical, *Rerum novarum* (1891), inspired some Catholic laymen to join their forces and to create 'European Christian democratic circles.' Giuseppe Toniolo was the first to elaborate the 'Christian concept of democracy.' According to Toniolo's definition, democracy "is a civil order wherein all social forces, juridical and economical, in the fullness of their hierarchical development, work for the common good, searching, as final result the advancement of the inferior classes."

The actual formation of the Christian democratic party in Italy took place immediately after World War I through the daring initiative of Luigi Sturzo, Alcide De Gasperi and Giuseppe Donati.

Originally the new party took the name of *Partito Popolare*. Reduced to inactivity and silence by fascism, the *Partito Popolare* revived and substantially contributed to the *resistenza* toward the end of World War II. After the war, with the new name of *Democrazia Cristiana*, the party of the Italian Catholics became the leading political force in Italy. From 1946 to the present, Italy has known great social, cultural, and economic progress, notwithstanding the apparent instability of its governments (almost fifty different governments in 44 years) thanks to the strength and unity of the *Democrazia Cristiana*.

The aim of the *Democrazia Cristiana* has always been that of using political power in order to pass laws, to build social and political structures, and to create a culture inspired by the principles of the Christian message. But it has not been an easy task, first of all because of some difficulties intrinsic to the very same concept of *Democrazia Cristiana*, where the adjective *Cristiana* could be understood either integrally or in a more liberal sense. In the first case it is believed that the solutions for political problems may be drawn directly from the gospel. In the second case it is asserted that the solutions of political problems requires the use of the mediation of patient analysis, of historical, social research, the study of political opportunity and feasibility. In the *Democrazia Cristiana* there has been a constant conflict between the two souls, the integral and the liberal. The integral prevailed during the 1950s and 1960s (De Gasperi, Fanfani); while the liberal soul became stronger in the 1970s and 1980s (Moro, Andreotti, de Mita). Another difficulty that Christian democratic parties encountered, especially in Italy, was that of preserving their autonomy from the Catholic church. From Leo XIII the church always recognized the autonomy of the state and of political parties. But the church cannot remain indifferent towards political decisions that touch on morality and religion, and that have to do with peace and justice, especially when they are taken by political leaders that proclaim to be Catholic and by a party that calls itself Christian which professes a lifestyle and culture inspired by the Christian message. Especially on the occasion of campaigns for political elections and for referendums (divorce and abortion), the statements made by the Catholic church have been taken by the enemies of the *Democrazia Cristiana* as illegitimate interference in the affairs of the state.

There is another consideration in evaluating the Italian religious situation after forty years during which the country has been ruled by the Christian democratic party: During this time did the religious situation improve or did it deteriorate? And if it has deteriorated, whose fault is it? In other words, has Italy become more or less democratic and more or less Christian?

The enemies of the *Democrazia Cristiana* and the secular press in general (which in Italy is very powerful) charge the *Democrazia Cristiana* for the widespread immorality that prevails today in political and social life in Italy. Certainly there is some truth in this charge. The party that rules a country for a long period of time is responsible for both the good and the bad that happens in that country. But what of the decline of religion in Italy? Is the *Democrazia Cristiana* also responsible for that?

In my opinion the *Democrazia Cristiana* has only an indirect responsibility, which consists in its choice to qualify itself so strongly and so openly religious, as a Christian and as the only Christian party in the country. This qualification has certainly favored the strategy of the other parties which sought to cut the religious roots of the Italian people in order to weaken their allegiance to the *Democrazia Cristiana*. In this way, the excessive presence of Christianity in the political life in Italy, in the end, backfired on (at least) the Catholic religion, if not on all of Christianity. Religion has been attacked with every means (mass media, laws passed by the government that discourage the teaching of religion in public schools, abolition of the financial support of the clergy, etc.). Hence, little by little, religion was widely eradicated from the soul of the Italian people.

SECULARIZATION OF SOCIETY AND PRIVATIZATION OF THE CHURCH

Subsequent to the French Revolution, European society—in the activities of politics, science, economics, and technology—has become more and more areligious, assuming an expression more formally secularized, and in some nations openly atheistic. God progressively vanishes from all cultural manifestations—from philosophy and politics, from morals and law, from literature and music. In fact, the situation worsened to such an extent that some extravagant thinker suggested that God ought even to be thrown out of theology (the 'death of God' theology).

Starting from the nineteenth century, the philosophers—those pundits who give theoretical expression to human self-awareness and speculative reasons for practical behavior—started to provide a wholly atheistic interpretation of the world and of history. Such an interpretation of the world and of history defines the causes of everything as immanent, intramundane and intrahistorical. The forces of nature, economic factors, the subconscious mind etc., became the new *arkai*, replacing the old metaphysical or religious principles. The famous and much disputed hermeneutics of Feuerbach, Marx, Engels, Nietzsche and more recently the hermeneutics of Bloch, Sartre, Marcuse, Adorno, Lukacs, and Gramsci, claim that atheism, which in the past was a privilege of the bourgeois society, has become a right also of the working class.

During the twentieth century most countries of Western Europe approved and endorsed constitutions in which God has become a mere byword and where everything is claimed to be grounded exclusively upon man (defined perhaps as the *homo faber*, as in the Italian Constitution). In recent years there has been some revival of religion not only in the United States but also in Europe. However, as it has been shown by G.F. Morra and A. Del Noce, such revival cannot be overestimated, since it by no means marks the end of the secularization of society and of the privatization of religion and of the church.

Jacques Audinet and Matthew Lamb recently completed some research on the cultural situation in France and Germany that is very significant and illuminating. From their studies, it appears that in France and Germany, culture has become religiously very poor and that religion has lost almost all its significance in the public expression of society.

According to Audinet, in France, religion as such no longer has 'droit de cité' (right of the city). In institutions and in social activities, any religious reference has been excluded from collective life:

> The State and the Churches are totally separated; there is no concordatary system, and the public institutions have nothing to do with religion. The world of politics, business, education is closed to every religious intervention. If the needs of social life require some factual agreement, as in the case of the school, the private and nonreligious character of such agreements will be stressed. In such a way, France seems fully to verify

Luckmann's hypothesis according to which in a technological society, religion becomes a private affair. As to the individual persons, be they believers or unbelievers, they seem willing to subscribe to this situation. Although this may look strange to a foreigner, the French Christian seems to be perfectly at ease in a society where God's name is never mentioned and a religious discussion appears to be prohibited, and where the question about one's own religious affiliation is never asked to anybody.[4]

In Germany, according to Lamb, religion has lost its position of cultural primacy, and has retired in the private ghetto. The Christian religion has been so reduced in stature, that presently it merely resembles aesthetic interludes, symbolic distractions and moral exhortations whose intention it is to reinforce the integration of the faithful back into the daily routine of secular society. The ultra-terrestrial kingdom of God has been trivialized in the private sector. Every manifestation of genuine social weight is repressed; credit is given only to the ideologies that preach the limitless progress of mankind. The weight of humanistic social and technological developments are indeed heavy and so, once in a while, the citizens feel free to take some small, corroborating dose of the religious 'opiate'.[5]

The religious situation in Italy, as we have previously seen, is not much better than in France and Germany, notwithstanding the presence of a very strong Christian Democratic Party. The studies of Sabino Aquaviva, Gian Franco Morra and other sociologists have shown that religion in Italy has become completely stifled by a secular culture. It has been turned into a strictly private affair. A number of causes fostered this situation. The astonishing conquests achieved by science and technology was one such cause. Great economical progress was another. But in particular, a major factor was the ceaseless animosity directed toward religion by liberal government before fascism and the enemies of the Christian Democrats subsequent to fascism. After World War II, on the cultural level, there has been an authentic dictatorship of the communists, socialists, republicans and liberals which forced the ruling party to assume a secularized position. Worst of all was the stupidity with which many Christian Democrats gladly accepted this sort of politics, convinced that this would safeguard the autonomy of political power in its confrontation within the region.

In conclusion, the general tendency in Europe during the twentieth century has been not only of keeping the church and the state distinct, as required by St. Thomas Aquinas, but to assign to the state every decision that has to do with the public, collective life of society and to reserve to the church only that area that has to do with the private, inner, spiritual life of the single person. Such an extensive secularization of society with the contemporary marginalization and privatization of religion was not without serious consequences for both culture and society. The gravest of all consequences has been the collapse of those moral values which constitute the main pillar of every culture and, therefore, of every society.

One century ago, Nietzsche had sought the transmutation of values through the destruction of metaphysics, ethics and religion. He knew he was making a foolish proposal, but in his prophetic intuition he foresaw that in a few decades his message would encounter fertile soil. Nietzsche promised the advent of the superman (*Übermensch*), a man who would abandon the camel's submissiveness and assume the boldness and arrogance of the lion. From the feeble, mediocre, obedient, religious, moralist, man would develop into an autonomous legislator of himself, one who is absolute master of his destiny, one who is beholden for his actions neither to God nor to society but only to himself. This complete subversion of value can only be achieved by the 'death of god.' This is truly the announcement of Zarathustra to mankind.

Nietzsche's prophecy today has become a harsh reality. In our culture and in our society God is truly dead, and with the death of God the hierarchy of values has been turned upside down. Absolute values have been destroyed and replaced with instrumental values; spiritual values have been obliterated and replaced with material values with the result that the value of life is rendered meaningless and society is transforming itself into one where brutality is the rule.

POLITICAL THEOLOGY: THE POLITICAL ENGAGEMENT OF THE CHURCH

Immediately after the Second Vatican Council, some Roman Catholic theologians, first in Europe and then in Latin America, strongly reacted against a cultural atmosphere which favored the privatization of Christian faith and the political disengagement of the church.

According to Johannes B. Metz, considered the founder of political theology, the church and its members cannot be indifferent and keep aloof from political affairs, for many reasons. First of all, man is by nature a 'political animal,' according to the classic definition of Aristotle. The political dimension is essential to every human being and, consequently, also to the Christian believer.

Second, the Christian message and Christian salvation do not concern the soul alone but the whole person. They do not regard only the individuals but also society, its structures and values. As a matter of fact, Jesus is not a private but a public personality, who openly faces religious and political problems. "His revolutionary message," writes Metz, "drew him into a mortal conflict with the public powers of his time. The cross is not raised in the *privatissimum* of the individual room nor in the *sanctissimum* of the religious field, but stretches out, beyond the barriers of the merely private and the precincts of the exclusively religious. The veil of the temple has been torn forever." According to Metz the critical attitude taken by Jesus toward the socio-political powers of his time, is a perennial task of theology. But, in Metz' view, it is impossible to draw directly from the Gospel political solutions for the problems of each concrete context. The Gospel is not in favor of any socio-political model or of some specific economic or social structure or form of government. Therefore, following the example of Jesus, theology and the church should act as 'critical institutions' over the actual political praxis, giving their contribution for improving it both negatively—condemning what is wrong or bad—and positively—by defending the dignity of man and the higher, spiritual, perennial values.

The basic principles of the political theology worked out by Metz were taken over by the Latin American theologians Gutierrez and Boff, who applied them to the situation of their continent, an extremely different situation than that of Europe. Europe has few areas of poverty; governments are liberal and democratic and assure justice and freedom to everybody. In Latin America many people live in misery, workless and homeless. Oppressed by hunger and ignorance, they are frequently deprived of elementary civil rights. In the face of such an intolerable situation, theology cannot be satisfied with critical measures and suggestions. It needs to become revolutionary: *teologia de la liberacion*. What is peculiar about liberation theology is a critical reflection on the human praxis (of people in general and of Christians in particular) in the light of Jesus' praxis and according to the needs of the Gospel.

According to Gutierrez and Leonardo and Clodovis Boff, for a political situation which is intolerable and which needs a radical change, theology can learn from Karl Marx (a viewpoint also shared by Dom Camara). Liberation theologians believe that Marxism is helpful above all for the social analyses of society.[6]

John Paul II has followed with deep concern the movement of liberation theology. He fully approves the main thesis of liberation theology: 'the option for the poor'. It is essentially the same option of Christ and his church. What the pope cannot approve of are some theoretical positions (the Marxist analysis of society) and some practical solutions (for instance, the class struggle).[7]

CONCLUSION

Today not only Europe but the whole world is going through a very serious crisis, an epochal crisis. We are moving beyond modernity and entering into postmodernity.

Consequently, in my opinion, the strongest effort of the church should now be addressed not so much to politics as to culture. Politics, after all, is just one aspect of culture.

Consequently, the main concern of the theologian ought not to be directed toward politics, but rather toward culture, since what we badly need today is not so much 'political' theology as 'cultural' theology.

What is most urgently needed by our society (in Europe, North and South America, Africa, and Asia) is a new culture which ought to be, as have been all the great cultures of the past, at the same time humanistic and religious. We need a planetary culture that works on the full humanization of mankind; but no true humanization is possible without God. Therefore the new culture needs also to be religious, it needs to be a divine-human culture. And this is the major lesson of Jesus Christ, the God-man, who has saved and divinized mankind.[8]

NOTES

1. St. Augustine, *De civitate Dei* XiV, 28.
2. St. Augustine, *De civitate Dei* XV, 5.
3. Gelasius, in Mansi VIII, c.31.
4. J. Audinet, "Une culture sans religion. Le cas de la France," in *Concilium* 1980, n. 16, 57-58.
5. M. Lamb, "Germania: il dibattito sul carattere mistico e politico della regione cristiana," *ibid* 108-109.
6. Cf. Cl. Boff, *Teologia e practica. Teologia do politico e suas mediacoes*, Petropolis: Vozes, 1978.
7. Cf. S. Congregazione per la dottrina della fede, "Istruzione su alcumi aspetti della 'teologia della liberazione'" Vatican City 6, VIII, 1984.
8. Cf. B. Mondin, *Una nuova cultura per una nuova società*, Milan: Massino, 1982.

SEVEN

THE PROTESTANT PERSPECTIVE WITH REGARD TO THE INTERRELATIONSHIP OF CHURCH AND STATE

Dean M. Kelley

PROTESTANT ROOTS OF LIBERAL DEMOCRACY

One of the favorite indoor sports in scholarly circles is to claim for a particular historical movement, school, or event the credit for initiating or enabling the development of modern democracy. Students of various religious traditions are not slow to join in this engagement. A signal contribution to this genre was initiated by a prominent group of American church leaders—including John R. Mott and Henry Sloane Coffin—in the 1940s. The group formed the Committee on Religious Tolerance, later related to the Federal Council of Churches. They commissioned Professor James Hastings Nichols of the University of Chicago to develop a historical analysis of the role of religious movements in the formation of democracy. Nichols' analysis, *Democracy and the Churches,* was published in 1951. The first chapter, entitled "The Religious Origins of

Liberal Democracy," found the religious origins of liberal democracy in one particular strand of Protestantism:

> Most Americans [have] been quite unaware of the fact that the moral dynamic of their democracy was the creation of one very specific Protestant ethical tradition, and that, with a few minor exceptions, it was the peculiar product of that single tradition. And without such roots the cut flowers of democratic parliaments, ballots, constitutions and the rest did not seem destined to bloom long in Germany or Japan or such lands as Latin America.[1]

This generalization may have seemed more obvious just after the close of World War II. But in the long sweep of history it can still be said that 'liberal democracy' has its shaky moments in many parts of the world where it has been tried in fitful spasms, even as it is struggling to come into being in others that have little experiential preparation for it.

Nichols did not see the cradle of liberal democracy in Lutheranism or high Anglicanism. "The characteristic political expression of both Reformation and Counter Reformation was absolute monarchy," he stated. Neither did he see it in Roman Catholicism:

> In Roman political ethics the tradition of divine-right monarchy was dominant, ... but not the sole school of thought. What of the ... anti-absolutists such as Bellarmine and Suarez? The Roman opponents of absolutism were generally more radical and violent than the Reformed. They were not constructively interested in responsible constitutional government. It was not accidental that nothing came of this Thomist "liberalism" but a series of political murders.... Bellarmine and Suarez believed monarchy to be the best form of government. They wished only to deny its *"divine"* right so as to remove in advance any theological defenses against deposition by the pope. The only restriction they opposed to growing monarchical absolutism was the right of clerical intervention, the very system whose failure was the original condition of the development of the national monarchies. If, as is sometimes alleged at Communion breakfasts, the American founders drew their political ideas from this Jesuit school, or from Thomas Aquinas, they should have confined their constructive actions to dispatching an Irishman to dirk George III.
>
> The pattern of monarchical Church government was still regnant even in these Jesuit opponents of divine right. Their mental image of the State was not the constitutionalism of the Reformed, but an absolutism like that of the Jesuit order. Such an order rests ultimately on popular sovereignty, on the deliberate compact of individuals hitherto "free and equal." Once having entered into the compact, however, the individual has alienated all rights of consent and review.... The rulers of the order, again, are elected, but, once elected, admit no restrictions on their absolute authority. This may not be divine-right monarchy, but still less is it constitutional or limited monarchy.

This Jesuit and Thomist political thought has less relation to liberal democracy than it has to the theories of the classical antidemocrat, Thomas Hobbes.[2]

Nichols quoted Harold Laski's dictum that "the Reformation was the real starting point of democratic ideas"[3] but made clear that it was not in the mini-monarchies of Lutheranism that it took form but in the strongholds of Calvinism:

> For amid the great sweep toward absolutism, which dominated Roman Catholic and Lutheran societies up to the nineteenth century, a contrary current toward constitutional limitations on monarchy or toward outright republicanism was also to be observed. This tradition shaped the life of Switzerland, Holland, Scotland, England, and the English colonies in America. All these countries were profoundly influenced by that type of Protestantism called Calvinistic or Reformed or Presbyterian.... The only enduring and successful constitutionalist revolutions of this period were carried out by Calvinists....
>
> There can be no doubt that the most essential motive in this struggle was the religious one.... "Civil rights are secondary, a means to an end, never successfully preserved either among Protestants or Catholics except where dangers to religious belief sharpen the determination to resist by a higher than utilitarian motive.... Political liberty is the residuary legatee of ecclesiastical animosities."[4]

But Calvin and his followers did not invent the idea of constitutionally limited government out of whole cloth. As the theologian John T. McNeill noted, "The fundamental ideas at the basis of their bold experimentation in representative church government came to them, consciously or unconsciously, from the conciliatory thinkers of the late Middle Ages."[5] ... "The very Protest of Spires of 1529, from which the name 'Protestantism' stems, was an appeal to the principle of the government of the Church by representative councils."[6]

The formative historical events by which this Calvinist vision was impressed upon civil structures were the federalism of the Dutch Republic following the deposition of Philip of Spain in 1581. This became, according to Father J.N. Figgis, the working model of free institutions to seventeenth century Europe,[7] and the Puritan Revolution in England of the 1640s and 1650s. It was here the seeds were sown that bore fruit in Philadelphia in 1787.

Not least among the new creations of this Puritan generation of Cromwellian origin was liberal democracy. Distinguished Anglicans such as William Temple and R.H. Tawney, as well as Roman

Catholics like Lord Acton and Christopher Dawson, have accounted Puritanism to be the most potent force in the shaping of modern Anglo-American democracy. Dawson's account is worth quoting:

> In England the pure Calvinist tradition was united with that of the Anabaptist and independent sects to produce a new movement which was political as well as religious and which marks the first appearance of genuine democracy in the modern world ... The Cromwellian Commonwealth, short-lived though it was, by the momentum of its religious impulse opened the way for a new type of civilization based on the freedom of the person and of conscience as rights conferred absolutely by God and Nature....
>
> The modern Western beliefs in progress, in the rights of man, and the duty of conforming political action to moral ideals, whatever they may owe to other influences, derive ultimately from the moral ideals of Puritanism and its faith in the possibility of the realization of the Holy Community on earth by the efforts of the elect.
>
> One may say that modern democracy was born in June, 1647, when at Newmarket and Triploe Heath the Army covenanted not to disband until its rights and liberties were assured. Democratic left-wing Puritanism had challenged theocratic right-wing Calvinism. A year later Colonel Pride "purged" the Parliament of Presbyterians and the Army democracy prepared to organize a new State and a new Church system for England.[8]

At the same time, on the other side of the Atlantic, similar winds were stirring from similar sources; the Congregationalist theocracy of Massachusetts Bay Colony was being challenged by left-wing rebellions.

> The first written constitution of the English-speaking world was the 'Fundamental Orders of Connecticut' of 1639. Drawn up by seceders from Massachusetts, these Orders set neither religious nor property qualifications on the franchise. Other refugees from the Bay Colony, led by Roger Williams, founded Rhode Island. Rhode Island had a strictly civil 'covenant', which explicitly used the word 'democratical' and provided for majority rule, government by consent, and 'due process' of law. Roger Williams was the American counterpart of John Lilburne, and the left-wing Puritans of Rhode Island the analogue of the democratic Puritans of Cromwell's army ...
>
> For a century and a half, thus, from 1640 to 1790, only one Christian tradition—that of Anglo-American Puritanism and Nonconformity—had nurtured a mature democratic political ethic. This orientation stood out in sharp contrast to the traditionalist authoritarianism of High Church Anglicanism and early Methodism, the conservative patriarchalism of German Lutheranism, and the divine-right absolutism of Roman Catholicism.[9]

Of course, great political systems are the result of the confluence of many streams of causality, and retrospectively picking out one strand from others can be a deceptively plausible exercise in partly artificial abstraction. Yet Nichols' analysis can serve as a quick reprise of the arguments that attribute to the Calvinist-Nonconformist stream of Protestantism a significant paternity in the birth of liberal democracy.

FIVE PROTESTANT VIEWS OF CHURCH AND STATE

As time moved on, the Federal Council of Churches in the United States merged with a dozen other ecumenical groups to form the National Council of Churches in 1950. The Committee on Religious Toleration became the Department of Religious Liberty, which I served as its third Executive Director, from 1960 to the present. In 1962 I interested Arthur Cohen of Holt, Rinehart and Winston in publishing a series of studies of church and state, the first and last of which appeared in 1964. It was Tom Sanders' classic *Protestant Concepts of Church and State*, which emphasized the point (already suggested by Nichols) that there is no such thing as 'The Protestant Perspective' on church and state, but rather a range of Protestant perspectives. He managed, by some Procrustean bunching, to reduce them to five and to describe those five with some clarity and richness.

But first Sanders noted "three fundamental elements of all Christian political theory," whether Roman Catholic, Eastern Orthodox or Protestant:

1. The dualism of church and state

2. The sovereignty of God over both

3. The mixed nature of the state as both good and evil[10]

Under the first heading, the 'two swords' or 'two powers' described by Pope Gelasius I in 494 A.D. became for Luther the 'two kingdoms' and for other Protestants even wider distancing between the temporal and the spiritual, the civil and the ecclesiastical. In American parlance, this has been characterized as the 'separation of church and state,' and has been widely imitated in varying degrees elsewhere. (It is by no means a simple or bicameral idea, and we shall return to it later.)

In the second category, divine sovereignty has usually meant to Christian thinkers (in Sanders' analysis) that:

1. The state may serve as an instrument of God's activity in history;

2. The political order is established for particular abiding purposes; and

3. If God is active in political and social institutions, he has a purpose for them which to some extent can be learned.[11]

It is in the third area that reality-testing and considerations of purity versus prudence result in a splintering of counsels upon the moral ambiguity of government: when and how one serves God rather than the demands of human authorities.

The five clusters of Protestant thought and practice that Sanders analyzed are Lutheran, Anabaptist, Quaker, 'Separationist' and 'Transformationist'. The first three are primarily historical, although they have their modern counterparts. The fourth and fifth are the increasingly dominant divisions (across denominational lines) into two prevailing—and countervailing—schools of thought in the 1960s in the United States.

THE LUTHERAN TRADITION

Luther divided humankind into two 'kingdoms' or 'regiments'— those who are "true believers in Christ and are subject to Christ.... These people need no secular sword or law...."—and those who are not. "All who are not Christian belong to the kingdom of the world and are under the law."[12] Government is instituted to keep the latter in order (though Luther also recognized that Christians are often sinners, too, and in similar need of governmental restraint and correction).

> God has established in both the worldly and spiritual kingdoms instruments through which he governs, the state and the church. The word that Luther most commonly used to refer to these is "regiment," literally "power" or "government."...
>
> Although the state governs for God in the secular kingdom, political authority alone does not encompass all the dimensions of worldly life. Rather, government is the apex of a series of relationships called "orders," in which people hold "offices." These orders may be natural or biological, such as the family; or cultural, such as one's work and schooling....
>
> Church and state, the spiritual and temporal governments, are unified by the sovereignty of God and the loyal submission of the believer to both, Luther speaks of the worldly regiment as the left hand of the kingdom, and the spiritual regiment as God's right hand; both belong to God.... Although

God is the efficient and final cause of both, they are different in nature, they have different commissions, stand in different relationships to God, and give expression to his sovereignty with completely different instruments.... They correspond to Luther's view of law and gospel. The law, though good as a part of creation in enabling natural man to live a tolerable life, is ineffectual for achieving salvation, for which the church holds responsibility. The gospel does not invalidate the law, but one must never confusedly regard the law as a legitimate means of [salvation]...

The state achieves its purposes through the ruler's use of law and the sword, the church its purposes through the word of the Bible and its preaching by the minister; the nature of the state is force and coercion, of the church, love and humility. All of these aspects must be kept sharply separated. The political ruler should not interfere in the religious life of [the] nation; similarly, ecclesiastical officials distort their function and violate God's will when they undertake political activity. Luther adamantly denied the use of law and the sword for the furtherance of the church's objectives, or humility and love for political purposes, since the state cannot preserve stability without coercion....

During his lifetime, Luther encountered two groups which, he felt, were especially flagrant in violating the design of God—the papacy and the Anabaptists. The former sought to use political instruments for religious objectives, and the latter tried to apply the norms of the gospel directly to politics.[13]

One of Luther's most fruitful insights into the way in which individuals were to fit themselves into the divine scheme was his doctrine of 'vocation' (*Beruf*). Roman Catholic thought had limited this term to the monastic or priestly function alone, implying that all other occupations were of lesser spiritual worth. But Luther taught that God calls individuals to serve him in secular stations as well. In fact, the Christian may feel a call to a secular office in which his or her gifts may be of unique service to the community. As Luther so aptly stated:

Therefore, should you see that there is a lack of hangmen, beadles, judges, lords, or princes, and find that you are qualified, you should offer your services and seek the place, that necessary government may by no means be despised and become inefficient or perish.[14]

In such a civil vocation, the Christian may even need to exercise the power of the sword against malefactors or enemies of the realm, and can conscientiously do so in love and humility as a necessary service to the neighbors for whose well-being he or she is responsible. The ethic of the Sermon on the Mount, while applicable to personal affairs, is not appropriate in carrying out the duties of the civil order. The Christian, however, ought not to be unthinking in carrying out those duties, but should be guided by such principles as those developed during the Middle Ages to distinguish the just war from the unjust. The Christian should not participate in the latter, even if it means defying the ruler. "If a Christian can heed Jesus' admonition to leave father and mother for the sake of God, then he can leave his ruler for the same reason. Luther did not justify rebellion or active resistance, but only [the Christian's] commitment to suffering through a conscience obedient to God, come what may."[15]

Luther was usually supportive of the interests of rulers (at least Protestant rulers) in the wars of his time because the survival of Protestantism was often at stake. He was vehement in denouncing the resort to violence by their subjects in the Peasants' Revolt: "Suffering, suffering; cross, cross! This and nothing else is the Christian law!"[16] Short of violence, Luther upheld the responsibility of Christians to criticize and denounce injustice, even if that brought retribution upon themselves: "The church's front line is wherever there are those who suffer unjustly."[17] But because of the political situation of the time, the churches that followed Luther tended to become increasingly subservient to the political regimes that had protected them, and Lutheran energies turned toward inward spirituality that culminated in the flourishing of Pietism in Protestant Europe in the late seventeenth and eighteenth centuries.

In America, Lutheranism resonated to the innovative teaching of the First Amendment because it moved in the direction of the differentiation of the two kingdoms or regiments and away from what some Lutherans saw as theocratic tendencies in Roman Catholicism and Calvinism.[18] But Lutherans were not comfortable with an impermeable separation between the two or a wholly secular understanding of the civic realm. In 1963 the Lutheran Church in America issued a study entitled "Church and State: A Lutheran Perspective" representing their outlook on the questions before us. Its thrust is summarized in the assertion, "We shall defend both the institutional separation and the functional interaction of church and state in the United States and Canada"[19] The two poles of this ambipolar manifesto were spelled out in the following particulars:

CHURCH AND STATE: THE PROTESTANT PERSPECTIVE

I. Institutional Separation

A. What is the nature and mission of the church under God?

1. The church proclaims God's Word through preaching and sacraments.
2. The church witnesses to God's Word through its worship and evangelism
3. The church witnesses to God's word through its Christian education and social ministry.

B. What is the nature and mission of the state under God?

1. The state establishes civil justice through the maintenance of law and order.
2. The state establishes civil justice through the protection of constitutional rights.
3. The state establishes civil justice through the promotion of the general welfare.[20]

Interestingly, the Lutheran Church's exposition bears no reference to the state's role in defending its citizens against aggression by other states, i.e., characterizing war. In characterizing the state, a typically Lutheran note is sounded in the study:

> The purpose of the state is to establish good order, peace and justice in a sinful world. In other words, its might must be enlisted in the service of right. But Christians should not expect love to replace justice in the operation of government. Civil authorities are not elected to run a pseudo-church on the basis of a culture-religion. The state's limited goal is earthly preservation under the law, not heavenly salvation under the gospel. Consequently, there is no "Christian" form of the state. While persons can be transformed by the gospel, institutions can only be reformed by the law. We can "Christianize" politicians and statesmen but not politics and the state. They are ordained by God to remain secular.[21]

The other half of the exposition continued:

II. Functional Interaction

A. How is the church helpful to the state?

1. The church relates to the interests of the state by offering intercessory prayers on its behalf.
2. The church relates to the interests of the state by encouraging responsible citizenship and government service on the part of its lay members.
3. The church relates to the interests of the state by holding it accountable to the sovereign law of God.
4. The church relates to the interests of the state by contributing to the civil consensus which supports it.
5. The church relates to the interests of the state by championing the human and civil rights of all its citizens.[22]

(While the incumbent functionaries of the state might not always view all of these ministrations of the church with unalloyed enthusiasm, they might in more reflective moments recognize them as contributing to the long range stability of 'liberal democracy.')

B. How is the state helpful to the church?

1. The state relates to the interests of the church by ensuring religious liberty for all.

2. The state relates to the interests of the church by acknowledging that the rights of man are not the creation of the state.

3. The state relates to the interests of the church by maintaining an attitude of 'wholesome neutrality' toward church bodies in the context of the religious pluralism of our culture.

4. The state relates to the interests of the church by providing incidental benefits on a nonpreferential basis in recognition of the church's civil services which are also of secular benefit to the community.

5. The state relates to the interests of the church by providing financial aid on a nonpreferential basis to church agencies engaged in the performance of social services which are also of secular benefit to the community.[23]

A secular cynic might observe that after a certain amount of abstract prolegomenon, the document arrives at the 'nitty-gritty' of who gets what at the 'bottom line.' Indeed, the statement takes care to spell that out under the concluding points 4 and 5:

4. Government may properly provide for churches and chaplains at military establishments and penal institutions, for the appointment of legislative chaplains and the praying of invocational prayers in legislative chambers, for tax exemptions for churches along with other educational, charitable and eleemosynary groups, for the nondevotional study of the Bible in public schools, and for nondiscriminatory aid in public welfare programs....

5. As population booms, problems grow, and costs soar, the state is gradually assuming its communal responsibilities more directly by taking over many of the social functions performed earlier by the church.

    The state is now willing to pay church agencies for many social services which are primarily of secular (rather than religious) benefit to the community, and which a welfare state would otherwise have to provide itself....

    Even where such state aid is constitutionally legal, however, it may not always be socially desirable or ethically advisable. The church and its agencies must therefore decide in each case (1) if the integrity of the church's witness requires that the church itself pay for a given service, or (2) if the church may accept funds from the state for such a service, or (3) if the church considers that a particular service is the peculiar responsibility of the state alone. Prudentially, of course, any institution of the church that is the recipient of such public funds must face the fact that it takes the risk of being subject to governmental direction if it becomes financially dependent upon governmental financing.[24]

Despite the concluding caveats, the Lutheran social agencies that are a significant element of the private nonprofit welfare sector in the U.S. have not hesitated to avail themselves of the willingness of the state "to pay church agencies for many social services." In fact, it may be that the heavy investment of the Lutheran communions in such welfare enterprises inspired and enabled this conclusion of the report rather than the other way around. In any event, it represents a prominent element in the Lutheran outlook on church-state issues in the U.S.

THE ANABAPTISTS AND MENNONITES

A very different strand of church-state tradition stems from the 'left wing of the Reformation'—the Anabaptist movements of the sixteenth century, one of the most seminal sources of historical innovation in many areas, secular as well as religious. Its very name arose from its radical response to a church-state problem. Since the time of the Christian triumph over the Hellenistic world, everyone was thought to be automatically enrolled in the ranks of Christendom by baptism as an infant. Thus one inherited before the age of discretion a predetermined religio-political role and responsibility that was expected and enforced by the civil authority as well as the spiritual. The Anabaptists believed that one must choose to be a Christian through the process of conversion, and that only then did baptism have real meaning. So they practiced 'believer's baptism' and disdained infant baptism. Since all who were thus baptized as adults had already been baptized as infants, this act put them in violation of a fifth-century Roman law that made rebaptism a capital offense. 'Anabaptist' means rebaptizer, and hundreds of them were executed for this 'crime,' many by drowning, in a hideous parody of baptism by immersion.[25]

The central tenet of the Anabaptists was *discipleship*, which they understood to mean following the teaching and example of the Lord Jesus Christ, replicating the way of life spelled out in the New Testament, reconstituting the pure community of the early Christian Church as the band of regenerated believers. As such they

155

could not continue in the state church nor associate with the errors of the fallen "world."

> Association with the state was at best sub-Christian, whereas the [gathered] church represented the kingdom of God. This despised group thus became the first Protestant advocates of a separation of church and state, not on rational, pragmatic, or political grounds, but as a consequence of a theology of discipleship and the [true] church as a community of disciples.... [T]hey could not tolerate the intrusion of the state in the internal life of the congregation.... The church is separated because the children of God's kingdom should have nothing to do with the wicked. By definition all those not in the believers' church are citizens of the kingdom of darkness.... The most obvious sign of the fallen church was its union with the state....[26]

The Anabaptists counseled obedience to the state as God's creation in all things not contrary to scripture. They paid taxes and rendered obligatory civic service such as the corvée, but would not hold office, serve in the army or take an oath. These reservations amply sufficed to stigmatize them as subversive of the civil order, and they were mercilessly persecuted by state and church, Catholic and Protestant. Their response was one of nonresistance, accepting martyrdom rather than striking back or violating conscience. Indeed, thousands of Anabaptists were slain, but in their case, as in many others, they found that "the blood of the martyrs is the seed of the church."

The gathered church of the Anabaptists was too poor to afford clergy, so all the (lay) members bore equal responsibility for the course of the congregation, the first systematic practice of inclusive democracy in church or state. When in doubt about the course that they should follow, they would search the scriptures together for guidance. In order to do this, they all had to be able to *read* the scriptures, so learning to read was one of their necessities—the first instance of universal common education within the small community over which they had control, before church or state evinced an interest in educating all its members. They would search the scriptures until the Holy Spirit guided them to a solution, which became apparent when they arrived at a consensus. That consensus was then binding on all of them thereafter, and those who defaulted or defected from it were subjected to the ban: they were treated as outsiders because they had left the community by their falling away and would no longer be treated as though still members until they repented and returned to the rule.

The Anabaptists, unlike the 'magisterial' Reformers, were zealous evangelists, and they spread their 'seditious' beliefs throughout Europe, despite the worst that church and state could do to stop them. The Swiss and South German Brethren were largely destroyed by persecution, but not before giving birth to the Hutterites in Moravia.[27] Dutch Mennonites and North German Brethren were able to survive, and refugees from all these groups, as well as the later Amish, spread to other lands, including Russia, Canada, the United States, and Paraguay. (Thirteen Mennonite families from Krefeld, Germany, founded Germantown, Pennsylvania, in 1683, one of the first of many communities in the U.S. of Anabaptist origin.)

In the New World, Anabaptists have tried to retain their unique cultus and culture against the constant and increasing inroads of assimilation, and have maintained their presence in rural sections of Pennsylvania, Ohio, Indiana, Iowa, and Canada, thanks in large part to their high birthrate and agrarian isolation. Theirs is the quintessentially 'sectarian' concept of church and state: that the task of the gathered community of Christ is to bear its pure witness in isolation from the 'world'—as 'light' rather than 'leaven'—a city set on a hill instead of an element of righteousness to be amalgamated with the baser metal of the unsaved. Asking only to be left alone, they continue their testimony as the Plain People, who do not aspire to wealth, fame, dominance, technological proficiency, or worldly 'success,' but to unresisting humility, patient husbandry, and unremitting discipleship.

THE QUAKERS

Superficially the Religious Society of Friends may seem so similar to the Anabaptist witness as scarcely to deserve a separate classification, but the similarity is more apparent than real. Both are known for their unwillingness to participate in war or other exercises of violence and their refusal to take an oath, but that is about as far as the resemblance reaches, and even that stance is taken for different reasons and with different objectives. The Quakers today are pacifists rather than nonresisters like the Mennonites.

As Reinhold Niebuhr has pointed out, nonviolence as a method for [attaining] political objectives is not the same as the nonresistance of Jesus' teaching, which is neither a method nor directed toward social goals. In this respect the Mennonites stand closer to the outlook of the Sermon on the Mount than do the Quakers....

Niebuhr [has] considered the Mennonite witness a genuine, admirable expression of Christianity, while castigating Quakerism for "heresy"; and Niebuhr has placed Quakers in the category of culture-Christians in his classification of Christian social attitudes.[28]

Quakers have not always been pacifists. In their formative period (1650-1660) under the leadership of George Fox they were theocrats, an element of left-wing Puritanism. Their central tenet was obedience to the Inner Light, the guidance of the Holy Spirit within each person, which took precedence over both reason and scripture. Thus they were essentially mystics rather than biblicists like the Anabaptists. They also believed that the Inner Light could lead believers to earthly perfection beyond the stain of sin, and that such perfected believers could bring in the Kingdom of God on earth, whereas the Anabaptists did not accept that humans are perfectible within history. The Quakers were thus eager to take a leading role in bringing in the Kingdom at the time of the Puritan Revolution. As Niebuhr noted:

The early Quakers were not nonresistants, nor did they hold doctrinaire convictions against coercion in government.... The Friends ... did not forbid Quakers to serve in the [Protector's] Army, and occasionally they urged Cromwell to fight for particular causes.... The Friends conditioned violence upon whether it advanced their theocratic and millenarian interests or not.... Just as they disrupted by violence church meetings that they considered idolatrous, so they willingly sanctioned war and coercion to advance the cause of the Lord.[29]

Quakers likewise had an estimate of the state very different from that of the Mennonites. Niebuhr continues:

Whereas the Anabaptists denied the religious relevance of government and abjured office holding, the Quakers interpreted government as a potential agency for effecting the will of God.... Unlike the Anabaptists they felt that political office had a direct relation to the will of God and could be perfected if authorities seriously obeyed God.[30]

Quakers, like Anabaptists, did refuse to take oaths of loyalty, and when Cromwell required such an oath of all soldiers and government employees in 1654, many Quakers were obliged to relinquish their civil and military positions. When that requirement was removed in 1659, some of them returned to office, and several Quakers were appointed commissioners of the militia.[31]

'Friends' were active champions of religious liberty, not by virtue of religious relativism or even (at first) respect for individual conscience, but in deference to the sovereignty of God, whose communications could be delivered through any person. Thus they advocated religious liberty for all, including "Jew, or Papist, or Turk, or heathen, or Protestant,"[31]—a radical notion, even for the radical period of the Puritan Civil War!

The Quaker movement at its inception was ardent for the complete transformation of England and the world. They pressed Cromwell and the Army to enforce the Puritan outlook by law. They directed their efforts against the instruments of religious oppression, opposing the collection of tithes for the support of an established clergy—or any clergy. They favored the separation of all religion from any type of relationship with the state, but equally demanded the enforcement of civil righteousness by law, urging abolition of capital punishment for theft; relief for the poor, hungry and widows; elimination of corruption in office-holding; punishment of excessive drinking, cheating, frivolity, entertainment on holidays, and Sabbath breaking; and ending of inequalities in the law.[33] When these reforms were not forthcoming, and, indeed, the Revolution subsided and was succeeded by the Restoration, Quakers became disillusioned and suffered a period of persecution under the later Stuart monarchs, which led to an era of Quaker quietism and withdrawal from political activity. Rather than the radical dualism of the Anabaptists, however, 'Friends' continued to see a continuum of religion and morality in civil society. Human beings ranged from depravity to perfection, with good and evil mixed in most, and could be drawn toward the righteous end of the spectrum by the influence of love and persuasion in a process of amelioration.[34]

In the twentieth century, both in England and the United States, many Quakers were attracted to the prevailing liberalism in theology and social thought that dominated mainstream Protestantism, although rural elements of Quakerism clung to evangelical and fundamentalist affinities. Several activist agencies instituted by Quakers, such as the American Friends Service Committee (1917), and the Friends Committee on National Legislation (1943), have been assiduous and effective in lobbying and in direct action in support of Quaker objectives, especially peace and relief of oppressed minority groups. They worked closely with Anabaptist-descended 'peace churches,' such as the Mennonites, Church of the Brethren, etc., in opposing conscription and supporting alternate service for conscientious objection to military service.[35]

Perhaps the most significant characteristic of Quakers today is their embrace of the Gandhian technique of non-violence called *satyagraha*, used as an effective method of political action. Civil disobedience "may be the best means to call a state to its obligations," said the Philadelphia Yearly Meeting of the Religious Society of Friends in 1943, and for some Quakers this commitment to a Hindu-created tactic has become almost the "reduction of the Christian faith to a new legalism, that of nonviolence, which is inviolable" as Sanders assessed it.[36]

Modern Quakers do not seem to have a systematic conceptual understanding of church-state relations—certainly not the one their founders had. Their view of the state has been focused mainly upon its role in advancing or obstructing peace, disarmament and the rights of pacifists, with little realistic attention to its responsibilities for restraining evil and protecting its populace from outside aggression. They have contributed a continuing critique of the propensity of governments in times of trouble to turn to violent means as a first instead of last resort and have explored and advocated many useful alternatives short of violence for conflict-resolution that have not yet begun to be adequately utilized. But on many of the currently controverted questions of church and state, the Quakers do not seem to have any salient views and indeed tend to view them as something of a distraction from the cause of peace.

THE SEPARATIONISTS

Sanders traced one of the two leading schools of church-state thought in the modern United States primarily to another strand of the leftwing Puritan movement of the early seventeenth century, the *Baptists* (not to be confused with the Anabaptists, with whom they had no organic connection of descent or alliance and little in common beyond congregational polity and believers' baptism). The central tenet of the Baptist movement was the independence and equality of each *congregation* of Christians, which in later encounters with Enlightenment rationalism and nineteenth century revivalism came to be subsumed under the broader concept of the 'soul-competency' of *individuals* to deal directly with God without the need of ecclesiastical intervention, a rather different idea, though having some similar outcomes.[37]

Sanders identified three sub-strands in left-wing Puritanism that tended toward separationism: (1) the millenarian stance of the Fifth Monarchy Men (which included some Baptists like Thomas Collier); (2) the natural-rights views of the Levellers, expressed in "An Appeal to Parliament" of March, 1647, and (3) the teachings of Roger Williams in his writings and activities on both sides of the Atlantic in the 1640s. From these various sources (which he traced in much greater detail) came ideas that shaped a new concept of government in England, though it did not come to stable fruition for several generations: 'liberal democracy.' Such thoughts as the sovereignty of the people, government by elected representatives, the limitation of power because of its corrupting tendencies, inviolable popular rights, and the free functioning of independent corporate groups[38] were initiated in the revolutionary ferment and became more and more widely accepted until by the time the American colonies declared their independence those ideas were endemic in the political awareness and expectations of British subjects. In fact, many of these formative ideas were appropriated from the organization and experience of the congregational life of the Separatists of the seventeenth century.[39] They were accustomed to electing their leaders in a congregational setting where each Christian had a voice and an equal vote.

With respect to church and state, the left-wing Separatists were led by the overthrow of Anglicanism (and the failure of the Puritans to take its place) to question the need for any established church at all. Since they had to choose and support their own ministers, they saw no reason why others should not do the same. And if there was no established church, there was no need for the government to collect tithes to pay its clergy, so they pressed for the abolition of tithes as well.

Roger Williams' contentions are well-known, though perhaps not as fully as they should be: he insisted that the civil magistrate's rightful responsibility did not extend to religious matters, that force should never be used to affect faith, and that all persons comporting themselves peaceably should be free to believe and practice whatever religion they chose—or none. Like most Puritans, however, the Separatists, like the Quakers, expected government to enforce secular canons of righteousness derived from general Christian teaching then common: no Sabbath-breaking, swearing, drinking, fornicating, gambling, etc. Such pressure for moral regulation Sanders considered inconsistent with the concept of separation of church and state. With the restoration of the monarchy in 1660, however, most of the Puritan arrangements were swept away, only to re-emerge in modified forms in unexpected places, such as in the American colonies, where the Great Awakenings of the eighteenth and the revivalism of the nineteenth centuries injected new evangelistic energies into the successors of the Separatists: the Baptists and Methodists of the frontier.

At the time of the formation of the new government of the newly independent colonies, Baptists and New Light Presbyterians were influential in ending or modifying colonial establishments, in which they did not share. They formed an unlikely and unstable alliance with the Enlightenment rationalists to overthrow Anglican and Congregationalist hegemony, beginning with the defeat of Patrick Henry's 'Bill Establishing a Provision for Teachers of the Christian Religion' in Virginia, thanks in large part to James Madison's 'Memorial and Remonstrance.' In its place was enacted Thomas Jefferson's 'Bill for Establishing Religious Freedom' in 1785.

After a short and chaotic life as a confederation, the thirteen American colonies drew up a new constitution in 1787 (or at least 12 of them did; Rhode Island refused to play) and it was ratified in 1788, containing an important church-state provision: that there would be *no religious test for (federal) public office under the new nation.* But several of the states ratified only with the assurance that a Bill of Rights would be added, so the First Congress in 1789 proposed a set of amendments, of which ten were ratified in 1791, forming the Bill of Rights of the Constitution of the United States. The first sixteen words represented a historic experiment in separating church and state: "Congress shall make no law respecting an establishment of religion or prohibiting the free exercise thereof." What those words are supposed to mean will occupy the remainder of this paper.

During the next century and a half, the Supreme Court of the United States had occasion to interpret the subject-matter of those words in about 22 decisions. The number is inexact because some failed to reach the merits, some did not specifically refer to the Religion Clause(s) of the First Amendment, some were consolidated cases, and at least two were later overturned. The reason for the relative desuetude of the proviso was that it refers solely to Congress, and most of the issues to which it might apply were within the jurisdiction of the states. Then in 1940, the Supreme Court held that the Free Exercise Clause applied also to the states and, in 1947, the No-Establishment Clause likewise. This opened the floodgates for church-state cases in the Supreme Court. Over 100 cases have been decided in the past half-century, or over eighty percent of the total church-state decisions in the history of the world's oldest functioning written constitution. Most of the decisions on Establishment have been such that have gladdened the Separationists and distressed their opponents. The Separationists attribute this outcome in part to their militancy.

Sanders recounted the formation of various Separationist alliances and their efforts to maintain and strengthen the 'wall' of 'absolute separation' between church and state. He also criticized (in some instances rightly) their anti-Catholic animus, which tended to distort the vision of their goal and distract them from objective issues. Whatever Roman Catholics favored, Separationists felt an obligation to oppose, almost irrespective of the merits. They imputed to the Roman Catholic church an imperialistic design on the American population and the U.S. Treasury, to gain religious dominance, public financing and political hegemony over the nation, claiming religious liberty for themselves while in the minority but reverting to the rule that 'error has no rights' when in the majority. At the same time, charged Sanders, the Separationists ignored the cultural 'establishment' of Protestantism and the many governmental accommodations from which Protestant institutions benefited.[40] He characterized Separationism as "historically the most significant of the Protestant positions considered ..., but paradoxically in its contemporary form ... the most questionable,"[41] since in his view it is still fighting the battles of a bygone era, resisting dangers no longer present and failing to respond to new conditions and opportunities.[42]

Sanders' view of then-contemporary Separationism was derived from the fulminations of such groups as Protestants and Other Americans United for Separation of Church and State (P.O.A.U.), an organization initiated in 1948 by the following individuals: Methodist Bishop G. Bromley Oxnam; Charles Clayton Morrison, editor of *The Christian Century*; Edwin McNeill Poteat, president of Colgate-Rochester Divinity School; John McKay, president of Princeton Theological Seminary; Louis D. Newton, president of the Southern Baptist Convention; Clyde Taylor of the National Association of Evangelicals; Frank Yost of the Seventh-Day Adventists; and Joseph M. Dawson, secretary of the Baptist Joint Committee on Public Affairs. Under its staff leaders of the 1950s and 1960s, Glenn Archer and C. Stanley Lowell, P.O.A.U. tended to take a paranoid view of the machinations of the Catholics (which, given the triumphalist pre-Vatican II stance of Cardinal Spellman and other Catholic leaders was not without some justification). Though P.O.A.U. did occasionally criticize some Protestant infringements of 'separation of church and state,' most of its efforts were directed against Catholic 'encroachments'— mainly attempts to obtain public funds for parochial schools.

Not until 1971 did the U.S. Supreme Court respond to Separationist complaints on this subject. Its conclusion was that the Establishment Clause of the First Amendment required that state action challenged on that score must have (1) a secular purpose, (2) a primary effect that neither aids nor hinders religion, and (3) no excessive entanglement between government and religion. Several state programs that aided parochial schools were found unconstitutional because government surveillance necessary to determine that only secular purposes and neutral effects were served by such aid would itself unavoidably create 'excessive entanglement' between religion and government[43]—an analysis that one or two justices have since referred to as 'Catch-22.' Nevertheless, this three-pronged test of establishment continues to be used today and has invalidated most forms of tax aid to parochial schools,[44] though not to church-related higher education.[45]

The court thus seemed to accede to the Separationists' demands with respect to tax aid for parochial schools. It likewise moved in a Separationist direction by banning prayers and devotional Bible reading in public schools.[46] The court also prohibited the posting of the Ten Commandments in public school classrooms[47] and the teaching of 'creation science.'[48] The court even prohibited instituting a moment of 'silent meditation and prayer' in public schools.[49]

There are some Separationists who have pressed for even stricter enforcement of the Establishment Clause with respect to ending the tax exemption of churches, military chaplaincies, legislative chaplaincies, creches and crosses on public property, 'In God We Trust' on currency and coins of the United States, the sending of an ambassador of the U.S. to the Vatican, the granting of federal surplus property to church-related institutions, and many other causes. However, these efforts (with a few exceptions such as the Vatican ambassador) have not been attributable to Protestant church groups so much as to advocacy agencies of the Jewish community (particularly the American Jewish Congress), the Unitarians, the American Civil Liberties Union, the American Humanist Association, and the public school establishment (National Education Association, Congress of Parent Teachers Associations, American Association of School Administrators, American Federation of Teachers, etc.), as well as the successor to P.O.A.U., Americans United (A.U.). Under its new leadership, A.U. has shed most of its anti-Catholic animus and is not a church-related organization.

At the time Sanders wrote, these ardent Separationist efforts were coming to be viewed with alarm by some Protestants, who launched (or revived) corrective efforts designed to reassert a less 'sectarian' view of the churches' relation to the state.

THE TRANSFORMATIONISTS

With this fifth and final strand of "Protestant Concepts of Church and State," we reach what Sanders evidently considered the culminating and perfecting deliverance of the Protestant community in the United States on this much-controverted topic. He traced it to the leaders of the Neo-Orthodox movement centering at Union Theological Seminary in New York City in the 1940s, led by Reinhold Niebuhr and John C. Bennett and the publication they launched, *Christianity and Crisis*, edited by Wayne Cowan. They were joined in their uneasiness about the Separationist position by many other individuals. Among them were

Luther Weigle (former dean of the Yale Divinity School), Henry Pitney Van Dusen (then president of Union Seminary), Merrimon Cuninggim (former dean of Perkins School of Theology and then director of the Danforth Foundation), F. Ernest Johnson (educator and researcher with the Federal Council of Churches) and others.

Sanders saw in them an effort to retain or recover the formative role of the churches in shaping the public policy of the commonwealth (including its government)—a role rejected by many *secular* Separationists, but never repudiated by Protestant advocates of separationism. Transformationism, Sanders felt, was a descendant from the 'theocratic' impulses of John Calvin, John Knox, and the English Puritans, led by Thomas Cartwright, Robert Baillie, and others. It reached its fullest embodiment, not in England, where the Restoration soon put an end to such idealism, but across the Atlantic in the Massachusetts Bay Colony. Although "the Massachusetts Puritans ... insisted on a separation of political and religious offices, so that the same person could not hold an important office in both church and state,"[51] the civil and the ecclesiastical arms cooperated so closely that the 'rule of God' was affirmed from the pulpit and enforced from the bench. Although this *de facto* theocracy eventually deteriorated, the Puritan spirit of religiously inspired rectitude persisted into the eighteenth century, invigorated by the Great Awakenings and inspired by Jonathan Edwards. It continued on into the nineteenth century with numerous movements of moral reform, many of them sparked by Lyman Beecher, leader of Connecticut Congregationalism.[51] These efforts were beset on one side by sectarian Separationists (such as the Baptists) and on the other by liberal rationalists and humanists (such as the Unitarians).

> Both Separationists and Unitarians opposed theocracy and vigorously advocated separation of church and state. Against both, the theocrats, having once accepted church-state independence, fought for the greatest possible christianization of society consistent with religious freedom. Religious symbols and holidays, exemption of churches from taxation, military and legislative chaplains, and the appreciation of religion by government represent the theocratic legacy.[52]

THE PRESENT SITUATION

Since Sanders wrote, the Separationists seemed to be in the ascendancy for a while, as we noted in the preceding section with respect to a number of Supreme Court decisions in the 1960s, 1970s and early 1980s. But the picture is not all one-sided: during that period the Court also rejected some of the most basic Separationist contentions. Since 1970, it has rebuffed the following separatist claims: that tax exemption of churches is a form of establishment of religion;[53] that the clergy may not hold public office;[54] that religious student clubs may not meet on a state university campus;[55] that the federal government may not give surplus property to a religious school (because federal taxpayers do not have standing to challenge that kind of action);[56] that a state may not grant tax deductibility for expenditures for (religious as well as public) general education;[57] that a state legislature may not employ a chaplain to lead it in prayer;[58] that a municipality may not erect a Christian nativity shrine as part of an array of (otherwise "secular") Christmas decorations;[59] that a blind student receiving state disability assistance may not use it to attend a Bible college;[60] that Congress cannot allow churches to hire their own members in preference to others;[61] and that Congress cannot provide for church-related welfare agencies to supply counseling to adolescents on sexual morality and teenage pregnancy.[62] In most of these cases the Supreme Court reversed the holdings of lower courts that such actions violated the Establishment Clause.

Since William Rehnquist succeeded Warren Burger as Chief Justice, and Justice Antonin Scalia came to the court in 1986, the Separationists have fared even worse. Only three Establishment Clause challenges have been upheld, and Rehnquist and Scalia dissented in all three, as did Justice Kennedy in the more recent two.[63] There is considerable dissatisfaction among some of the Justices—White, Rehnquist, Scalia and Kennedy—with the test of establishment expressed in *Lemon* (and also with the Free Exercise test in *Sherbert v. Vernor* and *Wisconsin v. Yoder*, which was stripped of independent force by these four justices, plus Justice Stevens, in *Employment Division of Oregon v. Smith*, 1990).[64] It is possible that we may see some significant reconstruction of the court's understanding of the religion clauses in the next few years.

"*SEPARATIONISM*" OR "*STATISM*"?

Notwithstanding this very mixed picture, some commentators still seem obsessed with fear of the Separationists and keep pressing for greater governmental 'accommodation' of religion. Michael McConnell of the University of Chicago Law School wrote an article recently entitled "Why 'Separation' Is Not the Key to Church-State Relations,"[65] which seemed curiously misdirected, like flogging a dead horse or calling alarm against a wolf that has long since left the vicinity. I responded in an article in the same issue entitled, "Statism, Not Separationism, is the Problem," in which I contended that the Supreme Court—particularly its most recent appointees—seems less concerned with 'separation of church and state' than with cutting back on the scope of both religion clauses (and many other elements of the Bill of Rights) in order to let the government govern without restriction by a lot of niggling constitutional limitations:

> Some of [the court's] members seem to feel that individuals should not have many rights that are judicially enforceable against the government.... That view, of course, would put the courts on the side of the strong against the weak and nullify the whole purpose of the Bill of Rights, which is to protect individual rights against government powers.[66]

SHIFTING ALLIANCES AND NEW PARTNERS

In the era of the 1990s, the old battle lines no longer seem so clear. In fact, alliances are shifting, and new combinations appear around new issues. For instance, Protestants of a wide spectrum of views joined together in a brief *amicus curiae* asking the Supreme Court to reverse a holding of the Second Circuit Court of Appeals that an abortion-rights group could attack the tax exemption of the Roman Catholic church for supporting right-to-life candidates for Congress (and opposing their opponents). Some of these groups disagree strenuously with the Roman Catholic church on abortion, but thought that no church's tax exemption should be jeopardized by its preaching and acting in furtherance of its moral beliefs, especially when it was fined $100,000 per day for refusing to turn over its internal records to its adversaries. Joining the National Council of Churches on this brief were the Baptist Joint Committee on Public Affairs, the Church of Jesus Christ of Latter-day Saints (Mormons), the Lutheran Church (Missouri Synod) and the National Association of Evangelicals. The Supreme Court reversed the lower court and remanded the case for reconsideration of the question whether the district court had jurisdiction to hear a third-party challenge to anyone's federal tax status, and the Second Circuit Court of Appeals finally dismissed the case.[67]

In another case, which challenged the provisions for government to contract with churches to provide teen counseling on sexual morality in the Adolescent Family Life Act, the U.S. Catholic Conference submitted a brief *amicus curiae* supporting the Act, siding with United Families of America—intervenor-defendants—represented by the Center for Law and Religious Freedom of the Christian Legal Society, an evangelical Protestant group. On the other side were briefs *amicus curiae* by the Baptist Joint Committee on Public Affairs and Americans United supporting the American Jewish Congress, plaintiff and cross-appellant opposing the Act. The latter may be a 'Separationist' combination, but Catholics and conservative Protestants represented a new alliance, one we may see more often in the future. (The court upheld the constitutionality of the Act 'on its face,' but remanded it for further proceedings 'as applied,' thus giving something to both sides.[68])

Another recent controversy produced a similar split. In 1981 the Supreme Court held that the University of Missouri could not bar student extracurricular religious clubs from a campus to which it had admitted all kinds of nonreligious clubs. The question next arose whether the same principle applied to public high schools. Three circuit courts of appeals have held that it does not,[69] but Congress in 1984 said in the Equal Access Act, that it does,[70] and the U.S. Supreme Court agreed with Congress.[71] Though technically a free-speech issue—whether a public school, having once created a limited open forum for student-initiated and student-led extracurricular clubs, can bar some clubs because of the content of their speech—it has stirred strong controversy on church-state grounds.

The Act was drafted by the Christian Legal Society and introduced by Senator Mark Hatfield (R.–Oregon) as a solution to the religion-in-public-schools impasse following the school prayer decisions of the 1960s. It was designed to permit students to pursue religious interests in their educational community without school sponsorship or supervision. Separationists viewed it as 'son of school prayer' and pointed with alarm to the possibility of revivalists and 'cults' getting a foot in the schoolhouse door in the guise of a 'student' religious 'club.' This alarmist view was expressed by the Lutheran Church in America and the American Lutheran Church,[72] the Anti-Defamation League of B'nai Brith, Americans United, and the ACLU, as well as the public-education establishment. On the other side were not only evangelicals, but several Protestant organizations that had been active over the years in opposing state-sponsored school prayer: the National Council of Churches and the Baptist Joint Committee on Public Affairs.

Those two bodies had also been instrumental in 1965 in supporting the child-benefit theory that permitted some benefits of the Elementary and Secondary Education Act of that year to go to children attending parochial schools (but not to the schools themselves). In so doing, they broke with the strict Separationists listed above. They resisted the efforts of Representatives Edith Green (D.–Oregon), Al Quie (R.–Minnesota), and Charles Goodell (R.–New York) to divide the Protestant and Catholic supporters of the bill and thus bring about its defeat. This 'church-state settlement' has been credited with making possible the enactment of the first substantial program of federal aid to education.[73]

In the 1988-1989 and the 1989-1990 sessions of Congress, a similar struggle occurred over the church-state aspects of the Act for Better Child-Care Services, which would provide more than one billion dollars for various child-care programs through the several states. In this instance, the Catholics were in disagreement with the major Protestant groups over the terms on which church-based child-care providers can be aided by the Act. The Catholics wanted a 'voucher'-type arrangement under which individual children would be given child-care certificates that could be used to pay 'tuition' to any child-care provider, including a church. The mainline Protestant churches (which are collectively the largest non-home-based providers of daycare in the country)—Presbyterian, Methodist, Lutheran, United Church of Christ, and Disciples of Christ (all members of the National Council of Churches)—were strong supporters of the bill. However, they did not want tax funds to be used for sectarian purposes. They were against churches hiring their own members as child-care workers with public money— a position the Catholics were resisting. In this instance, however, the Baptist Joint Committee found itself unable to support the bill at all because of what it considered inadequate church-state safeguards. The Jewish agencies seemed ready to support it. The ACLU was opposed. The public-education establishment was divided. (The evangelical Protestants were opposed to the entire proposition, since they saw federally aided child care as introducing government regulation into family life by enticing mothers out of the home to take jobs rather than minding their own children.)

The upshot of all this is that, since Sanders wrote, the 'Transformationist' wing divided into several sectors, as has the 'Separationist' wing. With the emergence of Reverend Jerry Falwell and the Moral Majority, a new resurgence of theocratic Transformationists has appeared, which seems aggressively inclined to 'Christianizing' America. One of the advocates of this effort is Pat Robertson, a Republican candidate for President in 1988, who in 1985 declared that the Supreme Court had ruled that 'this is a Christian nation' in an 1892 case that has never been overruled.[74] He seems determined to pursue that concept today.

Even farther out on the theocratic wing are "theonomists" like Rousas John Rushdoony. Others strongly supporting theonomy are the Christian Reconstructionist Movement, Tim LaHaye, Francis Schaeffer, and John Whitehead's Rutherford Institute and the Christian Law Association (not to be confused with the Christian Legal Society, which is a relatively centrist evangelical group). These folk are inclined to insist that the civil government can have no regulatory authority over churches or their ministries (such as Christian schools, even to the extent of obtaining the names of pupils enrolled therein). They seem to envision an almost 'extraterritorial' status for churches. They also have been active in radical action against abortion, such as 'Operation Rescue', devoted to blocking access to abortion clinics and even damaging the property of the clinics. The Christian Reconstructionists would like to enact the laws of the Bible (especially the Old Testament) as the law of the land, to be administered solely by born-again fundamentalist Christians.

The Moral Majority thrust, now supposedly decommissioned by Mr. Falwell, with its counterparts in the Religious Roundtable, chaired by Edward McAtteer, and Christian Voice, led by Robert Grant, is a vigorous 'transformationist' effort that flourished during the Reagan Administration. They are not quite as extreme as the theonomists, but are probably still the most energetic and atten-tion-getting branch of Protestant activists on the church-state front. However, Jeffrey Hadden maintained that they were never much more than a glorified media hype that had little significant grassroots support.

Not quite as far to the 'right' are the traditional evangelicals, led by the National Association of Evangelicals and the Christian Legal Society. Both of these groups cooperate congenially with ecumenical religious bodies on matters of mutual interest and par-ticipate actively in the Religious Liberty Committee (related to the National Council of Churches) which I staff. (The Religious Liberty Committee is the successor of the Department of Religious Liberty mentioned earlier.)

Somewhere in the middle are the mainline Protestant bodies of the National Council of Churches, whose inclinations are partly Transformationist, partly Separationist. They were active in orga-nizing church opposition to seven successive efforts to amend the Constitution to permit state-sponsored prayer and Bible reading in public schools, and were instrumental in defeating all seven of them, including the most recent effort led by former President Reagan in 1983. It failed to obtain the necessary two-thirds majori-ty votes required in the then Republican-controlled Senate, falling short by eleven votes. But they, the mainline Protestant bodies, are also insistent (and always have been) on the right of churches to seek to influence public policy in obedience to their understand-ing of the will of God. This led them to defend the Catholic Church's struggle against Abortion Rights Mobilization, referred to earlier. Some Protestant denominations, particularly Lutherans, as we have seen, defend the right of church-related institutions of welfare and (higher) education to share in governmentally financed programs of community service. The Baptists tend to be more inclined to the Separationist side of the spectrum, but even they are easily distinguishable from the strictest Separationists like the Unitarians and the ACLU.

THE MOST RECENT READING

A good index of the church-state inclinations of this middle-of-the-road cluster is provided by the most recent official action on a broad range of church-state issues. It was taken by one of the major religious bodies in the country, the 200th General Assembly of the Presbyterian Church (USA), in 1988. They adopted 55 policies in seven general areas. Outlined below are some of the policies:

A. The Right of Church Autonomy

1. Churches have a right of autonomy protected by the Free Exercise Clause of the First Amendment. Each worshipping community has the right to govern itself and order its life and activity free of government intervention.

B. Conduct Motivated by Conscience

1. Individuals should be excused from obeying laws of general application which violate their conscience except when "the gravest abuses endangering paramount interests [of the state] give occasion for permissible limitation ..."

C. Government Support for Religious Institutions

2. Government should not discriminate against religious institutions and agencies in the expenditure or administration of public funds, when the public purpose can be achieved by the religious group in a way that does not support or advance religion....

3. Since each state guarantees the right to a free public elementary and secondary education and maintains universally accessible institutions for that purpose, we oppose as a matter of public policy the use of substantial public funds to support private educational systems, including tax deductions or credits and use of educational vouchers.

D. Taxation and Religious Organizations

1. The state may not use its power to tax or to exempt from taxation to restrict, or place conditions on, the exercise of religion.

2. The state may not tax the central exercise of religion or property essential to the core functions of religions.

3. Special tax exemptions or burdens for the property and income of ministers or other church employees are inappropriate....

E. New Religions and Threats to Conversion

The right to choose one's own religion, and to change that choice, is the most fundamental religious liberty. This right must be vigorously protected from governmental intrusion or physical coercion, either by those seeking to convert or those seeking to prevent conversion.

F. Religious Expression in Public Places

1. Government must be neutral in matters of religion. It may not show preference for one religion over others, or for religion over non-religion.

2. Government may not engage in, sponsor, or lend its authority to religious expression or religious observance. We continue to oppose any constitutional amendment to permit public schools to sponsor prayer....

4. The display of religious symbols in connection with private speech and assembly in public places is appropriate and legal. We oppose the permanent or unattended display of religious symbols on public property as a violation of the religious neutrality required of government....

7. If a public secondary school permits genuinely extra-curricular student initiated group activities on non-instructional time, religious expression should be permitted, subject to the same regulations and restrictions.

G. Religious Participation in Public Life

1. The corporate entities and individual members of the Presbyterian Church (USA) are obliged by the religious faith and order they profess to participate in public life and become involved in the realm of politics.

2. Pastors and officials of the church, as well as lay members, have the right and the responsibility to stand for and hold public office when they feel called to do so....

6. We reject and oppose any attempts on the part of the church to exercise political authority or to use the political process to achieve governmental sponsorship of worship or religious practice.

(A complete copy of the Presbyterian policies is in the Appendix.)

It is significant that the Advisory Committee on Religious Liberty and Church/State Relations that drafted the report over the course of several years, though drawn from different parts of the country and various occupational settings (albeit predominantly clergy and attorneys) found itself arriving at an almost complete consensus on all of its recommendations except for section C, paragraph 3 (above), on which there was a minority report that would have entertained various possibilities of public funding of parochial education. That minority report was rejected by the Advisory Council on Church and Society, which transmitted the report to the General Assembly for adoption. In the legislative committee of the Assembly which deliberated for a day on the report, there was little resistance to the recommendations except for section D, paragraph 3 (above), which was opposed by some who (rightly) interpreted it to disapprove of the exemption from personal taxable income of the cash housing allowance of clergy (Section 107(b) of the Internal Revenue Code). However, that opposition was voted down by the full committee. The General Assembly adopted the Advisory Committee's original recommendations without revision. Thus the final policies represent a broad consensus of the governing body of a major Protestant communion (and probably of many other mainline Protestants in the U.S. at the time).

Nowhere in the 55 policies adopted by the Presbyterian General Assembly is there any reference to 'separation of church and state' as such. A few of the policies support 'Separationist' positions (section C, paragraph 3; section F, paragraph 1, 2, 4). Others support 'Transformationist' ones (section C, paragraph 2; section G, paragraph 1, 2). The main thrust supports both individual and collective free exercise of religion and the autonomy of church bodies in managing their own internal affairs without governmental interference. That thrust is not at odds with either Separationist or Transformationist wings of Protestantism, though the latter would want to press for greater public 'recognition' of religion (as in school prayer, etc.), whereas the former would want to bar tax funding for church related welfare programs and higher education.

Rather than 'separation of church and state', the Presbyterian statement envisions religion and government pursuing their distinctive functions independently of one another, but not without some interaction. The Presbyterian position favors regulation by the government in matters where public health and safety are at stake, influence on public policy by the church(es) in the same manner and degree that other groups of citizens seek to influence public policy, and occasional cooperation between the two in furtherance of the common good, but without special favors (or burdens) for religion in the process. That probably represents the central 'Protestant perspective' on church and state in the United States today for most practical purposes.

We can then view the following 'Protestant' spectrum:

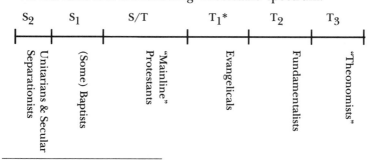

S_2 S_1 S/T T_1* T_2 T_3

Unitarians & Secular Separationists — (Some) Baptists — "Mainline" Protestants — Evangelicals — Fundamentalists — "Theonomists"

*Catholics form a spectrum of their own, but many of them would probably fit in at section T, para. 1 or 2.

APPENDIX

Excerpts from "God Alone Is Lord of the Conscience"
Report of the Committee on Religious Liberty and Church/State
Relations
General Assembly of the Presbyterian Church (USA)

A. The Right of Church Autonomy and Government Regulation of
Church Activity

The 200th General Assembly (1988) adopts the following affirmations:

1. Churches have a right of autonomy protected by the Free
Exercise clause of the First Amendment. Each worshipping community has the right to govern itself and order its life and activity
free of government intervention.

2. The government must assert a compelling interest and
demonstrate an imminent threat to public safety before the right
of autonomy may be set aside in specific instances and government
permitted to interfere with internal church activities. The need to
separate business activity from residential areas is not sufficient to
justify use of zoning regulations to prevent prayer meetings in private homes nor prohibit the use of the church building as a shelter
for the homeless.

3. Churches have a fundamental right to be free of government
infiltration. Court-approved wiretaps and searches of church
premises can only be made on a showing that evidence of crime
endangering public health or safety will be removed or destroyed
and that no other less intrusive means exist to satisfy the need to
preserve such evidence.

4. We concede the appropriateness of some governmental regulation of church activities in the interests of public health and safety. Fire and earthquake regulations and sanitary and building
codes may properly be made applicable to churches, provided that
they do not entail unreasonable cost, are genuinely health and
safety related, and are appropriate to the pattern of church activity
rather than a supposed secular analog. A church kitchen used a
few hours a month for church groups is not the same as a public
restaurant.

5. The government may not require a congregation to maintain a church structure because of its historical significance or subject it to proceedings in eminent domain in order to preserve a church structure. The church should make every effort to cooperate with efforts to preserve esthetics and architectural character, but must finally itself be the judge of what religious life and mission require concerning property and its use.

6. Internal disputes within churches, including disputes over church property, should be decided by the ecclesiastical authority recognized by both sides before the dispute arose. The application of so-called "neutral principles of law" by civil courts violates the right to autonomy of hierarchical and connectional churches.

7. Those who consent to be governed by a church, including its employees, should not be subject to governmental regulations. We reject the notion that minimum wage laws or other labor regulations may properly be applied to church organizations.

8. As a matter of faith and witness, the church has a moral duty to provide adequate compensation and safe working conditions for its employees and to offer employment without discrimination. The church should voluntarily meet or exceed the standards and practices required by law for non-religious employers.

9. Courts and public agencies called upon to assess the bona fides of a claim to protection under the First Amendment should not base their decision on traditional notions of religion but should give substantial deference to the self-understanding of that group.

B. Conduct Motivated by Conscience

The 200th General Assembly (1988) adopts the following affirmations:

1. Individuals should be excused from obeying laws of general application which violate their conscience except when "the gravest abuses endangering paramount interests give occasion for permissible limitation."

2. The legal defense of freedom of conscience must be conceived broadly enough to include freedom for the non-religious conscience.

3. The protection of religious conscience should not be limited to actions stemming from beliefs shared by all members of one's

religious group or to what is required by the creed or order of one's religious group. It includes practice that may be regarded as voluntary by one's religion as well as that which is individually derived.

4. The right of adults to refuse medical treatment for themselves on religious grounds should be upheld, but not their right to withhold medical care for their minor children when such treatment is deemed necessary to prevent death or permanent injury.

5. The diversity of understandings of different religious groups as to what constitutes health should be respected.

6. The right to observe the Sabbath and other days of religious obligation should be protected, but not to the significant material disadvantage of co-workers whose days of religious obligation are different or those who are not religiously affiliated.

7. The present selective service law, which requires that conscientious objectors be opposed to all wars, should be changed to allow exemption as well for those opposed only to participation in particular wars on the ground that they are unjust.

8. Not all employment discrimination can be reached by law. The church should be prepared to expose, analyze, and confront cases of discrimination in public or private employment based on religious conviction or status, as well as on grounds of race, religion, nationality, sex, or sexual orientation, and to provide aid and comfort to the victims.

9. Claims of Christian conscience should not be lightly or cynically made, and should be tested to the maximum extent possible by the counsel of the Christian community.

C. Government Support for Religious Institutions

The 200th General Assembly (1988) adopts the following affirmations:

1. Government payments on behalf of individuals under programs such as Medicare, Medicaid, and scholarship assistance, should without exception be available to clients and students at church-sponsored agencies and institutions on exactly the same terms as if those patients or clients were receiving their services from secular entities.

2. Government should not discriminate against religious institutions and agencies in the expenditure or administration of public

funds, when the public purpose can be achieved by the religious group in a way that does not support or advance religion. When public funds are made available to private agencies to meet welfare and social service needs, religious programs and agencies should not be excluded provided that:

a. the service is open to the public without discrimination on the basis of race, age, sex, religion, or national origin;

b. the service is administered without religious emphasis or content, or religious preference or other discrimination in employment or purchase of services;

c. no public funds are used by religiously controlled organizations to acquire permanent title to real property. Where existing religiously owned property requires minor modifications to meet specific requirements of the particular program and there are public funds expressly available for such purpose, they may be used by the church also; and

d. the religious organization or agency is subject to the same provisions for safety, general standards and licensing, qualifications of personnel, and financial accountability as other private agencies.

3. Since each state guarantees the right to a free public elementary and secondary education and maintains universally accessible institutions for that purpose, we oppose as a matter of public policy the use of substantial public funds to support private educational systems, including tax deductions or credits and use of educational vouchers.

4. Where government provides non-curricular services to both public and private schools that involve the itineration of public employees to the institutions, schools sponsored by religious organizations should not be excluded.

5. Tax deductions for contributions to religious agencies, or for payments to religious schools should they be enacted, should not be viewed as support or aid for religion. A policy decision by the state to refrain from taxing is not equivalent to a decision to appropriate public revenues.

6. Service ministries operated by or related to Presbyterian governing bodies, whether or not they receive public funds, should offer all service without restriction based on race, sex, religion, ethnic origin, or sexual orientation, and should conform to requisite

health and safety requirements and standards regarding licensing and personnel qualifications. Where such programs are expected to continue for considerable time, placing them under the control of independent community-based bodies should be carefully considered.

7. In light of the division within the religious and public life of this nation concerning government aid for religious schools, and the great significance of quality education for all our children, we urge continuing study and reflection on the whole subject at every level of the church. The child-benefit, purchase of service, and equal-treatment approaches in particular merit careful analysis, both in ongoing constitutional interpretation and in public policy considerations.

D. Taxation and Religious Organizations

The 200th General Assembly (1988) adopts the following affirmations:

1. The state may not use its power to tax or to exempt from taxation to restrict, or place conditions on, the exercise of religion.

2. The state may not tax the central exercise of religion or property essential to the core functions of religion. We hold that the application of the restrictions in Section 501(c)(3) of the Internal Revenue Code to the speech of the church and its leaders is an unconstitutional limitation on a central exercise of religion.

3. We support exemption of other church property and income as a matter of legislative policy. Such exemptions do not "establish" religion.

4. We concede that some properties and operations of religious organizations may be subjected to taxation by legislative act, but we will resist all efforts to do so by administrative determination, in the face of statutes that exempt churches from taxation, that some properties or activities wholly controlled and operated by the church as part of its mission are "non-religious."

5. We affirm the legitimacy of taxing unrelated business income and property used to generate such income.

6. Particular taxes or exclusions from taxes should treat religious organizations equally with charitable and non-profit organizations; religious organizations should not be singled out for either penalty or privilege except for the exemption of property essential to the core functions of religion.

7. Special tax exemptions or burdens for the property and income of ministers or other church employees are inappropriate. They should be phased out over a period long enough to accommodate the reliance of many churches on existing exemptions.

8. Payments to government for specific services billed separately to all property owners are not "taxes" and may legitimately be required of religious organizations at the same rate as for other property owners.

9. Churches should feel no obligation to make voluntary contributions in lieu of taxes, and all such contributions should be truly voluntary. They are not a *quid pro quo* for tax exemption.

E. New Religions and Threats to Conversion

The 200th General Assembly (1988) adopts the following affirmations:

1. The right to choose one's own religion, and to change that choice, is the most fundamental religious liberty. This right must be vigorously protected from governmental intrusion or physical coercion, either by those seeking to convert or those seeking to prevent conversion. This right should also be protected from fraud, but courts cannot evaluate claims of religious faith.

2. The church should be tolerant of other religions and respect their right to proselytize and practice their beliefs in accordance with the tenets of their faith.

3. We oppose judicial and legislative efforts to interfere with freely chosen and maintained religious commitments by legal adults, whether based on attempts to define legally undesirable "cult" religion, the use of conservator and guardian procedures, or reversal through legally authorized deprogramming.

4. We further oppose the use of civil law by persons disaffected, or disenchanted with their religious experience, unless plausible allegations of physical coercion or fraudulent claims related to empirical facts are present. The right of religious freedom carries responsibility for its exercise and the risk of disenchantment.

5. The church should provide counsel, education, and support for the family members and friends of those who have converted to a new faith or undergone a powerful religious experience, and should indicate understanding and continued openness to those who have converted.

F. Religious Expression in Public Places

The 200th General Assembly (1988) adopts the following affir-mations:

1. Government must be neutral in matters of religion. It may not show preference for one religion over others, for religion in general, or for religion over non-religion. While contact and con-versation between public officials and religious leaders on public policy issues are certainly appropriate, official institutional ties between government and religion are not. For that reason, we con-tinue to oppose the appointment of ambassadors to the Holy See of the Roman Catholic Church.

2. Government may not engage in, sponsor, or lend its authority to religious expression or religious observance. We continue to oppose any constitutional amendment to permit public schools to sponsor prayer.

3. Religious speech and assembly by private citizens and organi-zations, initiated by them, is protected both by the Free Exercise of Religion and the Free Speech clauses of the Constitution and can-not be excluded from public places.

4. The display of religious symbols in connection with private speech and assembly in public places is appropriate and legal. We oppose the permanent or unattended display of religious symbols on public property as a violation of the religious neutrality required of government.

5. Religious speech and assembly in public places may be regu-lated by government as to time, place, and manner, but only in a neutral manner and not to any greater extent than non-religious expression.

6. Statutes permitting "moments of silence" in public schools are not inherently unconstitutional, but should not be enacted because they are subject to misuse through pressures to allow state-sponsored prayer or endorse religion.

7. If a public secondary school permits genuinely extra-curric-ular student-initiated group activities in non-instructional time, religious expression should be permitted, subject to the same regulations and restrictions.

8. Public schools may constitutionally teach their students about religion in a neutral way. The incorporation of factual and objec-tive references to the role of religion when teaching history, social

studies, art, and literature is essential to a comprehensive and balanced education, and should be encouraged and assisted in every possible way.

9. Presbyterians should be particularly vigilant to protect the right to public religious expression for new and unpopular minority faiths, and should be sensitive to the faith and feelings of others in their own public expressions of faith.

G. Religious Participation in Public Life

The 200th General Assembly (1988) adopts the following affirmations:

1. The corporate entities and individual members of the Presbyterian Church (USA) are obliged by the religious faith and order they profess to participate in public life and become involved in the realm of politics.

2. Pastors and officials of the church, as well as lay members, have the right and responsibility to stand for and hold public office when they feel called to do so.

3. The "free exercise of religion" must be understood to include and protect the right to practice faith in public and private as well as the right to believe, and thus to include participation in public affairs by the individuals and church bodies for which such participation is an element of faith.

4. As part of the church's participation in public life, governing bodies of the Presbyterian Church (USA) at every level should speak out on public and political issues, taking care to articulate the moral and ethical implications of public policies and practices.

5. We recognize that speaking out on issues will sometimes constitute implicit support or opposition to particular candidates or parties, where policy and platform differences are clearly drawn. Since such differences are the vital core of the political process, church participation should not be curtailed on that account; but we believe that it is generally unwise and imprudent for the church explicitly to support or oppose specific candidates, except in unusual circumstances.

6. We reject and oppose any attempts on the part of the church to exercise political authority or to use the political process to achieve governmental sponsorship of worship or religious practice.

183

7. We oppose attempts by government to limit or deny religious participation in public life by statute or regulation, including Internal Revenue Service regulations on the amount or percentage of money used to influence legislation, and prohibition of church intervention in political campaigns. We will join with others, as occasion permits, to seek repeal of such regulations and statutes or a definite ruling by the Supreme Court on their constitutionality.

NOTES

1. Nichols, J.H. *Democracy and the Churches*, Phil., Westminster Press, 1951, 17-18.
2. Ibid., 26-27.
3. Ibid., 18.
4. Ibid., 18-19, quoting J.N. Figgis, *From Gerson to Grotius.*
5. Ibid., 23, quoting John T. McNeill, "Natural Law in the Teaching of the Reformers," *Journal of Religion*, July, 1946, 171.
6. Ibid., 23.
7. Ibid., 22.
8. Ibid., 29-31, quoting Dawson, C., "Religious Origins of European Disunity," *Dublin Review*, Oct., 1940, 151ff.
9. Ibid., 31, 41.
10. Sanders, T.G. *Protestant Concepts of Church and State*, (New York: Holt, Rinehart & Winston, 1964), 6.
11. Ibid., 9.
12. Ibid., 26, quoting Luther's "On Secular Authority."
13. Ibid., 29-31, passim.
14. Ibid., 35, quoting Luther's "On Secular Authority."
15. Ibid., 39.
16. Ibid., 41, quoting "Against the Robbing and Murdering Hordes of Peasants."
17. Ibid., 45-46, quoting Luther's "Table Talk."
18. Ibid., 62.
19. "Church and State: A Lutheran Perspective," Board of Social Ministry—Lutheran Church in America, 1963, 36, emphasis in original.
20. Ibid., 36-41, passim.
21. Ibid., 39.
22. Ibid., 41-43, passim.
23. Ibid., 43-47, passim
24. Ibid., 46.
25. Littell, Franklin H., *The Origins of Sectarian Protestantism.*, (New York: MacMillan, 1964).
26. Sanders, op. cit., 81-83, passim.

27. Littell, Franklin H., op. cit. 37, 39.
28. Sanders, op. cit., 153, 159, citing Niebuhr, *Christianity and Power Politics*, 10-12.
29. Ibid., 123.
30. Ibid., 124.
31. Ibid., 124-5.
32. Ibid., 120-121, quoting George Fox.
33. Ibid., 122-123.
34. Ibid., 131.
35. Ibid., 148-149.
36. Ibid., 153, 154.
37. Ibid., 171, 199-200.
38. Ibid., 174ff.
39. Ibid., 175-181, passim.
40. Ibid., 206-215, passim.
41. Ibid., 220.
42. Ibid., 221.
43. *Lemon* v. *Kurtzman*, 403 U.S. 602 (1971).
44. E.g., *Pearl* v. *Nyquist*, 413 U.S. 756 (1973); *Meek* v. *Pittenger*, 421 U.S. 349 (1975); *Wolman* v. *Walter*, 433 U.S. 229 (1977), *Aguilar* v. *Felton*, 473 U.S. 402 (1985).
45. *Tilton* v. *Richardson*, 403 U.S. 672 (1971); *Hunt* v. *McNair*, 413 U.S. 734 (1973); *Roemer* v. *Bd. of Public Works*, 426 U.S. 736 (1978).
46. *Engel* v. *Vitale*, 370 U.S. 421 (1962); *Abington Township* v. *Schempp*, 374 U.S. 203 (1963).
47. *Stone* v. *Graham*, 499 U.S. 39 (1980).
48. *Edwards* v. *Aguillard*, 107 S.Ct. 2573 (1987).
49. *Wallace* v. *Jaffree*, 472 U.S. 38 (1985).
50. Sanders, op. cit., 245.
51. Ibid., 247-251, passim.
52. Ibid, 253.
53. *Walz* v. *Tax Commission*, 397 U.S. 644 (1970).
54. *McDaniel* v. *Paty*, 435 U.S. 618 (1978).
55. *Widmar* v. *Vincent*, 454 U.S. 263 (1981).
56. *Valley Forge Christian College* v. *Americans United*, 454 U.S. 464 (1982).
57. *Mueller* v. *Allen*, 463 U.S. 388 (1983).
58. *Marsh* v. *Chambers*, 463 U.S. 783 (1983).
59. *Lynch* v. *Donnelly*, 465 U.S. 668 (1984).
60. *Witters* v. *Washington*, 474 U.S. 481 (1986).
61. *Corporation of the Presiding Bishop* v. *Amos*, 107 S.Ct. 2862 (1987).
62. *Kendrick* v. *Bowen*, 56 USLW 4819 (1988).
63. *Edwards* v. *Aguilard* (1987) and *Texas Monthly* v. *Bullock* (1989). All three dissented in *Allegheny County* v. *ACLU.* (1989).
64. State action burdening the free exercise of religion must be justified by a compelling state interest that can be served in no less intrusive way. 374 U.S. 398 (1963) and 406 U.S. 205 (1972).
65. *Christian Century*, Jan. 18, 1989, 43-47.
66. Kelley, D.M., "Statism, Not Separation, Is the Problem," *Christian Century*, loc. cit., 48-51.

MORALITY AND RELIGION

67. *United States Catholic Conference* v. *Abortion Rights Mobilization, Inc.*
68. *Bowen* v. *Kendrick*, 56 USLW 4818 (1988).
69. *Brandon* v. *Guilderland*, 635 F.2d (CA2, 1980), *Lubbock Civil Liberties Union* v. *Lubbock School District*, 669 F.2d 602 (CA5, 1982), and *Bender* v. *Williamsport*, 741 F.2d 538 (CA3, 1984), vacated for lack of standing of appellants, 106 S. Ct. 1326 (1986).
70. 20 U.S.C. § 4071 et seq.
71. The Equal Access was upheld in *Westside School District* v. *Mergens*, 1990.
72. This was probably due to the leadership of the Rev. Charles Bergstrom, their staff representative in Washington, who has been active in People for the American Way, an antifundamentalist secular advocacy group.
73. See Kelley, D.M., and George R. LaNoue, Jr., "The Church-State Settlement in the Federal Aid to Education Act," Gianella, Donald A., ed. *Religion and the Public Order*, 1965, (Villanova Univ., 1966), 110-160.
74. *Church of the Holy Trinity* v. *U.S.*, 143 U.S. 457 (1892).

EIGHT

CHURCH AND STATE RELATIONS: WHO IS CAESAR?

Alain Besançon

How has history interpreted Christ's word, "Give back to Caesar what is Caesar's and to God what is God's"? The word that needs to be emphasized here is Caesar. It connotes political power. In the eyes of the Jews, it was the 'paradigm' of an illegitimate power that weighed heavily on the chosen people. But in the eyes of the Roman world, of which Jewish Palestine was a part, this power had a legitimacy that some of the Jews readily accepted. Indeed, in the time of Christ, it had already received a philosophical sanction. This sovereignty began to organize itself as a compulsory form of religious worship, namely as the cult of the emperor. In this context, Caesar means the goals that an organized human society sets itself. Peace, justice, the defense of the empire—that is of the Roman world (*oikoumene*)—find their center and their incarnation, so to speak, in the person of Caesar.

When Celsius engaged in polemics with the Christians, he criticized them for considering themselves strangers to the world while profiting from the social and political order. They ought to pay a tribute of honor, he said, to the emperors who watched over this order. "Otherwise they would appear singularly ungrateful to these superior beings, for it is not right to partake of the advantages they proffer and not pay them any homage in return" (ch. 110).

In response, Christians drew attention to the fact that they did indeed pay homage: they prayed for the emperor, were he Nero,

Caligula or Diocletian. They prayed for him because his power—his 'potestas'—came from God and was legitimated in the mandate to preserve society, i.e., the political institution, despite the fact that, because of his hatred for Christianity, he also incarnated the power of the antichrist. But adoration, however, could be given only to the true God. They thus rendered to each his due, in accord with the fundamental legal principle confirmed by the Lord: *suum cuique.*

When the emperor converted to Christianity and the antichrist submitted to the authority of Christ, the same principle regulated the relationship between the church and the empire. In the east, where the empire had kept all its strength, the church preserved the ideal of the 'symphony'. In the west, after a protracted struggle, the church won a more secure independence. But having secured its rights in the spiritual order, it had to concede the rights owed to the temporal order. At the best of times, it did not challenge the legitimacy of the established order as long as the state allowed some room to the citizen who, while obeying the prince in all things, was free to give to God what was God's, both in worship and in moral life.

Once the Jewish people lost their independence, 'Give back to Caesar' came to mean obtaining a status that allowed the people to give back to God what is God's. The people paid taxes, were subjected to a limitation of sovereignty, and in return remained free to have the Torah. When the Jews lost their land and were forced to disperse, they had to renegotiate their status in less favorable circumstances. They then began to lead a kind of double life: as a Jew, hedged behind the Torah, and as a loyal subject for whom, as a Talmudic saying goes, "The law of the land is the law."

Even if this situation were to last for centuries, the Jews would still proclaim, 'Next year in Jerusalem'. They endured their situation in exile (Galut). Indeed, the people could be totally free and punctiliously observe the law only in the 'Promised Land.' Jewish people could, as they have done for centuries, abstain from politics in general. Frequently, politics was of consequence to the Jews only to the degree that it exposed them to persecution. Politics was reclaiming its rights but it did so in the midst of the people, within the framework determined by the law and Talmudic jurisprudence. The secular state of Israel itself could not create a constitution, for this constitution could not be anything other than the Torah.

As for the church, it does not have a law embracing all aspects of human life. It is the prince that makes the law and the fact that the prince happens to be a Christian—as was the case with the conversion of Constantine—does not necessarily simplify matters. In the first place, he is not fully a Christian, being a converted pagan. Almost all Christians, in fact, are in this situation. Second, he does not have to be a Christian, his mandate being that of a pagan emperor, namely to assure, from the human standpoint, the general welfare of his subjects. It is no concern of his whether they are Christians or not. If he desired to lead them to Christianity, he could not use coercive legislation which would automatically be unchristian. Political Augustinism—the *compelle intrare*—very soon comes up against moral limitations.

In other words, the church is forced to engage in politics. It has to do it for its own sake, '*more judaico*,' to protect its status and secure its internal freedom. The church has to do it in general because of its mission. Its vocation is to take care of all people, Christians and non-Christians, and it cannot be indifferent to their fate. Finally, the church has to do it for theoretical reasons, because it has to consider human nature, that is, as a political animal, and because, by virtue of the 'Incarnation,' it is the totality of this nature that is to be redeemed.

But the art of politics is problematic. Neither the church nor the Christian politician can claim any special gift of clairvoyance. The church can never be sure it is unmistakably promoting the general interest, let alone its own particular interest. In the history of the advances and setbacks of Christendom, we can perceive how decisive a sound or an unsound course of political action can be. If the church failed its mission in Persia, China, and Japan, and if it fulfilled it among the barbarians of northern Europe, of America, and Africa, it is largely due to whether its political decisions were sound or unsound. If half of Christendom fell to Islam in less than a century, it is, in the final analysis, due to the politics of the Christian empire.

It has happened that politics invade the church to the point of disfiguring it. Let us recall the situation in the fifteenth century when the church was being oppressed and was oppressing in its turn, when the clergy was being affected by the vicissitudes of secular politics and when politics was being infected by a political clergy. Then came the temptation to abandon politics. Let the church extricate itself once and for all from all these entanglements in order to dedicate itself solely to the things of the Father! Let the world follow its own course! This is perhaps an exaggeration of political Augustinism. The worldly government is perceived as a *latrocinium*, a den of thieves whose master is Satan.

Both the Roman Catholic church and the churches that emerged from the Reformation have been exposed to this temptation; they are all vulnerable on this score. Luther and the 'spirituali' are agreed to abandon the secular world to the princes, in effect to the Prince of this world. Freedom, according to Luther, is internal and the church is invisible. Ignatius and Calvin, on the contrary, have no compunction in drawing upon all the resources of politics. When Ignatius writes two different letters to remit to the pope, the one more in tune with the pope's mood, he is acting politically, according to the classic political tradition. Suarez practiced an *aggiornamento* (adjournment) over St. Thomas that Machiavelli had rendered necessary, and was later to outline the contours of the art of politics in which men like Richelieu, Mazarin, and Urban VII excelled.

But once again, the art of politics is a difficult one and Christian faith does not guarantee infallibility. A decision that may seem sound in the short term may turn out to be catastrophic later. It was the theologian Cardinal Retz who said that politics is not a choice between good and evil but between bad and worse. It is an ambiguous, a compromising art, and one can understand that the Russian Orthodox church, the only orthodox church not to have been reduced to servitude by the Ottoman Empire, allowed itself to be subjugated by the state. It adopted, through particularly humiliating modalities, a kind of hyperlutheranism which, it believed, would leave it in charge of the things of heaven. The Catholic church could never consent to such a capitulation. And it never ceased to practice politics, good or bad.

There is no need to recount here the whole story. The main difficulty the church encountered in the nineteenth century was the progressive emergence of new regimes which were moving by fits and starts toward modern democracy. The church had forged narrow secular ties with the monarchies. Perhaps it failed to extricate itself from these entanglements in good time. Rather than secure for itself a decent and acceptable place, the church, in France, Italy, and Spain, sometimes represented by the pope, sometimes by local episcopacies, tried to prevent the advent of the new political regime which was often lay, democratic, liberal, anti-clerical and antichristian in character. It succeeded more easily in Anglo-Saxon countries, first in the United States, then in Belgium, and in the low countries. But the remarkable thing is that the criticism of the political action of the church has been displaced through historical consciousness to become criticism of its social action. The church has been accused of 'taking sides with the rich,' of colluding with 'capitalism' and using the working class. However, an examination of the facts reveals something quite different. The church has been prematurely motivated by 'social' considerations. It was very aware of the misery of the masses, encountered daily in charitable institutions, hospitals, prisons, and schools. If the poor have separated themselves from the church, it is not because the church has abandoned them but rather because, in their desire to climb the social ladder, they have mimicked the impiety of the higher classes. Consequently, the political analysis that should have severely condemned the delay of the church to rally to the republic, the blunders in negotiating the status of Rome, or the mistakes of the Dreyfus Affair, has been directed instead toward a socialistic analysis which occulted the real weakness of Catholic politics. This erroneous diagnosis weighed heavily on the conscience and the political action of the church in the twentieth century.

In politics, mistakes are more striking than success. It is out of the question to pass a global judgment on the politics of the church in the twentieth century. However, nothing prevents us from pinpointing its main mistakes. I shall define this mistake thusly: in its desire to follow tradition and render unto Caesar what is Caesar's, the church blundered. In fact, it was giving away what was no longer Caesar's, to whom nothing was due.

Caesar symbolizes the normal political aspiration of humanity to found a society, to defend it, to assure its peace and to organize it according to the rule of law. These are limited and imperfect goals because they do not pretend to lead humankind to salvation.

These goals can be reached only to a relative degree, leaving unresolved injustice and other consequences of the sins of rulers and ruled alike.

Now, the twentieth century has witnessed the rise of political entities which arrogate to themselves different goals. They aspired to build a perfect society by destroying existing social relations. In this, they were following a doctrine which pretended to pinpoint the root cause of evil and provide a recipe for the final eradication of evil. They arrogated to themselves unlimited power to achieve this goal. Morality and law were subsumed under this doctrine and subordinated to the achievement of this grand design. In this way, killing was permissible, was even an obligation if, by eliminating one's enemies, one moved closer to the promised ideal.

Foundational to these new regimes is ideology. This is a new intellectual phenomenon born of the concatenation of two currents. One is the gnostic tradition, as old as Christianity itself, which injects ideology with the contempt of the created world and of the established society. The universe is the battleground for an implacable conflict between two principles, one good and the other evil. The task of the initiated gnostic is to exercise discernment between the two principles, to recognize their presence and their operation behind the fleeting phenomena of history in order that he may assure the triumph of the good principle and establish thereon a new heaven and a new earth. The other current is science—or what the ideologue believes to be science. Science is mobilized to provide the certainty intrinsic to truly scientific operations and thus guarantee the validity of the gnostic system. Science strips the gnosis of its religious character, or rather, buries it to the point of making it invisible even to the ideologue. The redemption of the world takes place in accordance with the laws of nature and the ideologue is convinced that he or she is simply applying the laws immanent in the world. In the final analysis, ideology is to be understood as a perversion of both religion and science. It is a perversion of religion because faith is supposedly infused by a pseudo-rational system, and of science which, transposed outside the realm from which it acquires certitude, is reduced to an imposture and charlatanism.

I have just described the foundation of two principalities of twentieth century history: Marxist-Leninist communism and

Hitler's nazism. But how was it that the church allowed itself to be partially deceived by both? In the 1920s and the 1930s, the Catholic church acutely felt the menace of communism and, through the popes, it formally condemned communism on several occasions. As the first targeted victim, the church has been more lucid on this point than the majority of secular powers. However, a slight error of perspective prevented the church from carrying its analysis to its natural conclusion. The church saw in Leninist communism the aggravation and monstrous prolongation of what it, sometimes in an exaggerated manner, had already recognized as evil: social democratic socialism and, before that, modern liberal democracy. The church failed to grasp immediately the radical novelty, the absolute originality of the communist principality. This is manifest even in the most profound condemnation of communism ever issued by a pope, the encyclical *Divini Redemptoris* of 1937.

The same week, Pius XI published *Mit Brennender Sorge* condemning nazism. However, this encyclical suffered from exactly the same flaw: it did not discern clearly enough the radical novelty of nazism. Nazism was classified in the same category with such regimes as Italian fascism, Spanish Francoism and Portuguese Salazarism. These authoritarian corporate regimes, totalitarian at times in their rhetoric, were far from being ideal but "in rendering to Caesar what was Caesar's," the church had made a deal with them and signed concordats. The church had failed to take account of the novel perversity of nazism and signed a concordat with Hitler, a stance bitterly regretted. In signing the concordat with Hitler, the Catholic church's judgment was blinded and hampered by its concern about the war, its concern for German Catholics, and a legitimate fear of communism. The church can certainly be blamed, after the war, for the relative silence it kept over certain Nazi crimes, notably the most terrifying of them all: the genocide of the Jews, the core evil of the Nazi doctrine, the one that should have affected the church the most, considering its Israelite origins. As often happens in politics, a seemingly insignificant mistake—in this case the concordat with Hitler—ended in disaster. The church in Europe emerged from the war morally weakened in contrast with its communist adversary, now more powerful than ever.

One can feel only admiration, therefore, for the politics of Pius XII. In that dangerous contingency, he firmly maintained the condemnation of communism, while accepting more sincerely than the church had ever done before the modern political regime and democracy. Inspired by him, distinguished Catholic statesmen like Gasperri, Adenauer, and Robert Schumann were able to create the peaceful and prosperous order in which Europe continues to thrive.

This recovery was very precarious, however. As a matter of fact, under the pressure of communism and the European intelligentsia, a few erroneous ideas took root in the church and were accepted as facts. One serious fallacy was an incorrect classification of twentieth century political systems. The Catholic church accepted the classification proposed by communist thinking: liberal capitalist systems; fascist capitalist systems (fascism, Francoism and nazism), and socialist systems (communism). A more accurate assessment of political systems would have been (1) liberal democratic systems, (2) authoritarian regimes (fascism, Francoism, etc.) and (3) totalitarian systems (nazism and communism).

The church also misjudged social systems. Instead of correctly classifying market economies and free societies as opposed to state dominated communist economies, the church accepted capitalism versus socialism. In other words, the church fell prey to Marxist-Leninist ideology. From this viewpoint all economic and social relations of the noncommunist world are subsumed under the concept of *capitalism*. The mode of production under communism was subsumed under the ideological definition of *socialism* (i.e., socialization of the means of production). The communist system, which crushes society under the ideological domination of the party, was perceived as the expression of a new type of society, the socialist society. In this way, Leninist socialism is not defined by what actually characterizes it—namely its political system—but by what, except in its false, ideological definition, does not characterize it: its social and economic relations.

The church accepted the idea of '*exploitation,*' that is the idea of a vicious 'structure' as being foundational to social exchanges. According to this paradigm, wealth comes from an unjust mechanism of economic distribution. Hence, '*exploitation*' governs socioeconomic relations within nations as well as among nations. Thus, the making of profit and the present wage distribution were automatically condemned. Exploitation was held totally responsible for the poverty of what was to be called the Third World.

All these ideas—and quite a few more—penetrated the Catholic Church by contagion with the surrounding Marxist milieu. They have perpetuated their own noxious life within the church and influenced ecclesiastical thinking almost in the very substance of faith itself. Let us limit ourselves to their impact on the political positions of the church.

In the social encyclicals of the nineteenth century, the magisterium consistently and symmetrically condemned liberalism as an economic doctrine and socialism. This symmetrical condemnation has shifted to apply to 'capitalism' and to 'socialism,' without much regard for the ideological and unreal nature of the concepts being contrasted. Capitalism is condemned as evil because it inherently contains a principle of injustice which works in favor of the rich at the expense of the poor. The injustice does not result from the sinful acts of the economic agents but from the very economic system itself. The magisterium thus speaks of 'unjust structures.' Socialism, on the other hand, is considered evil because it stifles personal initiative and freedom and notably because it is atheistic and abolishes religious freedom. However, the socialist system is credited with a striving toward justice and is not criticized intrinsically, in its very 'structure' but rather in its practice.

According to Cardinal Glemp, a communist government is not unqualified, in principle, to promote the common welfare of the country. All that is asked of it is that it respect individual rights—particularly religious freedom. To deem communism as capable of this is tantamount to saying that it is not 'intrinsically perverse,' as Pius XI and Pius XII asserted.

Communism was not condemned at the Second Vatican Council. The petition of more than 400 bishops to this effect was not examined or publicly discussed. It appears that a deal was struck between the Vatican and representatives of the Russian Orthodox church to block a condemnation of communism. In return, a delegation of the Moscow patriarchate would attend the Vatican Council as observers. From the time of that bargain in 1962, all reference to previous condemnations disappeared from the documents of the magisterium, and the word 'communism' itself was no longer mentioned.

Instead, allusion is made to 'ideologies' in the plural, thus suggesting a kind of vague and symmetrical diffusion of the phenomenon to avoid naming the only virulent and structured ideology, that of Marxist-Leninism. One also comes across the expression of the 'two materialisms': Western 'consumerism' was designated as 'practical,' and dialectical materialism was dubbed 'theoretical.' What we have here is a case of pure paralogism. Under the same concept of materialism are subsumed, on the one hand, the exaggerated desire for material goods which pervades the West and which would certainly exist in the East were these goods to be available, and on the other hand, the 'diamat' from which, as a doctrine, political power grows, and which must be considered as an absolute idealism. There is, between the 'two materialisms' the same relationship that exists between the barking dog and the constellation that bears its name.

Such a position gives rise to a dream of unity which is as utopian as the worldview that nourishes it is false. The primate Cardinal Wyszynski drew the attention of the Vatican Council to the irremediable dichotomy that ideological domination and what he called the "State of Diamat" introduced in humanity. In spite of his warning, the encyclical *Gaudium et Spes* displays in places the semi-Teilhardian vision of a world moving toward 'unification,' toward the 'standardization of customs,' the rise of humanism and 'progression of the sense of autonomy.'

The Second Vatican Council paralleled the emergence of one of the shallowest and most misleading terms of our time: the word *dialogue.* If 'dialogue' is the medium two individuals of good faith use to seek truth, well and good. But to fetishize the term, as happened, implies that dialogue must take place at all costs—even in cases where there is no common search for truth and where the only option left is fight, testimony and martyrdom. Christ did not dialogue with Pilate or the High Priest.

This persistence in the 'dialogical' imperative reveals also an erosion of the classic political principles to which the church has always had recourse. It also translates the humanitarian idea according to which—to quote an expression used by Cardinal Glemp—'life is the supreme value.' However, while measuring life as a precious gift, the Bible and the church have nevertheless taught that life can be sacrificed for higher goals like the salvation of the soul and confession of the true God. Furthermore, the church has always defended a just war, the civic struggle *pro aris et focis*, or simply to defend one's honor. This dialogic shift also betrays the Tolstoian notion that it is intrinsically wrong to have enemies and that the true Christian has friends only. In the Old Testament, the enemy is treated as an enemy. The New Testament urges that an enemy who remains an enemy should be treated like a friend—out of consideration for his human nature, and because God deals with his enemies in this manner. Tolstoyism refuses even to make the friend-foe distinction and places them together in the fold of universal goodness. This interpretation, mistakenly understood to be the sublime fulfillment of the gospel, means actually that the natural order is not realized but is destroyed by some pseudo-supernatural order. This convenes to a situation whereby the enemy is so formidable that he is in a position to veto his being identified as an enemy and described as such.

From this jumble of false ideas, dressed nonetheless in Christian garb, there emerges a condemnation of political action. Political action necessarily involves the choice of friends and enemies. This is followed by a struggle at the end of which either the enemy is rendered powerless or an agreement over mutual interests is reached, in which case the enemy ceases to be an enemy. But if one shrinks from political struggle, all that remains is to admit defeat. Or, if one has lost even the courage to admit defeat, one has to imagine that a settlement is still possible over mutual interests, even though one's adversary, by virtue of his ideology, refuses to grant that there can be commonality of interests between the section of humanity that is custodian of the promises of history and the part that is condemned by that same history. His ploy consists in deceiving the church by proffering false mutual interests—like peace and justice—as long as 'peace' and 'justice' mean the victory of communism.

If the church allows itself to be cornered on this terrain, if it shrinks from political struggle, it is left with the option of proffering an infra-political message. This is the social doctrine of the church, addressed primarily to the 'capitalist' world and complemented by the new doctrine of the rights of man addressed primarily to the 'socialist' world. The message is that the solution to the political problem is to be found in the pre-political relations that individuals forge ethically, and in social relations. The political battlefield is thus evacuated, abandoned to the enemy. It then becomes necessary to justify theologically such a capitulation. The church is driven toward the spiritualist temptation. Its own tradition provides it with numerous examples, the heretical character of which goes much farther than anything Savonarola or Luther could have said.

Laziness, pure and simple, equally supports this position. Unfortunately, ever since the French Revolution, the political decisions of the Catholic church have rarely been happy ones. Almost everywhere the church has lost its influence and political clout. Is it not tempting for it to voluntarily abandon a terrain from which, in spite of itself, it has been systematically ousted?

The accumulation of failures, the refusal to fight in places where it was most dangerous and most necessary, have created a political vacuum for the church. There is today an astonishing discrepancy between the precision and minutiae with which the magisterium handles the most delicate issues of sexual ethics and the vagueness in which the church leaves the faithful concerning the infinitely more general and fundamental questions touching the 'welfare of the city.' It was inevitable that this vacuum provoke a draught. In Latin America, where the communist experience was distant but injustices which fill daily life are immediate and violent, 'liberation theology emerged.' For an outside observer, the liberation theology boils down to a form of Marxism-Leninism which, instead of frankly and honestly eliminating Christian faith, recuperates and subordinates it. From the communist point of view, the liberation theology is a form of progress: it makes the ideological message more acceptable and more respectable to those that need to be converted. It is also a progress in falsehood. Solzhenitsyn has given to communism its true name: a lie. This lie perfects itself when, instead of openly attacking God, his people and his Messiah, it acts in their name and in their guise.

For having lacked discernment in dealing with Caesar, the church—or at least some of its representatives—lost sight of what Caesar really was. The church did not immediately realize that it was no longer dealing with Caesar but with something much worse of which it had no experience. Perhaps what led to this confusion is the fact that the church, in the course of the nineteenth century, developed the habit of undue moaning over its fate by blackening Caesar. Perhaps it came to believe that nazism and communism only served to confirm its pessimistic diagnosis. At the same time, it hoped that they were not going to prove worse than the state powers that have abused it in the past.

This misunderstanding had the consequence, however, of paralyzing the church and forcing it into a dishonorable silence. The crimes perpetrated by its silence were of unprecedented magnitude in human history. Furthermore, this misunderstanding disrupted the classic political sense of the church and prevented it from rendering to Caesar what is Caesar's, wherever Caesar remained Caesar. Hence these inopportune attacks on property, legitimate profit, the right to self-defense, and to a just war, areas in which the church could sometimes allow itself to move into the noncommunist world under the political and intellectual pressures of the communist world.

But how to call that which is no longer Caesar? It would appear that the recent development—first in Nicaragua and later the whole of the communist world, including Poland and the USSR—consists in capturing religious energies and in subverting faith to serve communist ideological regimes. This has served to push the church closer to its primitive experience and to the apocalyptic literature in which it translated this experience. In the course of the three centuries of its persecution, the church prayed for Caesar and denounced the antichrist. When it became clear that Caesar was no longer, but had wasted himself in a purely antichristian undertaking, there was nothing left but struggle and testimony. The truly prophetic act, as opposed to the pseudo-prophetic theology of liberation, is the courageous and wise act of calling the adversary an adversary. But this act, which we all await, must be preceded by a conversion of the intellect.

Indeed the disease that gnaws at the church is not the dissolution of morals nor the chilling of charity, but that of intellectual paralysis. Faced with the sheer magnitude of the rethinking to be undertaken, in the presence of the enormity of the dangers which would surface if the church confronted the situation as it actually is, it has often taken refuge in a form of intellectual abdication. For disinterested piety and all other virtues are inauthentic if they only serve as an escape from the task of intelligent discourse. The discourse on love is a mockery if it is not accompanied by a discourse on truth.

What twentieth century ideology (communism and nazism) threatens, first of all, is the order of nature: material nature as manifested in the physical bodies that have been mangled and destroyed; and spiritual nature in the falsification and perversion of reason and morality. Such is the character of the main attack. If it is equally effective against religion, it is because, in the final analysis, religion is a bulwark of nature.

In the critique of the national order, one must in no way make common cause with ideology. If one does so, one is caught between natural order and the unnatural order fabricated by ideology. Such a symmetrical opposition to both orders leads to utopianism. As for the natural order, the traditional indictment of its imperfection will be perverted by a radical ideological criticism aimed at destroying this natural order and replacing it by a new one. So far as the world of ideology is concerned, the contradiction between sordid reality and sublime goals will be exposed. In other words, according to the order of nature, a noble intent will be attributed to the ideological program but, if it is hostile to religion, then, according to the order of grace, it will be taxed with deficiency. As soon as it appropriates to itself a religious character, however, as in the case of the liberation theology, this last objection disappears. In effect one would then sanction the abolition of nature and eliminate as a consequence all possibility of grace.

If indeed this is the principal target of ideology, one can immediately see who are the allies of the church. It does not have any more unreliable ones than those, be they Christians, who aspire to moral sublimity and to disinterested spiritualism. And it has no surer allies than those who, be they agnostic, love the creation and love truth for its own sake.

NINE

RELIGION AND AMERICAN DEMOCRACY

A. James Reichley

Religion has always played a powerful and profound role in American politics. This is true both in the sense that churches and other religious groups have, at least on certain issues, substantially influenced public policy, and in the sense that religious belief has been a major source of the values, social attitudes, and moral assumptions on which American democracy is based.

At the policy formation level, the role of religious interest groups, measured in terms of direct participation, has never been more active than it is today. Offices on or near Capitol Hill in Washington representing the mainline Protestant denominations (Methodists, Presbyterians, Lutherans, Episcopalians, the United Church of Christ, and some smaller denominations) campaign vigorously for a wide variety of causes, ranging from abandonment of nuclear deterrence to saving the family farm. The Roman Catholic Church, the nation's largest single denomination, after long maintaining a low profile in national politics, has plunged into forceful involvement, first to secure enactment of a constitutional amendment to prohibit abortion, and more recently on a range of economic, foreign policy, and military issues. The Black Protestant churches, many of which formed originally as a result of racial discrimination in their parent denominations, continue to provide political leadership on civil rights and social justice issues. They increasingly take stands on other domestic and foreign policy concerns. Jewish social agencies, most of which are not tied directly to denominational bodies but which take moral direction from Jewish religious tradition, lobby in Washington and mobilize public opinion among their national constituencies with political skill and organizational efficiency as yet unmatched by other religious interest groups. White evangelical Protestants—nearly one-fifth of the total national population—have long been the 'sleeping giant of American politics.' They now have switched from traditional political passivity to sometimes clamorous activity, even to the extent of providing the base for a political 'movement' aimed at gaining control of the Republican party and ultimately the national government. Political involvements by other significant religious groups, including the Mormons, the Orthodox churches, and various Islamic bodies, have been more selective but generally are rising.

Perhaps all these signs of direct political participation by religious interest groups are to some degree misleading. It may be that as the religious groups increasingly go public in their political activities, they lose some of the access they, or their leaders, formerly enjoyed through the back corridors of political power. Such a change may well serve the overall health of democracy, and enhance the social integrity of the religious interest groups. But in terms of concrete results, increased political activity may be accompanied by actual decline in effective influence. (Or the decline may have come first, and been one of the spurs to increase in direct political action.) At the value-generating and nurturing level, there is less ambiguity: the role of religion has almost surely diminished. Americans remain by all measurable criteria (testimony to belief in God, church attendance, financial support of churches, and so forth) an unusually religious people among economically developed nations. More than ninety percent of Americans tell pollsters they identify with a particular religious faith, more than eighty percent say they believe in the divinity of Jesus, and about forty percent are found in church on any given Sunday morning—far higher figures than in any European country except Ireland or Poland. Private financial support of religion in the United States is also relatively high—though comparison is less meaningful because most other developed countries, including many in which few people go to church, still give public subsidies to established or otherwise qualifying denominations. "We are a religious people," Justice William Douglas wrote and repeated in Supreme Court decisions in the 1950s and 1960s on church-state issues, and by measurable standards of belief and behavior apparently it is still so.[1]

Yet few would contend that religion plays the role in the moral and cultural lives of Americans today that it did around the turn of the twentieth century, or even fifty years ago. Other transmitters of values, not necessarily hostile to religion, but often ostentatiously 'free' of its influence, or taking pains to avoid recognition of its existence, pound at individual consciousness. These secular value sources include: various segments of the news, advertising, and entertainment industries, particularly those centered on television, to which the average American now devotes almost as much time as to work or sleep; largely secularized public education; some forms of psychological therapy and government sponsored social planning; and the trickle down influence of an intelligentsia whose members, though usually without clear value structures of their own, predominantly reject transcendent purpose as a plausible existential principle. Religion probably creeps back in through some of these. But its role in most of them is small and probably dwindling. Americans today, therefore, are strongly influenced by secular value purveyors whose dominant personnel assume that religion is probably unnecessary, possibly socially harmful (because it foments bigotry and social division), and in any case, unbelievable.

Rising political activity among religious interest groups and decline in the influence of religion on the formation of public values are distinct but to some degree related developments. I will first consider the changing political participation by the churches. (In this essay, churches will be used as a generic term to signify all religious interest groups unless otherwise specified.)

FAITHS OF THE FOUNDERS

The United States, from the beginning, was pluralist in religion. Though Calvinist influence, conveyed by Congregationalists (Puritans), Presbyterians, and German and Dutch Reformed, was strong among the Founders, there were always competing tendencies and sects. These included: evangelical Baptists, particularly in

New England and along the western frontier; Quakers in Pennsylvania and Delaware; Lutherans, at first mainly in Pennsylvania; the resurgent liturgical tradition in the Anglican (later Episcopalian) Church; German pietist sects, like the Amish and the Brethren in Pennsylvania, and in the Shenandoah Valley of Virginia; the evangelical revival that in 1784 blossomed into American Methodism; Catholics, at first few in number, but a growing presence in New York, Maryland, and Pennsylvania; and a handful of Jews in places like Charleston, Newport, and New York City. An additional contributor to pluralism at the time of the Revolution was the influence of the European Enlightenment. A complex intellectual and social phenomenon, the Enlightenment in general rejected all revealed religion, or at least religion within the framework of orthodox Christianity, and substituted in its place reliance on human reason and belief in humanity's natural goodness.

Partly because of this fact of pluralism, the American founders determined that there should be no established religion for the nation as a whole—a very unusual undertaking for that time, or in fact for any previous time, anywhere in the world. It must quickly be added that the founders did not believe that the nation they were forming could get along without religion. Even those among them who were skeptical in their personal religious views, like Thomas Jefferson and Benjamin Franklin, were convinced that republican government rests on moral foundations that for most people must come from religion—by which they pretty much meant Christianity. They thought so much of religion that in the First Amendment to the Constitution they specifically guaranteed its free exercise—not simply as a general civil right, like privacy or travel, but as a faculty essential to the functioning of a republic, like free speech and a free press, also protected by the First Amendment. But the national government, they believed, partly because of existing pluralism and partly reflecting their observation of the corrupting effect of government on established churches in Europe, should play no part in sponsoring or financing or compelling adherence to any particular religion or to religion in general. They therefore balanced the free exercise clause of the First Amendment with an establishment clause—or more correctly, a no-establishment clause—prohibiting

Congress from making any "law regarding an establishment of religion."[2]

The First Amendment, like the rest of the Bill of Rights, applied when it was enacted only to the federal government. It contained nothing to prevent the states from maintaining established churches, and several among them in fact did so well into the nineteenth century. Gradually, established churches even at the state level were recognized to be contrary to the American public philosophy. The last of the state establishments, in Massachusetts, was disbanded in 1833. In the 1920s the Supreme Court began finding parts of the Bill of Rights in the Fourteenth Amendment, enacted at the end of the Civil War to prevent the states from discriminating against Blacks. In 1940 the Court at last extended the establishment clause to the states—causing social and judicial complications that are with us still.[3]

There was certainly nothing in the First Amendment to prevent the churches, or church officers, or clergy, from being politically active. Jefferson, who distrusted the clergy (partly because of his experience with the reactionary Catholic hierarchy in France while he was American ambassador in the 1780s), for a time favored a law to prohibit election of ministers or priests to public office. He was talked out of the idea by James Madison, who persuaded him it would infringe civil liberties. Some states passed laws against clergy holding elective office until such prohibitions were declared unconstitutional, on free exercise grounds, by the Supreme Court. Public opinion polls show that many Americans still believe that members of the clergy should not run for office. Despite this prejudice, or tradition, some churches and church leaders were deeply involved in politics, both openly and behind the scenes, from the earliest days of the republic.

CHURCHES AND POLITICAL ACTION

Among what Martin Marty has called the colonial 'Big Three'—Congregationalists, Presbyterians, and Anglicans—were included about three-fourths of the colonial population. The first two, expressing variants of Calvinism, were militant supporters of the Revolution. James Otis spoke of the Congregationalist clergy as his 'Black Regiment,' and Presbyterian clerics in western Pennsylvania urged loyalty to 'No King but King Jesus.' The Anglican clergy, on the other hand, were mainly Tory, and the Anglican Church in consequence, though it included George Washington and James Madison among its members, suffered a loss of following in the general public from which it never recovered. (The successor Episcopalian Church, however, has always had a disproportionate share among the political as well as financial elite—including President George Bush.)[4]

After enactment of the Constitution, Congregationalist and Episcopalian clergy were for the most part ardent Federalists—warning their parishioners against the evil effects to be expected from the political success of the supposed atheist, Jefferson. Presbyterians split between Federalists and Jeffersonian Republicans, while the more evangelical Baptists and Methodists were moved by anti-establishment and equalitarian sentiments to give strong backing to the Republicans (later to Democrats). When the slavery issue heated up in the 1840s and 1850s, many clergy in the north enlisted in the cause of abolition, even to the extent of advocating armed insurrection. During the Civil War, clergy were fiercely active on both sides.

In the final third of the nineteenth century, Protestant clergy in the north helped maintain Protestantism as the mass base of the Republican Party, supplementing the plea of Republican orators to 'vote the way you shot,' with appeals to 'vote the way we pray'. The Catholic Church, meanwhile, became a guiding presence within the Democratic Party in many big cities and industrial states, though usually playing little role in national politics. With the advent of the Social Gospel movement in mainline Protestantism around the turn of the century, an articulate minority of Protestant clergy became active on a wide spectrum of social reform issues, including prohibition of alcohol, woman's suffrage, overthrow of corrupt political machines, regulation of industry, and support for labor unions. Some of the Social Gospelers went the full distance to socialism, but most found outlet for their ideals through participation in the Progressive movement, which spared them from promoting revolution or even from collaborating with Democrats. On the issue of prohibition, Social Gospel Protestants were joined by more socially conservative Methodists and Baptists, forming a coalition that achieved enactment of the Eighteenth Amendment in 1919. During the New Deal period of the 1930s, economic reform received some support from both Protestant and Catholic clergy, as well as Jewish welfare agencies. Conservative evangelicals, discouraged by the failure of prohibition, became politically passive.

World War II brought increased involvement in Washington by most denominations, pitching in to help win the war—or, in the cases of pacifist churches like the Quakers and the Brethren, representing the interests of conscientious objectors among their members. After the war, many denominations built on these efforts to establish permanent Washington offices, at first to observe, and then actively to lobby (though most church representatives continue to avoid identification with the term—partly because of fear of upsetting the churches' tax exemptions). The creation of Israel in 1947 led Jewish agencies to step up already substantial political involvement. In the 1960s, Protestant, Catholic, and Jewish groups in Washington formed effective coalitions, first to support enactment of civil rights legislation (which Lyndon Johnson said could not have been passed without the help of the churches), and then to protest against the Vietnam War.

In the 1970s some of the religious groups active in politics encountered internal turbulence. Mainline Protestant denominations broadened their lobbying to cover so many causes that their agendas took on the look of platforms of national political parties. Conservatives and moderates within these denominations responded with alarm, and several internal reform groups were organized. The coalition of religious interest groups in Washington was hit by some divisive issues. The Supreme Court's decision declaring a constitutional right to abortion in 1973 stirred the nation's Catholic hierarchy to an unprecedented level of political activity. The issue placed strains on the relationship between the United States Catholic Conference and liberal Protestant and Jewish groups, some of which also had moral misgivings about abortion but were unwilling to join the bishops in advocating national prohibition. Growing criticism of Israel and support for the Palestinian cause among Protestant groups produced angry reaction from Jewish agencies.

The conservative evangelical churches, aroused from political passivity by perceived national moral decay, organized in groups like the Moral Majority that contested with liberal groups on almost every issue. Heavy involvement by religious interest groups on both sides in the presidential campaigns of 1980 and 1984 made the role of the churches in politics itself a highly visible public issue.

Each of the constellations of religious interest groups now faces particular sets of problems, as well as common problems relating to separation of church and state. Other essays in this books will deal at length with situations within particular groups. I will examine each major group briefly, concentrating on how the situation within the group affects the more general influence of religion on democratic society.

GROUPS THAT REMAIN COHESIVE

Among the major groups, the two that are now most internally cohesive on the group's political role are the Black churches and the Jewish agencies. Internal rivalries and differences over strategy and emphasis exist within both these groups. But most of their members continue at least to agree on a need for vigorous political representation of their group by institutionalized religion (or for the Jews, by institutions whose identity is rooted in religious tradition). Both continue predominantly on the liberal side of the political spectrum, specifically as parts of the Democratic coalition that was formed during the New Deal period.

These generalizations being made, it is worth noting that forces for change are at work among both Black churches and Jewish agencies. The political leadership of the Black community no longer comes almost entirely from the churches, as it did between the Civil War and the 1970s—although many Black political leaders, including Jesse Jackson, William Grey, and Andrew Young, are still drawn from the ministry. Many within the Black leadership, though more among the church leadership than among the newer secular political leadership, are increasingly restive over their community's almost monolithic loyalty to the Democratic party. Some Black leaders, including at times Jesse Jackson, speak of the option of forming a third party that could at least hold the balance of power in close elections. It is possible to imagine the political role of the churches at some point becoming a contentious issue in the Black community, and to foresee the possibility of substantial political division of Blacks among Democrats, adherents of a new third party, and even some Republicans. But neither of these possibilities is currently very active.

Political division within the Jewish community is more advanced. Some Jews have recently been critical of the current political leadership of Israel, and have moved a slight distance toward healing the rift that had developed over Middle Eastern policy between liberal Jews and liberals taking up the cause of the Palestinians. A larger contingent of Jews continues to be attracted, partly by concern for Israel, and partly by general belief in social order and moral rigor, toward political conservatism. The intellectual 'neoconservatives' who made a large contribution to the ideological foundations of the Reagan administration, and still exert some influence in the Bush administration, are for the most part Jewish. As a Jewish leader pointed out to me, declining belief among Jews in the moral and ideological superiority of liberalism, or socialism, opens the way for economic self-interest to pull some of them toward conservatism.[5]

And yet most Jews still hesitate to give up longstanding ties to liberalism and the Democratic Party. About two-thirds of Jewish voters supported Walter Mondale for president in 1984, and three-fourths backed Michael Dukakis (whose wife is of Jewish descent) in 1988. This is partly because Jews simply feel more comfortable with the Democrats. As a lobbyist for Jewish causes said, "Republican White Houses do not look Jewish." Beyond that, many Jews are convinced that the Republicans, whatever they may say for political purposes, in their hearts feel no special affection for Israel. The angry Jewish reaction to Secretary of State James Baker's speech on Middle Eastern policy to a pro-Israel interest group in the spring of 1989 was caused as much by the frostiness of Baker's manner as by the substance of what he said. Most of all, Jews are concerned by the presence of the so-called Religious New Right in the current Republican coalition. Many Jews would now feel at home in a moderately conservative political alignment, but most are not comfortable in a coalition that depends heavily on support from Christian fundamentalists.

MIXED SIGNALS FOR CATHOLICS

The situations within the other three major constellations of religious groups in the United States—Catholics, mainline Protestants, and evangelical Protestants—are more complex. Many leaders within the American Catholic hierarchy felt bruised and troubled by their experiences in the 1980 and 1984 presidential campaigns, particularly the latter. In 1988 the church moved back toward its more traditional low political profile. Catholic laity in 1988 divided about evenly between Bush and Dukakis after going for Reagan by small majorities in 1980 and 1984. In the last few congressional elections, Catholics have voted about 55 percent Democratic to 45 percent Republican—much lower Democratic margins than existed any time in American history before 1980. Catholics remain heavily Democratic in party identification, though by steadily declining margins.[6]

The international Catholic Church has usually been a bastion of moral conservatism, but the church in the United States has always espoused social and economic equalitarianism. Before the 1970s, the Democratic Party easily accommodated both these tendencies. Most Catholics over thirty, including most of the bishops, grew up in homes in which to be a good Catholic was to be a good Democrat. Since the early 1970s, however, sharp differences between traditional Catholic morality and the Democratic Party's liberal positions on issues of sexual and family morality (particularly the abortion issue but others as well), have weakened if not broken this tie.

Further complications were introduced in the 1980s when the bishops took distinctly liberal stands on economic, foreign policy, and military issues. Bishops identified as social conservatives testified before congressional committees in favor of liberal positions in other areas, such as nuclear disarmament and choice of weapons systems.

In 1984, some of the most visible Catholic cardinals and archbishops, including Krol in Philadelphia, O'Connor in New York, and Law in Boston, gave clear indications that in their view, abortion was the issue on which Catholics should vote, and that the Republicans were much closer to the Catholic position on this issue than the Democrats. No such signals were conveyed in 1988.

The Catholic Church in the United States seems still to be groping to find an appropriate and morally responsible social role in a democratic society in which it is an important but not dominant institution. The church clearly feels that it must accept more responsibility for the general conduct of American government than it did in the days when it represented a heavily outnumbered minority facing a barely tolerant Protestant majority—an 'immigrant church,' as Catholic commentators put it. But it is still guided by social prudence, and at least since the Second Vatican Council in the early 1960s, by ethical principle as well, to proceed with tact and respect for other moral voices.

The social role of Catholicism is made even more complex by the resurgence of moral and theological conservatism in the Vatican, and the resulting placement of theological conservatives in many places of authority within the American hierarchy. As yet this theological swing has not seemed to move the hierarchy toward political conservatism. But there is probably an inherent tendency for a hierarchical church, which Catholicism remains despite changes produced by Vatican II, to feel some natural affinity for politicians and political groups promoting social order and moral restraint—in other words, conservatives. On the other side, political conservatism in the United States has been associated with advocacy of market capitalism, traditionally viewed by the Vatican as a by-product of Protestantism and tainted by excessive individualism.[7]

THE DIVIDED HOUSE OF MAINLINE PROTESTANTISM

Mainline Protestantism, which through most of American history was the nation's semi-established faith, is currently even more at sea than Catholicism in searching for a morally viable social role. Since the 1960s representatives of the mainline denominations in Washington have positioned themselves at the extreme left of the political mainstream—and sometimes have seemed to move outside the mainstream altogether. During the Reagan presidency, mainline church offices reliably opposed administration policy on practically every issue: economic, social, foreign policy, and military. Mainline laities, in contrast, have remained for the most part at least moderately conservative and Republican. Large majorities of mainline church members voted for Reagan in 1980 and 1984, and for Bush in 1988.[8]

Mainline lobbyists are generally rated by political practitioners on Capitol Hill as less effective than those from Jewish or Catholic agencies—though more effective than the more recently arrived lobbyists for evangelical Protestant groups. The political skill of the mainline representatives, however, has been rising. They were generally credited with playing an important part in cutting off aid to the Nicaraguan contras during the final years of the Reagan administration—in part because on this issue they were perceived to have the support of a majority of their constituents.

Division between mainline denominational bureaucracies and laity on political orientation has been accompanied by steady and precipitous decline in church membership, recently accompanied by financial crises in several mainline denominations and agencies. The erosion of mainline membership has been widely studied by sociologists. Most of these studies have found little direct relationship between loss of membership and discontent among laities with the political activities of their denominations. Most church members, indeed, have until recently been hardly aware of the political stands being taken by their denominations at the national level, except in a few highly publicized instances. Political division, however, can hardly have helped the internal cohesion of the churches, and conservative opposition groups formed in some denominations are now making it more difficult for local church members to ignore the political activities carried on in their name. Probably the chief effect of liberal politicization of mainline denominations on member loyalty and enthusiasm remains that pointed out years ago by Dean Kelley—preoccupation with political and social issues has distracted some churches from the functions which are what most people chiefly seek from religion: discovery of meaning in existence and direct experience of God's grace and love.[9]

Mainline leaders and clergy who are convinced that political action is the principal means through which the church is currently called to carry out God's purpose, but who are not supported on the form or direction of this action by a majority of their members, certainly face a moral dilemma. Some have responded by welcoming further shrinkage of membership to a hard core who share the leadership's sense of political mission. Others are seeking to find in traditional Protestant theology— Calvinist, Lutheran, Anglican, and Wesleyan—roots for church revival that will enable mainline denominations to speak, not with unanimity, but with reasonable unity for a shared and Biblically founded moral point of view. There is no more important question for the future of American democratic society than the outcome of the search and debate now going on within the mainline denominations, which taken together still form the largest cultural group in the United States.

SECOND THOUGHTS AMONG EVANGELICALS

While the mainline Protestant denominations have been losing members and impact, their evangelical cousins have achieved spectacular growth. Though the social conservatism of most evangelical churches may have contributed to this advance, its most important source has been that the evangelicals have been doing relatively well at meeting Dean Kelley's tests of offering meaning and experience.

During the late 1970s, some evangelical leaders, particularly highly visible television preachers like Jerry Falwell and Pat Robertson, broke with the evangelicals' traditional rejection of church involvement in politics, which was based in part on a theological conviction that civil life is inherently corrupt and corrupting. The new breed of evangelists sought in the 1980s with remarkable success to lead their flocks to increased political involvement. With more activity has come a major shift in political direction. In the past, evangelicals participated in politics mainly through voting. They predominantly supported the Democratic party. During the 1980s this orientation has changed dramatically, producing eighty percent majorities among White evangelicals for Reagan in 1984 and Bush in 1988, and high levels of support for Republican congressional candidates. (Many Blacks are evangelical in religious practice and belief, but have followed a quite different political route.) The switch in political allegiance of the White evangelicals has probably been the single most important cause of the conservative trend of national politics during the 1980s.[10]

The apparent growth of the evangelicals' political clout persuaded Pat Robertson that in 1988 he could build on the base of the religious right to capture the Republican nomination for president and catapult himself into the White House. Robertson's failure was even more spectacular than the preceding political rise of the evangelicals. In not a single 1988 state primary did Robertson win more votes than George Bush, even among evangelicals.[11]

Robertson's defeat was accompanied by bad publicity generated for the evangelical movement by the escapades of other purveyors of television piety like Jim Bakker and Jimmy Swaggart. His defeat caused a rethinking of the political role among evangelicals as severe as the crisis faced by Catholics and mainline Protestants. Some evangelical leaders, such as Bob Jones, never wavered from the view that the church should stay clear of politics. These are now receiving a more receptive hearing. Other evangelicals, including some who were active in the Robertson campaign, persevere in the crusade to remake American society in the evangelicals' image. Still others seem to be groping toward a political role for evangelicals as part of a conservative coalition that they will influence but not dominate.

Evangelicals seem unlikely to return in large numbers to their former political passivity. Many of them have come to enjoy the social power and the attention of national leaders, received as a result of their political involvement. Evangelicals still have an unfinished social agenda they are determined to carry out— through federal judicial appointments from a friendly national administration if not through legislation. Whether they will be able to maintain the political unity they achieved in some elections in the 1980s is quite another question. Evangelicals in internal church matters have tended through their history to fracture, in part because their kind of religion has been built to a great extent around charismatic preachers (in the non-theological sense) with powerful egos. Particularly when their own leaders are directly involved, they seem to show a similar disposition in politics.

THE VALUE-NURTURING ROLE

Religious interest groups—past and present—played important roles in promoting particular causes in American politics. But the most important social and political role the churches performed, in my judgment, is the one often referred to by America's Founders: nurturing the moral values and assumptions on which American democracy is based.

Of course, there have been other sources for democratic values, notably the humanistic world view that was conceived by the Enlightenment. But humanism divorced from religion has never provided a convincing explanation within the limits of its own value system why the individual should over the long term give much weight against personal ends to the ends of unrelated others, or the needs of society as a whole. Some humanists have argued that human beings are natural altruists, whose instinctive benevolence is twisted and corrupted by the deprivations inflicted by class-structured society (or, in another version, by scarcity in nature before the advent of achievable affluence). But this claim has never been plausible to many, and is disputed by the persistence of evil in even the most materially affluent social settings.

Without moral principles of caring and sharing, democracy in the past has tended to fly apart into dog-eat-dog atomism, often followed by authoritarian reaction. Collectivists, including (but not limited to) Marxists, have dealt with this problem through the supposed revelation that the meaningful focus of human value is not the individual but the social whole, 'species being' as Marx termed it. This analysis is at least internally consistent, but it leads to a political end that is not democracy, but some form of authoritarianism, under which the welfare, or indeed the survival, of the individual is entirely secondary to the interest of the social collective. The practical results of this conclusion are now seen in the economic failure and governmental brutality of societies organized on collectivist principles in many parts of the world.[12]

Democracy requires a world view assigning fundamental value to both the individual human life and the society to which the individual belongs. The American founders believed, and social philosophers from Toqueville to Walter Berns and Robert Bellah have agreed, that religion is the only reliable source from which such a world view can come.

Some commentators argue that the experiences of some industrial democracies since World War II indicate that religion is not so necessary to democratic values. Religion seems to have declined sharply in most of the countries of western Europe. The same seems to be true in Japan. Yet democracy has functioned and has appeared to take hold in most of these countries. Have these developed democracies found a moral substitute for religion? It is too soon to tell. The residual moral effect of religion remains strong in most of them. If the influence of religion continues to recede, it seems quite possible that atomistic individualism, already on the rise, will sap their social vitality and cohesion. Also, democracy in many of these countries is, after all, not very old. Vulnerability to resurgence of new or old forms of authoritarianism is far from eliminated in some of them.

Nothing in contemporary experience has shown that the founding fathers were wrong in believing that democracy and republican government depend on moral values rooted in religion. But can religion continue to play this role?

THE EFFECTS OF POLITICAL ACTION

In the United States, increased direct political involvement by many of the churches has in some ways made it more difficult for them to perform their value-nurturing functions. Many Americans worry that an aggressive role by the churches in politics threatens religious freedom and social pluralism. Political disillusion within denominations inevitably undermines moral cohesion. The churches, moreover, are unlikely to possess expert competence in fields with major relevance to governmental problems, such as economics, international politics, or military strategy. If churches are shown to be wrong on substantive issues of economics or diplomacy, or mistaken in their predictions of behavior by foreign regimes, they risk loss of credibility on larger questions of social and moral value. Even on issues on which determination of who is right or wrong seems almost infinitely debatable, churches that act as party-line propagandists or political agents for a secular ideology tend to lose moral stature, sometimes even among those who support the ideology.

This is not to say that American churches should wholly abstain from political or social involvement. Memory of the temporizing responses of most of the German churches to the rise of nazism in the 1930s is too fresh for that. Even apart from clear threats to freedom and human decency, the churches have important roles to play in offering counsel on social and political issues in which moral questions are paramount or crucial. Civil rights issues are often of this kind. The abortion issue, which turns primarily on complex moral questions, is another example. The issue of nuclear arms, surely the most important political problem of our time, involves many highly technical scientific, diplomatic, and military components, but also turns on central moral determinations on which the churches are natural sources of counsel. Even economic issues, though often to a great extent pragmatic, involve basic moral judgments, such as the questions of how much social and economic inequality a democratic society should countenance, and where trade-offs should come between economic efficiency and social compassion.

The churches should have something to say on the moral aspects of these issues, but they usually undercut their effectiveness if they become involved in prescribing detailed political enactments. The differing public reactions to the letter of the Catholic bishops on nuclear disarmament issued in 1983, and to the bishops' subsequent letter in 1985 on economic policy, provide cases in point. The nuclear arms letter attracted certainly not uniform agreement, but high degrees of attention and respect. Though the bishops did not shrink from questions of application, they devoted themselves mainly to the extent to which the United States is morally justified in utilizing its capacity in nuclear weapons to deter war or to prevent intimidation by hostile military force. They spoke on matters on which most Catholics, and many non-Catholics, regarded them as specially authoritative and competent. In contrast, the letter on economic policy, while including some general moral directives, was substantially occupied with recommending particular policies. These policies often involved issues hotly debated among economists and within the political arena. Most people did not believe the bishops had any special expertise in solving these economic dilemmas. Hence, the letter had little impact on the general public and the political community.[13]

PROBLEMS OF PLURALISM

American pluralism poses more general problems beyond the obstacles to the churches' value-nurturing role caused by their current political activities. Can a nation that maintains no established church, and that regards religious pluralism as both socially inescapable and ethically desirable, confidently look to religion to generate and nurture its fundamental moral values? When the American Founders spoke of the nurturing function of religion, they thought primarily of Christianity—more specifically, Protestant Christianity (indeed, for some, specifically Protestant Christianity with a distinctly Calvinist flavor). In the second half of the twentieth century most of the public, as well as most commentators, regarded the religious basis of American social values as including virtually all forms of the entire 'Judeo-Christian tradition.' During the 1980s, there was growing immigration from countries in the Middle East and Asia. Most of these people follow faiths other than Christianity or Judaism. The 1980s also saw an inclination among some earlier inhabitants, including Native Americans, to return to or maintain other faiths. This created the awareness that even Judeo-Christianity does not embrace the full panoply of religions in the United States. In addition, a small but significant and gradually increasing share of Americans follow no religious faith whatever.

Most forms of Christianity and Judaism now practiced in the United States include among their doctrines theological and social concepts that give moral support to democracy. Among these concepts are the belief that God has endowed each human life with unique value; the belief that human beings have a social as well as personal responsibility to help fulfill God's purpose for the created universe; and the conviction that the realms of church and state are distinct, though not mutually exclusive. It is not so clear that all these concepts are held, or at least emphasized, by other forms of religion, and the first two of course have no standing whatever with persons who reject all religion. Even Islam, which like Christianity comes from a common Judaic root, seems to have little concept of distinction between the authorities of church and state. As a result, the value of religious freedom, a crucial support of modern democracy, does not appear to receive much reinforcement from Islamic tradition. (Some forms of Christianity and Judaism at other times and places, of course, have done no better.) In many Eastern and Native American religions, there does not seem to be much, if any, concept of a creator God endowing each human life with unique value. Many of these religions move in the other direction, submerging individuals in underlying cycles of existence or undifferentiated being—sometimes achieving profound spiritual or moral insights, but tending to undermine the significance of political freedom or the possibility of social progress. Totally materialist views of existence must find what support they can for democracy in the interplay of instinct and reason.

Some modern commentators, notably Robert Bellah, have sought escape from the problems created by religious pluralism by turning to Rousseau's idea of a civil religion. Advocates of civil religion claim that broad and vaguely stated religious concepts can, without acknowledging any particular religious faith, give a kind of transcendent reinforcement to values that are deemed useful to society. It is worth noting that Rousseau's formulation was meant to serve a political theory that was more collectivist and authoritarian than democratic. Apart from that, civil religion places the welfare of the state at the heart of human values, and is therefore easily manipulable by those holding political power. This was exemplified in ancient Rome where religion was turned into a device to maintain civic loyalty among the masses. In actual fact, civil religion, distinct from patriotism, has never played much role in American life. American politicians have drawn (and sometimes overdrawn) on religion to legitimatize their purposes. But the religion they invoke comes from sources outside American history or civil experience, and derives its force from these external origins.[14]

I cannot say that I see a simple solution to the problems posed by pluralism for maintenance of common democratic values. Perhaps all of the so-called higher religions, at least, provide support for a common body of ethical beliefs on which democracy can indiscriminately draw for social values, but the evidence on this is far from clear. The truth is, I think, that democratic values, at least historically, have rested largely on a Judeo-Christian foundation. Once the system of social values has been created, it may acquire a life of its own, to some degree enriched through contact with other sources. But if the Judeo-Christian roots were destroyed, the superstructure of democratic values could probably not persist for long. If this is true, the political system is to some extent dependent on a religious tradition, or traditions, not shared by all Americans.

COMPETING VALUE SOURCES

This circumstance in itself should not be particularly troublesome, so long as mutual respect and civility are maintained by persons within and outside the core traditions. But can we be sure the traditions of Judeo-Christianity will compete successfully in the future? Will the cacophony of values rising from secular sources— commercial advertising and entertainment, secularized schools, psychological therapy, public and private bureaucracies, the secular intelligentsia, etc.—dilute religion to impotence?

The importance of this question is to some extent eased by the fact that most of the major secular value sources (for now) at least endorse many of the values that also stem from Judeo-Christian sources: individual rights (with some disagreement about how these are defined), peace among nations, respect for positive law legitimately created, social fairness, and responsibility to help people in need.

There are, however, some discordant and potentially destructive notes. Some secular value sources in the United States, as in other western democracies, increasingly promote self-gratification as the primary human imperative. This is often presented as personal fulfillment, 'doing one's own thing,' career success, or single-minded pursuit and consumption of material things ('because I'm worth it,' as the television advertisements say). There has always been a place for self-fulfillment in the value systems of Christianity and Judaism, but if promoted to the exclusion of responsibility to others, to society, or to a higher level of judgment, it can be anticipated to lead very quickly to social chaos and 'the war of each against all.'

Other secular value sources—conveyed by public and private bureaucracies and uncritical application of quantitative research techniques—move in the opposite direction. These threaten to reduce the individual to identification with undifferentiated social masses. These sources foster such qualities as conformity, passivity, and individual and social inertia. Either of the above mentioned extremes (which unfortunately seem to aggravate each other rather than to provide offsetting effects), is potentially disastrous for democracy—indeed, for any kind of decent human existence.

A final harmful tendency of many of the secular value sources (many of which have positive effects as well) is to promote actual exclusion of religion as an available source of alternative values. The public stance of most promulgators of secular values in western democracies is to be tolerant of religion, even abstractly supportive of its practice. But they are bound to find that some of the values nurtured by Christianity and Judaism threaten their own value schemes—distracting individuals from unrelenting pursuit of self-gratification, or, against the other face of secularism, challenging imposition of social regimentation. Although religion is regarded with private hostility in some of the current power centers of American society, there is no evidence of any kind of secular conspiracy to suppress religious practice of belief. Religion, rather, is treated as an inconvenience, an uncomfortable presence to be ignored, or, even more damagingly, to be denatured into a facsimile of one or another form of secularism.

How is religion to respond? Not, I would suggest, with stridency. Efforts by religious interest groups to impose themselves on the public consciousness through raw exercise of political power would certainly, and justifiably, excite apprehension over revival of the authoritarian tendencies that religion itself has all too often displayed. It would raise fears of the kind of divisive social conflict that has ravaged places like Northern Ireland and Lebanon.

Yet religion must be true to itself, and present its perspective on the human situation with clarity and candor. Attempts to dilute the message, or messages, of religion, in order to make them more acceptable to secular sources, undercut religion's capacity to perform its unique functions—spiritual, moral, and existential, as well as social.

The outlook for the future of religion in modern democratic societies, even in the United States, cannot, on the basis of current social trends alone, be regarded as entirely hopeful. There are some positive signs, but also some inescapable negative indicators. But followers of the great religions that descend from Judaic roots—modern Judaism, Christianity, and Islam—have the advantage of believing that what happens in history depends finally on God's grace. We can therefore, while proceeding with prudence and vigor, afford to be less disturbed by the clamor of competing values and world views in modern society—no worse now, surely than at many times in the past. Ultimately, the essential question about Christianity or Judaism or any other religion, is not whether it is socially useful, but whether it is true. If the beliefs on which the traditions of Judeo-Christianity are based are true, their social effects will certainly be felt—in God's good time.

NOTES

1. *Religion in America* (Princeton Religious Research Center, 1982); *The Gallup Report* (May, 1985, and July, 1985); *Zorach v. Clausen*, 343 U.S. 313 (1951).
2. A. James Reichley, "Religion and the Constitution," in *Religion in American Politics*, Charles W. Dunn, ed. (Congressional Quarterly Press, 1989), 3-14.
3. *Cantwell v. Connecticut*, 310 U.S. 625 (1925).
4. Catherine L. Albanese, *Sons of the Fathers: The Civil Religion of the American Revolution* (Temple, 1976), 12 and 49.
5. Interview with Hyman Bookbinder.
6. *New York Times*, November 8, 1984, and November 10, 1988.
7. Thomas J. Reese, S.J., *Archbishop: Inside the Power Structure of the American Catholic Church* (Harper and Row, 1989), 307-348.
8. *New York Times*, November 8, 1984; Everett Carll Ladd, "The 1988 Elections: Continuation of the Post-New Deal System," *Political Science Quarterly* (Spring, 1989), 15.
9. Wade Clark Root and William McKinney, *American Mainline Religion: Its Changing Shape and Future* (Rutgers, 1988); Dean A. Hoge and David A. Roozen, eds., *"Understanding Church Growth and Decline: 1950-1978* (Pilgrim Press, 1979); Dean M. Kelley, *Why Conservative Churches Are Growing: A Study in Sociology of Religion* (Harper and Row, 1977), ix-xx, 134-35.
10. *New York Times*, November 8, 1984, and November 10, 1988.
11. *Wall Street Journal*, March 9, 1988.
12. Karl Marx, *Essential Writings*, Frederic L. Bender, ed. (Harper and Row, 1972), 66.
13. *Pastoral Letter on War and Peace* (National Conference of Catholic Bishops, 1983): *Economic Justice for All: Pastoral Letter on Catholic Social Teaching and the U.S. Economy* (National Conference of Catholic Bishops, 1985).
14. Robert Bellah, "Civil Religion in America," *Daedalus* (Winter, 1967), 1-21. Bellah refines and modifies his argument in Bellah, Richard Marsden, William M. Sullivan, Ann Swidler, and Steven M. Tipton, *Habits of the Heart: Individualism and Commitment in American Life* (University of California Press, 1985).

TEN

CATHOLICISM AND DEMOCRACY: THE "OTHER TWENTIETH-CENTURY REVOLUTION"

George Weigel

In a conversation early in the 1980s, Sir Michael Howard, the Regius Professor of Modern History at Oxford, allowed as how there had been two great revolutions in the twentieth century. The first took place when Lenin's Bolsheviks expropriated the Russian people's revolution in November 1917. The second was going on even as we spoke: the transformation of the Roman Catholic Church from a bastion of the *ancien régime* into perhaps the world's foremost institutional defender of human rights. It was a fascinating reading of the history of our century. One also sensed, in Sir Michael's story, just the slightest hint of an element of surprise: Fancy the Vatican as defender of the rights of man!

There are, to be sure, reasons to be surprised by the contemporary Vatican's aggressive defense of human rights, and by Pope John Paul II's endorsement of democracy as the form of government which best coheres with the Church's vision of "integral human development." In the worlds of political power, those "surprised" would have to include the late Leonid Brezhnev (puzzled by the concurrent rise of *Solidarnosc* and the election of a Polish pope), Ferdinand Marcos, Augusto Pinochet, and the leaders of the Czechoslovak Communist Party. On the other hand (and viewed with perhaps more clarity in historical retrospect), key themes in classic Catholic social ethics—personalism, the common good, and the principle of "subsidiarity" —seem not merely congruent with democracy but pointed positively toward the evolution of liberal democratic forms of governance.

That, of course, would come as news indeed to Popes Gregory XVI or Pius IX, whose attitudes in the nineteenth century toward liberal democracy were rather chilly, at best. What has happened, between then and now, between the mid-nineteenth and late twentieth centuries, between an official Catholic skepticism about democracy that bordered on hostility and a Catholic endorsement of democracy that not only threatens tyrants, but actually helps to topple them?

THE MID-NINETEENTH CENTURY ARGUMENT

The hostility of official Roman Catholicism's papal magisterium to the liberal concepts of the "rights of man" as defined in the French Revolution's creed and to the liberal democratic state is well-known to all students of the period, and is neatly encapsulated in that last of the condemned propositions in Pius IX's 1864 *Syllabus of Errors*, namely, that "the Roman Pontiff can and should reconcile himself to and agree with progress, liberalism, and modern civilization." What is perhaps less well-known is that Pius IX, Giovanni Maria Mastai-Ferretti, was elected in 1846 as a reforming pope with a more tolerant attitude toward modern thought and institutions than his predecessor, Gregory XVI (1831-46) who in the 1832 and 1834 encyclicals *Mirari Vos* and *Sinculari Nos* had flatly condemned liberalism (including "this false and absurd maxim, or better, this madness, that everyone should have and practice freedom of conscience") as essentially irreligious.[1] In any case, events—particularly the Italian *Risorgimento*, whose liberal anticlerical leadership made no pretense about its intention to dislodge traditional church authority throughout Italy—hardened Pius IX in his views such that by the time of the First Vatican Council (1869-70), the pope, who had been elected 23 years earlier as something of a reformer had become, throughout the world, the very symbol of intransigent resistance to the ideas and institutions of modernity.[2]

While there were undoubtedly personal factors involved in the retrenchment strategy of Pius IX, it seems far more fruitful to focus on the substantive reasons why official Catholicism found itself in resistance to the "liberal project" in the nineteenth century. At least three suggest themselves to this observer.

First, one should not discount the enduring effects of the shock that the French Revolution sent through European Catholicism—a shock of perhaps greater intensity than any the Church had absorbed since the Reformation. There was, to be sure, the crazed bloodiness of the Terror itself. But beyond that, and beyond even Napoleon's persecution of Pope Pius VII, the leadership of Roman Catholicism saw the lingering specter of Jacobinism as an ideological force that threatened the very foundations of European civilization.[3] That civilization, in its "public" aspects, had been rooted in the notion that states, as well as individual men, were accountable to transcendent moral norms (generally held to be revealed by a God who was sovereign over states as well as over individuals). By its defiant insistence on the autonomous reason of man as the first, and indeed only, principle of political organization, Jacobinism threatened not simply the position of the Church as mediator between the sovereign God and his creatures; the anticlerical laicism imbedded in Jacobinism was a problem, to be sure, but it was not the fundamental threat. No, in the Church's view, and not without reason, the Jacobin spirit inevitably led to the implosion and consequent collapse of civilization in mobocracy, or what J.R. Talmon has called "totalitarian democracy."[4] Thus a damning equation become hardened in the minds of a Church leadership which had long identified not merely its institutional prerogatives but civilization itself with the moral understandings that (in however attenuated a form) underlay the structures of the *ancien regime*: liberalism = Jacobinism = (anticlericalism + The Terror + anarchy). Discriminating or not, fair or not, the brush of Robespierre tarred the revolutionaries of 1848, the leaders of the Italian *Risorgimento* (Cavour, Mazzini, Garibaldi, etc.), and in fact the entire "liberal" project in Europe.[5]

The second factor which colored the mid-nineteenth century Church's appraisal of "liberalism" and democracy was the Church's own internal situation. The "answer" which Roman Catholicism devised to the political threat posed by the rise of post-monarchical states in Europe and to the advance of "liberal" ideas was centralization: the radical concentration of effective authority over virtually all matters, great and small, in the person (and, of course, staff) of the Roman pontiff. The pope would be the sole judge of orthodoxy and orthopraxies; the pope would manage the Church's affairs with sovereign states through an expanding network of papal diplomats, concordat arrangements, and so forth. *Ubi Petrus, ibi ecclesia* ("Where there is Peter, there is the Church") is an ancient theological maxim. But it was given new breadth in the nineteenth century in response to the ideological (and indeed physical) threats posed by the forces of what the *Syllabus* called "progress, liberalism, and modern civilization."

There is, of course, an irony, here: the Church's answer to the threat of "progress, liberalism, and modern civilization" was to adopt a quintessentially modern structure, i.e., one that was highly centralized and bureaucratically controlled. Be that irony as it may, though, the new emphasis on centralized authority, coupled with the traditional understanding of the divinely-given prerogatives of the Roman pontiff and further complicated by the dependence of the Papal States (pre-1870) on European monarchs for physical security, combined to create a situation in which the Church's leadership was rather unlikely to feel much of a sense of affinity with liberal democracy. In terms of the sociology of knowledge, the conditions-for-the-possibility of a Roman pontiff looking with much favor on liberal democracy were not, to put it mildly, in place.

In the third place, and as if the above were not enough by way of barriers to rapprochement, "liberalism" in the latter part of the nineteenth century was widely (and not altogether inaccurately) perceived in Vatican circles as a package deal that included Darwinism (which seemed to threaten the distinctiveness of human beings in creation), "higher criticism" or the "historical-critical method" (which seemed to challenge the integrity of the Bible and its status as the revealed word of God), and socialism (which seemed to threaten the Church's traditional teaching on the right of private property). To these perceived threats in the order of ideas must be added the physical threat of revolutionary Marxism as it showed itself in, say, the 1870 Paris Commune.

The most fundamental reason for the Church's resistance to the liberal democratic project in the nineteenth century should not, though, be located on this institutional/ideological axis. The institutional threats noted above were real, in both corporate and personal terms (ask Pius VII or Pius IX); and those threats did act as a kind of filter through which ideas and events were, in some cases, misperceived. All of that can be conceded. But beneath it all lay, I believe, an evangelical concern.

Rightly or wrongly, the central leadership of nineteenth century Roman Catholicism truly believed that religious liberty—a key plank in the platform of liberal democracy—would inevitably lead to religious indifference and, given the right circumstances, to hostility toward religion on the part of governments. The secularization of Western Europe in the nineteenth century was a complicated business,[6] and it would be a grave historical error to attribute it solely (or even primarily) to the collapse of the old altar-and-throne arrangements that was obtained at the Peace of Westphalia ending the European wars of religion in 1648. On the other hand, and from the Vatican's point of view at that time, secularization proceeded apace with the collapse of those arrangements. Those of us with the luxury of hindsight should be perhaps less quick to dismiss as mindless the inferences that were drawn. As for the breakdown of altar-and-throne eventually leading to hostility toward religion on the part of governments, there was, at the beginning of the nineteenth century, the Napoleonic persecution of the Church. After 1870 there was the pressing problem of the violently anticlerical Third French Republic, in the face of which it was all too easy to read the historical record backward, from the depredations of the Commune and the later anticlericalism of the Third Republic, to the *Declaration des Droits de L'Homme et du Citoyen.*

One cannot, in short, dismiss Roman resistance to the liberal democratic project as merely institutional self-interest. Some liberal democratic states put grave difficulties in the path of the Church's evangelical and sacramental mission, and larger conclusions (appropriate or otherwise) were shortly drawn.

On the other hand, it should also be conceded that the Roman authorities were slow to seize the opportunities presented by what might be called the "Catholic Whig" tradition, which looks to Thomas Aquinas for its inspiration and which had, in Lord Acton, a powerful spokesman in the mid- and late-nineteenth century.

Given his views (largely negative) on the utility of the definition of papal infallibility at the First Vatican Council (itself, an act of defiance against the epistemological spirit of the age), Acton was an unlikely broker of this tradition, which taught the possibility of genuine progress in history when that progress is mediated through rightly-ordered public institutions holding themselves accountable to transcendent moral norms. In any case, the Catholic Whig tradition—a revolutionary liberal tradition in its own right, if in sharp contrast to the Jacobinism with which the Vatican typically associated liberalism—would not have all that long to wait, as history goes, for its moment to arrive.

THE TURN TOWARD DEMOCRACY BEGINS

What accounts for the shift in official Catholic teaching in the period from 1864 to 1965, between the rejection of the modern constitutional state in the *Syllabus of Errors* and the Second Vatican Council's acceptance of the juridical state in the *Declaration on Religious Freedom*? There were, clearly, any number of factors in play. But one strikes me as particularly important; and that was the fact of America. In the United States, the Church was confronted with a liberal society and liberal-democratic state that were good for Roman Catholics. In America, religious liberty and the constitutional separation of church and state had not led to religious indifferentism, but to a vibrant Catholicism which still (unlike its European counterparts) held the allegiance of the working class. Moreover, while anti-Catholicism was a fact of life in the United States (Arthur Schlesinger, Sr., once told the dean of American Catholic historians, John Tracy Ellis, that "I regard the prejudice against your Church as the deepest bias in the history of the American people")[7], the U.S. government had never come close (save perhaps in the case of the Church of Jesus Christ of Latter-day Saints) to conducting an overt program of persecution on the basis of religious conviction.

This was, as can be imagined, somewhat difficult to handle for those in Rome who were still committed to a restoration of the *ancien regime* or even those who were simply skeptical about the American experiment. A bold, public attempt to press the argument for religious liberty and liberal democracy in Rome itself took place on March 25, 1887, when the newly-created Cardinal James Gibbons of Baltimore took possession of his titular Church of Santa Maria in Trastevere and preached to his Roman congregation in these terms:

> ... Scarcely were the United States formed when Pius VI, of happy memory, established there the Catholic hierarchy and appointed the illustrious John Carroll first Bishop of Baltimore. This event, so important to us, occurred less than a hundred years ago.... our Catholic community in those days numbered only a few thousand souls ... and were served by the merest handful of priests. Thanks to the fructifying grace of God, the grain of mustard seed then planted has grown to be a large tree, spreading its branches over the length and width of our fair land.... For their great progress under God and the fostering care of the Holy See we are indebted in no small decree to the civil liberty we enjoy in our enlightened republic.
>
> Our Holy Father, Leo XIII, in his luminous encyclical on the constitution of Christian States, declares that the Church is not committed to any particular form of civil government. She adapts to all; she leavens all with the sacred leaven of the Gospel. She has lived under absolute empires; she thrives under constitutional monarchies; she grows and expands under the free republic. She has often, indeed, been hampered in her divine mission and has had to struggle for a footing wherever despotism has cast its dark shadow...but in the genial air of liberty she blossoms like the rose!
>
> For myself, as a citizen of the United States, and without closing my eyes to our defects as a nation, I proclaim, with a deep sense of pride and gratitude, and in this great capital of Christendom, that I belong to a country where the civil government holds over us the aegis of its protection without interfering in the legitimate exercise of our sublime mission as ministers of the Gospel of Jesus Christ.
>
> Our country has liberty without license, authority without despotism.... But, while we are acknowledged to have a free government, we do not, perhaps, receive due credit for possessing also a strong government. Yes, our nation is strong, and her strength lies, under Providence, in the majesty and supremacy of the law, in the loyalty of her citizens to that law, and in the affection of our people for their free institutions....[8]

Gibbons' proud assertions sound mild to our ears, but in their own day they were intended as a manifesto and a challenge, and were understood, by contemporary celebrants and detractors alike, to have been such. As Gerald Fogarty, SJ, puts it, "Here was the gauntlet of the benefit of American religious liberty thrown down by the new world to the old...."[9]

Pope Leo XIII (1878-1903) was happy to acknowledge the practical benefits of the American arrangement in the American circumstance, but he was not yet prepared to concede the moral superiority of the liberal (i.e., confessionally neutral) state over the classic European arrangements. In his 1895 encyclical letter to the

American hierarchy, *Longinqua Oceani,* Leo cautioned against any temptation to universalize the American experience and experiment:

> ... the Church amongst you, unopposed by the Constitution and government of your nation, fettered by no hostile legislation, protected against violence by the common laws and the impartiality of the tribunals, is free to live and act without hindrance. Yet, though all this is true, it would be very erroneous to draw the conclusion that in America is to be sought the type of the most desirable status of the Church, or that it would be universally lawful or expedient for State and Church to be, as in America, dissevered and divorced. The fact that Catholicity with you is in good condition, nay, is even enjoying a prosperous growth, is by all means to be attributed to the fecundity with which God has endowed his Church, in virtue of which unless men or circumstances interfere, she spontaneously expands and propagates herself; but she would bring forth more abundant fruits if, in addition to liberty, she enjoyed, the favor of the laws and the patronage of the public authority.[10]

Thus the situation in the late nineteenth century: as to the American arrangement, i.e., the liberal democratic, confessionally-neutral state, *tolerari potest:* "it could be tolerated." Indeed, the accomplishments of the Church under such a new arrangement could be forthrightly and gratefully acknowledged. This was a step ahead. We have come a distance from the rejectionist posture of Pius IX and the *Syllabus.* But we have yet to reach the stage at which the confessionally-neutral state which acknowledges the right of religious liberty as an inalienable right of human beings as such, prior to their status as citizens, is preferred to a benign altar-and-throne (or altar-and-desk) arrangement.

The path to that more developed position, which is the basis of the contemporary Catholic rapprochement with liberal democracy, would be traversed over the next sixty years. The vigor of American Catholicism continued to play a role, by way of example, in insuring that the issue remained alive. One would also have to take due account of the effect of the (providential) loss of the Papal States. Absent this direct political responsibility, popes from Leo XIII on were in a more advantageous position to consider, from a far less encumbered theological and practical position, the relative merits of various forms of modern governance. And, as the nineteenth century gave way to the twentieth, other realities of modern life began to influence the Church's perspective. Among the most significant were the following:

The rise of totalitarianism, in both its Leninist and fascist forms and in the threat posed to Roman Catholicism by both of these demonic modern political movements, led the Church not only to look toward the democracies for protection but to look toward democracy itself as an antidote to the totalitarian temptation. This was particularly true in the immediate post-World War II period, when Vatican diplomacy, often working closely with American diplomats and occupation forces, worked to strengthen Christian Democratic parties in Germany and Italy. In the Italian case, this represented a shift indeed, for Pope Pius XI (1922-39) had summarily ended the proto-Christian Democratic experiment led by Don Luigi Sturzo in the early twentieth century with most unfortunate results.[11] In any event, Christian Democracy, in theory and in practice, seemed to many Vatican minds (including that of Giovanni Battista Montini, later Pope Paul VI) as the best available alternative to either Leninist or fascist totalitarianism, in a world where even constitutional monarchy was clearly on the wane. Montini was influenced in this judgment by his regard for the philosophical work of the French neo-Thomist Jacques Maritain, whose *Christianity and Democracy*, written during the summer of 1942, became a kind of theoretical manifesto for the Christian Democratic movement.[12]

This turn toward the Christian Democratic alternative was also facilitated by the recession of the cruder forms of anticlericalism among European liberals and by the terrible revelation of the difference-in-kind between liberals and radicals that was occasioned by the ferocities of totalitarian persecution. The Vatican may still have had its differences with liberals, but after the ruthless persecution of Christianity under Lenin and Stalin, the Ukrainian terror famine, and the Holocaust it was no longer possible to even suggest that modern radical dictators such as Stalin and Hitler were but exceptionally virulent forms of a general liberal virus. In the French situation, cooperative efforts during World War II between Catholic intellectuals and a few religious leaders on the one hand and the wider Resistance movement (with its secularist and Marxist leadership) on the other, helped break down some of the stereotypes (in both directions) that had plagued life under the Third Republic.[13] In Italy, the tradition of Don Sturzo, incarnated in such major post-war figures as de Gasperi and Moro, could be reclaimed, just as in Germany Konrad Adenauer was able to tap the Christian Democratic tradition of the old Catholic Center party.[14] In the post-World War II period, then, there were new facts of national and international life which validated Gibbons' thesis beyond the borders of the United States and which created the sociological conditions for the possibility of retrieving Pius VII's views on the compatibility of Catholicism and democracy.

Finally, and perhaps most significantly in terms of the history of ideas, the evolution of Catholic social teaching itself pushed the Church toward a more positive appraisal of liberal democracy. The key development here was Pius XI's emphasis on the "principle of subsidiarity," a principle that was central to the pope's teaching in *Quadragesimo Anno*, issued in 1931 for the fortieth anniversary of Leo XIII's groundbreaking social encyclical *Rerum Novarum*. The key passage in Pius XI's letter was the following:

> It is true, as history clearly shows, that because of changed circumstances much that formerly was performed by small associations can now be accomplished only by larger ones. Nevertheless, it is a fixed and unchangeable principle, most basic in social philosophy, immoveable and unalterable, that, just as it is wrong to take away from individuals what they can accomplish by their own ability and effort and then entrust it to a community, so it is an injury and at the same time both a serious evil and a disturbance of right order to assign to a larger and higher society what can be performed successfully by smaller and lower communities. The reason is that all social activity, of its very power and nature, should supply help [*subsidium*] to the members of the social body, but may never destroy or absorb them.
>
> The state, then, should leave to these smaller groups the settlement of business and problems of minor importance, which would otherwise greatly distract it. Thus it will carry out with greater freedom, power, and success the tasks belonging to it alone, because it alone is qualified to perform them: directing, watching, stimulating, and restraining, as circumstances suggest or necessity demands. Let those in power, therefore, be convinced that the more faithfully this principle of subsidiary function is followed and a graded hierarchical order exists among the various associations, the greater also will be both social authority and social efficiency, and the happier and more prosperous too will be the condition of the commonwealth.[15]

As it has worked itself out in subsequent Catholic social teaching, the "principle of subsidiarity" has consisted of the following substantive elements:

• The individual human person is both the source and the end of society: *civitas propter cives non cives propter civitatem.*

• Yet the human person is "naturally" social and can achieve the fullness of human development only in human communities; this is sometimes referred to, particularly in analyses of the writings of John Paul II, as the "principle of solidarity."

• The purpose of social relationships and human communities is to give help [*subsidium*] to individuals as they pursue, freely, their obligation to work for their own human development. Thus the state or society should not, save in exceptional circumstances, replace or displace this individual self-responsibility; the society and the state provide, as it were, conditions for the possibility of the exercise of self-responsibility.

• There is a hierarchy of communities in human society; larger, "higher" communities are to provide help (*subsidium*), in the manner noted above, to smaller or "lower" communities.

• *Positively* the principle of subsidiarity means that all communities should encourage and enable (not merely permit) individuals to exercise their self-responsibility, and larger communities should do this for smaller communities. Put another way, decision-making responsibility in society should rest at the "lowest" possible level, commensurate with the effective pursuit of the common good.[16]

• *Negatively* the principle means that communities must not deprive individuals, nor larger communities deprive smaller communities, of the opportunity to do what they can for themselves.

Subsidiarity, in other words, is a formal principle "by which to regulate competencies between individual and communities and between smaller and larger communities." Because it is a formal principle, its precise meaning "on the ground" will differ according to circumstances; because it is rooted in "the metaphysics of the person, it applies to the life of every society."[17]

There is both a historical and substantive connection between the identification of the "principle of subsidiarity" and the Roman Catholic Church's increasingly positive appraisal of democracy in the mid-twentieth century. Historically, the very concept of "subsidiarity" was developed in the German *Koenigswinterer Kreis*, a group of Catholic intellectuals interested in questions of political economy who deeply influenced both the author of *Quadragesimo Anno*, the Jesuit Oswald von Nell-Breuning, and the evolution of Christian Democracy in pre- and post-war Germany.[18] The substantive connection was closely related to the historical connection. *Quadragesimo*

Anno was written under the lengthening shadow of totalitarianism and collectivism. If its predecessor encyclical, *Rerum Novarum*, had been written, at least in part, to warn against the dangers inherent in Manchesterian liberalism, *Quadragesimo Anno* was written in response to the threat posed by the overweening pretensions of the modern state:[19] thus the importance of the principle of "subsidiarity," which sought, *inter alia*, to set clear boundaries to state power. The question then arises: under modern circumstances, what form of governance is most likely to acknowledge, in practice as well as in principle or rhetoric, the limited role of the state, the moral and social importance of what Burke called the "small platoons," and the principle of *civitas propter cives?* A number of theoretical possibilities come to mind, but in actual historical practice, it is liberal democracies which best meet the test of these moral criteria. That was not precisely what Pius XI, with his "corporatist" vision, had in mind in 1931, but it was certainly what Pope Pius XII (1939-58) had in mind by the mid-1940s: not as a universalizable principle of political organization, but as the best available modern alternative in what a later generation would call the "developed world."

VATICAN II ON CHURCH AND STATE

The proximate origins of what I have termed elsewhere the "Catholic human rights revolution," which led in turn to the Church's new appreciation for and overt support of the democratic revolution in world politics, should be located in the Second Vatican Council's 1965 *Declaration on Religious Freedom* so aptly styled, in its Latin title, *Dignitatis Humanae Personae* [hereinafter, DHP]. The Declaration was itself a child of the American experience and experiment, and a brief sketch of that background is in order.

The chief intellectual architect of DHP was the American Jesuit theologian John Courtney Murray. Beginning in the late 1940s, Murray conceived and orchestrated a creative extension of Catholic church/state theory. To make a complex story drastically brief, the official Roman position, when Murray first took up the topic, was precisely where Leo XIII had left it in *Longinqua Oceani*: the "thesis," or preferred arrangement, was the legal establishment of Catholicism on either the classic altar-and-throne or modern Francoist models; the American arrangement, i.e., religious liberty for all in a confessionally-neutral state, was a tolerable "hypothesis," the "toleration" of which included work on the part of the local Church in question for the day when it, too, would enjoy the benefits of state support. The "thesis" arrangement, with its rejection of religious liberty as a fundamental human right, was grounded on the maxim that "error has no rights" and was defended by prominent American Catholic theologians like Joseph Clifford Fenton and Francis Connell, C.SS.R. of the Catholic University of America and the *American Ecclesiastical Review.*[20]

Murray's challenge to this position and his creative extension of Catholic church/state theory involved a classically Murrayesque maneuver, i.e., the retrieval and development of an old and largely forgotten current in Catholic thought which antedated the medieval altar-and-throne model. Murray found the *locus classicus* of this forgotten current in a letter sent by Pope Gelasius I to the Byzantine emperor Anastasius in 494, in which the pope had written, "Two there are, august emperor, by which this world is ruled on title of original and sovereign right—the consecrated authority of the priesthood and the royal power." As I have written elsewhere about this modest but crucial statement,

> This was not a radical 'two kingdoms' construct so much as a declaration of independence for both Church and state. The Church's freedom to exercise its ministry of truth and charity was a limit on the powers of government; the state's lack of authority in matters spiritual 'desacralized' politics and by doing so, opened up the possibility of a politics of consent in place of the politics of divine right or the politics of coercion. The Gelasian tradition frowned on a unita Church/state system for the sake of the integrity of both religion and politics.[21]

After considerable theological and ecclesiastical-political maneuvering, Murray's Gelasian retrieval prevailed at Vatican II and, enriched by a personalized philosophical approach which taught that persons had rights, whether their opinions were erroneous, was incorporated into DHP, with a palpable effect on the Church's subsequent stance toward democracy.

The connection here—between the definition of religious freedom as a fundamental human right and the affirmation of democratic forms of governance—has to do with the very nature of religious freedom itself, for religious freedom has both an "interior" meaning and a "public" meaning.

The "interior meaning" of religious freedom can be stated in these terms: Because human beings have an innate capacity for thinking, doing, and choosing and an innate drive for meaning and value, freedom to pursue that quest for meaning and value, without coercion, is a fundamental requisite for a truly human life. This innate quest for meaning and value, which is the basic dynamic of what John Paul II has called the "interior freedom" of the human person, is the object or end of that "human right" which we call the "right of religious freedom." The right of religious freedom, in other words, is the juridical expression of this basic claim about the constitutive elements and dynamic of human being in the world. One can argue, then, that religious freedom— as the Council put it, the claim that "all men are to be immune from coercion on the part of individuals or of social groups and of any human power, in such wise that in matters religious no one is to be forced to act in a manner contrary to his beliefs"[22]—is the most fundamental of human rights, because it is the claim that corresponds to the most radically human dimension of human being in the world. This brings us, in short order, to the "public meaning" of religious freedom. On the personalized analysis above, religious freedom can be considered a "prepolitical" human right: it is the condition for the possibility of a *polis* structured in accordance with the inherent human dignity of the persons who are its citizens. Thus the right of religious freedom establishes a fundamental barrier between the person and the state which is essential to a just *polis*. The state is not omni-competent, and one of the reasons we know that is that the right of religious freedom is the juridical expression of the "pre-political" fact that there is a *sanctum sanctorum* within every human person wherein coercive power (most especially coercive state power) may not tread.

The right of religious freedom—which includes, as the Council taught, the claim that "No one is to be restrained from acting in accordance with his own beliefs, whether privately or publicly whether alone or in association with others, within due limits"[23]—is also helpful in establishing that distinction between "society" and "the state" which is fundamental to the liberal democratic project. Democracy, in theory and in practice, rests upon the understandings that society is prior to the state, and that the state exists to serve society, not the other way around.

Social institutions[24] have a logical, historical, and one might even say ontological priority over institutions of government; among the many social institutions which have persistently claimed this distinctive priority are religious institutions and, in the Gelasian tradition, the Christian Church. Thus the public dimension of the right of religious freedom is a crucial barrier against the totalitarian temptation, in either its Leninist or mobocracy forms. Some things in a democracy—indeed, the very things that are the building blocks of democracy, i.e., basic human rights—are not up for a vote. Democratic politics is not merely procedural politics; democracies are *substantive* experiments whose successful working out requires certain habits (virtues) and attitudes, in addition to the usual democratic procedures. The public meaning of the right of religious freedom reminds us of this, in and out of season. And thus the importance of the right of religious freedom for unbelievers as well as believers, for the secularized American new class elite as well as for the ninety percent of the American people who remain stubbornly religious.[25]

In short, and as Murray himself put it, at Vatican II and in the *Declaration on Religious Freedom*, Roman Catholicism embraced "the political doctrine of ... the juridical state ... [i.e.] government as constitutional and limited in function—its primary function being juridical, namely, the protection and promotion of the rights of man and the facilitation of the performance of man's native duties."[26] The juridical or constitutional state ruled by consent, not by coercion or by claims of "divine right." The state itself stood under the judgment of moral norms that transcended it, moral norms whose constitutional and/or legal expression could be found in "bills of rights." Moreover, religious liberty, constitutionally and legally protected, desacralized politics and thereby opened up the possibility of a politics of consent. Where in the modern world could such constitutionally-regulated, limited, consensual states be found? The question posed seemed to answer itself: in liberal democratic states.

Thus the path to an official Roman Catholic affirmation of democracy had been cleared, and indeed the obligatory ends of a morally-worthy democratic *polis* specified, in this American shaped development of doctrine on the matter of the fundamental human right of religious freedom.

THE CONTEMPORARY DISCUSSION

Pope John Paul II (1978-) has deepened and intellectually extended the Catholic human rights revolution during his pontificate, not least by explicitly connecting it to the democratic revolution in world politics.

This extension undoubtedly reflects the pope's personal experience in Poland, where the "parchment barriers" (as Madison would have called them) of communist "constitutions" and other forms of political flim-flam have illustrated precisely how important it is that rights be secured by the structure of governmental institutions, as well as by the habits and attitudes of a people. Here, again, we see how the totalitarian project in the twentieth century has been, paradoxically, a prod to the extension and evolution of Catholic social teaching.

John Paul II has also had to contend with the phenomenon of the various "theologies of liberation." While liberation theology is a reality vastly more complex (and, just possibly, of considerably less long-term importance) than has typically been presented in the American secular media, the sundry theologies of liberation share a pronounced skepticism, at times verging on hostility, to what they often term the "bourgeois formalism" of liberal democracy. Whether liberation theology represents a genuinely distinctive phenomenon in Catholic history, or whether it is the old Iberian fondness for altar-and-throne arrangements in a unitary state moved from right to left on the political spectrum, is an intriguing question, the full exploration of which is beyond the scope of this paper. What is clear is that, by the early 1980s, the theologies of liberation had evolved, in this matter of Catholicism and democracy, along a rather different path than that taken by the Roman magisterium.

Closing the widening breach between official Catholic social teaching and the theologies of liberation, and challenging the currents in the latter which were most out-of-phase with the developments sketched above, was the task undertaken by the Congregation for the Doctrine of the Faith in its two "instructions" on liberation theology, the first published in 1984 and the second in 1986.

The 1984 "Instruction on Certain Aspects of the 'Theology of Liberation,'" issued by the Congregation with the pope's personal authority, acknowledged that liberation was an important theme in Christian theology, frankly faced the overwhelming facts of poverty and degradation in much of Latin America, and argued that the Church indeed had a special love for and responsibility to the poor. On the other hand, the Instruction rejected a number of themes which had been key teachings of the various theologies of liberation. Among these themes the Instruction cited the primary location of sin in social, economic, and political structures; the class struggle model of society and history and related analyses of "structural violence"; the subordination of the individual to the collectivity; the transformation of the concepts of "good" and "evil" into strictly political categories, and the subsequent loss of a sense of transcendent dimension to the moral life; the concept of a partisan Church; and an "exclusively political interpretation" of the salvific meaning of the death of Christ.[27]

But for our purposes here, the most crucial passage in the 1984 Instruction was the following:

> One needs to be on guard against the politicization of existence, which, misunderstanding the entire meaning of the Kingdom of God and the transcendence of the person, begins to sacralize politics and betray the religion of the people in favor of the projects of the revolution.[28]

In short, the theologies of liberation had broken with the modern retrieval of the Gelasian tradition as it had evolved in the teaching of the Second Vatican Council and the social teaching of John Paul II. Against the core dynamic of the Catholic human rights revolution, the theologies of liberation were proposing, in effect, a flight from pluralism and a return to the monism of the past—this time buttressed by the allegedly "scientific" accomplishments of "Marxist social analysis." And with monism came, inevitably, the use of coercive state power against individuals and against the Church. The politics of consent were, again, being threatened by the politics of coercion.

The 1986 "Instruction on Christian Freedom and Liberation" pushed the official Roman discussion even further toward an open endorsement of the moral superiority of democratic politics in this passage:

> ... There can only be authentic development in a social and political system which respects freedoms and fosters them through the participation of

everyone. This participation can take different forms; it is necessary in order to guarantee a proper pluralism in institutions and in social initiatives. It ensures, notably by a real separation between the powers of the State, the exercise of human rights, also protecting them against possible abuses on the part of the public powers. No one can be excluded from this participation in social and political life for reasons of sex, race, color, social condition, language, or religion....

When the political authorities regulate the exercise of freedoms, they cannot use the pretext of the demands of public order and security in order to curtail those freedoms systematically. Nor can the alleged principle of national security, or a narrowly economic outlook, or a totalitarian conception of social life, prevail over the value of freedom and its rights.[29]

The politicization of the Gospel—its reduction to a partisan, mundane program—and the re-sacralization of politics were decisively rejected by the 1984 Instruction. The 1986 Instruction taught that participatory politics was morally superior to the politics of vanguards, whether aristocratic or Marxist-Leninist. The linkage between these themes and the positive task of democracy-building was made in late 1987 by the encyclical *Sollicitudo Rei Socialis.*

Sollicitudo's portrait of the grim situation of Third World countries was based on a more complex analysis than could be found in the encyclical it was written to commemorate, Paul VI's *Populorum Progressio* (1968). Where Paul tended to locate primary (some would say, virtually exclusive) responsibility for "underdevelopment" in the "developed" world, John Paul II argued that responsibility for the world's underclass was not unilinear and involved "undoubtedly grave instances of omissions on the part of the developing countries themselves, and especially on the part of those holding economic and political power."[30] In a more positive vein (and here extending the Catholic human rights revolution in explicitly structural/political terms), John Paul II taught that economic development would be impossible without the evolution of what would be called, in Western terms, the "civil society," or in the pope's own words, "the developing nations themselves should favor the self-affirmation of each citizen, through access to a wider culture and a free flow of information."[31]

But the enhanced moral and cultural skills of a people were not enough, the pope continued. Important as they were, they would not yield "integral human development" if the peoples in question remained the vassals or victims of inept, hidebound, ideologically rigid, and/or kleptocratic dictatorships. Thus true development required that Third World countries "reform certain unjust structures, and in particular their political institutions, in order to replace corrupt, dictatorial, and authoritarian forms of government by democratic and participatory ones."[32]

In short, in *Sollicitudo Rei Socialis* the formal leadership of the Roman Catholic Church reconfirmed its support for the democratic revolution in world politics. As John Paul II said of this striking phenomenon of the 1980s, "This is a process which we hope will spread and grow stronger. For the health of a political community—as expressed in the free and responsible participation of all citizens in public affairs, in the rule of law, and in respect for and promotion of human rights—is the necessary condition and sure guarantee of the development of the whole individual and of all people."[33] *Sollicitudo* in fact brought Catholic social theory into congruence with Catholic social practice during the pontificate of John Paul II. Whether the locale has been El Salvador, Chile, Nicaragua, Paraguay, Poland, the Philippines, South Korea, or sub-Saharan Africa, John Paul II's has been a consistent voice of support (and, in Poland, rather more than that) on behalf of the replacement of "corrupt, dictatorial and authoritarian forms of government" by "democratic and participatory ones." And as for criticism that his preaching on behalf of human rights and democracy constituted an unbecoming interference in politics, the pope had this to say to a reporter who asked him about such carping, while pope and press were enroute to Chile and Paraguay in 1987: "Yes, yes, I am not the evangelizer of democracy, I am the evangelizer of the Gospel. To the Gospel message, of course, belongs all the problems of human rights, and if democracy means human rights it also belongs to the message of the Church."[34] From religious conversion, to moral norms, to institutions and patterns of governance: the pope's sense of priorities is clear, but the connection between Catholic social teaching and the democratic revolution is, too.

None of which should be taken to suggest, of course, that the Church of the 1990s and beyond will be an uncritical or naive celebrant of the democratic possibility. John Paul II made clear, in his pastoral visit to the United States in 1987, that democratic polities must always remind themselves of the transcendent norms of judgment to which they hold themselves open. Most particularly, today, this means deepening the democracies' understanding of human freedom. As the pope put it in 1987, speaking of the United States,

> Among the many admirable values of this country there is one that stands out in particular. It is freedom. The concept of freedom is part of the very fabric of this nation as a political community of free people. Freedom is a great gift, a blessing of God.
>
> From the beginning of America, freedom was directed to forming a well-ordered society and to promoting its peaceful life. Freedom was channelled to the fullness of human life, to the preservation of human dignity, and to the safeguarding of human rights. An experience of ordered freedom is truly part of the history of this land.
>
> This is the freedom that America is called upon to live and guard and transmit. She is called to exercise it in such a way that it will also benefit the cause of freedom in other nations and among other peoples.[35]

And thus did the Bishop of Rome endorse the moral intention of the American experiment in the categories of the Catholic Whig tradition, as exemplified by Acton and his postulate that freedom is not a matter of doing what you want, but of having the right to do what you ought.

Cardinal Joseph Ratzinger, prefect of the Congregation for the Doctrine of the Faith and chief intellectual architect of its two "instructions" on Christian freedom and liberation, has been another challenging critic of the gap between intention and performance in the established democracies. Ratzinger, like John Courtney Murray, is particularly concerned that "democracy" not be reduced to what the American Jesuit would have called "an ensemble of procedures" with no substantive foundation. As the Cardinal put it in a 1979 essay,

> ... democracy is by its nature linked to *eunomia*, to the validity of good law, and can only remain democracy in such a relationship. Democracy in this way is never the mere domination of majorities, and the mechanism whereby majorities are provided must be guided by the common rule of *nomos*, of what internally is law, that is under the rule of values that form a binding presupposition for the majority too....
>
> ...democracy is only capable of functioning when conscience is functioning, and ... this latter has nothing to say if it is not guided and influenced by the fundamental moral values of Christianity, values which are capable of

realization even in the absence of any specific acknowledgement of Christianity and indeed in the context of non-Christian religion.[36]

These developments in Catholic social teaching and the Church's theology have had significant effects "on the ground," as papal teaching and Catholic reformist practice have, in a variety of locales, become a powerful support for the democratic revolution—and a means for keeping that revolution from spilling over into anarchy. Catholic lay organizations, supported by their local bishops and by the Holy See, have proven an indispensable part of the democratic transitions in Spain and Portugal. The Church is clearly aligned on the side of democracy is Latin America, to the discomfort of caudillos right and left. In Poland, Czechoslovakia, and Lithuania, the Church is at the forefront of the democratic churnings in the world's last empire. In East Asia, the Church was the chief domestic institutional support for the democratic insurgency that toppled Ferdinand Marcos and installed Corazon Aquino, and church leaders and laity played important roles in the transition to democracy in South Korea. This complex pattern of activism was buttressed by, even as it influenced, the Church's moral case for the democratic alternative—a case that combined idealism and realism in an impressively sophisticated mix.

And thus Sir Michael Howard's identification of the "other twentieth century revolution" seemed, by the end of the 1980s, not quite so surprising after all and in fact remarkably prescient.

ISSUES FOR THE FUTURE

The dialectic between the evolution of Catholic social teaching and the democratic revolution can be expected to continue. Among the issues that may rise to the front of the intellectual agenda are the following.

Catholic social teaching, in the United States and in Rome, should more fully integrate the experience of the American Founding—including the Founders' and Framers' philosophical justification for their revolutionary activity—into its reflection on the quest for human freedom. There remains a tendency in Rome to view the modern history of that quest through primarily Continental filters. Thus the seminal 1986 "Instruction on Christian Freedom and Liberation" could argue that "it was above all ... at the French Revolution that the call to freedom rang out with full force. Since that time, many have regarded future history as an irresistible process of liberation inevitably leading to an age in which man, totally free at last, will enjoy happiness on this earth."[37]

Yet there was another revolutionary tradition in the late eighteenth century—a revolutionary tradition which was, contrary to that of 1789, a deliberate extension of rather than a repudiation of the central political tradition of the West: the revolution of 1776 and 1787, the revolution that began with the declaration of "inalienable Nature's God" and was channeled into the process of Constitution-making.

The current historiography of the American Founding stresses that the Founders and Framers, far from being the radical Lockean individualists and libertarian Smithite merchants portrayed by Vernon Louis Parrington and Charles Beard, were in fact thoroughly convinced that the success of the American experiment required a citizenry that would live the life of "... public virtue, public liberty, [the] public happiness of republicanism, the humane sociability of the Scottish Enlightenment." For the American Founders and Framers, in other words, "the concept of public virtue stood at or near the center of 'republicanism.'" The American Founders and Framers were moral realists, not antinomians; knowing that all men were sinners, they tried to devise "republican institutions which could preserve liberty in virtue's absence."[38]

This moral realism of the Founders and Framers is, of course, not identical with the Catholic social ethical tradition of moderate realism as developed by Augustine and Aquinas.[39] But there would seem to be important points of connection between the two—a point emphasized by such giants of the American Church as John Carroll, John England, James Gibbons, John Ireland, and John Courtney Murray. Thus an intense conversation with the leadership of the universal Church, as it continues to reflect on the political/institutional implications of the Catholic human rights revolution, needs to take place and ought to focus at least some of its attention on the dialectic between the American experience of democratic republicanism and the public philosophy undergirding (or failing to undergird) the experiment launched in 1776 and 1787.

If that point is not particularly well-understood in Rome today, the problem may lie not primarily with Rome but with the successors of Carroll and Gibbons in the American episcopate and with the successors of Murray among American Catholic intellectuals. In both quarters today one finds a disturbing phenomenon: men and women who insist on being American Catholics, but who deep down are profoundly skeptical about, indeed in some cases overtly hostile to, the American experiment.[40] In short, the current episcopal and intellectual leadership of the Church in the United States has not completed the task begun by Gibbons in his 1887 sermon at Santa Maria in Trastevere. It is time to take that task up again—for the sake of the moral deepening of the American experiment, and for the sake of the evolution of Catholic social teaching.

The argument with the various theologies of liberation must continue. The Vatican "instructions" of 1984 and 1986—and the democratic revolution itself in Latin America—have had a beneficial impact on this front. In an interview with the *New York Times* in the summer of 1988, for example, Father Gustavo Gutierrez of Peru, widely-recognized as the father of liberation theology, distanced himself from those of his brethren who deprecate the accomplishments of Latin America's nascent democracies as but "bourgeois formalism." "Experience with dictatorship," Father Gutierrez said, "has made liberation theologians more appreciative of political rights." So, too, have the "changes in Marxist and socialist thinking" in Eastern Europe.[41] So, too, one suspects, have the Vatican "instructions" of 1984 and 1986, and the social teaching of John Paul II, in his encyclicals and during his pastoral visits to Latin America.

In short, it is now possible to imagine a "second-phase" or "third-phase" liberation theology which supports, rather than deprecates, the democratic revolution and the possibilities it holds out for the empowerment of the poor. But to "imagine" such a development and to find it are, of course, two different things. Today, a "liberation theology of democracy" is a possibility, not a reality.[42] And so a continued conversation, which is sure to be brisk, remains in order.

Problems of religious liberty—and thus of the rightordering of political communities—are showing up more frequently in the Church's interface with other world religions. Buddhists in Nepal, militant Hindus in India, and above all Islamic fundamentalists throughout Africa and Asia are now impeding, with various degrees of persecutorial vigor, the evangelical and sacramental mission of the Church.

These confrontations raise intriguing new questions for the Catholic human rights revolution and the Church's support for democratic transitions. In many Asian and African locales, or even in a quasi-Western nation such as Haiti, the cultural roots of democracy seem scanty, at best. The Church, like democrats throughout the world, has to explore a number of questions here: What are the cultural prerequisites for successful transitions to democracy? Can these cultural building-blocks of the politics of participation and consent be enhanced or strengthened by the "intervention" (the term is used neutrally) of "external" religious forces?

Islam, Buddhism, and Hinduism are complex bodies of religious thought: What currents within them are supportive of democratic politics? What currents are opposed? What is the "correlation of forces," to borrow from the Marxists, between supporters and opponents?

Catholicism is now formally committed to a strategy of "inculturation" in its missionary work.[43] What is the relationship, if any, between the "inculturation" of the Gospel and the "inculturation" of human rights norms and political institutions generally perceived in Third World arenas to be "Western"—and thus suspect? How, in other words, does the Church concretely give expression to John Paul II's comment (n. 34 above) that "To the Gospel message belongs all the problems of human rights, and if democracy means human rights it also belongs to the message of the Church"—and do so without appearing to be the agent of "Western cultural imperialism"?

In sum, then, the new official Roman Catholic support for the democratic revolution in world politics raises at least as many question as it answers, for both theology and political theory, for evangelization and political action. The "other revolution" will, it seems, be an ongoing one.

NOTES

1. From *Mirari Vos*, as cited and discussed in Roger Aubert, et al., *History of the Church VIII: The Church Between Revolution and Restoration* (New York: Crossroad, 1981), 286-92.

    The historical and sociological context of Gregory XVI's condemnation is well summarized by Rodger Charles, SJ.: "Gregory XVI was a temporal ruler faced with a revolt in his own dominions, a revolt which was in the name of a liberalism which … was in practice anti-clerical and anti-Christian…. The Pope could not accept state indifferentism in matters of religion, nor grant liberty of conscience while these implied positive anti-clerical and anti-Christian attitudes. Liberty of the press and separation of the church and the state were likewise rejected absolutely because of their secularist implications. This was the essence of the papal dilemma: popes, as vicars of Christ, could hardly recommend policies which, if put into practice in their own states, would link them [i.e., the popes] with them and ideas both anti-clerical and anti-religious. Only when the question of temporal power of the papacy had been solved … could the situation satisfactorily be resolved." *The Social Teaching of Vatican II* (San Francisco: Ignatius Press, 1982), 239.

2. For a portrait of Pius IX that usefully complexities many of the regnant stereotypes, cf. E.E.Y. Hales, *Pio Nono: A Study in European Politics and Religion in the Nineteenth Century* (London: Eyre & Spottiswoode, 1954).

3. The Holy See was not, of course, alone in this judgment, although the logic of concern varied from institution to institution. Cf. Henry A. Kissinger, *A World Restored: Metternich, Castlereagh and the Problems of Peace, 1912-1922* (Boston: Houghton Mifflin, 1973).

4. For a discussion of this point, cf. John Courtney Murray, *We Hold These Truths: Catholic Reflections on the American Proposition* (New York: Doubleday Image Books, 1964), 40 ff. The danger in question was encapsulated in the Abbe Sieyes' defense of the replacement of the old States-General by the revolutionary National assembly: "The nation exists before all, it is the origin of everything, it is the law itself." (Cited in Conor Cruise O'Brien, "A Lost Chance to Save the Jews?" *New York Review of Books*, April 27, 1989 27. O'Brien correctly identifies the Jacobin current as the forerunner of twentieth century totalitarianism and chillingly cites the German theologian Gerhard Kittel [a "moderate"] who wrote in 1933, in *Die Judenfrage*, that "'Justice' is not an abstraction but something which grows out of the blood and soil and history of a *Volk*." O'Brien could, of course, have cited any number of Leninist *mots* to this effect, too).

5. Pope Pius VII (1800-23) was an interesting countercase. Despite his personal suffering at the hands of Napoleon, Pius VII was not so thoroughly soured on the "liberal project" as his successors Leo XII, Gregory XVI, and Pius IX. As Cardinal Luigi Barnaba Chiaramonti, Pius VII was a compromise candidate at the conclave of 1800, but one who had shown his moderate colors at Christmas 1797, when he shocked his conservative congregants with a sermon in which he

declared there to be no necessary conflict between Christianity and democracy. As pope, Pius VII and his secretary of state, the brilliant Cardinal Ercole Consalvi, tried to "blend administrative, judicial, and financial reforms on the liberal French model with the antiquated papal system"—an effort at cross-breeding that "exasperated reactionaries and progressives alike, and led to serious revolts" (J.N.D. Kelly, *The Oxford Dictionary of Popes* [Oxford: Oxford University Press, 1986], 302-304). Pius VII's modest reforms were rolled back by his successor Leo XII (1823-29), who also took up again the rhetorical cudgels against liberalism. Thus ended what might be called the Chiaramonti/Consalvi experiment in rapprochement between Roman Catholicism and the liberalizing reforms of the day. For the next fifty years, conservative retrenchment would dominate Vatican policy and the notion of "conservative reform" pioneered by Pius VII and Consalvi would fall by the wayside.

6. Cf. Owen Chadwick, *The Secularization of the European Mind in the 19th Century* (Cambridge: Cambridge University Press, 1975).

7. Cited in John Tracy Ellis, *American Catholicism*, 2nd edition, revised (Chicago: University of Chicago Press, 1969), 151.

8. "Cardinal Gibbons on Church and State," No. 129 in *Documents of American Catholic History*, vol. 2, ed. John Tracy Ellis, (Wilmington: Michael Glazier, 1987), 462-63 [emphasis added].

9. Gerald P. Fogarty, SJ, *The Vatican and the American Hierarchy from 1870 to 1965* (Wilmington: Michael Glazier, 1985), 41.

10. *Longinqua Oceani*, in *Documents of American Catholic History*, vol. 2, 502.

11. Cf. Anthony Rhodes, *The Vatican in the Age of the Dictators, 1922-1945* (New York: Holt, Rinehart and Winston, 1973), 14-15.

12. Cf. Jacques Maritain, *Christianity and Democracy* (San Francisco: Ignatius Press, 1986). Maritain had an interesting historical perspective on the events through which he was living, in exile in the United States: "We are looking on at the liquidation of what is known as the 'modern world' which ceased to be modern a quarter of a century ago when the First World War marked its entry into the past. The question is: in what will this liquidation result? ... [T]he tremendous historical fund of energy and truth accumulated for centuries is still available to human freedom, the forces of renewal are on the alert and it is still up to us to make sure that this catastrophe of the modern world is not a regression to the perverted aping of the Ancient Regime or the Middle Ages and that it does not wind up in the totalitarian putrefaction of the German New Order. It is up to us rather to see that it emerges in a new and truly creative age, where man, in suffering and hope, will resume his journey toward the conquest of freedom." 11, 17.

13. The divisions in pre-war French society are well-captured, in fictional form, in Piers Paul Read, *The Free Frenchman* (New York: Ivy Books, 1986).

14. One should also note, with an eye to 1992, the connection between these national Christian Democratic movements and the movement for West European integration that led to the Common Market and the European Parliament.

15. Cited in Joseph A. Komonchak, "Subsidiarity in the Church: The State of the Question," *The Jurist* 48 (1988), 299.

16. Is there a connection between the principle of subsidiarity and the American concept of "federalism" here? It would be going considerably out of bounds to

suggest that Madison's concept of federalism, as suggested in *Federalist 10* and *Federalist 51*, was informed by that classic Catholic social theory which eventually evolved the principle of subsidiarity; Madison should not be taken as a kind of proto-Pius XI. Indeed, *Federalist 10* and *Federalist 51* endorse decentralized decision-making not as an expression of human possibility, but as a remedy for human defects (the "defect of faction"). On the other hand, one can argue that federal arrangements (irrespective of their political-philosophical rationale) are one possible expression, in history, of the "principle of subsidiarity." One could possibly go further, and suggest that the principle of subsidiarity establishes a firmer moral-cultural and indeed philosophical foundation for federal arrangements than Madison's "let a thousand factions bloom," so to speak, that no one of them may become oppressively dominant. Grounded as it is in an ontology of the person that links being and acting and that regards human community as rooted in the social nature of the human person, the principle of subsidiarity might provide a more satisfactory basis for federalism than the voluntarism with which Madison is (wrongfully, in my view often charged, but of which some of his successors in American political theory (principally the "progressivist" historians of the Parrington/Beard school) are surely guilty.

17. These definitions, as well as the schema above, are adapted from Komonchak, "subsidiarity in the church."

18. On the *Koenigswinterer Kreis*, cf. Franz H. Mueller, *The Church and the Social Question* (Washington: American Enterprise Institute, 1984), 116-17.

19. On this distinction between the two encyclicals, cf. ibid., 214.

20. For a detailed examination of the Murray/Fenton/Connel controversy, cf. Donald Pelotte, *John Courtney Murray: Theologian in Conflict* (New York: Paulist Press, 1975).

21. *Catholicism and the Renewal of American Democracy* (New York: Paulist Press, 1989), 86.

22. *Dignitatis Humanae Personae*, 2.

23. Ibid.

24. Chief among these "prior" social institutions and the fundamental values they incarnate are what Murray called the *res sacrae in temporalibus*, those "sacred things in man's secular life" of which the Church had been the traditional guardian:

"... man's relation to God and to the church, the inner unity of human personality as citizen and Christian but one man, the integrity of the human body, the husband-wife relationship, the political obligation, the moral values inherent in economic and cultural activity as aspects of human life, the works of justice and charity which are the necessary expressions of the Christian and human spirit, and finally that patrimony of ideas which are the basis of civilized life—the ideas of law and right, of political power and the obligations of citizenship, of property, etc." (John Courtney Murray, "Paul Blanshard and the New Nativism," *The Month* [new series] 5:4 [April 1951], 244.)

26. For a fuller discussion of the "interior" and "public" meanings of religious freedom, cf. my essay, "Religious Freedom: The First Human Right," in *This World* 21 (Spring 1988), 31-58.

26. John Courtney Murray, SJ, "The Issue of Church and State at Vatican Council II, *Theological Studies* 27:4 (December 1966), 586.

27. For a fuller discussion of the instruction, and references, cf. my *Tranquillitas Ordinis: The Present Failure and Future Promise of American Catholic Thought on War and Peace* (New York: Oxford University Press, 1987), 291ff.
28. Instruction on Certain Aspects of the "Theology of Liberation," 17.
29. Instruction on Christian Freedom and Liberation, 95.
30. *Sollicitudo Rei Socialis*, 16.
31. Ibid., 44.
32. Ibid.
33. Ibid.
34. Quoted in *New York Times*, April 6, 1987.
35. Cited in *Origins* 17:15 (September 25, 1987).
36. Joseph Ratzinger, "Europe: A Heritage with Obligations for Christians," in *Church, Ecumenism and Politics* (New York: Crossroad, 1988), 228-29, 234.
37. Instruction on Christian Freedom and Liberation, 6.
38. William Lee Miller, *The First Liberty: Religion and the American Republic* (New York: Knopf, 1986), 145-46.
39. For the Catholic tradition of "moderate realism" in social ethics, cf. my *Tranquillitas Ordinis*, 25-45.
40. Cf. my chapter "The Jacobin Temptation in American Catholicism—The Worlds of the *National Catholic Reporter*," in *Catholicism and the Renewal of American Democracy*, 47-69.
41. *New York Times*, July 27, 1988.
42. Such a second- or third-phase liberation theology would also have to address the liberation of Latin American economies, and individual Latin Americans, from the crushing weight of mercantilism regulation and bureaucracy. One important test of the reality of a second- or third-phase liberation theology will be its openness to the analysis and prescriptions of, say, Hernando de Soto in *The Other Path* (New York: Harper & Row, 1989). One point of connection between de Soto's empirical studies on entrepreneurship and the evolution of Catholic social teaching may be found in *Sollicitudo Rei Socialis*, where John Paul II defends the "right of economic initiative" as an essential component of integral human development.
43. "Inculturation ... refers to the central and dynamic principle governing the Christian missionary outreach to peoples not yet evangelized, or among whom the church is not yet rooted firmly and indigenously. More commonly, this is known as the principle of catholicity, or accommodation, or adaptation, or indigenization, or contextualization ... [T]he principle of inculturation may be traced to its earliest articulation in St. Paul's great debate with the Jewish Christians [who] ... erroneously confused their new faith with their own ethnic conventions, cultural practices and local laws which they wished to impose upon all non-Jewish converts to Christianity.... [In contemporary terms, the principle means that if the Church] is to become a universally visible and intelligible sign of humankind's unity and salvation ... [it] must learn to experience and express itself through the cultural riches not only of Western peoples but of all peoples" (Eugene Hillman, "Inculturation," in Joseph A. Komonchak, Mary Collins, and Dermot A. Lane, eds., *The New Dictionary of Theology* [Wilmington: Michael Glazier, 1987], 510-12).

ELEVEN

LIBERALISM IN TENSION WITH CULTURE*

John Carroll

Has liberalism strengthened or weakened the moral culture of the West? That is my question. Let us start concretely. The rock of stability in modern Western societies has been the political constitution and its institutions. One wing of this is the law, the judiciary and the courts. The other is parliamentary democracy, on which I first want to concentrate. A key test of liberalism is the significance of its role in the development of parliamentary democracy. I will examine this question in relation to the inception of parliamentary democracy in England, focusing on its foundation and historical development.

Let us define our topic before we proceed further: Liberalism is an entire metaphysics of man, deriving from the axiom that the rational autonomous individual is the constituent element in human society. The individual is also the most important element. The more free a person is to pursue his happiness, the better this world will be. Liberalism is a derivative of humanism. In the words of Pico della Mirandola, "We can become what we will." Human beings possess free will, and applying this will in tandem with intelligence, one can benefit as an individual as well as improve society. The liberal view was given some ethical weight by Kant

---

* The author has developed this theme more broadly in his book titled *Humanism: The Rebirth and Wreck of Western Culture* (1992).

weight by Kant, with his insistence that human beings are ends in themselves. If there is a liberal ethics, its central principle is that it is wrong to use another human being entirely as a means to an end, for that would be to deny his autonomy, and thereby his dignity as an individual.

The evolution of parliamentary democracy took most of the five-hundred year humanist epoch, which began around 1500 A.D. It was largely complete by 1867 when Walter Bagehot published his enduringly insightful analysis of its workings, *The English Constitution*. Although the system has often loosely been called liberal-democratic, liberalism and the middle class played a minor role in its formation. The steady development from the absolutism of Henry VIII to the constitutional monarchy of Victoria was largely due to the success with which the aristocracy steadily wrestled power from the monarch, and then consolidated that power in parliament. This in itself was surprising. A parliament is quite unlike the typical aristocratic model of governing, the oligarchy or federation of powerful nobles. The more time passed, the more this came to be so. By the nineteenth century, parliament's executive and legislative decisions were being made by a committee, the Cabinet, under the charge of a powerful chairman, the Prime Minister, who was elected by the collegiate of the majority party in the parliament.

The liberal-democratic influence on this history was in citizens electing their representatives, and having the further check on those in power through a free press, public opinion, and free associations or pressure groups—as Tocqueville stressed in his great study contrasting aristocratic and democratic political forms. This was a liberal-humanist derivative, giving special power to each "I" among the citizenry. It depends on assumptions: the capacity of each adult to reason, to think intelligently about government, to have freedom to do what one thinks is right—i.e., liberty. The Protestant stress on the preeminence of the individual's conscience played an important part in the turbulent seventeenth century. A further liberal-humanist derivative, the belief in merit, was also important. Hence, ability rather than social background or personal patronage became the deciding factor as to who should occupy public office.

An ethic was still required in politics, and this was largely Protestant. A just politics depends on conscience, individuals acting honestly for a good higher than that of their own egos: the nation. It depends on vocational commitment. The heroic figure of Abraham Lincoln in American political imagery illustrates the point. Moreover, the Protestant ethic became more necessary as the aristocratic code of honor receded, with its obligation that nobles devote some of their time to politics in an honorary capacity. Without either of these ethics, politics degenerates into a chaos of competing pressure groups, deals, buying off, and before long—corruption.

Parliamentary democracy depended for its success on other basic factors. Among these were a respect for tradition, and the practical manifestation of that in an independent judiciary, a legal system independent of the political system, with its own history and tradition, and its own collective conscience. In the crises of English political history, reliance on a long established constitution and its legal forms thwarted any tyrannical moves by the monarch. This factor is neither Protestant nor liberal. Indeed it is at odds with liberalism, as Edmund Burke pointed out in his polemic against the French Revolution. The wisdom inherent in the English political system by the end of the eighteenth century had little to do with reason and ideals about progress and the 'rights of man,' or the arrogance of the humanist 'We can become what we will.' The English wisdom, rather had to do with good instincts and healthy prejudices, a respect for what generations had slowly and sometimes painfully built. In other words, parliamentary democracy depended in good part for its stability on an anti-liberal skepticism about the power of human reason and a conservative warmth and attachment to custom and tradition.

The European aristocracies had a real culture, with authority and weight. It was founded on ancestors, blood lines, family portraits on the walls, heirlooms of swords and decorations from wars, and stories of generations of valor. This was clan culture consolidated in property, the ancestral home, a tribe of dependents, and the status of the family title, all engraved in a fixed social hierarchy with king above, and commoners beneath. The Reformation created its own quite different real culture. Liberal-humanism, however, never succeeded on its own. While it had its own unique and trenchant ideals, it never managed to grow roots. It was a parasitic form that to survive had to feed off strengths external to it. There had been Christian humanism, exemplified by Erasmus, still tied to the Catholic umbilical cord. There was aristocratic humanism. The Renaissance created the glittering humanist fantasy, but once it lost its Christian root, the ethic it sought to ground itself in was not its own; it was aristocratic. The ideal of the gentleman is in fact a hybrid of humanist notions integrated into an aristocratic core.

The third and last parasitic form was Puritan humanism, the case of the bourgeoisie. Bourgeois culture had a tendency to swing backward and forward between Protestant and aristocratic poles, especially in England where the class organization of society survived longest. In the nineteenth century, sons from a hardworking middle-class entrepreneurial background would often, in entering Oxford or Cambridge, soon distance themselves from their Puritan home backgrounds and take to aristocratic habits, under the influence of the poise, confidence and style of the upper-class gentlemen. Their fathers, for whom the harsh Calvinist God was now little more than a distant ancestral ghost, usually approved. By this time, in France and Germany, the aristocratic presence was weaker and the bourgeoisie compensated by making culture a much stronger ideal.

My argument then is that liberalism on its own is not a real cultural entity. What is real culture? The distinctive sign that it exists is that people have a place to stand, metaphysically speaking, that does not move under their feet. The test of culture was put by Archimedes: "Give me a place to stand, and I will move the earth." This means roots. It means gravity. It means unquestioned faith in a 'No!', without doubt. It was what Luther needed in order to assert his own 'Here I stand.' It is the foundation of honor, and as every real culture has taught, the dishonorable life is not worth living. Honor takes precedence over happiness, it places a limit on pleasure. Real culture stakes in limits which will not give, whatever the pressure.

Liberalism on its own is the French Revolution, where reason and free will combined to build a political utopia from the ground up, having annihilated all the traditional constraints of inherited wealth, status, power and prejudice—all hierarchy and custom. What resulted was not virtue and happiness, but the Reign of Terror and Napoleon, with two million Frenchmen killed for no reason. Liberalism on its own is scientific research into anything and everything. In 1982 in Australia, in the name of progress and intellectual curiosity, rat eggs were fertilized with human sperm. Liberalism on its own is the free press without censorship, with no reason for propriety, which could quite easily lead to (and fairly soon) mass-circulation daily newspapers devoted to pornography. Why not? Liberalism is incapable on its own of defending any 'No.' Everything is negotiable in the name of freedom, of the rights of the autonomous and rational individual to follow his every pleasure.

Liberalism on its own is not a real culture. Worse, it is a destroyer of culture. However, it has made lasting and significant contributions to Western society when it has worked in alliance with one or another of the two real cultural forms whose unconscious influence has survived in modernity—the aristocratic and the Protestant. There are three separate contributions that liberalism has helped to make. The first has been to the political system, as already discussed. In the formative English case, it must have been some liberal sentiments, probably imbibed from the strong and independent legal tradition rooted in common law, that inclined politically successful aristocrats to channel new powers into parliament rather than a closed oligarchy. Moreover, the major reforms of the nineteenth century were notably under the influence of liberal ideas. These included the extension of the franchise, and the evolution of the party, cabinet and prime ministerial leadership model to increase the stability of government, and to consolidate merit as the principle of promotion. Here was liberalism in alliance, on the one hand, with an essentially aristocratic institution, underpinned by the character ideal of the 'gentleman' code of honor. On the other hand, there was the Protestant ethic with its emphasis on duty, selfless hard work and honesty. In summary, it can be said that liberalism leavened a weighty cultural lump.

The second liberal contribution was in the economic sphere. By the late twentieth century we have seen many different possible systems for the production and distribution of goods and services in industrial civilization. From this, we can conclude that the free market, for all its imperfections, is by far the best at creating prosperity, and a prosperity that is reasonably just. The free market is the material correlate of liberalism, both interpreted and affirmed by its leading theorists from Adam Smith onward.

The third liberal contribution has been to the conduct of daily life. The ideal of the autonomous individual—articulated by Kant in the 'moral imperative' to treat every man as an end in himself— has produced a fairly just daily life. The individual is more than a cog in the economic and social machine, according to liberalism. In exhorting us to take the rights of other individuals seriously, liberalism has enhanced the quality of life in the modern West. This is another instance, however, where the liberal contribution was benign only because it worked within a context of cultural checks, independent of it.

There is another area of great social importance in which liberal-humanism has played a key role: education. The example is peculiarly instructive in that liberal ideas initially exerted an improving influence, but once they gained sway they turned destructive. There is a long tradition in political thought that argues that the ideal institution strikes a balance between liberty and authority, or in the categories I am employing here, liberty and culture. The history of schooling over the last century and a half exhibits a tipping of the scales from too much authority to a golden mean, and then in recent decades a further swing into too much liberty.

Again, I wish to focus on England, where the clash of the different cultural forms has been most obvious. English education, dominated by Oxford and Cambridge, and the Public Schools, remained essentially aristocratic until well into the twentieth century. For instance, it was not until the 1930s that the humanist value on 'culture' made any headway in the Public Schools. A key difference between England and France or Germany was the enduring vitality of a social hierarchy led by a confident upper class, one which was open to the middle class with money. One could gain entry to this upper class through sending sons, and eventually daughters, to Public School. Those elite schools had the aim of developing 'character,' which they did mainly through an emphasis on sport and a Spartan disciplinary regimen, which had special effect because they were boarding institutions that had total control of their pupils. Their curriculum well into the twentieth century was mainly the rote learning of the ancient classics. They were not greatly interested in whether their students learned much. The main nineteenth century reform, exemplified by Thomas Arnold's Rugby, was the addition of a severe evangelical Protestantism, infusing the character ideal with piety: the school's task was now to turn out more godly, morally superior gentlemen with a strong sense of civic duty.

The Public Schools retained their aristocratic goal of reinforcing the class hierarchy. Character was not simply to be pious and good: it should have 'tone.' There was an inviolable code of how to speak and behave, what views to hold, and with whom to associate. Here was the crucible for the intensely coercive formation of the small, exclusive caste that dominated English society and occupied almost all its important offices. In this system there was no need for the liberal-humanist ideals of culture, knowledge and the trained intellect.

The great achievement of the English Public Schools was the development of 'character,' the turning out of young men with a commanding sense of public duty and the personal values of the Puritan gentleman. There followed a period between about 1920 and 1960 when the Spartan rituals were moderated in a liberal direction, and learning became important. If it had been possible to resist the democratizing drift of the surrounding culture, and hold schools in this moment as a force for stability and continuity, then it would be fair to chalk this up as another liberal contribution to Western well-being. This was not to be, and character was slowly drowned in an increasing academicism. One of the darker implications of this story is that education and learning may be deeply at odds with each other. I mean education in the sense of the old Plato of the *Laws*:

> Education is the rightly disciplined state of pleasures and pains whereby a man, from this first beginnings on, will abhor what he should abhor and relish what he should relish.

My overall conclusion is thus two-sided. First, the West has benefited from liberalism in three important ways. Liberalism contributed considerably to the development of our political institutions, our economic system, and the humane conduct of everyday life. This is an achievement not lightly to be dismissed. Second, liberalism played a gravely destructive role in other key areas of our culture. The schooling example illustrates a typical pattern. In the first instance, liberalism loosens up an institution and makes it more supportive of individual initiative and development. Liberalism is, however, wildly contagious. Before long it starts to undermine the cultural limits that have kept its own anarchic spirit in check. In the end all limits are gone, and we have cultural decadence in the modern Western mode, in the liberal mode.

TWELVE

SEXUAL MORALITY AND THE LIBERAL CONSENSUS

Roger Scruton

The liberal view of the state requires government by consent. The most plausible version of this requirement formulates the test of legitimacy in these terms: The legitimate state is the one that each individual citizen would consent to, in those circumstances where consent derives solely from the principles of rational choice. In our time the most famous exponent of that idea has been Rawls, but it can be recognized, in one form or another, as fundamental to Enlightenment thinking. The state ought therefore to be neutral regarding all those matters over which rational people might reasonably disagree. By a wholly natural movement of thought, the liberal tends to conclude that morality and its enforcement are no business of the state. To make the state into the guardian of morality is to give privileges to a particular morality, and therefore to those individuals who subscribe to it. But other individuals, whose values differ from those endorsed by the high command, may be equally reasonable in affirming them, and equally entitled to live as their conscience dictates. They could never rationally consent to an order that forbids this right, and therefore no such order can be countenanced. The only conceivable liberal order is one that remains morally neutral, standing above and beyond those particular 'conceptions of the good' which motivate the various ways of life that are subsumed by it.

Inherent in that argument is the assumption that rational beings may reasonably differ concerning the requirements of morality. Kant denied the assumption, on the grounds that moral principles emerge directly and necessarily from the autonomous exercise of practical reason, and that every rational being will, in those circumstances where his reason is unclouded, spontaneously affirm a common moral code. Moral neutrality seems to follow from the liberal view of the state, only on the assumption that the ordinary principles of rational choice—principles which every individual can be expected to endorse—do not fully determine the content of morality. That is the assumption made by Rawls, and by many other liberal thinkers. It is an assumption that is easily made, given the manifest fact that ordinary people, even though rational, must invariably be prompted by something other than reason—a religion, for example—if they are to have a clear idea of right and wrong. A problem then arises for the liberal world view. These ancillary forces which turn us to the moral life are not as a rule tolerant of rivals. They are not 'experimental' attitudes. On the contrary, they derive their power from an authority that countenances no alternative. God's will cannot be countermanded, and once revealed, cannot be disobeyed. The very fact that it provides the certainty which reason never offers makes religion immune to argument, and intolerant of those who reject its counsels.

Faced with this dilemma, the liberal conscience tends to turn in one of two directions: either it reverts to the metaphysical morality of Kant, affirming that reason alone determines the content of morality, or it retreats by degrees from the moral view of things, replacing praise and condemnation with an easy toleration which, while rotten with guilt feelings, denies the reality of guilt. Neither solution is comfortable. The first has the unwelcome consequence that the state is, after all, entitled to enforce the moral code—whatever it might be—that spontaneously emerges from the exercise of reason. The second has the equally unwelcome consequence that no merely human power can be allowed to impede man's corruption, but that every 'option', however repugnant, is but another form that liberty may take.

An illustration of the liberal dilemma is provided by homosexuality—a practice which has often been condemned, but which is now permitted wherever the liberal conscience holds sway. It is true that the liberal is not obliged to countenance every human impulse. He will argue that some fragments of traditional morality can be reconstructed on principles, and endorsed and upheld by the law. It has always been central to the liberal idea that rational beings will not consent to be harmed by their neighbors, so that practices which threaten harm can be outlawed and the implicit agreement of everyone safely assumed. But aside from forbidding murder, violence, and theft, this way of thinking leaves us powerless to determine the path of others' salvation. So vague is the concept of 'harm' that it is never clear what activities can be condemned by it. Do we condemn homosexuality because it might lead to disease? Or do we condemn the disease? In the latter case, our moral obligation is not to refrain from buggery, but to look for a prophylactic against the effects of it. The moral status of the act becomes incalculable: best, therefore, to permit it, for fear of losing that most precious of political commodities, the consent of the one with whom we disagree.

Although a liberal may find homosexuality 'distasteful,' therefore, he tends to regard this as an individual prejudice of no intrinsic moral interest. Distaste is not the same as disapproval, and disapproval must always be withheld until the case is proved. The legacy of this world view (if I may so describe it) has been confusion. For while ordinary people have little sympathy with homosexuality, they hesitate to describe it in the terms which otherwise would come so naturally to them, as immoral. In an age of liberal consensus, nobody is more severely censured (and censored) than the anti-liberal. With the growth of proselytizing homosexuality, which seeks to enter schools and households with the liberating message that there are rival 'orientations,' the situation has arisen in which parents seek desperately to shield their children from an influence which they are forbidden to condemn. The result is part of the inevitable unhappiness of humanity, when the liberal conscience rules over it.

I shall consider the case of homosexuality since I believe not only that it is of primary importance at the present time, but also that it leads us, when properly considered, to an important insight into morality. The terms 'moral' and 'immoral' have traditionally been used more of sexual conduct than conduct of any other kind. Under the influence of liberal ideas, however, they have been gradually voided of their sexual application. Instead, the terms 'moral' and 'immoral' are reserved for those relatively undemanding areas in which toleration comes easily, and in which the liberal conscience is naturally at home. These are areas of calculation, where cost and benefit seem clear. (Hence the peculiar examples in books of moral philosophy: ought I to visit Aunty Jane in the hospital, or ought I instead to attend the meeting of the Academic Council? Ought I to shoot the intruder now, or ought I to wait until I know that he is armed? In these dilemmas the great question is avoided—what sort of person should I be? This may be a religious question, but it is also at the root of the two most vivid secular moralities that I know—those of Aristotle and Nietzsche.)

Traditional sexual morality tends to lean on two kinds of teaching: the theological, which advises us that the body is God's image, and must therefore not be defiled; and the familial, which tells us that the sexual act is not what it appears to be (a project for individual pleasure), but a commitment which includes others who are not party to it, and indeed who may not yet be born. The Catholic Church has emphasized both those ideas, and described the hidden *telos* of the sexual act as the generation of children. On that radical view all actions—including contraception—which sever the act from its God-given purpose, are immoral. They disavow our primary commitments and allow us to put our own gratification ahead of the obligation to life.

It is difficult to make the Catholic teaching clear—even as fine a mind as Professor Anscombe's has notoriously failed to do so. Nevertheless, it seems to capture a worry that is already familiar to readers of *Brave New World*, and to all who have followed with alarm the insolent proposals for 'genetic engineering' which have so exhilarated the liberal imagination in recent years. If children can be made in laboratories, and by methods which bear no relation to the love-making of their parents, what remains of those commitments which tie the generations to each other and give us a motive, in our most urgent ventures toward the Other, to safeguard the world for those who have not yet entered it?

Attempts have been made to reconstruct the idea of commitment on purely individualistic premises, without reference to the dead and the unborn who have such an interest in our conduct.

Chastity, for instance, may be defended as the virtue which prepares us for love, and for the consolations upon which our happiness depends. (I have developed this argument in *Sexual Desire*.) We might all therefore have reason to control our sexual impulses, in order to reap the greater benefit of consolation. But such an argument hardly seems to capture the weight, or the urgency, of our moral interdictions. Moreover, this argument is powerless to rule against homosexuality: it forbids promiscuity only, something that the wiser proponents of 'the love that dares not speak its name' have in any case always condemned.

The issue becomes clearer when we recognize that there is a distinction between the first-person and the third-person view of agency, and that liberalism, for commendable reasons, has always taken the first-person view as fundamental. For the liberal, the question of social order is the question of my choice—whether I would, in real or ideal conditions, consent to it. Hence the only reasons relevant to the legitimacy of a practice are the reasons individual agents might have for permitting or forbidding it. From this first-person point of view, given 'risk and uncertainty,' the constraints of traditional morality appear to have an arbitrary—or at any rate a nonrational—character. From the first-person point of view, traditional morality consists of sacrifices or 'uncompensated costs.' One purpose of religion is to convert these costs into notional benefits—rewards stored up in heaven, or yet heavier costs foregone in purgatory and hell. But when we lose religious belief (and liberalism is historically a consequence of that loss), it becomes hard to see why the costs of moral sacrifice should be incurred at all.

But there is also the third-person view of moral agency—the view which sees our actions from outside, and which does not limit its perspective to those features of a situation that can provide a reason for me, here, now. The third-person perspective can arise in two ways: first as the perspective that others take of my action; second, as the perspective that I might take, were I to step outside the limits imposed by my present motivation and see my action in the context of my life as a whole.

From the point of view of others, the sacrifice required by morality may be a social benefit. Consider the Spartans at Thermopylae. They were motivated by honor, which commanded them to stand and die. No selfish calculation could conceivably recommend that course of action. Their first-person reasoning, therefore, which started from the absolute interdiction of dishonorable conduct, may seem arbitrary, even irrational—certainly not something that a liberal could recommend to others. On the other hand, the motive of honor, and the disposition to sacrifice one's life for honor's sake, are useful to the social organism that instills them. A society which can count on these motives has—as the historical experience of the Greeks demonstrates—an immense evolutionary advantage over its rivals. And a society which, like that prevailing in the last days of Rome, is devoid of the spirit of sacrifice, will fall to the first competitor. Those obvious (if shocking) truths provide some justification for a moral education which instills the motive of honor in its pupils.

This third-person perspective on action is not the prerogative of the third person. I can adopt such a perspective on my own action. In doing so, I may find reasons for the cultivation of motives which I presently do not have, but which serve my long-term interest. This, I believe, is the leading idea of Aristotle's *Nicomachean Ethics*. For Aristotle, the self-sacrificing motives, which have *to kalon* as their goal, serve not only society, but also the individual. However, to discern this is not within the power of everyone: It is not given to the ordinary person to understand that happiness lies in the exercise of virtue, and that one therefore has reason to acquire the self-sacrificing motive. Since a person's practical reasoning must begin from motives that he presently has, it will never be possible for the unphilosophical person, lacking the motive of honor, to acquire that motive by his own reasoning powers. Nor will he, acting in a spirit of calculation, approximate his conduct to that of the virtuous individual. However, suppose Aristotle is right. Suppose that happiness is our final goal, the obtaining of which justifies every labor expended in the pursuit of it. Suppose that happiness is 'an activity of the soul in accordance with virtue.' And suppose that virtue is the disposition to pursue what is honorable, regardless of countervailing desires. If this is so, then we are right to instill the motive of honor, even in those people who do not presently possess it, and who, from the first-person point of view, can find no reason to act as honor requires. We are justified not only for society's sake, but for the individual's sake as well.

Such thoughts provide the foundation for an illiberal morality— or at least, for an illiberal moral education. The principal questions are twofold: Can we instill motives, such as honor, in those who do not possess them? And can we do so without violating some other moral imperative, for example, without violating their rights? We shall return later to these questions.

The hostility to the homosexual act derives from a feeling of revulsion. This revulsion is an instance of a more general reaction to what we might call unseemly visions of the flesh. It is a curious fact that certain uses and aspects of our bodies arouse the most violent reactions. Obscenity is an illustration: the sense, which we may find extremely hard to justify, that certain things cannot be looked at, cannot even be thought of. Obscene things display someone as threatened, overcome, or extinguished in his body. Our fear of obscenity, like our curiosity toward it, parallels our fear and curiosity toward death.

Sexual revulsion is manifest too in the feeling of shame, described by Scheler as a *Schutzgefühl*—a protective feeling, whereby the self guards itself against invasion. A woman, whose sexual feeling, once aroused, attaches her immovably to its object, clearly has a reason to hesitate. She therefore has reason to acquire those *Schutzgefühle*, of which shame is one, that guard her against any hasty indulgence.

The ordinary person's revulsion against homosexuality can be seen as another such *Schutzgefühl*, a feeling which protects one from activities which one might otherwise engage in. From the liberal point of view, the question of homosexuality takes a straightforward form: Are there reasons why one who wishes to engage in homosexual practices should refrain from doing so? Whichever way the argument goes (for the liberal can be dissuaded from an 'option' if the costs are high), the homosexual act is purged of the aura of sin which was previously attached to it. Buggery is at worst inadvisable. For the traditional conscience, the question takes a different form: thinking about homosexuality starts from the premise of revulsion, an absolute interdiction which blocks off the path to indulgence. The question is no longer whether the benefits of transgression outweigh the costs—one of the costs presumably being the guilt feelings which one's *Schutzgefühl* will almost certainly inflict on one. For revulsion is one of those motives that bring calculation to an end. Like the motive of honor, it defines its object as forbidden. I may go against my revulsion, but the revulsion is not to be measured on the scale of costs, and is not overridden even when defied. It possesses the categorical character of moral sentiments generally. The question is whether the feeling can be justified: is there a reason to instill this kind of revulsion against the homosexual act? And can we do so without violating other moral imperatives? I believe that the answer to both these questions is yes.

First let us consider the interests of society. What are the social benefits of retaining, and the social costs of abolishing, the *Schutzgefühl* that forbids homosexual intercourse? The social arguments for the traditional view are, I believe, of four kinds.

PRESERVATION OF GENERATIONAL FAMILY BONDS

First, traditional sexual morality instills and reinforces an idea of the sexually normal. This idea has a social function of reinforcing the desire of one generation to sacrifice itself for the next. The family embodies this spirit of sacrifice, transforming sexual attraction into a commitment to offspring, and at the same time, a commitment to home. Sexual feeling acquires a solemn character: those unborn have an interest in it, and this interest is transformed into a sense of eternity, which inhabits the sexual passion itself. 'Normal' sexual feeling is forever. To mark this 'eternal' quality, sexual unions are traditionally enshrined in vows, rather than in contracts. 'Normal' sexual feeling comes to enjoy the dignity of a sacrament.

The liberal view, by contrast, sees the sexual transaction as an agreement between consenting adults, who write the terms of the contract according to their own desires. Other generations are not intrinsically involved in their transaction, and become involved only if the parties desire. The sexual act loses its solemnity, and the sacrifices which some people (the 'straights') feel mysteriously impelled to undertake for the sake of future generations seem optional and arbitrary. Why go to such trouble merely for the sake of sexual pleasure?

The idea that homebuilding is the normal result, and the justifying goal, of sexual attraction is so widespread and enduring, that we might be tempted to conclude—on grounds of natural selection—

that my functional justification of it is empirically confirmed. At any rate, its loss cannot be in the interests of society. On the contrary, society, whose hopes lie with those unborn, has a reason to avoid any developments which tend to sever sexual passion from the commitment to future generations. Surely, then, the easy permission of homosexual union—as an 'orientation,' on a par with that which leads to the raising of children—offers a threat to social continuity.

TRUE SEXUAL LOVE AS A SPIRITUAL AWAKENING

According to the traditional conception, the sexual act involves the passing of a threshold, a moving outward from the self, into a realm that is partly unknown. The body of the Other is a mystery, whose secrets are unlocked by the charm of desire. Sexual possession is also a spiritual awakening; a peculiar sense of responsibility comes from knowing that you have awakened feelings that you do not understand. The heterosexual therefore makes himself vulnerable in the sexual act, and is a solicitor for love and understanding. This experience is hard to describe in philosophical idiom, although it is familiar enough from poetry. Once the possibility of homosexual intercourse is freely admitted, however, what remains of it? Again, it becomes a 'residue'—a discardable option. The body of the homosexual's beloved belongs to the same kind as his own, there is no mystery in its arousal, nor in the desire that animates it. It is not truly 'Other.' It lacks the inviolable character which attaches (for a man) to the body of woman and vice versa. To deal with it there is no need for love or understanding, nor is there a mystery to be unlocked. The loss of the revulsion against homosexuality therefore takes us one step further along the road to the de-sanctifying of the human body. It becomes easier to see the sexual act as an animal performance, rather than a spiritual journey. Again, for reasons already implied, it would seem that society has an interest in preventing such a loss.

PROMISCUITY AS A RESULT OF DEVIATION

Perhaps as a consequence of that loss, there is, in homosexual union—especially that between men—a tendency toward promiscuity. Unimpeded by the shame which governs women, unhindered by the awe which attends woman's awakening, the male homosexual hastens to arouse in another those feelings which he knows in himself. The natural predatoriness of the male is shared by both partners, and the body of the one holds no mystery for the other. When the experience of the other is so familiar and predictable, it can easily become the subject of a contract, and if both parties consent, why should the contract not be acted upon? It is surely no accident, therefore, that male homosexuals are promiscuous, once they have lost the *Schutzgefühl* which forbids their desire. The result of promiscuity is to void the sexual relation of commitment. No society, therefore, has an interest in permitting it.

RENUNCIATION AS A SOCIAL GOOD

It is undeniable that a certain number of people in any generation, especially men, are attracted to their own sex, and especially to children of their own sex. The *Schutzgefühl* prevents them from expressing their desire, and perhaps even from overtly acknowledging it. Indeed, it turns them against their sexuality, and directs them along the path of renunciation. At the same time, in searching for an outlet for their now 'sublimated' feelings, they tend more and more to take an interest in the young. They become priests, teachers, scoutmasters, and so on. They acquire the character of 'father' to everyone's children, and their role in that of *paideia*, in the Greek sense. If you were to wonder why it is that homosexual impulses are reproduced in human societies, then here is a functional explanation: societies benefit from the emergence of a priestly class, which in turn benefits from sublimated homosexual feeling, and the vow of chastity that enshrines it. Homosexuality can confer this beneficial effect, however, only if the homosexual act is the object of revulsion.

I have sketched four lines of justification that might be offered for the *Schutzgefühl* forbidding homosexual intercourse. They are by no means conclusive: nor could a conclusive third-person argument be mounted for any of our *Schutzgefühle*. For the facts about society are hard to grasp. (Consider, for example, how we might justify our revulsion against pedophilia.) It is also a further question whether the *Schutzgefühl* is in the interests not only of society but of the individual. Maybe those things which further the well-being of society also further the well-being of its normal member. But that does not give us what Aristotle promised, namely, an argument to show that the individual must have certain motives if he is to be happy (if he is to flourish according to his nature). When people condemn homosexuality as unnatural they are implying that such arguments exist.

I suggest that the individual does indeed have an interest in being sexually normal according to the traditional conception. For he has an interest in all of the following: in tying sexual desire to love, and love to commitment, in viewing sexual union as a vow and a sacrament, in feeling the urge to sacrifice oneself for one's children, and to make a home for them. He has an interest in living cleanly and chastely, governed by sentiments of responsibility and awe toward the body of one's companion. And he has a reason to acquire those feelings—revulsion against promiscuity, homosexuality, bestiality, pedophilia, and obscenity—which keep him on the path of decency, and which reassure him of the innocence of his pleasures. He has an interest in all this, because he needs that which can easily be acquired by no other way, unless it be the way of renunciation and *paideia*: knowledge of one's proximity to, and right conduct toward, the rising generation. All people need the love of children, and all people need to confirm their values and their lives in terms of what they transmit to their successors. This is part of moral certainty; and without moral certainty humanity is prey to unassuageable guilt.

That is only a sketch. It depends upon assumptions (defended elsewhere) about the nature of sexual desire. But if it were true, it would follow that we must, if we can, instill in children the feelings of revulsion that guide them to the normal path. But can we do this without infringing upon any other moral imperative? It seems evident that we can. For sexual revulsion is pliable. Although it is founded in natural facts, such as the mechanism of sexual selection, it is everywhere reshaped by education. People are taught to feel ashamed of certain acts, by the opprobrium and ridicule that is heaped upon those who overtly perform them. However, can such a method of education coexist with the 'respect for persons' which lies at the heart of the liberal world view? In one sense, yes: for the condemnation and shaming of those who overtly engage in homosexual behavior is compatible with the view that each has a right to live as he wishes *in private*. It has always been a requirement of sexual morality that public scandal be avoided, and private practice concealed. The distinction between the private and the public is indeed integral to any sexual morality that could commend itself to the normal conscience. If one says that those things which are done privately should be condoned publicly—as Diogenes did, when asked why he masturbated in full view of passers-by—then one will soon come to the conclusion that there is no such thing as sexual morality, but only irrational feelings of distaste. On the other hand, one may concede that certain acts are shameful, and must therefore be concealed if they are to be performed at all. One can maintain this and still believe that we have no right to cross another's threshold, into that world of 'rights' where he alone is sovereign, so as to prevent him from doing certain actions. That surely was the traditional position, in its most civilized form. It is a position, however, which liberalism renounced, when it lost its sense of shame. It then found no reason against advocating that which it could find no reason to suppress.

But now we must part company with the liberal viewpoint. For suppose my contentions are right. Suppose the *Schutzgefühl* forbidding homosexual intercourse is in the interest of society, and also of the individuals who compose it. It is nevertheless true that the arguments for this are hard to understand, especially when expressed in the secular and abstract form given to them here. No unphilosophical rational being would come naturally to reject the homosexual 'option,' if he did not already possess revulsion for it—at least, not by reasoning. Nor would he, lacking that feeling, have any sense either of the sinfulness of the homosexual act, or of the desirability of avoiding it. Only if the revulsion is implanted by means which bypass reflective powers, could he ever come to see the point of the traditional interdiction. In formative years, therefore, he must be subject to an education process which could never be justified from liberal premises. Our moral education cannot be a purely 'enlightened' and 'enlightening' one. It cannot be simply a matter of teaching to calculate the long term profit and the loss, while leaving our desires to develop independently. It must involve an 'endarkened' and 'endarkening' component, by which we are taught precisely to cease calculations, and to regard certain paths as forbidden—as places where neither profit nor loss has authority. There is no force like religion, for endarkening the mind in this way.

If such a moral education is ever to be justified, however, we will have to abandon the liberal concept of society. For a society which serves the happiness of its members would then contain a component that could not be a part of the social contract. It would involve practices which close options that a liberal must regard as open, and which could not be recommended purely on the basis of the first-person reasoning of any and every agent. Only those who share the favored revulsions, or who have worked through the arduous reasoning that justifies them, will see that they have a reason to accept such a society and to live within its institutions.

THIRTEEN

MORAL EDUCATION IN SOME ENGLISH-SPEAKING SOCIETIES: ANTINOMIAN AND FUNDAMENTALIST CHALLENGES

Geoffrey Partington

In countries such as Britain, Australia and the United States, three main coalitions can be perceived in the field of moral education: the first, traditionalist, dogmatic or fundamentalist; the second, attached to what Robert Bellah (1975) termed 'civil religion'—the ethos of the early twentieth century American schoolhouse, the Australian government school, or the English LEA-maintained school; and the third, antinomian, opposed to any notion of a binding universal moral law. For most of the twentieth century government school systems in English-speaking countries accepted, implicitly at least, a series of moral prescriptions and proscriptions based loosely on traditional Judeo-Christian teaching, but without specific commitment to any religious doctrine. This type of civil religion was rejected by the Roman Catholic Church and by most of its adherents. But it was found satisfactory by the overwhelming majority of Protestants, including fundamentalists, whose forerunners had indeed often taken the lead in opposing dogmatic teaching in schools (the dogma being that of established churches they considered to be in error). During the 1960s antinomianism began to undermine forms of civil religion in government schools in Britain, Australia, and the United States. During that period larger numbers of protestant fundamentalists turned away from government schools. This process has continued by and large for the last quarter of a century. Antinomianism, sometimes in the form of 'Values Clarification,' is making further advances, although not as much as many antinomians would wish. Meanwhile, fundamentalists are becoming increasingly alienated from government schools. Upholders of the besieged civil religion are unsure as to whether fundamentalism or antinomianism is the greatest threat to their hopes for the government school as a moral agency influencing the overwhelming majority of the population.

PROTESTANT FUNDAMENTALISM

Most Protestant fundamentalists for most of the twentieth century found government schools in the United Kingdom, the United States, or Australia adequate for their children. This was not because their own specific doctrines were taught in them, but because schools contained little, if anything, directly repugnant to their beliefs. Typically, short passages of the Bible were read daily or weekly, usually without commentary. Christianity was mentioned with respect, and the public morality propagated was highly compatible with Christian beliefs. For that matter, the moral injunctions offered by Roman Catholic schools, as distinct from the 'Catholic atmosphere' deemed essential by Rome, were broadly similar to those of the government schools. The 'Victorian virtues' were not rejected by British, Irish, American, or Australian Catholics, who claimed indeed that their schools were best at inculcating them. Equally, Roman Catholics, although considering secular schools sinful in their omissions, could not attack them, as they did later, for sins of commission, such as nonjudgmental teaching about contraception or abortion, since such matters did not enter the curriculum.

Before the late 1960s, government schools made few intrusions into the realms of private belief and family relationships, certainly not enough to alarm most Protestant fundamentalists. Their worries about schools were largely confined to the apparently conflicting claims of science and of revealed religion, numerous battles being fought on the 'Genesis vs. Darwin' front. Protestant fundamentalist schools in America and Australia rapidly expanded over the last two decades. This expansion originated not so much as a positive initiative aimed at taking salvation to others, than as a defensive reaction to increasing antinomianism in many government school systems. It is true many Protestant fundamentalist families reacted in dismay or horror to the intrusive power of the new mass media, bearing messages deeply inimical to their beliefs. Fundamentalists looked to the school more than in the past as an agency to counteract those influences. There was a strong correlation between the success of antinomianism within government schools and the fundamentalist flight from them. Once established, some fundamentalist Protestant schools attracted other parents, fearful that poor standards of work and conduct in their neighborhood government schools would have negative effects on their children. In general, however, nonfundamentalist parents sought a less dogmatic alternative, including Roman Catholic schools, which by the 1980s had typically a less pervasive religious atmosphere than that of the new fundamentalist schools.

Before the antinomian successes in the post-1970 era in government school systems, many antinomians favored alternative schools both within and outside of government schools. During the 1980s, antinomian opinion became increasingly hostile not only to any governmental funding for Protestant fundamentalist schools, but to their very existence. The minimal antinomian demand is that such schools should be subjected to governmental controls which would, in effect, destroy their distinctive character. Despite antinomian hostilities, Peshkin (1989, 48-9) acknowledges that Protestant fundamentalist students:

> achieve above-average scores on national tests, they receive good instruction in English; and they are taught by hardworking, dedicated teachers. Christian schools create a safe environment in physical and moral terms; they emphasize character training; they promote a sense of community; and according to my data, their students are noted for their low alienation and also for personal qualities that make them attractive to local employers.

Peshkin expressed alarm, however, that such students (1989, 51):

are taught to see the world in the dichotomized terms of us and them, with the clear-cut good guys—the born-again brethren—learning to stay separate on principle from the clear-cut bad guys—the rest of us ... children readily acquired the terms for stereotyping: secular humanist, Satan, and the world, on the one hand, and believer, born-again, and Christian on the other.

Pushkin (1989, 52) values "the principled protection of aberrant institutions," which, as he rightly says, "is not commonly found elsewhere in the world" (that is, outside the United States and other liberal democracies). He holds such principled protection to be "bred in the bones of our society" and "integral to the particular form we give pluralism." But he obviously had to struggle hard before rejecting the case that there is a 'compelling interest' requiring state intervention to forbid the indoctrinative practices engaged in by Protestant fundamentalist schools. He was especially disturbed by the pledge imposed on its teachers by the Bethany Baptist Academy,

> I affirm that I am a born-again Christian believing the Bible to be the inspired Word of God without contradiction or error in its original languages. I believe that every Christian should be separated from worldly habits.

Peshkin, one assumes, is a sensitive defender of the attenuated civil religion, rather than an antinomian. But many antinomians, including many leading officials in government school systems in Australia and other English-speaking countries, unlike Peshkin consider that there is a 'compelling interest' on governments to regulate and if necessary suppress Protestant fundamentalist schools.

ISLAMIC FUNDAMENTALISM
Like Protestant fundamentalists and Roman Catholics before them, many recent Muslim immigrants into English-speaking countries seek an education for their children which provides relevant secular knowledge within a framework of traditional belief. For Muslims who conform to the *Sunna*, the obstacles to achieving this aim are even greater than for Christians, Protestant or Catholic. This is not only because they are in countries little influenced by their own religious traditions but because Islam has remained a total way of life which allows no leeway to individuals or institutions.

Unlike many Christian missionaries and nearly all their anthropological successors, Islam seeks to remain aloof from local error or deviation, and rejects syncretic compromises. Islam is, in principle, deeply opposed to the pluralist ideas that it sometimes invokes when seeking rights or status within non-Islamic societies. Islam makes no concessions to earlier or later cultures or beliefs, and even opposes the translation of its sacred texts into languages other than Arabic. Specific education demands typically made by Muslims include: single sex schools after the age of puberty; traditionally appropriate dress for each sex; distinctive sex roles to be taught in accord with the Koran; science teaching in accord with the Koran; prohibition of representational art, especially of the human figure; prohibition of many Western forms of music; provision of *Halal* food and of facilities for ritual absolution.

Clearly compliance with such demands would leave children ignorant of much of the cultural life of Western societies to a much greater extent than do distinctive requirements in any Christian or Jewish schools. Furthermore, the Muslim demands cited are merely limited examples of what follows from the belief that education as a whole be based on Islamic belief. Islam requires the rote learning of the whole Koran by early adolescence and mastery of the classical Arabic in which it is written. As Mervyn Hiskett notes (1988, 6), the *Ulema* means by education "a devotion to study—Islamic law, Koran studies, Arabic language, Arabic literature, Islamic history, in their numerous branches—that can and often does take up a whole lifetime." Education, to a Muslim, is not a few periods of teaching about Islam within a multifaith social studies or religious studies syllabus.

Demands by Muslims in English-speaking countries for full freedom to found Islamic schools and for financial and other support from governments on comparable terms to aid given to Christian and Jewish schools are based in part on Islam's claims to truth—which are not admitted within the civil religion, by antinomianism or by Christian fundamentalists—and partly on pluralist arguments (which Muslims would not entertain in Islamic societies). Yet, although it is always right to expose double standards, such an exposure does not in itself enable us to decide which cultural and educational niches western societies should, in their own interests, afford to Islamic, or indeed to Christian, fundamentalists.

Ironically, Protestant fundamentalists in Britain may ultimately fare worse than Muslims at the hands not only of antinomians, but of the exponents of civil religion and of some established Christian churches, including the established Church of England. This liberal Christian commitment to 'multiculturalism' leads them to bend over backward to demonstrate their concern that there should be no discrimination against other creeds, whereas they are stern in their admonitions against dogmatism and prejudice in the indigenous population. In Australia, antinomian educators love to show their superiority to ethnocentric judgment by fulsome praise of the deeply spiritual character of Aboriginal Dreamtime myths— even though these consist in little else but murder, rape and incest—while demonstrating their commitment to rationality by deriding the literal acceptance of Genesis by Christian fundamentalists.

CIVIL RELIGION AND ANTINOMIANISM

Had major Islamic migrations to Western societies taken place a generation earlier, severe problems of mutual accommodation would still have arisen. Yet, even setting aside the increased Islamic militancy (of which the Iranian Revolution is only one example), the difficulties would have been less acute before the victories of antinomianism which caused Christian fundamentalist alienation from many government school systems. Bellah's civil religion, like any defensible morality in a modern pluralist society, was based on a fusion of two main bodies of ideas valued in Western thought: one, the desirability of freeing individuals from an unthinking acceptance of tradition; and the other, the desirability of fostering traditions and customs prerequisite for an open society. There was, is, and must always be, considerable tension between these two sets of goods, but without cultural and moral critique, there is stagnation and decay. And without adherence to a cultural and moral framework there is rapid collapse and destruction. It is only in 'bourgeois society' that individuality, diversity and pluralism have historically had much space. Yet countercultural criticism of 'bourgeois society's' allegedly sordid and mean characteristics developed early among writers and artists before gaining a progressively stronger hold over the academy. The battlefields of World War I and the Great Depression strengthened condemnation of 'capitalism' as the cause of the massacre of the dead and the misery of the living. Yet fears of fascism on the left and communism on the right, together with the deprivations and sufferings of another great war, limited the scope of antinomianism, which is the child of prosperity and plenty, not of dearth and hardship. The bearers of contemporary antinomianism have not been workers or peasants, but university students and their teachers, not factory girls but professionally qualified women and well-to-do housewives.

During the nineteenth century would-be reformers were rarely antinomian, but rather sought to persuade or coerce the unrespectable poor, and often the unrespectable aristocracy too, to adopt moral constraint in sex, drink, and much besides. As Brigette and Peter Berger noted (1984, 17) "bourgeois women in England and America were the shock troops of the various movements that sought to evangelize other classes with the blessings of the middle-class ethos." The task of gentling the children of the masses was spearheaded by women teachers, who would have been amazed that their feminist successors could deem their efforts illegitimate impositions on working-class groups with their own equally valid moral and cognitive norms. By the 1960s, antinomians in the professions and the academy were able, in ways as opposed to those of earlier radical reformers as to those of fundamentalist Christians, to redefine membership of a family as a matter of individual contract, which might justifiably and without penalty be broken by any one party without provocation by another. As expectations of the physical and psychic pleasures derivable from sexual relationships were heightened, as marriages consequently became increasingly fragile, and as previously illicit sexual practices emerged from privacy into public advocacy, so public educational authorities began to discard all attempts to present any human relationships as more natural or normative than others. These new tendencies were much more repugnant to Christian and Islamic fundamentalists than those which existed previously.

At first sight, the success of Values Clarification and many other similar forms of permissive pedagogy, seemed simply evidence that government schools had abandoned prescription or proscription, explicit or implicit. But every removal of limits not only creates new limits but implies new values; the new antinomian presbyters are often old priests writ large. The apparent successes of antinomianism may best be seen as the result of a two-stage operation. The initial victory of moral relativism over traditional norms is followed by the establishment of new norms. These may relate to trivialities of nonsexist pronouns or to the new orthodoxy of the evil nature of the traditional family, disfigured as it apparently was and is, not only by sexual oppression of wives by husbands, but also by sexual abuse of daughters by fathers.

In Australian schools during the 1980s, earlier forms of sex education, developed by the Family Life Movement and combining knowledge of human biology with advocacy of sexual restraint and chastity, were widely rejected as outmoded and backward. The superintendent of the South Australian Department of Education, Malcolm McArthur, was not thought extreme, as he would have been two decades earlier, in attacking early attempts at 'health education' as "heavily moralistic in tone and apparently designed to scare people" (1983, 28). In those benighted times young people were "panicked into driving slowly or out of sexual promiscuity or perhaps away from experimentation with drugs."

The new approach was spearheaded in Australia by the 1984 *Teaching About Sex: The Australian Experience*, edited by Wendy McCarthy. In this educational best-seller, Diana Wyndham of the Social Welfare Research Center of the University of New South Wales endorsed (1984, 112) Wardell Pomeroy's claim that masturbation is "not only harmless but it is positively good and healthy and should be encouraged because it helps young people to grow up sexually in a natural way." Wyndham, echoing McArthur, denounced earlier modes of sex education because they "emphasized the horrors of illegitimate pregnancy and venereal disease which were waiting ... to punish any teenager who dared to be sexually active." Antinomians now commonly describe premature sexual experience as being 'sexually active,' which sound much more positive and lively than being sexually passive. Another of McCarthy's contributors, Thea Mendelsohn, the education officer of the Family Planning Association of Western Australia, advanced many of the positions which distress not only many Protestant fundamentalists but a wide range of objectors to the antinomian revolution in sex education. Such objectors are described by Mendelsohn as a "vociferous and ugly minority," as "a legacy of the past" whose beliefs "are in their death throes." They are "repressionist authoritarian groups" whose "main attraction is comic value." But she warns her comrades that the "dirty and undemocratic tactics" of this minority may enable them "to force their will on the whole of the community." Mendelsohn's classic advice is to refuse to "dignify the opposition by acknowledging it and bolstering its press ... to debate with them is a futile exercise ... They will have their say, and loudly too, but invariably their outbursts provoke more allies to come forward from the ranks of the moderate."

The materials of AIDS Education offered by the South Australian Education Department (1987, 14) are prefaced by the statement that "no distinction has been made to separate homosexuality and heterosexuality." As is typically the case in AIDS Education materials produced by state education departments in Australia, this one serves to legitimize the most dangerous sexual practices: young adolescents are advised to use condoms during sodomy and to ensure that only clean needles are used if and when they inject themselves with illegal drugs. Apart from the utterly nonprudential nature of such approaches and admonitions, it is hardly surprising that from a moral standpoint they proved repugnant to many families, especially perhaps to those holding fundamentalist beliefs. In the United Kingdom during the 1980s similar sorts of sex education materials deeply affronted recently arrived Islamic families as well as the many indigenous families holding either positive Christian beliefs or civil religious ethics derived from Christianity and Judaism.

During the first stage of the antinomian operation, all are victims. The best-selling 1980s Australian publication on classroom management, Maurice Balson's *Understanding Classroom Behavior*, maintains (1988, 7) that "all difficulties encountered in classrooms, homes, offices, and elsewhere are mistakes in human relationships." In addition (1988, 17-18) "in almost all cases it is the behavior of the other children which is the source of a particular child's problems ... the so-called 'poor student' or 'problem student' is that way because of the behavior of other children." Of course, each one of the "other children" is similarly exculpated from any blame for mistaken behavior, which is never to be conceived as bad conduct. Balson claims (1988, 38) that "parents are the initial cause of a child's discouragement," which then leads to the mistaken behavior, while (1988, 40) "peers are also a source of discouragement (since) children are encouraged to excel." In

Balson's view, punishment of children is not only wrong but bound to fail. He argues (1988, 40) that "a student who badly beats a smaller child will be punished and told what a horrible person he is (the sexist pronoun is evidently acceptable in this context) ... a child who steals money from lockers will be punished and reminded of his moral violation. All these punishments are ineffective." Whole groups of the 'disadvantaged,' including *a fortiori* disadvantaged children, are relieved of any personal responsibility for their actions, however destructive to themselves or to others, on the grounds that they are victims of an unjust and inegalitarian society. This position is supported by thinkers suffused by antinomianism, including many of nominally Christian belief and indeed many prominent figures in church hierarchies. Yet the denial of responsibility for one's deeds renders invalid any attribution of virtue as well as of blame. It represents a deep and deplorable contrast with the former civil religion, which retained a quasi-Christian sense of the capacity of human beings for sin as well as for good works, let alone with traditional Christian morality.

The second stage in the antinomian agenda usually begins only after the first stage is well underway. The first stage drives out traditional values and creates a normative vacuum. But the two stages may also coexist, the first as the mode of public argument and the second, the mode of interior dialogue within the reconstructionist group. During stage two it is revealed that not all are victims but that there exist the really wicked who commit absolute evil. Industrial polluters, exploiters of nature, hunters of the fauna, loggers of the trees, advocates of the use of nuclear energy, tobacco companies, multinational companies and many other embodiments of evil are exposed to children in their schools for ritual denunciation and exorcism. Stereotyping, instead of being denounced, becomes obligatory, as in the case of education against sexual abuse, in which infants are warned against the dangers of 'bad touches' from fathers, male relatives and family friends, as well as male strangers.

Sidney Simon and the 'Values Clarifiers,' and to a lesser extent Lawrence Kohlberg and his followers, persuaded many adherents of civil religion in the schools that acutely controversial moral issues could be introduced into the classrooms without leading to indoctrination or divisiveness. This was done as an answer to reasonable fears suspecting previous curriculum of indoctrination and divisiveness. Sensitive and controversial questions could, they claimed, be considered by school students in a value-free way through enquiry and discovery. For the probing teacher, this opened up a wider range of topics to expose to children's minds. As Simon and Clark pointed out (1975, 32), 'the immorality of morality,' the beliefs of traditional morality, could best be overcome by "probing deeply into individuals who have private thoughts." Encounter-group techniques and sensitivity training were deployed on those children reluctant to reveal their innermost thoughts. By a process which many still fail to understand, an initial renunciation of indoctrination or moral molding proved to be a means by which antinomian teachers could first assault hostile values. They did so with impunity in the name of open debate and value freedom. Thus they created space in which to advance alternative values in the name of social justice. Like the Puritans in Samuel Butler's *Hudibras,* antinomians,

> Compound for sins they are inclin'd to
> By damning those they have no mind to.

Liberal tolerance is displayed towards sodomy, but stern abolitionism condemns smoking.

What has taken place in many Western government school systems may be open to dispute. It can be seen as a victory of antinomianism or viewed as the gradual replacement of one normative order by another. The ensuing corruption is less open to dispute. Concomitant with the collapse of civil religion within schools is an unprecedented rise in sexual diseases, divorce, illegitimate births, abortion, and suicide. Although *post hoc* does not in itself, of course, entail *propter hoc,* from the standpoint of Christian fundamentalist parents, or of Muslim parents, the moral ethos of the typical government school in most English-speaking countries is much more alarming than it was thirty years ago.

WHICH WAY FORWARD?

There is little reason for us to wish to return to a closed society or to one in which accepted belief faces no systematic challenge. Liberal capitalism inevitably generates new forms of modernity, social mobility and choice of ways of life, as well as new material goods. A balance between liberty and moral order is never easy to achieve in such a society, but try to achieve it we must. Schools are a vital part of any such engagement. We should be encouraged by the thought that from the time of Adam Smith to the 1960s, Britain and several similar societies had fair success in reconciling wider individual freedom with the propagation of moral norms. This included the belief that only within family structures could young or old find the best conditions for personal security and for the development of a wide area of individual autonomy.

This essay considers the plight of two groups which find the rapid changes associated with modernity especially difficult to negotiate. These two groups—Protestant fundamentalists and Muslims—feel deeply that governmental school systems are hostile to much they hold dear. Yet not only Protestant fundamentalists and Muslims have cause for alarm as the 'bag of virtues' (to use Willard Waller's derisive phrase) is discarded by government systems that were previous adherents. The discomfiture of religious factions should not delight us. We may not believe in Muslim tenets. We may wish that Protestant fundamentalists would accept the Bible as a series of diverse historical texts which present the nature of God and of morality in different and indeed incompatible ways. Yet much of what horrifies them should also disturb adherents of the civil religion. This included 'secular-humanists' who, like me, cannot hold, however much they may respect, the religious beliefs of their upbringing. This is not to imply that there is nothing disturbing in some fundamentalist responses to moral malaise—the enemy is always on two sides, at least.

A two-pronged policy seems necessary. First, government schools should once again give very high priority to habituating children into basic prudential virtues, such as truth-telling, fidelity to promises, honesty, self-control (including sexual restraint), industriousness, perseverance, and the like. Richard Peters' claim (*King and Parekh*, 1986, 2) that "the palace of reason has to be entered by the courtyard of habit" could scarcely be more true. Both by example and by appropriate explanation, government schools should instill in children the conviction that other persons have valid interests of equal importance to their own and strengthen in them the will to act accordingly. Teachers must cease to exalt 'self esteem' as the prime virtue and to recall the value of shame and remorse in moral life. Government schools should also foster a pride in those legal and political traditions and institutions that have made the English-speaking liberal democracies so attractive to migrants from every continent. If any school or school system complains at these injunctions on the grounds that they already perform them to the full, so much the better and so much easier the task ahead of us.

Strengthening prudence and morality in government schools along the lines suggested above would be good for our children and for our nations. It might also help to retain fundamentalist Protestant and Muslim families in those schools and even attract some to them, since there is nothing in the moral agenda proposed contrary to their religious beliefs. Indeed much of it is entirely in accordance with their own moral precepts. On the other hand, it is evident that for many families such a prudential moral education is insufficient and that only a school imbued with their own religious convictions will suffice. The second prong of the proposed policy is that there should be wider parental choice of school, including Islamic schools and fundamentalist Christian schools, comparable to that for Anglican, Roman Catholic, or indeed government schools. It would be best if all schools received their support from governments indirectly through parental vouchers rather than through direct governmental financing, but that is a secondary consideration here. It is possible that new schools would in such circumstances be opened by antinomians who consider even the current ethos of government schools too restrictive, as well as by fundamentalists who consider them too lax. Provided that adequate protection is offered to children in all schools against acts, or incitement to acts, contrary to the criminal law, choice of school for parents should be as wide as possible.

In the history of Australian education, the deepest conflicts were those over state aid for nongovernment schools. Whatever the initial rights and wrongs, there can be no dispute that for some three generations, Roman Catholic parents in Australia felt the deepest resentment against a system in which they had to pay taxes for other people's schools, yet were denied any public support for their own. This resentment, rather than the continued existence of separate Roman Catholic schools, created harmful divisions which poisoned many branches of Australian life. These divisions have almost entirely disappeared in only three decades of renewed government support for Catholic and other religious schools. Similar alienation followed the ending of government aid for nongovernment schools in other English-speaking countries. Hence, we should not exclude financial support for Christian fundamentalist or Muslim schools operating within the law. Such exclusion only strengthens feelings of alienation from the political system with which we surely wish them to fully associate themselves.

Dangers arise from both antinomian and fundamentalist pressures. Some may consider the moral subversion of the first less harmful than the illiberal dogmatism of the second, an opinion I certainly once held myself, although no longer. Although antinomianism often uses democratic language, its attraction is to the classes, especially to the intellectuals, rather than to the masses. Religious fundamentalism, particularly that of Islam, has a mass appeal. There is every danger of a massive alienation from the best Western traditions. This alienation could extend to large numbers of young people born in the United Kingdom and other English-speaking countries, not just to their overseas-born parents. I deeply appreciate the good faith of those, such as Raymond Honeyford (1987) who consider the answer to the problem to be direct initiation of Muslim boys and girls into life in a pluralist liberal-democracy. But I fear the evidence, including Honeyford's persecution, does not favor direct assimilation. Indeed, he inadvertently created an alliance, albeit opportunistic and temporary, between antinomian and Islamic opponents of his wish to give Islamic children a thorough grounding in the traditional values of English society.

Honeyford argued that the first priority is to inculcate in Muslim children feelings of affection and loyalty for countries which are now their homelands as a result of the deliberate choice of their families. But this is only likely to be achieved by making major concessions in culture and education. It should not horrify us that aspects of our Western societies, such as acceptance of homosexual and lesbian relationships as equal normatively to monogamous unions between man and woman, are rejected by Muslims, or by fundamentalist Christians. Some of these are pathological malformations anyway. There are other features of our ways of life that we should strive to persuade all newcomers to adopt, including equal access of women to public and professional life.

Despite the power of Islam, it is very likely that the attractions of many of the better aspects of Western culture will exert great influence on Muslim youth, especially perhaps girls, many of whom will prefer the position of women in our societies to that in traditional Islam. There will very likely be sharp and continuing culture conflicts among Muslim families, but we cannot prevent that. What we can and must prevent is the creation or the strengthening of a unified hostility among Muslims toward the host society. A much wider degree of religious autonomy would be very important in fostering a sense of roots in the new society. An efficient public examination system, based on a wide and liberal curriculum, is the pathway to professional success. Hence, there should be considerable parental pressure on fundamentalist schools, including Islamic ones, to support a broader education as opposed to extreme cultural compartmentalization and anti-intellectual tendencies. Perhaps we should take some hope from the obvious ability of millions of students in the Soviet Union, China, and Eastern Europe to rise above indoctrinative schools and allied social agencies. Dogmatic religion too may be tempered by appropriate studies prescribed by a national curriculum as the pathway to professional advancement. It even may be that burgeoning fundamentalism, Christian or Muslim, will help stiffen the defense of some of the moral norms which were integral to civil religion but have been all but submerged in the antinomian floodtide. More assuredly, we would be utterly foolish if we not only did not try to win over some of the great traditionalist religious forces among us for the defense of a liberal-democratic order, but unnecessarily made them fertile recruiting grounds for its enemies.

REFERENCES

Balson, M. (1988). *Understanding Classroom Behavior.* Hawthorn, Victoria: Australian Council for Educational Research.

Bellah, R.N. (1975). *The Broken Contract: American Civil Religion in a Time of Trial.* New York: Seabury Press.

Berger, B. and Berger, P. (1983). *The War Over the Family: Capturing the Middle Ground.* Harmondsworth: Penguin Books.

Hiskett, M. (1988). *Schooling for British Muslims: Integrated, Opted-Out or Denominational?* London: Social Affairs Unit.

Honeyford, R. (1987). *Integration or Disintegration.* London: Claridge Press.

King, P. and Parekh, B.C. eds. *Politics and Experience.* London: Cambridge University Press.

McArthur, M. (1983). 'Sex Education—too little and too late.' *Pivot* (Adelaide), 10:5.

McCarthy, W. ed. (1984). *Teaching About Sex: The Australian Experience.* Sydney: George Allen and Unwin.

Peshkin, A. (1989). 'Fundamentalist Christian Schools: Should They Be Regulated?' in *Educational Policy,* 3. 1: 45-56.

Simon, S.B. and Clark, J, (1975). *More Values Clarification.* San Diego: Pennant Press.

South Australian Education Department, (1987). *A Teaching Pack for Education about AIDS.* Adelaide: Government Printer.

FOURTEEN

THE RIGHT TO BE LEFT ALONE IS A RIGHT TO BE NO ONE

Morton A. Kaplan

James Reichley, Battista Mondin, and others among the authors of the chapters on religion and liberal democracy make a strong case for the importance of Judeo-Christian values in the development and maintenance of liberal democracy. They believe that it thrived only because society superimposed religious values on the democratic system and that democracy is being undermined by the spread of humanistic values.

It may be the case that a particular humanistic value—the Millsian concept that the individual should be free to do whatever does not directly harm others—may have an unfortunate impact on liberal democracy, although it is surely more benign than the Hobbesian individualistic alternative. But both individualistic positions are based on inapt philosophical and sociological analyses. Religion may remain in practice an important support for liberal democracy if appropriate humanistic supports are difficult to understand. Still it is important to show that humanistic values, properly understood, are consistent with liberal democracy.

I shall develop the position in this chapter that a correct understanding of the nature of human identity leads to a humanistic position that is consistent with liberal democracy. The reader may note how consistent this humanistic position is with the Catholic concept of subsidiarity as George Weigel portrays it. It is not unrelated to Aristotle's argument in the Ethics, although I would regard happiness as a byproduct of natural human activity that is related to good identities in a good society rather than as an end in itself. I shall explore this problem by analyzing a so-called human right—the right to be left alone with respect to those human actions that do not directly harm others—and by showing how it fails to take account of the nature of human personality and social identity.

The 'right to be left alone' with respect to social and moral matters is a currently popular position. Although the Supreme Court in its decision on the use of contraceptives—*Griswold vs. Connecticut*—defended privacy only in this particular matter, it increasingly has moved to an acknowledged generalized defense of privacy. The doctrine of privacy, however, is counterproductive as a generalized doctrine. This is a fault that can be attributed to its abstract treatment of freedom of choice. It fails to come to terms with the complex interrelationships between self and society that make the concept of individual choice meaningful. Hence, rather than supporting, it undermines, and *in extremis* would dissolve, that individual autonomy and human freedom it attempts to serve. In effect, it would serve no one, for the self—the subject of ethical discourse—that freedom serves would be minimized.

The doctrine of the 'right to be left alone' is dangerously seductive because we tend to restrict our attention to the many instances of freedom of choice that enhance human life in our society. There are clear and convincing reasons to support the 'right to be left alone' within some limits. Those limits are less restrictive in a pluralistic society such as ours than in a more culturally homogeneous society.

The rules that governed a more parochial America—for instance, the criminal law under which a Wisconsin married woman was recently convicted of adultery—cannot be imposed without social warfare on contemporary Americans. Because such rules remain important to such important institutions as the family, we must rely on social sanctions to preserve institutional strength. However, we threaten these and other vital institutions gravely if we transform the 'right to be left alone' into a generalized Constitutional doctrine.

The Millsian doctrine—that we should be free to do those things that do not harm others—fails to do justice to how identifications and conceptions of self develop within societies. And it misunderstands how the human mind works in solving problems. Because Mill misunderstood these processes, he also failed to understand that the generalization of the right of privacy—in his terms, the right to do anything that does not harm others—is destructive of the very values it is designed to implement.

In making my argument, I shall neglect some obvious cases of harm to others that arise under the doctrine. Excessive drinking or smoking, the taking of mind-altering drugs, and homosexual anal sex, for instance, impose huge costs on society in terms of medical costs and lost productivity. But these huge financial costs—possibly more than sufficient to balance the budget or to pay for important capital programs—pale into insignificance when weighed against other costs that are imposed.

The Millsian doctrine is severely flawed with respect to its implicit account of the ways in which the human mind works. The utilitarian thesis—even apart from its question-begging concept of utility—assumed that the mind was some sort of calculating machine: if correctly adjusted, it could make the calculations required for a utilitarian determination. However, the mind is a complex and dynamic interpretative system which depends, for adequate functioning, upon a balance of complementary but conflicting interpretative schemas, each of which becomes dysfunctional and pathological if used excessively. Rule-following and adjustment to circumstances are the two interpretative orientations or perspectives that play a primary role in the operations of mind and that are relevant to the following discussion.

The conflicts between considerations that affect human choices are inherent even in the simplest of systems that invoke more than one goal orientation. Air raid warning systems, for instance, must meet only two simple requirements: they must give notice of raids and they should not be subject to false alarms.

However, there is no simple or perfect way to balance these considerations. A system that never was subject to false alarms would fail to report many air raids. And an alarm system that would not give false alarms would miss many actual raids. Thus, a system compromise is necessary that does not follow from a unique and clear criterion. It should provide some reasonable mix of the two considerations. And this is true also of more complex systems with more complex requirements such as social and personality systems. No single principle can be generalized or absolutized without significant harm to society and the individuals who are members of it. And no unique criterion can determine the weight to be given to the considerations.

I have examined these matters elsewhere from both an ontological and a cybernetic point of view.* The categories of pathology most relevant to the discussion that follows are the compulsive/obsessive, which depends upon rigid adherence to strict rules, and the hysteric, which loses itself in the needs of the moment. Mental dysfunctions occur when minds tip too far in the direction either of rule-following or adjustment to circumstances.

There is no such thing as a veridical path that is distinct from some balancing of rules and the desires that are related to specific circumstances. External social constraints and internal inhibitions are the complements to the enticements and opportunities that social structure, personality, and environment provide. They are required to diminish the likelihood of pathology and to preserve the integrity of the self that makes choices. The Japanese culture is shame-oriented. It permits a strong sense of identification but submerges the individual within the group. The nineteenth century American culture was guilt-oriented. As long as there was a hegemonic culture, it permitted a strong sense of identity that was consistent with considerable freedom for individual variance where key cultural values were not involved.

Difficult problems arose when the American culture became pluralistic because of inconsistencies between the frames of reference of different social groupings. Transstable personalities**

---

*See Chapter 5, "Ontological Dysfunctions of Mind," in Morton A. Kaplan, *Alienation and Identification*, The Free Press, New York, 1976, pp.131ff. A revised account of my cybernetic account of information handling is given in Chapter 8, "The Mechanisms of Regulation," in Morton A. Kaplan, *Macropolitics*, Aldine Publishing Company, Chicago, 1969, pp.137ff. The inherently complementary character of rule-based and consequence-based calculations is analyzed in Morton A. Kaplan, *Science, Language, and the Human Condition*, revised edition, Paragon House Publishers, New York, 1989, pp. 174ff.

**Kaplan, *Alienation and Identification*, pp.166ff.

are able to maintain a strong sense of identity in pluralistic cultures by adjusting expectations and behavior to different settings.
But there are few transstable personalities. And there is a tendency, which has become increasingly manifest in contemporary
American culture, to invoke a doctrine of freedom of choice,
regardless of the setting in which one finds oneself, that is responsive to the idiosyncratic needs of an isolated self. This can be
inhibited only by an appropriate balance of internal and external
constraints.

The deleterious transformations that are occurring in the
American culture are supported by two concepts that are inherent
in the Millsian doctrine and that are widely believed. The Millsian
doctrine assumes that individuals can make choices that do not
change the choices that others face, hence, that they are cost-free
to others if they do not directly harm them. It also assumes that
the chooser is not changed by the choices that are made. Neither
is the case.

It was no accident that Spartan nobles wanted to be warriors,
that Dutch burghers developed bourgeois values, that contemporary children present their parents with what their peers do and
get as justifiable grounds for their own demands, or that few would
consider wearing a banner denouncing religion in a church. In
the society in which we are acculturated, a fairly stable set of values
and expectations plays a major role in the formation of our self
and of its sense of identity. That self and its sense of identity provide the framework within which choices can be reasoned about.

When change occurs, the meanings attached to choice also
change and operate with uncertainty. Is bowing to a superior a
sign of respect or one of self-denigration? If the former is the case,
bowing does not decrease self-esteem. However, if a Japanese
rejects this cultural value and does not bow, he preserves his self-
esteem only at the cost of hurting his superior's self-esteem. When
a culture is in flux, the meanings of transactions become uncertain
and harm cannot be avoided.

When the cultural guideposts change rapidly, anarchy—rather
than reasoned choice—is more likely. The conceptions of self that
guide choice become increasingly uncertain. This is even more
true of children, who are easily influenced by the practices that
they observe or read about, than it is of adults. If rapid change is

accompanied by the idea of the 'right to be left alone,' it would not be surprising if many adults, let alone children, believe there are no unacceptable social limits.

Some meanings are in flux in any complex society, but there is some limit beyond which changes in meanings call into question the social arrangements that make a body of consistent meanings possible. However, reasonably consistent meanings are integral to the sense and identification of the self and, hence, of its autonomy and freedom. Identity weakens and choice begins to relate to a less definite individual when the structure of meanings—providing context for individual meanings—weakens.

Every society, even the simplest, requires sets of understood rules that underlie expectations. When a wolf loses in combat to another wolf, it saves its life by lying supine and permitting the other wolf to urinate on it. If not hard-wired, this agonistic behavior is close to such. Humans have much greater flexibility. But even modern man has taboos.

For instance, we could use the meat from nondiseased recently dead humans to feed starving people, but an effective taboo operates to prevent this. Is that taboo irrational? Perhaps. But then again, perhaps it sustains, or at least helps to sustain, other important inhibitions in the treatment of other humans. It would be a serious mistake to test this possibility except perhaps under the hardest circumstances. We cannot reason about it abstractly and in isolation from the web of understandings that underpins the culture without gravely distorting or rendering senseless the conclusions we reach.

From birth to death the individual develops a sense of self as it interacts with others who provide support and constraint. Both constraint and support are required if the self is to have coherence through time and, hence, to be a focus for decisions that respond to more than transient pressures.

These supports and constraints transform potentially dangerous and antisocial impulses by constructing a web of sentiments and understandings that focus behavior. The supports provide assurance that one is not alone and that mutual expectations characterize one's society. They permit the postponement of pleasure in favor of longer-term goals and provide incentives to take into account the needs of others. The constraints promise sanctions of various kinds if one does not respond positively to the socially appropriate expectations of others. This complex network of supports and constraints sets the cultural terms for what freedom means for individuals in a particular kind of society.

Later Roman society was decadent. Its elites gorged themselves with food and vomited it to eat still more. One of the purposes of the training at West Point is to develop in cadets a sense of self that excludes the sybaritic life. The function of an army is to be ready to defend the nation. It is not desirable to have generals who, by indulging themselves, display a lack of that self-discipline that is essential in combat. Even if a particular general is an exception, acceptance of such conduct might legitimate it and other behaviors that would erode the fighting quality of the armed forces. Civil society is not an army. The narrow standards that apply in armies are inappropriate for civil society, particularly if it is pluralistic. But it does not follow that no limits apply even if behavior does not directly and immediately harm others. There is a limit beyond which the absence of agreed standards would defeat attempts to develop coherent selves that can make meaningful choices.

Foucault captures much support for his proposition that every culture exercises power over its members, hence that their similarities in undermining freedom outweigh their differences. However, Foucault fails to understand that every freedom is supported by a corollary constraint. This is true even at the simplest level of mechanics. An object is not free to roll unless it is roundish in shape. An individual is not free to think rationally if under the influence of mind-altering substances. A concert artist is not free to perform except under the constraint of long hours of tedious practice.

The freedom of human beings depends upon cultural constraints. The meaning and worth of human freedom in a society are intimately related to the types of human beings that are nurtured by its internal and external constraints. To state that American democracy nurtures better individuals and more freedom than a Nazi concentration camp would seem not worth stating were it not for the confusion spread by Foucault. Few contemporary Russian intellectuals would be taken in by his formulations.

On the other hand, the thesis that one should be 'free to be left alone' arises from examining the possible consequences of a particular novel freedom from within the framework of a relatively stable world of expectations. It may be possible to accommodate a small number of new freedoms without harm, depending on their impact on the web of cultural meanings. Yet it is surely not possible to analyze or to accommodate the program 'to be left alone' in whole or in large part, for that would be sufficient to invalidate the analysis or to disrupt the stable expectations that characterize any particular society.

The desire to be free of any constraint is not merely the desire to be free of any dominating society. In effect, it is the desire to be free of any set of individual characteristics that might constitute being human. It is pure fancy to suggest, as Derrida did, that anyone would want to be rid of the constraints of language. These are a minimal condition for communication with oneself let alone with others. That way lies madness.

If the system of constraints and supports is evanescent very early in life, a sociopathic personality may result that is innocent of concern for, or even understanding of, the reality of others. Such individuals probably lack the neuronic interconnections that are required for bonding to other individuals and moral behavior. The nonrational inhibitions that restrain most of us will not be present.

In addition to supports, even the most 'normal' individuals require constraints in the form of social sanctions in the absence of which they are most likely to lose their sense of appropriate limits. Dictators begin to lose their sense of reality, at least in part, because they are insulated from opposition and the need to test their views against those of others. And those who are less than the best, or who are faced with desperate circumstances, may be containable, if at all, only by the force of law. An open season for actions that do not directly harm others would contribute to personality dysfunctions with respect to behavior and morals by insulating individuals from the constraints that sustain our 'normality.'

The process by means of which one develops an identity and sense of self is one in which limits are tested. This is typical of, but not limited to, adolescent behavior. It serves two immediate functions: to learn what the limits are and to test the veracity of the declaratory beliefs of authority figures. It produces the dynamic and evolving framework of expectations that make possible complex society and the identifications that fit particular societies.

And the more complex and pluralistic the society, the more this process is lifelong.

A social system and a personality system that did not exclude some patterns of behavior—even if they did not injure others—would undermine the system of rules that are required for a good sense of identity. The literally infinite complexity of deciding each issue on its merits would founder when standards were absent. The infinity of considerations would overwhelm our ability to make decisions. They would be unrelated to our individual concept of our self in the absence of which freedom of choice loses its importance.

If, for instance, every social rule—whether to bow to superiors, to dress for dinner, and so forth—was subject to personal calculation, society would be in danger of collapse. But that is the direction in which the Millsian doctrine pushes us. Not all the norms of a society can, or should, be sustained by law. But a system will optimize its functionality and the autonomy of its members only when law is supplemented by effective social sanctions. When important institutions seek to render reasonable limits ineffective and they are supported rather than challenged by social elites, a time of trouble lies ahead for a society.

The rules that guide decisions constitute the data that tell us who we are because we then are the kinds of individuals who behave in certain given ways in certain kinds of situations. For instance, we are not the kind of person who copies someone else's paper when teacher turns his back. Such rules provide a matrix within which change can be assimilated and concepts of the self adjusted without loss of identity.

It is highly likely that many of the asocial and antisocial activities of the current period—including drug abuse and widespread dishonesty—are caused in part by the philosophy which underlies the concept of a generalized right of privacy. When standards erode to this point, the very conception of the absence of, or even the capability to conceive of, direct harm to others will be seriously diminished. For instance, at what point does consensual sadism weaken the barriers against nonconsensual sadism? Are pictures of bullwhips in anuses or adults urinating into each other's mouths, as in the Mapplethorpe exhibit, really harmless? Even if these activities occur behind private walls, the effects might become significant if it becomes widely known that they occur and are permissible. This is even more true if they win awards and are regarded highly. If one wanted to break down the minds of other individuals, would not a barrage of material of this type, or knowledge about it, be effective? What does it say of a society that so many of the elite defend or even stage such exhibits?

Moreover, continued experimentation of this kind is likely to break down the personalities that engage in these actions. The Marquis de Sade, apart from the harm he did to others, did harm to his own personality. He transformed it in dysfunctional ways by exercising his 'freedom' of choice.

The Manson group was not a totally illegitimate offspring of this philosophy. The motto of the sixties was 'the greening of America.' 'Doing one's own thing' was the new golden rule. Timothy Leary was telling us in *Playboy* magazine how taking drugs would raise us to a new level of consciousness at which we could perceive the flow of the individual atoms in our bodies. It is the generation of the sixties that is the greatest force behind the dysfunctional changes that are occurring in American society today.

When the sense of identity is gone, either people pursue immediate wants or, to escape confusion and indecision, they turn themselves over to a leader who can reinforce his sense of power only by formulating more and more bizarre demands. If the Manson group was an extreme result of this philosophy, it was such only because other internal and external constraints had not broken down as completely in other elements of society.

On the other hand, the conception that we can return to the stringent standards of the Anglo-Saxon culture of the nineteenth century ignores the pluralism and complexity of modern American society. The strains such an austere standard would impose would rival, and possibly surpass, those of prohibition. For reasons already stated, no perfect solution is possible because the requirements are incompatible. Therefore, some compromise solution is required.

No abstract principle can decide these issues, for all involve important tradeoffs. Moreover, in most situations in modern society, some balance between considerations is required. Therefore, two different arenas of compromise are relevant. One is the social and political, and the other is the judicial. In the former arenas, competing social forces will mobilize and seek support. They will win or lose depending upon the balance of social forces and their ability to influence legislation. This process, if it does not forfend all deleterious change, at least tends to limit the amount and speed of change and, thus, to provide time for absorption and readjustment of the sense of identity. Furthermore, if the society acts with discretion and good judgment, great damage may be avoided. If discretion and good judgment are not employed, there may be an overreaction. But this may be better than no reaction. These problems largely can be avoided if social agencies act with good judgment and a sense of public responsibility. The cultural framework for a stable self identity requires a compromised balance. One needs freedom of experimentation that leaves open room to consider change. Yet too much freedom can lead to an anarchy of expression that removes the likelihood of the integrity of self. This compromise between freedom and restraint is threatened when 'social elites' and 'panels that award' fail to distinguish between the spheres in which something is permissible and those in which it is not.

The other arena is the judicial. It is undemocratic for the Court to recognize a new right of privacy that still lacks predominant and sustained support—let alone while it remains a minority point of view. Even if the Justices of the Supreme Court had the qualities of Plato's guardians—and it is painfully obvious that they lack the requisite social and political knowledge and philosophical skills—it would be a mistake for the Court to play this role. Even Plato's philosopher kings would succumb to the heady wine of power and, like autocrats, would lose their own bearing. Because no rules would guide their decisions, other than the rule to produce the best results, they would be driven to extreme and idiosyncratic invention by the lack of context for their judgments. It is immoral to accelerate these dangerous tendencies by 'legitimating' them. This is particularly the case when the legitimation is in the form of a general principle—while proclaiming the philosophy of flower children as the law of the land. Instead, the emphasis of the Court should be on slowing down precipitate legislative change.

Justice Marshall of the United States Supreme Court is a major supporter of the right to generalized privacy. Justice Brennan, was also a major supporter until he retired in 1990. The two justices apparently saw themselves as men with a vision that they believed to be clearly correct and that they were obligated to impose on the Constitution. These are dangerously self-righteous blinders. They provide evidence that the two justices lost their sense of identification as neutral interpreters of the Constitution.

Even if inevitable difficulties of interpretation make neutral interpretation an impossible ideal it is still an important constraint on juridical behavior. Tendentious interpretations are particularly dangerous when pursued by justices who lack an adequate understanding of the complex interactions between individual personalities and social and political institutions.

The popularity of legal theorists such as Ronald Dworkin is an implicit comment on the quality of contemporary legal theory. Apart from the jurisprudential and philosophical infirmities of Dworkin's theory, his concept of autonomy runs no deeper than the definition one could find in an ordinary dictionary. It is as unrelated as was the earlier Millsian doctrine to the sociopsychological factors that make autonomy a meaningful concept.

From a moral standpoint, we do owe respect to the opinions of others. But that respect is limited by our mutual obligation to observe boundaries that have a reasonable relationship to the needs of the society and of the individuals in it.

As a person who likes to do things my own way, I am sympathetic to the concept of being 'left alone.' In the best society, internal inhibition would be the chief means for regulating individual conduct. I surely do not wish to see individuals reduced to creatures of either state or society in which conformity to generalized mediocrity becomes the rule.

But we also need to recognize that voluntary inhibitions often are insufficient. The concept of the individual is meaningless in the absence of society. The self and its identifications are the product of transactions with others. Hence, it is not possible or desirable entirely to eliminate external sanctioning.

Individual and society are symbiotic. I am a professor, but not a nineteenth-century German professor. I do not expect my students to stand when I enter the room and I want them to challenge my opinions. Introduce my other roles as husband, editor, and so forth, and one begins to understand who and what I am. In my understanding of myself—which is always subject to reevaluation in new situations and when faced by new types of choices—I find my own grounds for autonomous choice.

Were I to be forced out of my roles into a strange society, I would have to remake and refind myself. Force me out of a system of meaningful constraints and I would begin to lose the sense of identity without which the freedom to choose is meaningless. I would become a rudderless ship adjusting to momentary pressures without a sense of the pattern of life I wish to lead. It is this most terrible condition, even worse than death, that the concentration camp imposed on its victims. Will we impose it on ourselves in willful surrender to one-sided doctrine?

No society can prevent harm to its members that results either from individual or collective action. Most tax laws, for instance, will do immense harm to some because no general statements, no matter how carefully written, can take into account all possible contingencies. No matter how great the care we take to avoid such consequences, almost invariably a tax law will drive some individuals out of a business or a job that represents a lifetime of accomplishment and that is essential to their sense of identification. Life is filled with tragic dilemmas that we can attempt to ameliorate but that we cannot entirely avoid.

Because this is so, what we owe each other is an orderly regimen manifesting care for the equities and the values that are involved. This kind of care reinforces values and identifications that protect our freedoms. These are the values that would be threatened by extreme application of 'the right to be left alone.'

Ask not whom it would threaten, for it would threaten each of us in our ability to be who and what we are. Sinclair Lewis once wrote a book entitled *It Can't Happen Here*. In it, fascism came to America in the guise of antifascism. 'The right to be left alone' contains a greater threat to individuality and the freedom to choose than fascism or communism ever posed. If carried to term, it would threaten the dissolution of the organized self. And it would do so without providing a big brother against whom we could build internalized defenses of the kind that broke out into manifest activity in Eastern Europe and the former Soviet Union.

FIFTEEN

MORALS IN POST-COMMUNIST SOCIETIES — THE CASE OF POLAND[1]

Milowit Kuninski

In recent years we have been witnessing the collapse of communism in eastern and central Europe and in the former Soviet Union, although in some cases the pace of the decay is not uniform and we can see some delays and, at times, even regression.

The process of decline of the communist system, although almost completely unexpected not only to outsiders but also to those living inside the system, is an inevitable and natural phenomenon. Its decline has nothing to do with historical determinism but rather is much like a natural reaction of an immunological system against a parasitic disease.

The organistic metaphor may seem old-fashioned but in this particular case is quite appropriate. Communism is like a parasitic leviathan invented and constructed by man, preying upon the living body of society. At the same time, it gives certain symbiotic advantages to some of its parts. Now, the engorged leviathan, instead of growing stronger at the expense of those it enslaved, is losing vigor and power. It is wasting away, but is not yet dead. We must remember Tiananmen Square in June of 1989, and University Square in Bucharest in December 1989 and June 1990.

The events in Poland, Hungary, Czechoslovakia, Rumania, the Baltic and other eastern European countries since the Berlin Wall fell were consequences of their efforts to survive as nations. They represent day-to-day resistance against communism's parasitic consumption.

The changes which led to the spectacular overthrow of communist regimes in 'velvet' or bloody ways were not essentially of a political nature. These changes were grounded in moral firmness, religious commitment, yet also in despair.

Communism's fatal symptoms were visible for many years:

1. the systematic loss of legitimacy of communist regimes in terms of ideology, economic efficiency, rule of law, and even in terms of *Realpolitik* (in eastern Europe, local communist leaders hinted frequently that their rule was better and more liberal than direct Moscow rule or a military intervention);

2. the loss of the cold war by the USSR and its weakening international role as a superpower, leading to its loss of control over satellite countries;

3. a growing technological (hi-tech) gap between centrally planned and free-market economies;

4. the collapse of centrally planned economies in terms of meeting consumer and international economic competition demands;

5. the diminishing role of a centrally planned economy: emergence of enterprise and quasi-market relations, uncontrolled by the central planning body, and the emergence of industrial lobbies pressing for state subsidies and thus influencing the central plan;

6. routinization of totalitarianism, to use Max Weber's term, through corruption: existence of a large black market and private business deals (based on bribery and exchange of services) between members of the communist bureaucracy and certain social groups such as petty businessmen, individual farmers or managers of socialistic, monopolistic enterprises; this led to emergence of 'grey areas' which tended to blur relations between rulers and the ruled; i.e., rejection of 'revolutionary' asceticism and honesty;

7. in certain cases (Poland, Hungary) the black market and its close relationship with the government (or more generally with

nomenklatura) led to changes of definitions of property rights, paving the way to restoration of private property via recognition of equality before the law of different types of property such as state, cooperative and private property;[2]

8. growth of communist pragmatism in dealing with economic, social and internal political issues leading to the slow destruction of the utopian idea of the 'New Man' and the 'New Perfect Society';

9. the growing significance of institutionalized religion and churches in private and public life (Poland being the most spectacular example but also Czechoslovakia, East Germany, and some republics in the USSR);

10. a growing gap between the young generation's demands and the system's abilities to meet them: small diversity of the labor market, low standards of consumer goods, lack of guaranteed personal and political liberties, lack of freedom of association and free speech, destruction of the spirit of self-responsibility;

11. spreading religious devotion among the young generation and intellectuals;

12. the revitalization of traditional institutions and their moral values: family, parish, local community, educational institutions etc., but also of a national identity (sometimes combined with nationalism and xenophobia);

13. futile attempts to weaken and eventually destroy such an independent institution as the Roman Catholic church in Poland, and, on the other hand, necessity for the communists to negotiate with the church certain arrangements before introducing them into political life;

14. an increasing discrepancy of private and official, party-controlled public spheres of life leading to the appearance of substitutes for the public sphere (independent or underground activities) linked with the communist party loss of control over large sections of society: the rebelled intellectuals and the young generation, mushrooming independent institutions (lectures, theatrical performances, discussions, meetings, etc.) under or without the church umbrella, not only in Poland but also in East Germany, Hungary, and partly in Czechoslovakia; independent education; publishing houses (press, books, pamphlets—with a high circulation and which have become influential among different social

groups—not necessarily intelligentsia) in Poland as well as in Hungary; and, in the end, independent social and political movements such as the most influential and powerful, Solidarity in Poland, Chart 77 in Czechoslovakia, the Democratic Forum in Hungary, as well as political proto-parties like the Confederation of Independent Poland (founded in 1979).[3]

The short life of communism is only a brief episode in the long history of Russia and the East-Central European nations. These nations fought stubbornly to sustain and recover in full their authentic life founded upon traditional moral values and institutions. They sought to erect—or in some cases rebuild—western political institutional arrangements and sound economies. This is an imperative lesson for those in the west who are engaged in endeavors which undermine the moral and intellectual framework of their societies and challenge the legitimacy of their political order.

The trouble is that utopian seekers want the 'elusive better' rather than the 'solid good.' These idealists fail to view the collapse of communism in eastern and central Europe as an *experimentum crucis* of nonviability. They see it as only a proof of the nonfeasibility of the Stalinist variant of communism.[4] Their prototype of 'democratic socialism' has never been put to the test. Nor will it be in the future, because any kind of socialism or communism proven to be a failure will not be, naturally, a confirmation of a collapse of 'their socialism.' Therefore, they are dedicated, without hesitation, to a critique of western cultural and political traditions and institutions. They make endless efforts to establish socialist institutions within liberal societies, unwittingly building an edifice similar (contrary to their hopes and expectations) to the one they watch crumbling in the east.

Significant effects of this endeavor can be seen, for example, in western educational systems which for many years have been losing their traditional axiological underpinnings: a disinterested pursuit of truth; noninstrumentality of education; a focus on *maieutical* moulding of immature minds; a sense of intellectual mastery and authority; the influence of a Rousseauian pedagogy aimed at romantic self-expression; an overemphasis on technology and behaviorism; an abrogation of authority; and a propagation of intellectual egalitarianism.

Post-communist societies have freed themselves from the illusion of the 'third road' and are attempting to introduce or reestablish capitalism and democracy as practiced in most developed western countries. Still, some people in the West are dreaming of establishing a true version of socialism with the use of democratic political machinery and a democratic social infrastructure. What does this mean of the negative experiment and failure of communism? Are the sufferings of millions meaningless? Is the degradation of politics, culture and the natural environment untranslatable into western mentality? Are western democracies bound to repeat and live through the totalitarian affliction? One can only hope that the exemplary resistance of those who have no illusions about any kind of socialism—be it hardcore Stalinism or softcore socialism—will be a good lesson for those perplexed.

There are basic affinities between those who have defeated communism and those who resist its influence in western societies. The similarities are grounded in a certain common moral, intellectual, and political tradition. The fundamental difference lies in that those who struggled within the communist regimes depended mainly on morals, hoping that one day they will be followed by politics (which has happened only recently). Those who defend traditional western values in the west have been using political machinery and other free society institutions such as the free press or legislation to protect those values. Especially in education, the most socialist institution in western democracies, we can see a growing reaction against the abuses and foibles of the educational systems in the United States, Canada, United Kingdom, Australia, and France.[5]

Liberal, as well as so-called communist societies, have some common understanding of moral values such as individual freedom and responsibility, individual courage, honesty, family love, friendship, a sense of solidarity with the oppressed, etc. Although in both types of societies those values have eroded, it is too simplistic to claim that there is a direct correlation between liberal or totalitarian political and social orders and the decadence of moral values. Moral values tend to decay because of man's fundamental imperfection; they must be constantly supported and nurtured.

Excessive individualism is one of the main roots weakening the moral and religious foundations of liberal societies. There is a false idea of individual freedom as being equal to total individual self-dependence. There is an accompanying lack of responsibility for long-term results of an individual's actions. There is also too much focus on individual desires and appetites. The secularization of western societies—combined with that individualism—is regarded sometimes as an irreversible trend. However, I do not consider the decline of morals and religion to be irreversible. I doubt, nevertheless, whether trends of such complex phenomena can be properly measured. It is then quite probable that secularization is a temporary phenomenon.

The real moral core of western civilization has not been destroyed totally because there is a social fabric indispensable for its survival: family life, religion, work, and education. All are still alive even if in some sections of free societies they have been attacked by an ideological or hedonistic disease. There are people in the west who are fully aware of the dangers of leftist ideologies or of state idolatry. The problem is whether their rational arguments are sufficiently strong to correct those perplexed minds that still favor socialism.

Albeit the oppression in some communist countries like Hungary or Poland has decreased in the last several years, the moral foundations of the societies living under communist regimes were under constant pressure. One can detect easily how painful is the transition from communism to liberal order because morals were influenced by the totalitarian environment. There is a striving for the new free life fueled by the bad reminders of communism. At the same time, the backward habits formed by the communist ambience obstruct quick political, economic and social changes, making the whole process of transition very painful. Nevertheless, it is undeniable that, though weakened by an inhumane system, morals and basic social institutions such as family, parish and church—as well as things like an independent intellectual life—remained the fundamental source of spiritual strength of the people. These things made possible the protection of their self-identity and finally the overthrow of communist totalitarianism.

While pointing to the significance of morals for the resistance of societies against communism, I do not want to claim that morals and habits are sustained better when they are defended and sometimes even suffered for. It is widely known that people in communist societies were affected and corrupted by its immoral nature. They were corrupted by day-to-day concessions—made to the rules of the system—in order to survive, to live slightly better, or to improve life for their children. Communism is obviously not the best means to protect moral values. However, a defense of morals is even more stubborn when people make errors or moral compromises. They want to expiate their misdeeds, atone and redress them, and improve themselves. Without a sense of guilt, expiation, atonement and redress, it would be hard to understand the simple dialectics of the life of weak and fallible people. Moral and religious values are not functionally determined by oppression because they are autonomous. Nevertheless, oppression may well strengthen people's will to defend what they cherish, simply because values are better perceived as significant when they are under threat. Oppression can also weaken people's resistance and make those values rot when the social fabric in which they flourish is deliberately destroyed. Those values lose their autonomy and become instrumental in resistance against tyranny.

MORALS AND SOCIAL ORDER

It is true that the most important value of free societies is individual freedom. It is quite obvious that people living under communist regimes, when resisting oppression, had always in mind an idea of individual freedom and dreamed of the day it would be possible to live in their societies enjoying it. When the dream came true, people became more and more aware that the freedom they struggled for must be treated very carefully if it was not to be abused. It then becomes practically evident what great political philosophers have long noted—that individual freedom needs rules or principles guiding individual exercise of that freedom.

It may seem obvious that individual freedom needs some protection in the form of law; for the rule of law is indispensable for the sustainment of individual freedom. In other words, for an individual to be free, one needs guaranteed a broad protected sphere of liberty within which one may act as one pleases without being bothered or coerced by another's arbitrary will or the state action. But it is also clear that the law is necessary for the proper exercise of freedom which makes it compatible with a peaceful social order.

What is also needed, however, are moral rules. Friedrich A. von Hayek in his famous book *Law, Legislation and Liberty* argued very convincingly that law and morals—together with individual freedom—are products of a very long historical evolutionary process and therefore are mutually dependent. Morals and law are essential both to avoid abuses of freedom and for the maintenance of social order.

Nevertheless, in liberal societies there has been a split between morals and law, due to legislation substituting for the law grown out of customs and tradition. That led to an illusion that rational legislation and proper actions of legislative bodies are sufficient for the protection of individual freedom and social order, and that freedom itself is a result of legislation. Individual freedom, however, emerged out of moral rules and judiciary decisions under common law and therefore is a product of evolving tradition. Morals, together with law, set boundaries within which individual actions are performed in a peaceful way and interlock in a form of social order.

The negative effects of divorcing morals from law lie in their impact on people's conduct and eventually on their moral behavior and opinions.

There are many situations in western countries in which politicians, members of legislative bodies and even judges appeal to masses and/or respond to noisy 'minorities' and powerful media which pretend to express *vox populi*. In this way, certain unknown 'needs' are created for political reasons, or deviant lifestyles become legally sanctioned. In both cases law, recognizing almost any form of freedom, lays new moral standards in the form of positive rights which expand very quickly. They stimulate and liberate different desires and needs, while traditional morals, usually backed by transcendental authority, curbed them. In the long run, traditional morals will protect social order against destruction. In many cases, what is made legitimate is the weaker part of man's nature: his lack of discipline, his selfishness, and his passions.

On the other hand, in communist societies, ideologically loaded 'progressive' legislation and ubiquitous one-party state intervention affected family life (encouraging divorces, and one-parent families, or destroying responsibility for one's own children), blurred the sense of private and public property, disintegrated individual responsibility through the constitutional guarantees of the right to work and destroyed intermediary institutions which should exist between family and the state. In communist countries, the party used the law as an instrument of control over society. They did this through stimulation of new attitudes destructive of traditional morals, customs and institutions, thus making people almost completely dependent on the state and its agencies.

The law was the main means of creating the 'New Man.' This was an individual alienated from family, local community, parish and nation, deprived of private property, and therefore almost completely controlled by the omnipotent party.

While the communist party institutionalized liberation 'from the top,' the western counterpart is a liberation 'from the bottom.' It is more grassroots, demanded by intellectuals and public opinion, and incited by politicians seeking public fame and support. Both kinds of liberation meet, however, at a certain point. When grass-root tendencies in western countries to use state machinery to 'liberate' people grow, and states increase control over vast areas of social life, they achieve a level of control comparable with that exercised in the communist countries.

Moral rules are foundational to social order when they are supported by congruent law, even if there are sometimes conflicts between the two normative systems.

CIVIL SOCIETY UNDER COMMUNIST RULE

On a global scale, in the part of Europe dominated by Soviet rule, there was a transition from a formerly existing civil society to its truncated form, opposed to the alien communist state and its institutions. The genuine civil society, which existed in more or less mature forms in central and eastern Europe, was destroyed during the first five to seven years of communist rule after 1945.

A genuine civil society is a complex social formation which evolved spontaneously in different forms and institutions: families, free associations, private property, the rule of law and legitimate government. The crippled civil society was a result of deliberate and destructive enterprise by imposing control over institutions and ways of human conduct which sedimented and lasted for many generations. In the first case, government or state and its apparatus is accepted as legitimate through charisma, tradition, or legal procedures, as Max Weber put it. In the second case, government by force—whether resulting from a *coup d'état* or implemented by alien revolutionary military intervention—must seek its legitimacy in an ideology or gnosis, as Alain Besançon put it. This gnosis grounds its claims to power in a theory of irreversible historical trends which leads to a new form of society and government or state. In the latter case, the communist state expands at the expense of civil society; in the former, the state is a natural completion of the developing civil society.

There is no contradiction between genuine civil society and the government or state. They are its institutions, created and controlled by it. Deformed and reduced to its ill form, civil society in communism is an object of state actions. Therefore there is a fundamental incongruity between them, a constant conflict in which the state aims to subordinate civil society, and eventually to annihilate it.

Georg W. Hegel, in his *Philosophy of Right*, differentiated between a civil society and a state. Civil society was, for him, a realm of individuals, self-interest, and private law, ruled by an invisible hand, while the state was an embodiment of rationality, law and ethics. Although the Hegelian state was regarded as the necessary fulfillment of the civil society, his differentiation is useful when speaking of communist societies.

The communist state is no longer responsible for the maintenance of institutions which control its own activities (elective parliament, independent judiciary); it is no longer under public control and loses its legal and moral underpinnings. The disorganized, atomized and weakened civil society is no longer a Lockean or even Hegelian network of relationships. Deprived of its legal and economic institutions or free associations, civil society becomes an amorphous mass of families confronted with the almighty state. Its existence is confined to a moral dimension.

What are the basic features of that moral dimension? How was it possible that morals enabled the survival of the reduced civil society? Did morals have a fundamental significance for the rebirth of the genuine civil society?

To answer these questions it is necessary to point to certain traditional institutions which were natural niches in which morals survived and prevailed. With social life reduced to the moral dimension and its institutional framework, morals were partly distorted by being a substitute for other dimensions of social life, and especially for the public sphere.

The basic contradiction between the communist state and a civil society leads not only to the reduction of civil society to its moral dimension. It also creates an opposition between the private sphere, in which moral rules have significance, and the public sphere, in which moral rules are only somewhat valid or nonexistent. The 'private-public' and 'moral-immoral' dilemmas were combined with a very sharp contradistinction between morals and politics. Morals are confined to the private sphere; politics belong wholly to the public and therefore immoral.

This moral attitude to all forms of social life has troublesome effects on the re-emerging genuine civil society life. The reconstruction of the public sphere, politics and natural relationships between civil society and the state/government is significantly sealed with this reduced moral posture.

MORALS—PRIVATE AND PUBLIC SPHERES

Family and the closest circle of friends were, in a natural way, domains in which an individual, living in an omnipotent communist state, felt at home and relatively free. In the network of these bonds, basic moral principles were regarded as fully valid: honesty, veracity, mutual aid, solidarity, altruism, etc. However, those whom an individual knew less well were treated with less rigid moral principles and less important moral duties. In that sense, communism was equal to a revival of tribal mentality and behavior.[6]

In the case of contacts with the state officials, the basic principle was survival: avoid them or make them friendly and useful. The aliens, especially representatives of the regime—if they were not members of your own family or your close friends—were regarded with suspicion and fear. But they could also be potentially useful in a life full of hardships. They had access to certain privileges, goods, services, and the like.

However, it is not enough to say that an individual lived in two different dominions: private-moral and public-immoral. In fact, it was life in which boundaries of the private sphere (based on face-to-face relationships) were extended into the public sphere to change official and lamentably useless relations into a private, intimate, negotiable pattern of bonds. Thus in much of the social interaction in communist countries, vast 'grey areas' emerged, in which concessions and compromises were made and instrumental attitudes substituted for rigid moral principles. While within family life altruism prevailed, in the relations with the outer world, people adopted quite easily principles of corruption, which, however, were at the same time partly similar to principles of contract.

However useful for daily life, the instrumental attitude had some dangerous effects, although they were generally not obvious. Corruption and myriads of private mafia-type bonds softened and tamed the cruelty of the communist regime, but at the same time prolonged its existence through the expansion of mutual advantage spheres. In the long run, they not only corrupted the communist power structure but also permanently changed the attitudes of many of its members. This paved the way for certain systemic changes like the slow introduction of free market arrangements, which, among others, would make corruption more legitimate. Nevertheless, the most dangerous result of the routinization of totalitarianism (institutionalized corruption) was an immoral attitude toward the state within it in general, to politics, and especially to law, which people accepted as a sheer expression of one-party state interests. When one looks at the events in eastern bloc nations since the fall of the Berlin Wall, it seems quite probable that those corrupted areas determined a decrease of mutual hatred and anxiety between people (civil society) and state apparatus (*nomenklatura*). They cushioned the transition from communism to the threshold of democracy. In those countries like Rumania, where corruption was a phenomenon contained within both spheres separately or deeply hidden, with undeveloped 'grey areas,' the transition had a dramatic, revolutionary, and bloody form.

Now the changes we witness in the post-communist countries are inevitably sealed with this rotten posture to the public sphere, primarily in politics.[7]

Among specific features of Polish communism was a big private sector in the agricultural industry. Some seventy percent of farmlands were, for the last forty years, in the hands of individual farmers (with the majority of farms having less than three hectares). In other communist countries almost all farms were made collective or nationalized.

In a way, civil society, almost totally reduced to its moral dimen-sion, survived due to the private property of farmland. Rural communities are widely known for their traditional morals, reli-giosity, group cohesion and fundamental moral, psychosocial, and economic significance of family life (the lower divorce ratio in comparison with urban areas, for example). The people in the countryside are very religious and the role of the Catholic church in the life of peasant communities in Poland was crucial. The church was a center of public life in villages. Here is an anecdotal image of a Polish village in which three persons figured most sig-nificantly: the parson, the doctor, and the party secretary.

Thus, in Polish rural communities lived a large section of soci-ety which was not only accustomed to hard work but also accus-tomed to thinking in terms of investments and profits. However, the most important aspect of private property of farmland was a nearly mystical attitude toward land inherited from ancestors, and an almost sacred foundation of family life. While the rest of Polish economy (except for very small private businesses in industry and service) was run inefficiently by the state, Polish individual farmers lived in a way that was closer to their counterparts in western Europe. Their integrity and sense of independence, plus basic moral principles and traditional religiosity made them free and independent of state policies. The Polish countryside was then a niche of industrious and free people.

The contrast between the private and public sphere was weaker there than in the urban areas. There were two main reasons for that, the first of which was mentioned earlier: corruption and the blur between the sharp distinctions of the private and the public. The other reason was even more interesting: in the rural areas people, forced by circumstances, for centuries have organized themselves to solve certain local problems or to participate in local investments. These rudiments of public life survived communist havoc. Occasionally they were very important because they helped to articulate needs and expectations concerning the public good and added to the integrity of a local community.

The public good on the national level was beyond practical undertakings and rather vaguely perceived, while the public good on the local level was easy to define and perceive. The public sphere then was usually confined to such local endeavors as:

construction of schools, roads, post offices, water supplies, or gas pipes. More ambitious plans of more open-minded people reaching beyond the local horizon were blocked as politically dangerous by the local party bosses because they could undermine the myth of the party omnipotence. Even small local initiatives were sometimes taken over by the party to prove its 'indispensable' role in governing the country. Here again, compromise was the daily norm.

The private ownership of farmland, houses, and agricultural machines were necessary but not sufficient reasons for a fully free agricultural market. With the constraints on selling and buying farmland (combined with the deliberate policies aimed at bargain purchases of individual farms by inefficient run state farms), the state monopoly on wholesale prices, cheap credit, and subsidies on farm product prices were kept on a fairly decent level. However, they were not high enough to meet farmers' expectations.

This state protectionism with hidden intentions to nationalize agriculture in the long run guaranteed social peace in the countryside.

New policies of the Solidarity-led government aimed at the reduction of hyperinflation turned out to be unbearable to many individual farmers. They could not accept a 40 percent interest rate on credit and the abolishment of guaranteed minimum prices on farm products. They demanded cheaper credit, subsidies, and interventionist state purchases of agricultural products to keep their prices at a fairly high level.

The question arises whether their economic rationality, an exception in an irrationally led economy, and close connections between the moral and economic side of life were only illusions. Were individual farmers naturally free entrepreneurs or were they dependent on state subsidies?

The reaction of farmers to new economic policies was understandable: of course they were not eager to pay more than they were accustomed to. There were, however, interesting differences in responses to the new economic conditions. Those running small farms on the verge of unproductivity supported subsidies while those with bigger farms turned out to be more flexible. It became also evident that monopolistic structures in the wholesale market tend to keep low prices on farm products when buying them from farmers and selling them at very high prices to retailers. Those farmers who are against wholesale monopoly are right because its abrogation will pave the way for real market forces. Those, however, who demand subsidies do not understand that their focus should be on dismantling state control over agriculture rather than on reinforcing it. On the other hand, farmers' trade unions seem to be more radical and noisy in their demands than the farmers themselves.

This may mean that morals of self-reliant farmers were also affected by state control and interventionism and weakened their sense of independence.

Nevertheless, we should not exaggerate the frictions during the process of adaptation. They are painful and must have emerged after a short period of satisfaction with the major change of the political situation. It seems quite probable that we will witness real changes leading to fully free markets in agriculture. But the price of transition will be high: bankruptcy of many (some estimate one million) inefficient small farms. The syndrome of private ownership of land and traditional morals will decline. The integrity of families and local communities affected by the economic changes will also be reshaped.

A study of the second large social group—blue collar workers—revealed a number of specific features of their moral life and attitudes toward private and public spheres. Most of them came to cities from the countryside in the early stage of the communist industrialization. They were attracted by wages and prospects of a quick move up the career ladder, better education, and the easier city life.

This planned change of social structure, enforced by vertical and horizontal social mobility, had devastating results on their morals, integrity, and sense of identity. Separated from their traditional communities and families they needed some time to adapt. And they quite naturally, sometimes unconsciously, fell back on moral principles, customs, and the mentality of their families in the countryside, mixing them up with new habits molded by new circumstances of city life: anonymity and lack of social control. Many of them were lured by the change of their social status which they, quite rightly, associated with the new regime, and therefore accepted it, although not without some doubts.

It turned out quite soon, however, that their social and moral background, namely traditional religiosity ('backward' from the point of view of the new regime) was very strong. Those alleged socialist workers, members of the progressive social class, had a very unprogressive mentality and demanded churches in their 'socialistic' modern cities. Traditional commitments turned out to be stronger than the new ideology. Even party members were mostly religious and we had strange hybrids—Catholic-communists. It was a very important fact because even though there were substantial changes in their mentality, the core of their morals remained traditional and religious-based. This kind of cohabitation between Catholicism and communism seems impossible since both systems of thought and values are contradictory. There are only two possible ways of achieving a compromise: liberation or other progressive theology which perverts Christianity, and a less sophisticated eastern European solution: institutionalized religion subordinated to the communist regime (Russia, Rumania, Bulgaria) or 'moral schizophrenia.' In the latter case, the two systems are regarded as different but compatible because they operate in two insulated spheres: private and public. One could have been, especially recently, a disciplined party member in his factory during party conventions, etc., but on Sundays, Christmas, Easter, baptism, and the first communion of children, a good Catholic. Due to separation of the two dominions it was possible to behave officially as a good comrade and unofficially as a good parishioner.

The majority, however, were plagued by a different schizophrenia between private and public life. In the private sphere of one's home, with one's family, one followed the ten commandments. In the public sphere of the factory one pursued survival instincts, leaving principles at home—cheating one's managers, stealing, idling, etc. The deterioration of the moral aspect of work, part of the public sphere, was "a disease of Polish work," as Father Joseph Tischner put it. It was due to a topsy-turvy economy which was claimed to be guided by morals (distributive justice) but in fact was subordinated to ideological and political priorities: products being wasted however paid for. Under such circumstances where there was no direct link between good work and good wages people tended to find opportunities to work illegally on a black market where they were paid better. To earn more money for living in this way they had to use unscrupulously state factory tools or raw materials.[8]

There was the private sphere based on altruism, and the public sphere based on corroded self-interest. This did not lead to prosperity at all. Then there was the illegal public sphere of quasi-market relationships in which contract and profit prevailed. The more natural work within the black market was condemned as contrary to law and socialist principles; the dummy-work was officially praised but deplored by the workers. The good was illegal and immoral, the bad was legal and moral. The only way to change it was to turn to a free market economy.

Nevertheless, such a change of minds was not easy. Self-management was the prevailing idea among those workers who could not accept the abnormalities and immoral nature of communist mismanagement. Confronted constantly with incompetent party *nomenklatura*, workers quite easily came up with a simple solution: "Instead of party bosses, we ourselves can run our factories." The circumstances encouraged group solidarity and collective resistance against *nomenklatura* and then against the communist system as such. They fueled also workers' commitment to equality and social justice.

The moral pattern was used to perceive the most unacceptable traits of the system. Therefore, the corruption among workers connected with a black market was also deplored as a symptom of systemic illness. On the whole, the experience of industrial work in communism led to moral condemnation of totalitarianism and to efforts aiming at its overthrow. Traditional patriotic teachings of the Polish Catholic church added to this mixture of trade unionism, patriotism, and Catholicism. Intellectuals also played their role in the stimulation of workers' group and national identity.

Thus, Solidarity as a trade-union and a social movement which emerged out of this moral position had a very strong moral touch. However, its strength was not only rooted in morals but also in deep contradictions between them and the party—perceived in moral terms. This tension between deep hatred toward the system vs. moral principles gave rise to the amazing result of a self constrained and moral revolution against the system. The martyrdom of Father Jerzy Popieluszko, a chaplain of Warsaw steelworkers murdered by secret police agents, encouraged this self-constrained, non-violent struggle. Popieluszko was the embodiment of a principle: defeat evil with good.

With this moral world view shaped mostly by the pressure of the system, a short period of revival of the public sphere during the first Solidarity era (1980-1981) and its re-emergence in 1989, it is understandable that workers' responses to the economic and political situation were and will be differentiated.

First of all, workers are not a homogenous social class in a Marxist sense (large groups determined by their relation to the means of production). Some of them may easily adapt to market exigencies as businesses they work in already fit better into the new economic regime. The others, like coal miners, confronted with growing unemployment in unproductive sectors of the economy, may resist pro-market policies and stick to the idea of self-management and/or demand state subsidies.

Second, new political circumstances intervened. Sprouting democracies which extend the political public sphere will encourage political emancipation of workers, paving the way for their active share in the political process (which can be observed in civic committees but also in emerging political parties). This leads to a better grounding of the new political system.

Third, a developing democracy is still under threat by those groups which are endangered by unemployment. They may block economic changes through democratic activity or by staging strikes eagerly backed by the former communist trade unions playing on the fear of unemployment and stimulating an egalitarian mindset.

With the widely open public sphere, tensions and conflicts are emerging. It would be naive to predict that morals will guarantee their peaceful solutions. As is true with other social groups, workers will have to learn by experience new political habits, first of all, a compromise. In the period of reshaping political culture there is always the church and its moral authority and political wisdom to rely on.

There is also another social group which has been growing rapidly: small businessmen. Under communist rule, they were always threatened by arbitrary taxation leading to their bankruptcy. At the same time, they were able to make profits and to raise the living standards of their families. Their life was not reduced only to private sphere and a narrow moral dimension; they lived also in the public sphere of business, cooperating with the state sector of economy as well as with other private Polish or foreign companies. They were not fully free from corruption. They had to bribe state officials to avoid arbitrary administrative decisions and taxation or disadvantageous interpretations of socialist law. Still, they managed to survive in both the private and public spheres without making too many compromises with their morals. They kept to the moral principle of contract, which connects those spheres. They fully backed the political changes of 1989 and 1990 (albeit they could live in a peaceful way with the communist regime) because new economic policies and the new law gave them more opportunities and a sense of stability for the future.

Intellectuals, who form a part of a specific eastern European and Russian social group—the *intelligentsia*—played a crucial role in the postwar history of Poland. Some of them were responsible for the intellectual justification of the communist rule, and took part in purges in scientific and cultural institutions. They propagated the new ideology through the media and literature, contaminated the minds of younger generations, and tried to destroy religion and traditional morals. Finally, most of them rejected the system for intellectual, political, moral, and religious reasons.[9] The intellectuals turned out to be more sensitive to a new ideology while other social groups adapted to the system in order to survive. This sensitivity was connected with weak self-confidence and integrity, a tendency to alienate themselves, to overvalue their role, and to seek for power over a society which they simply deplored or hated. They were addicted to a new quasi-public sphere, especially politics, sometimes ruining their private sphere, rejecting family and traditional morality like worn-out shoes.

After some time it became evident that on the political scene they were only puppets and the intellectual depth of the new ideology was a mirage. Thus former communists or fellow travelers made another U-turn and came back to the old and proven morals. Those intellectuals who had close bonds with the church or gravitated toward it were much wiser and happier. They never neglected the private sphere and morals and found a parallel public sphere in the church. Cautiously, with certain compromises but not in conflict with their morals, they managed to make Catholic intellectual life flourish, constantly backed and defended by the church.

Both types of intellectuals had another institution which was a shelter and depository of basic intellectual and moral values: universities. These institutions were also infected with the communist disease, but they were able to survive and to save the ideal and practice of the pursuit of truth. With large numbers of intellectual *nouveaux riches* or simply idiots who crowded on the universities because of their political commitment, universities were still communities organized to achieve their main goal: a search for truth.

Again, traditional values (both moral and intellectual), suppressed for some time, turned out to be strong enough to survive and re-emerge. This would not have been possible without an older generation of scholars who never neglected their intellectual duties and who were depositories of the traditional ideas of university and scholarly work. Even though persecuted and banned from universities, they kept teaching and doing their research.[10]

Due to their strength, a new generation of scholars was educated and they form the real intellectual and moral core of Polish universities today. This struggle for truth was linked to their care for university customs and traditions. They knew very well that without a traditional institutional framework, Polish intellectual life would have been lamentably impoverished.

THE CHURCH AND THE SUBSTITUTES FOR THE PUBLIC SPHERE

It is a cliché to say that the Roman Catholic church played a decisive role in the survival of the rudiments of civil society under communist rule. It is necessary, however, to point to certain basic focuses of its activities.

In the public sphere, politics, economy, culture, and science are based on institutions which are the framework of the information exchange. The circulation of information in a modern society is a necessary condition of its existence. It is needed in political decision making, in economic conduct, and in culture and science which enable people to develop their professional skills, their personalities, and to raise their living standards. The communist destruction of the authentic public sphere, even if pursued with good intentions of founding a better political order, is based on the idea of total control of the civil society in order to achieve a presupposed aim: the New Society. Therefore, the main attack was made on all channels of information. Political and intellectual debate was suppressed by censorship. Its institutional framework of voluntary associations were banned. A 'commanded' economy—in which information was sent from one center to peripheries of the system—was substituted for spontaneous circulation of information on the market. Instead there were dummy political institutions—parliament, parties, government and ministries—which pretended to be similar to their counterparts in democratic countries. There were dummy political debates, a dummy free press, dummy trade unions, etc. All pretended to solve all kinds of problems. The main effort of civil society to defend itself was then focused on reconstruction of the information framework: underground printing and publishing houses. Even for a moral dimension, some information channels were necessary. Cultural transmission from generation to generation via family life was very important. But some means for communication on an inter-family or social level were also needed.

The Catholic church provided such channels of information in a traditional form of religious instruction for children, youth, and adults. The church provided patronage over systematic help for the disabled. In this way certain forms of voluntary associations were re-introduced. The people's needs were provided by parish committees through the organization of parish cultural life: public discussions, lectures of leading intellectuals, art exhibitions, and major events such as Weeks of Christian Culture on the diocese level which influenced thousands of people. The expansion of church activity had a step-by-step, cautious character. What was impossible for the church to provide was a vivid political life. One cannot have substitutes for main political institutions. However, political discussions which took place under the church umbrella turned out to be very important in the real political life during 1989. The Catholic church had a very clear idea of the crucial significance of the public sphere for civil society. It was deeply rooted in its traditional idea of subsidiarity, of many intermediary institutions—schools, universities, associations, parishes, local communities, press, etc.—which form a full and complex formation of the civil society crowned by the state and political system. The church then backed many initiatives which gave many opportunities for Catholics to participate in communist political institutions like the parliament (*Sejm*) to influence them and to express the position of the church and the majority of citizens. The church protected the independent Catholic press which tended to counterbalance the rest of the party-controlled media. The compromises were necessary. The Catholic press was censored meticulously, but from the point of view of the people, its existence was even more convincing proof of the non-authenticity of the party press.

In its struggle for an independent public sphere in different forms, the Catholic church also protected the Catholic University in Lublin (founded in 1918), the Pontifical Academy of Theology in Cracow, and various seminaries in many dioceses as well as a small number of Catholic secondary schools and elementary schools, including those for the disabled.

The new political situation of 1989 put the church in a different and perhaps even more difficult position. It ceased to be the main independent institution in a constant confrontation with the communist system. Now it supports the new government, and at the same time must calm down tensions which are connected with pro-market economic policies. In other words, it must find a position which would give it opportunities to mediate between government and some social groups. With the re-emergence of the public sphere, the Catholic church became one of many very important institutions within the public sphere.

The church is now worried whether religiosity under the communist regime was an expression of people's discontent with totalitarianism, or was it a deeper rooted, authentic phenomenon. As for the time being, we still notice a high abundance during masses and even more invigorated parish life. Civic committees in many cases use church facilities for their activities, underscoring the church's commitment to the public sphere. But this arrangement is temporary. With the growing number of political parties and inevitable splits, civic committees may evolve toward a political party or parties, thus ending the the close connection between the church and political movements. Their relationship will likely be suppressed because they may be dangerous for both parties concerned.

MORALS AND POLITICS

The developments which led to the overthrow of communist regimes in eastern and central Europe were more of a moral nature than political one. Politics are therefore a natural and subsequent step after a phase when morals were the main motive of activities.

Certainly the thesis is not an original one. The motivations of resistance to and struggle against communism are obvious. However indispensable for a sound social life, morals can hinder the political process. I do not mean that morals and politics are in opposition. On the contrary, I think morals are the necessary foundation of politics. However, under circumstances in which morals are confined mostly to the private sphere, since there is no natural transmission from it to the public sphere, morals turn out to be insufficient in providing the necessary political 'know-how.'

Politics is a way of negotiating a proportional share in power of different interests and establishing consensus and stability of social order.[11] Totalitarian 'politics' are alien to this idea of politics, which is as old as Aristotle's *Politics*, because it excludes other interests from the political arena. There is no consensus; only suppression of different interests, which gives an illusion of a stable political order. Another chimera of totalitarian politics is its efficiency based on a presumption that politics is a science which explains and makes predictions possible and therefore effective actions. This idea of short-term politics neglects long-run effects of political activities. Thus totalitarian politics turned out to be inefficient in the last resort because it was shortsighted, although it pretended to be based on necessary laws of social evolution.

Genuine politics is an endeavor focused on short-term results, but is based on moral principles, customs, and habits which emerge out of experience. They form its epistemological infrastructure which makes the politics efficient in the long term. Moral principles add to the stable political order.[12] In communist societies, morals replaced politics. Politics were synonymous with crime, violence, falsehood, arrogance, ignorance, and, finally, inefficiency.

The main social movements in eastern Europe which ousted the communists were based on morals with rather vague ideas about functioning of political institutions. Morals were strong enough to resist the totalitarian oppression, but now they must be followed by politics. This means that they partly must change themselves. Complex and subtle links between morals and politics transform moral perspective. Morals, if they are to expand to a public sphere and give grounding to politics, must adapt to this new domain of exercise and cease to be tribal. The morals must elevate to meet the needs of a complex society. This takes time. Morally motivated politicians must be very careful not to permeate their politics with personal views. Yet they must not abandon morals completely when pursuing what they naively consider politics, (i.e., efficient and quick reconstruction of a free society). The subtle balance between morals and politics, the private and public sphere, is something worth painstaking effort if we want not only to recover part of the political tradition of the region but also fit better to the rest of a free world.

NOTES

1. I am indebted to Professor R. Wayne Shute, Department of Educational Leadership, Brigham Young University, Provo, Utah, USA, for his friendly critical and stylistic remarks which helped me a lot in preparing the final version of this paper during my stay there in July 1990. I am also grateful to the staff of the Department for their kind assistance.
2. Mikhail Gorbachev came up with the same idea of equality under the law of different kinds of property during the last Soviet Communist Party Congress in July 1990. It seems like an introductory step to the full recognition of private property—a fundamental condition of a free market economy.
3. Taking into consideration these symptoms which in certain cases were present only partly, one was able to predict certain events in the short run. I managed to do it in the summer of 1989, anticipating major sociopolitical changes in Czechoslovakia and the Baltic countries. My cues were simple and obvious: growing religiosity (in the case of rather secular Bohemia it was even more significant) and striving for religious freedom: a nationwide action of signing a petition claiming the right to religious freedom and the Catholic church authority to ordain priests and bishops in Czechoslovakia and traditional Catholic or Protestant religiosity and commitment to western culture in the Baltic countries.
4. Mikhail Gorbachev gave exactly the same interpretation and assessment of recent changes in the ex-communist countries. When addressing the 28th Soviet Communist Party Congress in July 1990 he said that only "a variation of Stalin's authoritarian bureaucratic system" had collapsed in Eastern Europe. His reasons for giving this utterly nonsensical statement, if we take into consideration such countries as Poland or Hungary which got rid of Stalinism some twenty years ago even if they were still communist by certain criteria, are clear: he was trying to save as much as possible of the dilapidating empire without loosing

his position of the Secretary General of the Communist Party. Some leftists in the West, however, are still fascinated with the nebulous idea of building a new political system and liberating millions of the oppressed apparently living in their phantasmagoric minds. Cf. also: Kenneth Minogue "Societies Collapse, Faiths Linger On", in: *Encounter*, March 1990, 3-16.

5. Cf. for example: Bruce Cooper and R. Wayne Shute *Training for School Management: Lessons from the American Experience*, Bedford Way Papers 35, Institute of Education, University of London, London 1988; David Solway *Education Lost. Reflections on Contemporary Pedagogical Practice*, The Ontario Institute for Studies on Education, Ontario 1989; Caroline Cox *Standards in English Schools* (with M. Pomian-Srzednicki); D. O'Keeffe (ed.) *The Wayward Curriculum: A Cause for Parent's Concern?* The Social Affairs Unit 1986, and the same author's *The Wayward Elite: A Critique of British Teacher-Education*, Adam Smith Institute, London 1990; Roger Scruton (with Angela Ellis-Jones and Dennis O'Keeffe) *Education and Indoctrination: An Attempt at Definition and a Review of Social and Political Implications*, Education Research Centre 1985; Isabelle Stal and Françoise Thom *Schools for Barbarians*, transl. by Ken Connolly, with a foreword by Alain Besançon, (London and Lexington: The Claridge Press, 1988).

6. Cf. Friedrich Hayek's distinction between the tribal face-to-face society and the great society or extended order in his *Law, Legislation and Liberty*.

7. In Poland we could see lack of confidence that the political process is not a fake like politics under communist rule. It is significant how often people describe the new government and newly appointed officials as a new *nomenklatura*. It is not enough to say that former communists labeled their political opponents in this particular way. Had it not an appeal to those who used to think in terms of morals it would not be so popular. In this context relatively low voting frequency (general party free elections in 1989—62%, local free elections in 1990— around 42%) may be interpreted as an expression of cautiousness towards politics and the newly emerged establishment.

On the other hand this negative attitude toward politics is also fueled by the still operative old communist *nomenklatura* on lower levels of the economic system and public administration.

8. In the last decade Hungarian communists revealed quite a lot of common sense when they allowed people to use factory equipment to produce for their own customers. The deal was: you must work for the state eight hours and then you may work on your own. For some time this arrangement worked but the gap between low efficiency in case of serf labor for the state and high productivity of work for the quasi-market became so big that the only thing which could have been done was the total change of economy.

9. Cf. Jacek Kuron *Wina i wiara. Do i od komunizmu* ("Guilt and Faith. To and from Communism"), Biblioteka Kwartalnika *Krytyka*, Niezalezna Oficyna Wydawnicza, 3rd ed., Warszawa 1990.

10. An outstanding Polish sociologist Stanislaw Ossowski taught sociology in the early fifties at private seminars, when this discipline was officially banned.

11. Cf. Bernard Crick *In Defense of Politics*, (Harmondsworth: Penguin, 1964).

12. Cf. Michael Oakeshott "Rationalism in Politics," (London and New York: Methuen, 1989).

SIXTEEN

RELIGION AND DEMOCRATIC CULTURE

Gordon L. Anderson

A GLOBAL CULTURE IN FORMATION

The global trend toward pluralism and liberal democracy has been influenced by global communication, transportation, and economic interdependence. The electronic media, such as Cable News Network (CNN), are bringing about the collapse of traditional center-periphery models of control, which also require control of information.[1] Modern empires and wars have caused migrations of people from one cultural sphere to another; Christian, Islamic, Buddhist, and other peoples are living together in many parts of the world. Scientific thought has challenged all of the world religions. The political changes in Eastern Europe and South Africa reflect the present worldwide acceptance of democracy as the normative form of political organization.

The previous essays of this book make it abundantly clear that our present democracies are quite troubled on the issues of moral education and religion. Serious challenges to the ideals of justice, prosperity, and freedom are posed: the rise of religious hostility, ethnocentrism, racism, a growing underclass, high rates of teenage pregnancy, drug addiction, and corruption in government, business, and all areas of leadership. For liberal democracy to prosper in our emerging global culture, it is not adequate to relativize the questions of moral values. While this may have been a popular approach among American pluralists in the 1960s and 1970s, it is an irresponsible approach, an escape from hard controversial issues. Moral education and religion must be faced squarely in liberal democracies, if they are to succeed in this period of globalization.

The current period in human history has parallels to what Karl Jaspers called the 'axial age' in human civilization. That age, which occurred from roughly 700 B.C. until the time of Christ, involved the collision of traditional clan and kinship societies and the establishment of major cultural spheres. Today the speed of our cultural collisions have increased because of instantaneous global communication and rapid transportation systems. The major world religions and cultural spheres are now confronting one another as a world culture emerges. This is forcing a reassessment of traditional religions and a search for values which can be globally accepted.

THE ROLE OF NATURAL LAW IN GLOBAL VALUES

The main question for developing human values is, "What do we believe about the nature and purpose of human life?" This question has been answered with various degrees of accuracy by the cultures and civilizations which have preceded us.

In the early tribal and clan societies there was often a mystical worship of nature. In some of these societies the various gods were related to wind, rain, forests and other natural forces or elements. In monotheistic religions, God is viewed as single creator of all existence who made human beings for a purpose. The relationship to God in Judaism and Islam is mediated by God's prophets through revelation. In Aristotle's unmoved mover there is an attempt to integrate a first cause with laws observable in the world, natural law. In Taoism, the Tao is a symbol of a principle of harmonized polarity and movement which underlies all of nature. These early views of the nature and purpose of existence varied in the degree to which their justification was religious, scientific, or philosophical. They also used different concepts and terms to describe some of the same phenomena.

Western civilization is built on a fusion of Christian, Greek, and Roman thought. In St. Augustine we have a rational integration of biblical revelation with the speculative neoplatonism of his day.

St. Thomas Aquinas brought together the medieval synthesis of Christian doctrine and Aristotelian science.

In Western civilization, there has always been a tension between faith, revelation and tradition on the one hand, and reason and science on the other. This has caused a kind of schizophrenia in world view. Science was often viewed negatively by the church. Alchemy and ancient wisdom were frequently called the work of the devil. After the rise of modern scientific methods, some discoveries which did not fit into the official world view of the church were frequently viewed as a threat. After the publication of Galileo's *Dialogues* (1632) and Newton's *Principia* (1687) a great rift between the Catholic church and science came into existence. In the modern period, many who supported traditional dogmas attacked modernism; on the other hand, those who viewed science as the final authority opposed revelation, metaphysics, and tradition.

One aspect of the eighteenth-century world view, was that of natural law. The natural law theologians and deists developed a world view in which God, the creator of the universe, was understood in terms consistent with the Newtonian science of the day. Argumentation was different from the Aristotelian analysis based on function and purpose in that empirical observation and mathematical laws formed the basis of truth. Freemasonry promoted this type of world view and influenced many of the most prominent liberal thinkers of the age. The United States was begun by men who were influenced by this view and expressed natural law in terms of 'self-evident truths.'[2]

In the nineteenth-century, natural law lost its influence on liberal thought. At the end of the eighteenth century, Immanuel Kant proposed the idea of a religious a priori which was distinct from scientific inquiry. In his view, this a priori was the 'Moral Law.' Friedriech Schleiermacher, often called the father of modern theology, used Kant's line of argument in his theory that religion had to do with feelings, and ultimately the feeling of dependence upon God. This was a conscious effort to systematically separate empirically verifiable phenomena from religion. Then one of the strongest criticisms of the 'Argument from Design' was launched by Darwinists who believed that random selection and mutation, rather than purpose, was the reason for the way things are in the world.

The twentieth century inherited the Enlightenment view of 'value neutrality' or 'value relativity' with respect to science. G.E. Moore built on the philosophical heritage from Descartes, who posited an unbridgeable chasm between the mind and the world. Moore developed Hume's statement that one could not argue from an 'is' to an 'ought' into the 'naturalistic fallacy' thesis. This laid to rest natural law as a basis for human values or activity in the minds of many scholars.[3]

At the time of the founding of the United States, the drafters of the Constitution sought to give legitimacy to human law by correspondence to natural law. This gave the law a respect which today it no longer enjoys. Law, previously associated with righteousness, has become viewed as mere human legality. Like Kuninski's distinction between law and legislation, law is no longer something related to divine life or necessary principle, but arbitrarily instituted by human beings to shift money from one pocket to another. In order to regain respect for human law, a new consciousness in which the natural or transcendent laws of the universe, of which human laws are a reflection, is required.

A NEW MORAL VALUE SYSTEM

At the threshold of the twenty-first century the need to integrate science and values has gained paramount importance. The natural law espoused by America's founders in the Constitution had wide acceptance across Christian denominations as well as by men and women of learning.[4] It was a unifying concept among the religious pluralism in the United States. However, it was distinctly a product of the Christian civilization and a particular scientific age.[5] In the global community, the religious traditions are much more diverse. However, it is now recognized that all people are interrelated within one global ecosystem. All are subject to the same physical and natural forces. The 1990s have been called the environmental decade. A new understanding of natural law is emerging and can be developed to provide a similar cross-cultural cohesive element in the coming world civilization.

The teaching of values in schools must be significantly clarified and improved. Those universal values based on natural structures of existence common to all people should be taught by the schools with confidence. The particular elements of inherited cultures cannot be taught as absolutes by democratic governments or by public schools, but neither can they be ignored. Teachers must clearly distinguish between those values based on faith and those based on knowledge. However, those values held by faith should receive respect, not ridicule or condemnation.

DISTINGUISHING UNIVERSAL AND PARTICULAR VALUES

It may be that one cannot use logic to reason from an 'is' to an 'ought,' but one can start with the basic human desire to live. The right to life is considered the most basic of human rights. More importantly, biological life is a necessary prerequisite for the pursuit of the 'good life.' Given this necessity, it follows that natural laws which govern human life must be valued. Each dimension or subsystem of human life has values which correspond to its structure of existence. There are general or absolute values which are required for maintaining the existing system. There are also, in higher order systems, realms of freedom where particular values can be applied.

For the scientist, as with Aristotle, biologically based values are the most visible general values which can be empirically validated. There are features characteristic of all people: for example, breathing, eating, and sleeping. Air, food, and a resting place, which are biologically required to continue life, can be called 'goods,' if life itself is valued.

There is a realm of freedom which allows sets of particular values to enter. Here values are varied; they relate to "taste" and inherited values. For example, while all require food, how much food, what kind of food, and how the food is prepared are variables whose nature is not explicit. Each individual and each society has freedom in their choice. In a free pluralistic society, it can be taught in public schools that all people should eat, and eat 'well.' However, it would be inappropriate to define 'well' in absolute terms. One cannot teach that Chinese ought to eat European food or that Jews ought to eat pork. If one knows that eating a particular food could poison the body and cause death, it is appropriate to teach in a pluralistic society that eating such a food is 'bad.'

While the biologist may easily speak of universal values, the anthropologist or social scientist will focus on the relative or particular. While the biological dimension is a foundation for human values, it is only one aspect of human life.

The human being is also a social being. This dimension is linked to biological processes of growth. Every human being must go through a process of nurture to maturity. A baby, left on its own in nature, is not equipped to survive. Parents and teachers are required to nourish and educate the young. This makes human beings essentially and universally social beings from birth. Because dependency is a feature of childhood, the survival of children places an obligation on others. Adult responsibility is a social necessity. Free actions frequently have social consequences which require responsibility. The initial exercise of freedom by lovers, the choice to engage in sexual relations, which in itself may be viewed as a particular good, can have the consequence of creating a child. The parents become bound to a new structure of relations, partly created by themselves and partly derived from a law of nature. Taking responsibility for the care of their child is a moral rather than a material necessity. While most parents naturally love their children, the children can be abandoned, abused, or enslaved. While the content of "good" raising of a child is largely a matter of character, tradition, and faith, the necessity of a general obligation to raise children is a matter of knowledge.

Another universal social feature of human beings is communication. Communication is most noticeably accomplished through language, spoken or in other forms. Like food, language is universally valued. However, the spoken word and particular forms of communication may vary from group to group.

The human being is also a rational being. This aspect of human life also contains universal and particular characteristics. For example, it is a universal feature of reason to seek justice. However, to some people justice means equality of value in the eyes of God or the Law; to others it is equal opportunity; to still others it is equal ownership of wealth. In whatever particular way justice is envisioned, the fact that human beings compare their freedom, wealth, and other goods with each other is a universal feature of reason which transcends races and cultures.

Details about other aspects of human life could be discussed, but the method should by now be clear; each dimension of life has general and particular characteristics, and therefore needs and values, which correspond to it. The problem faced in liberal democracies is how to maximize attainment of the universal necessities of all human beings and at the same time minimize the forceful imposition of particular values. The absolutization of particular 'goods' by the leaders is felt as oppression by citizens who do not value the same particulars.

MORAL LEADERSHIP IN THE GLOBAL COMMUNITY

Leaders and responsible citizens in traditional societies undergo training that extends beyond rational knowledge or economic skills. The Jewish Bar Mitzvah, which literally means 'Son of the Commandment,' involves knowledge of, and application of social rule for behavior. The Ten Commandments given by Moses and recorded in the Old Testament are rules of ethical conduct, the first two involving one's relation to God and the remaining eight involving one's relationship to others. The Bar Mitzvah is a rite of passage into adulthood for the Jewish young man and occurs about the time of puberty at age thirteen.

Likewise, the Christian confirmation is a similar process but it focuses on the teachings of Jesus and the doctrines of the Christian church. The teaching of Jesus was a moral teaching. In his famous 'Sermon on the Mount,' Jesus taught basic virtues of humility, forgiveness, charity, and love. In both the Jewish and Christian traditions the initiates are taught that they will be 'blessed' if they behave in one way and 'cursed' if they behave in another.

Other traditional societies which existed over several centuries have had rites of passage to adulthood. The cave society in France, about 10,000 B.C., left pictorial remnants of their rites of passage in which young men were brought by their mothers and covered by branches, symbolizing the death of the dependent world of their mothers. Emerging from the branches, they began training by elders in the world of responsibility for the community.[6] Similar rituals are typical of homogenous face-to-face societies. Through the ritual process, the initiate learns the traditions, basic economic skills, and loyalty to the community.

The final act of graduation in the male ritual process frequently involves a test of loyalty in which the initiate shows he is willing to place his own life at risk for the sake of the community. The legends and folktales in which the hero slays the dragon before being qualified to marry the princess are examples of what people who will have to live under his leadership believe his ultimate motives should be. All people want leaders who place the needs of the community above their own. Jesus Christ has been widely accepted as savior by millions of people because he selflessly died for the sake of the world.

The development of moral leadership through a ritual process in liberal democracies which are religiously diverse is one of the most serious challenges they face. None of the previous traditions is equipped to prepare moral leadership for a pluralistic global society. Furthermore, modern democracies guarantee religious liberties which preclude the possibility of one tradition being chosen as normative. What can be a solution?

The founders of the American democracy believed that the families and the churches had a responsibility to provide education and to inculcate moral virtue. In their lively experiment, the government was the 'head' and religion the 'heart' of the society.[7] The extent to which this arrangement has worked has, to a large degree, depended upon whether existing family and religious institutions succeeded in producing citizens of moral integrity, living for the sake of others.

The arrangement has never completely worked. The 1960s, symbolized by the slogan 'Do your own thing,' was a failure of religion to lead popular culture in America. The 1970s and 1980s brought further moral decline with the 1970s called the 'me' generation and the 1980s called the 'just me' or 'yuppie' generation. Responsible positions of civil service became 'government jobs.' Elected positions for popular representation became 'positions of power.'[8] Less efficient government and higher taxes were the result. Without a proper 'heart,' the 'head' became a parasite, rather than a guide for the body. In the world of finance and banking, traditional religious cautions against borrowing and usury went largely unheeded until the entire savings and loan industry collapsed.

In the 1820s there was already strong evidence that religion was not educating enough of America's young people. The frontier nation was made up of immigrants from the Old World who often threw off old ways or lived in isolated and unpopulated areas. While there is a strongly religious history of the American people, only ten to twenty percent of the total population were full church members in 1820.[9] A high percentage of young people were illiterate. This failure of religion, by itself, to educate American youth led to the need to establish public schools by the 1850s. The 'civil religion' promoted in the public schools, combined with the more traditional moral education in private schools, helped to create a liberal society which was reasonably religious and moral. However, in recent years the public schools have been beset by both antinomian and fundamentalist challenges.[10] The public schools have appeared more a moral battlefield laying youth to waste than a place of character development that traditional societies have found integral to their very existence.

THE CHALLENGE TO JUDEO-CHRISTIANITY IN THE AMERICAN EXPERIMENT

The moral problems of the American experiment are complex. Perhaps some responsibility is due to the framers of the Constitution who had an overly optimistic vision of the abilities of religions, which had previously been state religions, to operate in a pluralistic and secular environment. Perhaps some of the blame can be laid to urbanization. Thomas Jefferson prophesied;

> I think our governments will remain virtuous for many centuries, as long as they are chiefly agricultural; and this as long as there shall be vacant lands in any part of America. When [people] get piled upon one another in large cities, as in Europe, they will become corrupt as in Europe.[11]

The frontier thesis developed by Frederick Jackson Turner saw the success of the pioneer in

> "The fierce love of freedom, the strength that came from hewing out a home, making a school and a church and creating a higher future for his family."[12]

The hardships and risks in bringing one's family to the New World was in itself a rite of passage which separated the brave and those with a burning desire for liberty from the others in the Old World.

The established religions have not been able to adjust to the new situation of pluralism easily. As Professor Weiler has explained: Judaism is based on the Torah, which is the law of a nation. It is not possible for the Torah to function as the law of a modern liberal democracy. The alternatives are (1) assimilation as individuals, (2) secular nationalism, (3) self-ghettoization, or (4) nationalist-religious fundamentalism. Should Judaism adjust enough to solve the church-state problem in liberal democracies it would be a different religion.[13] Islamic law faces a similar predicament.

Catholicism developed in the feudal period and contains feudal structures within its own organization but is not wed to political law in the way Judaism has been wed to the Torah. While the Catholic church itself is organized hierarchically, the pronouncements of popes and bishops on liberal democracy have often been positive. Battista John Mondin has observed, however, that in twentieth-century Europe the church has generally assigned responsibility for public life to the state, leading to a collapse of moral values in the culture.[14]

George Weigel is optimistic about the creative dialogue in the Catholic church in America. The American experiment, based on 'unalienable rights' given by 'Nature,' he explains, was a revolution for freedom which was far from radical individualistic and libertarian. Rather, it contained a moral realism with important points of connection to the Catholic tradition. Further, liberation theology has challenged the bishops to address issues of public policy. Weigel is hopeful that this theology can develop into a new phase which supports democratic ideals.[15] There are many American Catholics who feel that the moral decline in America and the decline in influence of protestantism in public life will provide a new opportunity for the Catholic church, a 'Catholic Moment.'[16]

Modernity, nevertheless, poses serious challenges to the Catholic church. Even in Poland, the strong traditions in rural areas may have survived more as a defense against communist oppression than in an encounter with modernity. In the West it is difficult to convince a young man or woman to join a monastery or order which requires vows of celibacy, poverty, and obedience. Eastern European democracies will gain from the experience of the West. However, the tenuous dialogue between the Catholic church and the modern world is far from a solution to the problem of developing moral leadership in pluralist societies.

The protestant tradition is a religious development in the modern era and contains democratic elements in its core. Rather than the church as sole mediator of the divine life of citizens, protestants developed a community of faith in which Christ comes directly to each believer. The community is available to support the individual in his or her faith, but essentially the moral life springs from within. This corresponds to the need for individuals to take personal responsibility in a democracy.

However, protestants are highly divided on moral and social issues. The spectrum of attitudes toward church-state relations documented by Dean Kelly is one clear example. Although protestants are the strongest advocates of democracy, and although they are more likely to accept the viewpoints of modern science, they have no unified institutional or moral tradition. Since interpretation of the Bible is in the end a personal matter, protestants have supported many conflicting ethical practices. Jesus Christ has been called both the world's first Marxist and the world's greatest businessman. Since he did not have a family or lead a society in his own lifetime, he provides no norm for many concrete family or social structures. The projection thesis developed by Ludwig Feuerbach[17] seems to make a lot of sense to the skeptic.

Friedreich Schleiermacher may have thought he was doing a service to theology by carving out a religious domain which science could not coopt or attack. Unfortunately, during World Wars I and II, protestants failed to challenge policies of the state because that was not considered the domain of religion. The National Council of Churches (NCC) in the U.S.A., and the World Council of Churches, when they attempted to become socially relevant, applied insights from the social sciences and the humanities, often sympathizing with Marxists in revolutionary struggle for the poor against their oppressors. By 1970 the radical theologies, such as the 'death of God,' 'the secular city,' and the theologies of liberation were too revolutionary for traditional Christian believers to follow. When the NCC began targeting financial aid to revolutionary groups, the member churches reduced their financial contributions, weakening the whole protestant ecumenical movement.

In the 1970s and 1980s Christian fundamentalism rose to fill a moral and emotional vacuum left by less influential mainline (now called 'old-line') protestant denominations. These protestant fundamentalists, while loosely forming the 'moral majority' which backed Ronald Reagan for the U.S. presidency, fragmented and divided in the late 1980s with the scandals surrounding many of their charismatic leaders. The future of the protestant churches is one of continued decline in the foreseeable future. The Jehovah's Witnesses and the Mormons, both autochthonous American religions, may be the notable exceptions to this downward trend. In 1980, the nearly 55 million Roman Catholics outnumbered by at least ten million the combined membership of all churches in the NCC, including the orthodox membership.[18]

The United States is not the 'Christian nation' it once was. There is continued population growth among Muslims, Buddhists, Hindus, and various new religions in America. There is little hope for finding universal moral values based on particular religious revelations in the near future.

TEACHING ALL TRADITIONS IS BETTER THAN TEACHING NONE

The conclusion the author has drawn from the situation described above is that public schools, in a climate of moral disagreement and quandary, would better educate young people if they taught all of the major traditions in the society rather than none of them. Traditionally, the age of puberty is the age where young people begin to make moral judgements. With the physical ability to create new human life through sexual relations comes a fundamental responsibility for self-control. Further, modern brain research shows that basic human behavioral habits are formed by this age.[19] In addition, how can we expect autonomous preparation of the self in colleges and universities from young people who have not developed a sense of purpose, personal and social worth, and self-control? Not to teach moral values, to teach that values are relative, or to teach that material values are superior to the spiritual, leaves young people morally vacuous and seriously handicapped.

Since it is not possible to have an official national religious tradition, the public schools could promote the general principles one can glean from history and science as well as to hold up the various traditional approaches to particular moral and lifestyle questions as attempts to create a good society. Further, it is not enough for an uncommitted relativist or skeptic to represent other traditions; each tradition should be taught by someone committed to it. This will help young people to wrestle with major religious issues at a time in their life when they need to mature morally. Further, in order to become a leader in a pluralistic society, it is helpful to understand all of its citizens on an emotional or religious level. A young person will be able to integrate the plurality of values his or her society has inherited at a more basic level than those adults who come from one of the narrower traditions.

Many parents may cringe at this proposal, not wanting their children polluted by what they believe to be false doctrines at a tender age. This is a natural parental concern. It would only be fair, therefore, to make private religious schools a real option. A real option means 'financially' possible for the parents. It is the belief of this author that it might take an educational voucher system, tax rebates, or some subsidy to children in the underclasses to make this a reality. Whether a school could really equip the youth to succeed and excel in leadership positions would be known by its fruits. Within one generation, most parents would be sending their children to the schools which best equipped their children to meet the moral leadership challenges as well as to acquire economic skills.

THE CULTURE OF THE GLOBAL DEMOCRATIC COMMUNITY

The culture of the global democratic community is in an embryonic form as the cultures of the various geographic areas collide with one another. Nevertheless, a global culture is forming, and that culture will become more identifiable as truth as the received traditions of the world's great civilizations are forged on the anvil of history. What seem today to be irreconcilable differences between often hostile religious believers will tomorrow seem to be petty disputes between narrow believers.

Traditions are always in flux. They change as their bearers encounter new reality. Today the reality of global community will impact on the traditions of all who experience it. Those traditions will change to account for the new reality and may develop more in common than in opposition.

The history of the National Council of Churches in the U.S.A. is an example of one phase in the epigenesis of the tradition of the approaching global culture. The predecessor organizations, the Foreign Missions Conference, begun in 1893, and the Federal Council of Churches, organized in 1908, originated as ecumenical forums to address common problems facing the churches. In the case of missions, there were similar problems that all missionaries faced when operating in foreign cultures with non-Christian governments and leaders. In the case of the Federal Council of Churches, there were common concerns at home regarding industrial justice, world peace, and poverty.

When these bodies were begun, questions of doctrine or ritual, which had always divided the denominations, were off limits.[20] Like other voluntary societies in pluralistic America, social leaders and concerned citizens united to attempt to solve major challenges common to them in their present culture. They put past differences aside. As these ecumenical bodies developed, a new ecumenical culture with its own institutions and common doctrine developed. The experience of World Wars I and II shook the foundations of all Christian theology. The ideas of Karl Barth, Reinhold Niebuhr, Paul Tillich, and other great minds helped all members of the ecumenical movement shape a common world view. At the Stockholm Conference in 1927 the 'Commission on Faith and Order' was established for doctrinal dialogue. Fifty years later, liberal protestants turned to the Commissions on Faith and Order in the National and World Council of Churches for official new orthodox policy.[21]

The neo-orthodoxy of the World Council of Churches was explicitly challenged at the Nairobi conference in 1975. It was there that some Third World Christian leaders challenged the 'Graeco-Roman-Germanic Christ' of Karl Barth. The collision of Protestant denominations at the turn of the twentieth century had led to a certain conception of Christian culture which was promoted in the news magazine *The Christian Century.* That cultural tradition is fading with the century as global religious dialogue and issues of global civilization force the ecumenical tradition into broader transformation.

Similarly, the ideological warfare between capitalism and communism has turned into constructive dialogue as both the American and Soviet empires of the late twentieth century have begun to collapse from the weight of rationalized society in which both, in retrospect, have had a naive faith. It is likely that the common experience of the key global players in our emerging global culture will force serious thinkers in both the United States and the Soviet Union to draw conclusions similar to each other but in conflict with the conclusions drawn by people in the Third and Fourth Worlds. Other cultures, too, will undergo their own epigenesis. The Africans, the Buddhists, and the Latin Americans will each have their own course of adjustment to global society.

The trends toward a global cultural outlook will continue to reflect the growing interdependent world human beings experience. As that experience is shared, succeeding generations will articulate new expressions of truth. This is the present chapter in the ongoing and dynamic story of the development of human culture.

This story of cultural evolution does not necessarily have a happy ending. Even as the great empires of the twentieth century meld together in peace, they both wallow in corruption, declining productivity, and moral decay. The key to the future is not just the expression of truth which resides in people—it is in the character of the people themselves. Is the rationalized society capable of producing leaders of moral integrity? Richard L. Rubenstein has convincingly argued that it was secularization which allowed leaders like Hitler and Stalin, who were not legitimated by transcendent principles, to claim self-legitimation. This distinguished them from traditional leaders who were legitimated by their conformity to the transcendent principles of their culture. The human spirit senses the vacuity of rational culture, yet the modern mind knows the shortcomings of inherited religious traditions.

The present generation owes it to the future generations to provide the best opportunities to wrestle with the inherited cultural traditions of the world in the new environment of a global community. The questions of God, of absolute and relative values, and the description of natural laws of the universe to which we are all bound, should be taught with sincerity and humility to our young people as well as we can comprehend them. It is most important for the elders and leaders of the present period in history, like the elders of the primitive cave society, the Jewish rabbis, and the Christian ministers to practice the highest example of a good life they can attain, and that it conform to the principles they teach. It has been a mistake to think that rationality or technology, with all the promises they hold for humanity, could somehow allow human beings to become less human than their forebears and yet prosper.

NOTES

1. Richard L. Rubenstein, "Toward a New World Culture in the 21st Century," *International Journal on World Peace*, vol. VI, No. 4 (Oct-Dec, 1989), 31-43.
2. "When in the course of human events, it becomes necessary for one people to dissolve the political bands which have connected them with another, and to assume among the Powers of the earth, the separate and equal station to which the Laws of Nature and Nature's God entitle them, a decent respect to the opinions of mankind requires that they should declare the causes which impel them to the separation.

    We hold these truths to be self-evident, that all men are created equal, that they are endowed by their Creator with certain unalienable rights, that among these are Life, Liberty, and the pursuit of Happiness."

    From *The Declaration of Independence*, July 4, 1776.
3. G.E. Moore, *Principia Ethica* (New York: Cambridge University Press, 1959), 46-47.
4. Based on a study of the Virginia debates on religious freedom, the classic conception given by historian Sidney E. Mead in "One's opinion about the duty which we owe to our creator, and the manner of discharging it. *The Lively Experiment* (New York: Harper & Row, 1976), 57.
5. The total Jewish population in America in 1776 was no more than 2,500 a small minority indeed. The number of Catholics in 1790 was 35,000 out of a total white population of 3,172,006.
6. Leonel L. Mitchell, *The Meaning of Ritual* (New York: Paulist Press, 1977), 11-13. Her discussion is based on the work of Johannes Maringer, *The Gods of Prehistoric Man*.7.
7. Sydney E. Mead, *The Lively Experiment: The Shaping of Christianity in America*, 38-41.
8. Gordon S. Jones and John A. Marini, *The Imperial Congress* (New York: Pharos Books, 1988). This book document the shifts in attitude and power in the Congress which has led to a crisis in the American political system. While a political solution is possible, it will take more leadership.
9. Sidney E. Mead, op. cit., 67.
10. Geoffrey Partington, "Moral Education in Some English Speaking Societies: Antinomian and Fundamentalist Challenges." Paper presented at The Fourth International Congress of Professors World Peace Academy, London UK, August 25-29, 1989.
11. Thomas Jefferson to James Madison, letter from Paris, December 20, 1787. Cited in *The Papers of Thomas Jefferson*, ed. Julian P. Boyd (Princeton, New Jersey: Princeton University Press, 1958), vol. 12, 440.

12. Frederick Jackson Turner from a paper given in Chicago in 1893. Cited from Ralph Henry Gabriel, *The Course of American Democratic Thought* (New York: The Ronald Press, 1956), 321.

13. Gershon Weiler, "The Jewish Perspective on the Interrelationship of Church and State," presented at The Fourth International Congress of Professors World Peace Academy, London UK, August 25-29, 1989.

14. Battista Mondin, "Religion and Politics from a Roman Catholic Perspective," Paper presented at The Fourth International Congress of Professors World Peace Academy, London UK, August 25-29, 1989.

16. George Weigel, *Catholicism and the Renewal of American Democracy* (New York: Paulist Press, 1989), 204-214.

17. Ludwig Feuerbach, *The Essence of Christianity*, translated by George Elliot (New York: Harper & Row, 1957). Original in German, 1843.

18. Arie R. Brouwer, "The Real Crisis at the NCC," *The Christian Century*, June 27-July 4, 1990, 633.

19. Jose Delgado, "Transracial Structuring of the Brain," *International Journal on World Peace*, vol. IV, No. 2 (April-June, 1987), 55-57.

20. Samuel McCrea Cavert, *Church Cooperation and Unity in America, 1900-1970* (New York: Association Press, 1970), 34-35.

21. In 1977 the General Board of the NCCC-USA asked the Commission on Faith and Order to provide a theological assessment of human rights issues. They were also asked to determine whether new churches applying to membership in the NCCC-USA, such as the Unification Church, could pass a test of orthodoxy. Ironically, such a judgment had been explicitly avoided when the churches initially organized.

CONTRIBUTORS

Gordon L. Anderson is Secretary General of the Professors World Peace Academy in New York, Lecturer in Religion and Society at the Unification Theological Seminary in Barrytown, New York, and Associate Editor of the *International Journal on World Peace*.

Alain Besançon is director of studies at the Ecole des Hautes Etudes en Sciences Sociales, Paris and a columnist for *L'Express*.

John Carroll is Professor of Sociology at LaTrobe University in Australia. He has written more widely on the rise and fall of humanism in his book *The Wreck of Western Culture*.

Robert Grant is Professor of English Literature at the University of Glasgow in Scotland.

Morton A. Kaplan is Distinguished Service Professor of Political Science emeritus for the University of Chicago. He is also the Editor and Publisher of *The World & I* magazine in Washington, D.C.

Dean M. Kelley is Director for Religious Liberty of the National Council of Churches (USA). He has published numerous books on church and state relations in the United States.

Milowit Kuninski is lecturer on History of Philosophy and Political Philosophy at the Jagiellonian University in Cracow, Poland. He has published Max Weber's sociology and on moral education in post-communist societies.

David J. Levy is professor at Middlesex Polytechnic in England.

Batista Mondin is Dean of the Faculty of Philosophy at the Urban Pontifical University in Rome, President of the Italian Association of Philosophy Instructors, an ordained priest, and author of over fifty books in several languages.

Geoffrey Partington is Senior Lecturer in Education at the Flinders University of South Australia. He holds several posts in voluntary organizations established to improve and support public education in Australia and he is the author of numerous articles on excellence and values in education.

Michael J. Perry is Professor of Law at Northwestern University in Chicago.

A. James Reichley is a Senior Fellow at the Brookings Institution in Washington, D.C. He was formerly political editor of *Fortune* and a member of the White House staff under President Ford. He is author of *Conservatives in an Age of Change* (1981), *Religion and American Public Life* (1985), and the *Party Politics and American Democracy.*

Roger Scruton is Professor of Aesthetics at Birbeck College in London. He is author of several books in Aesthetics, Culture, and Philosophy, and is Editor of *The Salisbury Review.*

George Weigel is President of the Ethics and Public Policy Center in Washington, D.C. His most recent books include *Catholicism and the Renewal of American Democracy* and *American Interests, American Purposes:Moral Reasoning and U.S. Foreign Policy.*

Gershon Weiler is Professor of Philosophy at Tel Aviv University in Israel. He has held posts at Trinity College, Dublin, Australian National University, and La Trobe University. He has published numerous books and articles on philosophy, language, and Jewish society, and is a fellow of the World Academy of Art and Science.

INDEX

A

abortion-rights, 168
Abortion Rights Mobilization, 172, 186
Ackerman, Bruce, 3, 42-43, 46-49, 52-54, 57, 61-62, 65-66, 68
Act for Better Child-Care Services, 170
Acton, Lord, 148, 227-228, 242
Adenauer, 194, 232
Adolescent Family Life Act, 169
Adorno, 138
advertising, 203, 219
Advisory Committee on Religious Liberty and Church/State Relations, 174
Advisory Council on Church and Society, 174
Africa, 142, 189, 241, 246, 329
altruism, 23, 83, 313-314, 319
American Association of School Administrators, 165
American Civil Liberties Union (ACLU), 165, 170-172, 185
American Federation of Teachers, 165
American Friends Service Committee, 159
American Humanist Association, 165
American Jewish Congress, 165, 169
American Lutheran Church (*see also* Lutheranism), 170
Americans United (A.U.), 164-165, 169-170, 185
Amish, 157, 204
Anabaptists, 5-6, 148, 150-151, 155-160
anarcho-aristotelianism, 36
Anastasius I, 109
Andreotti, 136
angels, rebellious, 4, 129
Anglican Church (*see also* Episcopal Church), 146-148, 161-162, 204-206, 212, 285

animal recognition, 93
Anti-Defamation League of B'nai Brith, 170
antichrist, 188, 199
anticlericalism, 8, 225, 227, 231
Aquaviva, Sabino, 139
Aquinas, St. Thomas, 4, 128, 131, 140, 146, 227, 244, 331
Archer, Glenn, 164
Arendt, Hannah, 30
Aristotelian ideal, 31
Aristotle, 2, 10, 30, 35, 38-39, 70, 75-76, 80, 102, 132, 141, 262, 264, 268, 290, 325, 330, 333
Arrow paradox, 102
Ashby, Ross, 102
Asia, 142, 217, 243, 246
assimilation, 4, 89, 124, 157, 286, 338
atheists, 6
Audinet, Jacques, 138, 143
Augustine, St., 128-130
Austria, 33, 135
Austria-Hungary, 34
authoritarian regime, 6, 9, 34, 64, 90, 97, 100, 193-194, 215, 219, 221, 241, 280, 326
authoritarianism, 6, 34, 148, 215
autonomy
    as element of the principle of subsidiarity, 8
    clergy's right to, 131
    compatibility with egoism, 20
    Dworkin's concept of, 300
    human capacity for, 91-92
    in communist society, 309
    in Judaism, 112-113, 124
    in liberal democracy, 95, 102
    in liberalism, 21, 252
    in society, 297
    in Vatican II, 196

M

ART FORMS
AND CIVIC LIFE
IN THE
LATE ROMAN EMPIRE

ART
FORMS
AND
CIVIC LIFE

IN THE

LATE ROMAN EMPIRE

By H. P. L'ORANGE

PRINCETON, NEW JERSEY

PRINCETON UNIVERSITY PRESS

1965

This book is a translation from the Norwegian
of *Fra Principat til Dominat*, published simultaneously
in 1958 by H. Aschehoug & Co.
(W. Nygaard), Oslo, Norway, and P. A. Norstedt &
Söners Förlag, Stockholm, Sweden

Publication of this book has been aided
by the Whitney Darrow Publication Reserve Fund
of Princeton University Press

Printed in the United States of America
by Princeton University Press,
Princeton, New Jersey

FOREWORD

AT AN early point in my studies of Late Antiquity I was struck by the marked similarity between the way in which the late antique state was organized and the predominating types of composition in both the figurative art and the architecture of that period. In my writings over the approximately thirty years I have devoted to the study of Late Antiquity, I have repeatedly drawn attention to the fact that the disintegration of the traditional society of the earlier empire—the Principate—and the consequent establishment of a new order during the late antique empire—the Dominate—were accompanied in the realm of art around A.D. 300 by a corresponding disintegration of classical tradition and the emergence of a new form of expression. The same "system" expressed itself with the same structural patterns in the life of practical organization and in art.

In order to examine this problem on a broader basis and to undertake a comparative structural analysis as indicated above, I was granted in 1952 the Hoff-Farmand Scholarship by the University of Oslo. Circumstances led to interruptions and postponements which prevented me from completing the research until 1958. The work was published in Norwegian in 1958 with a grant from the Svenska Humanistiska Förbundet by P. A. Norstedt & Söners Förlag (Stockholm) and by H. Aschehoug & Co. (Oslo).

I wish to express my gratitude to the University of Oslo for the Hoff-Farmand Scholarship, to the Svenska Humanistiska Förbundet, to Princeton University Press, which in the present edition publishes the work in English, and finally to Professor Erik Sjöqvist and Professor Irving Lavin for their interest in the book and to Dr. and Mrs. Knut Berg, who generously translated it into English.

H. P. L.

ACKNOWLEDGMENTS

For objects owned by collections or museums, the proprietor supplied the photograph unless another source is acknowledged. In other cases, acknowledgment is made to the following:

Alinari: Figs. 10, 67
Alinari-Anderson: Figs. 17, 33, 35, 36, 51, 53
Deutsches Archaölogisches Institut, Rom: Figs. 2, 3, 18-21, 30, 32, 37-39, 42-47, 50, 60, 62-65
Fototeca Unione, Rome: Figs. 5-7, 9
Istituto di Norvegia in Roma: Fig. 15
Middelthon, C.: Fig. 34
Teigen, K.: Fig. 52
Vasari, Rome: Fig. 4

CONTENTS

STRUCTURAL CHANGES
IN LATE ANTIQUITY

I. CIVIC LIFE AND THE STATE

THE everyday life of the average man—his whole political, economic, and social life—was transformed during Late Antiquity. The free and natural forms of the early Empire, the multiplicity and the variation of life under a decentralized administration, was replaced by homogeneity and uniformity under an ever-present and increasingly more centralized hierarchy of civil officials. Characteristic of the earliest period of the Principate was the infinite variety in the modes of life on the local level, the vigorous natural growth of the towns, the provinces, and the land districts of the enormous Empire, the self-development and natural rounding-off of civic life in individual urban communities (*municipia*), each with its own municipal government and administration. Late Antiquity leveled and regulated these forms of free growth, the community organizations were absorbed into the compact, all-powerful state.

The equalization, standardization, and centralization had already begun under Trajan. Jurisdictionally, the provinces arose to the level of Italy, which gradually lost its preeminence. The development tended towards a complete equalization of all the Roman provinces. The imperial idea won out over the old city-state of Rome and the old national state of Italy. As early as Hadrian, the Roman army had been recruited from all the provinces of the realm, and simultaneous with this provincialization of the army, the border districts were Romanized, again a step toward uniformity. The *Constitutio Antoniniana* of Caracalla from A.D. 212, which gave Roman citizenship to all free subjects of the Empire, is a confirmation of this new situation.

In the field of practical organization this advancing equalization of powers, this leveling, and this massive

3

consolidation of all elements, becomes apparent above all in the relations between the state and the municipalities. The great wars of Trajan had been an economic strain which had disrupted the finances of the cities; the central administration, therefore, placed imperial commissars in many municipalities to correct these disorders. Furthermore, ten-man committees were appointed by the city councils—*decemprimi* in the West, δεκάπρωτοι in the East—in order to enable the central power through such committees to intervene more quickly in the internal affairs of the municipality.[1] It was characteristic of the whole subsequent development that public offices in the municipalities—for example, the city councils and the ten-man committees—were burdened with state responsibilities, taking thereby the form of compulsory state service (what Romans called *munus* and Greeks, λειτουργία). This change in the character of the municipal office struck at the organic expression of the particular way of life in the world of classical antiquity—city government.[2] At the beginning of the third century A.D., great jurists such as Papinianus, Callistratus, Ulpianus, put into practice the theory of the municipal *munera* and gave this system its legal foundation.[3] City officials

[1] E. Kornemann, *Weltgeschichte des Mittelmeerraumes*, ii, Munich, 1949, p. 117.

[2] F. Oertel, *CAH*, xii, p. 259.

[3] In the *vita* of Antoninus Pius we read that the Emperor deprived a number of people who did not work of their wages, saying that there was nothing meaner and more heartless than the man who lived off the state without giving anything in return (*dicens nihil esse sordidius, immo crudelius, quam si rem publicam is adroderet qui nihil in eam suo labore conferret*). *Script. hist. aug., vita Pii*, 7. Here for the first time in world history is proclaimed the officially controlled duty of all citizens to work (Kornemann, *op.cit.*, p. 158). This is a step in the direction of state socialism, in sharp contrast to the individualism in economic theory of earlier times. "The replacement of one economic system by the other, and the substitution of a new civilization and

and wealthy council members now became personally responsible, in a way hitherto unknown, for the state revenue. Above all they were responsible with their personal fortunes for the collection of the taxes assessed in their city. Eventually, all who were not exempt in order to perform other state duties, such as military duty, had to take on municipal *munera*—financial, intellectual, physical, etc.—each according to his capacity and ability. Both the wealth and those who possessed it were bound to specific local *munera*, thereby becoming immovable.[4]

In so far as the free guilds (*collegia*) performed a vital task for the state, they too were encroached upon by the central authorities. They were now organized into corporations (*corpora*) and were obliged to render specific services to the state. The ship-owners (*navicularii*) and the corn-merchants thus were, for example, required to supply Rome with provisions, and the building trade had also to assume the duties of the fire brigade. Freedom of work was thus replaced by the obligation to work for the state and, through the transformation of the free trades into hereditary *munus*, people became bound to their professions and to their dwelling places. A similar *immobilization* occurred also in the social and economic life of the rural population. On the large estates (*latifundia*) and on the enormous imperial domains, there emerged a new class of small tenant farmers (*coloni*), who became ascripted leaseholders under the landowners (*possessores*) or their vassals.[5]

The end result of this development was an unchangeable, firmly crystallized order. All classes, or at least all except the privileged class, were bound to their

---

attitude toward life for the old took more than a century and a half. It was completed by the end of the III century, but the beginnings go back to the earliest years of the II century" (Oertel, *op.cit.*, p. 256).

[4] Kornemann, *op.cit.*, p. 158.   [5] *Ibid.*, p. 159.

professions, "the peasant farmer to his land and forced labor, the state-employed worker to his workshop, the trader, including the *navicularius*, to his business or his corporation, the small property-owner to his duties in connection with the *munera*, the large property owner to the curia, the soldier to his military service, and so on."[6] The individual no longer lived independently but within the state. He was no longer seen in his natural environment within life's organic groupings, in lively harmony with his surroundings, but as a firmly incorporated immovable part in the cadre of the state. As with the individual, so also with the communities. The municipalities no longer lived within themselves, but in the state; we no longer see them in vigorous self-growth, but firmly incorporated into the great symmetrical order of the state. In contrast to the organic expansion based on the concrete and individual life, so to speak, along an elementary growth line reaching upward from below, we now find an orientation directed downward from above, a higher order descends and is implanted into the elements—"an orientation is imposed from above upon the whole social and economic order."[7] The characteristic feature of this higher order is the uniform simplification, the coordination of equal elements and the crystallic consolidation of the whole. Everywhere the finer social differentiations disappear and the sharp edges and the broad planes of the blocklike mass of the state break through. The rich articulation which distinguished the life of the Principate had been lost forever. The individuals and the natural civic organisms in which they were grouped, more and more seemed to disappear into the massive and monotonous formations envisioned by the central administration as supporting walls for the Dominate's state structure.

[6] Oertel, *op.cit.*, p. 268.   [7] *Ibid.*, pp. 254 ff.

Civic Life and the State

The increasing standardization and equalization of life, the blocklife fusion of the civic organisms, was revealed characteristically in the increasing militarization of society—indeed in the whole way of life. The soldier-emperors' simplification of the government according to a military pattern was followed by a general militarization of the civil service and an assimilation of the civil into martial law (*castrensis jurisdictio*).[8] The whole administration of the state was increasingly organized and conceived according to military categories. Civil service was regarded as military service. Every civil servant, from the highest to the lowest, counted as an officer or a soldier. In all *officia* (public office), there are, according to Lactantius, *milites* (soldiers), and their service is a *militia* (war service).[9] The wages for civil officials are *stipendia* (soldier's pay). Subordinate civil servants are *cohortales*, i.e., belonging to a *cohors* (a military detachment). As the civil service was commonly called *militia*, a new name—*militia armata*—had to be invented to distinguish military service.[10]

Such a martial conception regarding civil servants demonstrates that the state demanded the same discipline and obedience of its civil administration as that which was required of the army. Before the highest authority, the *dominus*, every form of protest is silenced. His bidding is a command to be obeyed blindly. The people subordinate themselves, each and every one without exception, *en bloc* to this command. It is this unconditional, mass obedience which suggests the associations with the soldier, the military unit, and thereby with the whole militaristic

[8] S. L. Miller, *CAH*, xii, pp. 28 ff.

[9] *De mort. pers.*, 31.

[10] W. Seston, *Dioclétien et la Tétrarchie*, Paris, 1946, pp. 347 f. (hereafter referred to as "Seston"); A. Alföldi, "Insignen und Tracht der römischen Kaiser," *Mitteilungen des Deutschen Archäolog. Instituts, Röm. Abt.*, 50, 1935, pp. 64 f.; Kornemann, *op.cit.*, pp. 257 f.

terminology. Even Christian obedience of the period expresses itself, characteristically enough, in this style; God's servants are *milites Christi*.

This military way of life, which also becomes apparent in the imperial art and architecture of the period, is in the strictest accord with the peculiar pattern of the Dominate. The military aspect of man, that is, exactly the aspect which binds him to rank and file, letting him disappear as a person into a number within a unit, into a solid block, into a sum of uniform elements. Militarization, therefore, marks the basic characteristic in the form structure of the Dominate, in sharp contrast to the earlier Empire. The contrast between the military and the civil orders is just the contrast between mechanical coordination and organic grouping, between the natural formations in free life and a massive alignment in rank and square, between individual, natural motions and movements *en bloc*. Both in community life and in art the large block formations and mass movements now appeared ever more clearly behind the continually thinning veil of traditional antique forms.

II. ARCHITECTURAL FORMS

T HE same profound contrast between the Principate and the Dominate which we have found in organized society is also apparent in art. In this chapter we shall limit our comparisons to architecture, and the transformation of form, which takes place here, may be described briefly in the following way.

As the classical orders disintegrate during the Roman Empire, buildings lose their organic corporality, the clear articulation of their parts, and the functional relationships among them; they are gradually dissolved into a system of plain, simple walls. Here again, we see the characteristic transition from organic articulation of a well-differentiated structure to an abstract simplification in great planes and lines. To make this transformation clear it is first necessary to characterize the classical conception of architecture.

When the classical Greek fashioned something, he required of the form that it give the clearest possible expression of the object's particular function. A vase, for instance, is a container which has the special ability to enclose a liquid and hold its mass in balance. This function is physically expressed in the form of a Greek vase and is reflected in its decoration. No column is found in which the column's function—that of being a support—and no capital is found in which the capital's function—that of absorbing and transmuting pressure between the architrave and the column—is stamped with such objective clarity as in Greek architecture. One might say that the plastic form is brought forth from deep within the object itself. The form is organic, immanent.

Thus, the classical artist does not bring the form to an object from without or above, but brings it forth from

9

1. Columns and entablature, Parthenon, Acropolis of Athens

within the object itself. It is, therefore, characteristic of classical art that it is guided by the idea of a natural beauty inherent in the object; of a perfection which pervades the very smallest detail of it and which the artist, the architect, or the craftsman himself can bring forth from the object, and indeed can measure and determine numerically. Plutarch speaks of exactness of the beautiful: κάλλους ἀκρίβεια.[1] The classical architectural ornament can illustrate this conception (Figs. 1, 2).

Thus the constitution of ideal systems of proportion is a typical expression of classical art and architecture. From a given measure in the plan—for example, the distance from column to column—a number of other measurements can be determined: the proportions of the rafter system and thereby of the roof—even the proportions of sections of the building which are neither seen together with, nor are directly dependent on the columns. In the same way that the individual type of a

[1] Plutarch, *Perikles*, 13.

2. Architectural ornament, Erechtheum, Acropolis of Athens

living being determines the form of each single part of it, so the principle for the whole structure of the classical building is contained within each single element of it. In each of the three classical orders—the Doric, the Ionic, and the Corinthian—the building grows and unfolds in accordance with an organic law analogous to that which reigns in living nature.

It is precisely because the classical building is such an organic and self-sustained, such an autarchical, entity that it refuses to submit to larger architectural compositions. Often on sacred sites the classical temples stand with peculiar recalcitrance beside one another, each with its own orientation determined by its god or cult, by sacred portents and signs in the temple ground (Fig. 3). Each building defies superior order of axiality, symmetry, or unity of direction.

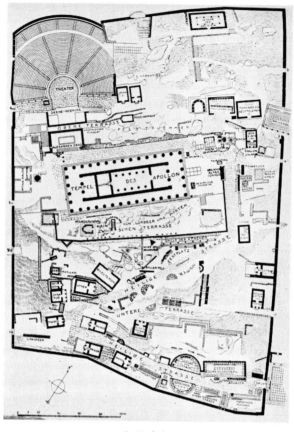

3. Delphi

This organic and autonomous life, this supreme development from within of each part, of each ornament of the building, was lost during the Hellenistic-Roman evolution which followed. The individual building was continually subordinated to a dominating, all-embracing architectural plan in which each structure is coordinated in relation to the axis of the whole, thus becoming a dependent part of a larger complex.[1] The axiality of the layout, for instance of the imperial fora of Rome (Fig. 4), forces one into the central axis of the square where

[1] H. Kähler, *Wandlungen der antiken Form*, Munich, 1949, pp. 13 f.

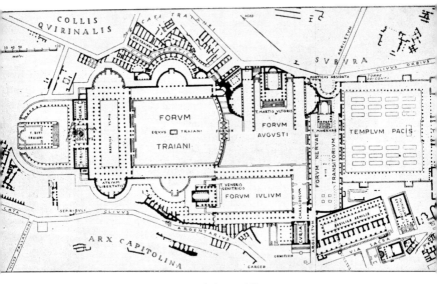

4. Imperial *fora* of Rome

one is faced by the towering temple façade.[2] The final
goal of this whole development was not reached until
Late Antiquity. We shall soon see how the Dominate
standardized, subordinated, and symmetrized all the single
building organisms in accordance with large and strict
axes of the whole architectural composition.

But with the subordination of the buildings to these
axes, the individual structural units dissolve and disappear
into the total architectural design; they lose their firm inner organization, their vivid proportionality, and the
clear articulation of their separate parts. Characteristic of
the whole development is the assimilation and mixing
together of the three classical building orders. Architectural decoration no longer depends upon an order that is
an organic system of ornament encompassing the whole
building.

Antiquity's sensitivity to the inner life of the architectural detail, its plastic beauty and expressiveness, gives
way (Fig. 13). The traditional décor, friezes and architec-

[2] H. Kähler, *op.cit.*, pp. 15 ff.

13

5. Market of Trajan, Rome

tural ornament, is absorbed more or less completely by
the massive wall. The eye is no longer fixed upon the
separate building parts. This is the reason why the flood
of antique *spolia*, i.e., building parts taken from earlier
monuments, are admitted into the architecture of Late
Antiquity, where they may be reemployed for essentially
different architectural purposes, unhampered by their
original tectonic function. From around A.D. 300, and on
into the Middle Ages, are thus put side by side building
elements taken from utterly dissimilar monuments, belonging to the most diverse systems of ornamentation and
having had widely different functions. It even happens, for
example, that the bases of columns are used as capitals.
And it must be emphasized that this did not occur during
a period of technical falling-off, but during one of the
most glorious epochs in the history of ancient architecture.
The extensive use of *spolia* has, with good reason, been .

14

6. Curia of Diocletian, Rome

compared with the contemporary trend towards the use of prefabricated building parts, especially capitals, which are mass-produced without having originally been intended for any particular building. Like the *spolia*, these prefabricated parts also often have to be cut or trimmed before they can be placed in architectural bond. The point of the matter is that the clearly defined form and function of each separate building element is no longer felt. Undisturbed by arbitrarily cut elements or a helter-skelter of undigested *spolia*, the eye glides over the architectural forms, follows the great movements of the masses, the grandiose rise of the vaults and the endless flights of monotonously divided walls. Characteristically abstract, peculiarly far-seeing and therefore summary, the glance skips over detail and articulation in order to rest with mass and dimension.

It is well known that during the Roman period—

7. Basilica of Constantine, Trier

and particularly evident in the western world—a new system of construction came into use. In place of the traditional column-architrave architecture appears the new archivolt- or arcade-architecture. Characteristic of this architecture, until the end of the third century A.D., is the breaking up and articulation of the archivolt façade by the elements of the classical building orders, thus the arcades are enclosed in a frame-work of column-architrave architecture. This is the well-known system of which we have an early example in the Roman Tabularium (78 B.C.) and which is infinitely repeated in both monumental and utilitarian architecture; for example, in the brick façade of the Market di Trajan in Rome (Fig. 5). Where constructions in *opus quadratum* are concerned,

16

8. Santa Sabina, Rome, ca. A.D. 425

the elements of this décor are generally incorporated into the wall itself with the half-columns and the flat beams projecting only in low relief from the wall surface. However, especially in the second and the third century A.D., this architectural décor is separated from the walls with detached columns supporting an entablature returned back to the wall, thus appearing as a magnificent screen in front of the building, as can be seen, for example, in Roman triumphal arches. At the end of the third century there was a strong reaction against this traditional system of decoration. Especially in the West the splendid column decoration vanishes and the classical articulation by column and architrave more or less disappears from the archivolt construction.

Structural Changes in Late Antiquity

Typical of the new architectural style are thus the large continuous wall surfaces, interrupted only by the functional wall-supports which, by more frequent repetition, give a firm, monotonous division of the wall through the regular and uniform passage along it of large arches and flat pilaster strips. In the Senate building of Diocletian at the Forum Romanum (Fig. 6), the great wall surface of the façade, crowned by a simple gable, is broken only by the portal and three large windows; strong corner pillars support the high walls. In Constantine's Basilica in Trier (Fig. 7, cf. Fig. 8), the outer walls are strengthened by arcadelike projections, which—as regular as the archivolts of an aqueduct and unrestrained by traditional decoration—run along the plain walls.[3]

Exactly as the architecture here throws off the traditional column-architrave decoration, the contemporary figurative art, as we shall see, drops the traditional patterns of composition. In contemporary portraiture the individual modeling sinks into the surface and the whole physiognomical complex is simplified into a crystalline regular totality, just as the plastic articulation of the building structure disappears into the great continuous wall surfaces.

[3] A. Boëthius has made fundamental studies in this late antique architecture in, for example, *Roman and Greek Town Architecture* (Göteborgs Högskolas Arsskrift, 54, 1948: 3); *Stadsbebyggelsen i Roms Hamnstad Ostia* (Göteborgs Högskolas Årsskrift, 57, 1951:2).

III. THE SPIRITUAL BACKGROUND

IN OUR comments upon architecture in the previous chapter the transformation of form appears mainly in a rather negative light: namely, the dissolution of the classical building structure. A positive side of this transformation is a new experience of space, a new feeling for the interior itself, which is an expression of the new spirit of the time. An appreciation of this positive side makes it possible for us to meet with a better understanding the peculiarly abstract—as it were, the distant glance which we have continually encountered in Late Antiquity.

It is of decisive importance that the large and simple wall surfaces of the new architectural style act as clearly defined space-enclosing boundaries in quite a different way from the much divided structural forms which they displace, thus in a new way making the unified interior manifest (Fig. 9). As the plastic decoration disappears into smooth walls, simple planes now enclose a clear and unified interior. It is in this interior that the eye now becomes immersed. Architecture becomes introspective. The building structure is reduced to a mere shell surrounding what is encompassed. It becomes no more than the enclosure of space.[1] Let us illustrate this with an example.

An important innovation which presumably first becomes common in the architecture of the third and fourth century—seen, for example, in the Christian basilica —is a continuous stretch of wall which now rises above the row of columns (Fig. 10). Such a construction is in conflict with the fundamental principles of classical archi-

[1] The new room architecture of the Empire is excellently described by G. von Kaschnitz-Weinberg, "Vergleichende Studien zur italisch-römischen Struktur," *Mitteilungen des Deutschen Archäolog. Instituts, Röm. Abt.*, 59, 1944, pp. 89 ff.

9. Interior of the Curia of Diocletian, Rome

tecture. The classical principle is to indicate the equilibrium of forces in the interaction between the supporting
column and the heavy load of the architrave. A further
construction above the rows of columns can, according

20

to the classical rule, only repeat this interplay between column and entablature, as seen, for instance, in the two-story rows of columns in the interior of the classical temple (Fig. 11). Now, with the massive wall replacing the organically muscular system of rows of columns and entablature recurring over one another, the classically organized building structure disappears behind a merely space-enclosing wall. The columns are withdrawn into the wall they support and are subordinated to the new crystalline totality of space. Everything now serves this interior. Above all, light is the space-creating element and models in its various intensities the different parts of the interior. In the Christian basilica, for example, the superstructure appears with radiant luminosity in contrast to the twilight of the lower zone which becomes even dimmer in the aisles.

In this transformation of the architectural forms during the Roman Empire we study in reality the profound human conversion from the "corporal beauty" of classical tradition to the transcendent contemplation indicative of the Middle Ages. One renounces the whole corporeal building—the columns, friezes, architectural ornament, the whole décor which Vitruvius still considered the *dignitas* of architecture—in order to immerse oneself in incorporeal space, in the insubstantial, intangible interior filled with light and shadow. From the clear, plastic definition of form one turns toward the realm of the abstract: a turning which, better than anything else, characterizes the whole attitude toward life in Late Antiquity.

Plastic art too is marked by this new attitude. It is thus significant that sculpture toward Late Antiquity adopts a technique that abolishes plastic form as such. While in classical times the whole modeling was accomplished by the chisel, one now finds a decidedly wider use of the

10. Interior of Santa Sabina, Rome, ca. A.D. 425

running drill. What does not such a change signify for the whole creative process! The chisel works out the tangible form, it follows flexibly all the ridges and hollows, all the ripples of the plastic surface (for example, Fig. 14). The drill on the other hand, works illusionally, it does not follow the tangible form but leaves a glimmer of lighted marble edges between sharp, shadow-dark drill grooves (for example, Figs. 22, 33, 34). With this technique the body loses its substantiality, it disintegrates: we are anxious lest it shrink to nothing and vanish. Also in architectural ornamentation we find this profound transformation of form. Examine, side by side (Figs. 12 and 13), an antae-capital from Didymaion by Milet, and a piece of a cornice, from the palace of Diocletian in Spalato;[2] compare the wonderful plastic, full-bodied egg-and-dart motif in the classical capital with the bodiless *clair-obscure* of the same ornament in the late antique cornice.

At the same time that the form thereby becomes increasingly insubstantial, it gradually loses its individual nature and becomes steadily more standardized, but with an ever more firmly crystallized significance. There is a

[2] Kähler, *op.cit.*, pl. 27a, pp. 60 ff.

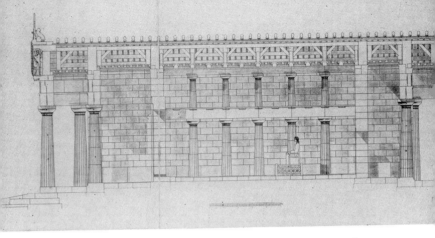

11. Temple of Aphaia, Aigina, early v cent. B.C., reconstruction
(Furtwängler)

movement away from lifelike nature to abstract types,
from plastic articulation to conceptual generalization,
from the corporeal to the symbolic. A higher meaning
is implanted in the object, which more and more is reduced to a shell enclosing this meaningful core, more
and more becomes a sign referring to a thought—and, as
a sign, always identical, formula-like, stereotype.

Choose as an example such a central ornamental motif
as the spiral rinceau of Late Antiquity and early mediaeval times (Fig. 15). It is now no longer a natural
growth as it was in the classical tradition (Fig. 14): the
stalk has become a lifeless band twining up into abstract,
uniform circles, the whole plant an ornament without
growth and lifelike nature. But this ornament encloses
a new "interior," a new content, it has a life outside the
order of nature; the rinceau blossoms forth into crosses,
or it grows out of a chalice, or something similar, and
thus becomes filled with new meaning. "I am the vine,
ye are the branches" (John 5:15). As the vine loses its
individual "object-nature," it becomes condensed to a
symbol. It is precisely this which is characteristic of the
transformation from Antiquity to the Middle Ages: the

23

12. Classical architectural ornament, early v cent. B.C.

objects lose their natural substance, their bodily volume, their concrete lifelike reality, but in return enclose a new "interior," a meaningful core, they become symbols and conceptual expressions. It is as if the natural objects flee from living perception and as if in their flight they are contracted to increasingly summary and simplified figures until, in the end, they remain only as fixed points of meaning in the distance. These distant points of meaning, this multitude of stars in the sky of abstraction, is what Late Antiquity's distant glance is contemplating.

Look at the portrayal of man in the Middle Ages. Face and body are simplified to certain significant types; they become vehicles of certain symbols and signs, of certain fixed formulae of expression, of certain sacred attributes or certain insignia of state, all adhering to a higher and perpetual order into which the fleeting human being has entered. We choose as an example one of the well-known processions of saints represented on the nave walls of Sant'Apollinare Nuovo in Ravenna (Figs. 17, 67), and compare them with the famous imperial procession on the Ara Pacis from the time of Augustus (Fig.

24

13. Late antique architectural ornament, ca. A.D. 300

16). Spiritlike and seemingly bodiless, the saints float past our eyes against a homogeneous background of symbolic palms of victory, each as a uniform element in an endless row: equal in height, with the same figure and with the same step, in the same venerable pallium costume, varied only in its detail, bearing the wreath of martyrdom, haloed, each of a singularly solemn, wide-eyed type which, for the beholder in Antiquity, was associated with the idea of man become divine (pp. 123 f.). Thus, the natural individuality recedes before a meaningful stereotype which characterizes the essence of the saints and indicates their place in an eternal hierarchical order. In the same way, the individualistic portraits of the emperors disappear, as we shall see (pp. 121 f.), in such depersonalized images, in a "sacred type" (τύπος ἱερός),[3] representing the Imperial Majesty itself. The emperors therefore become "alike" in the same way as the saints: the very idea of the *divina maiestas* penetrates and transforms the facial features. Man's image is formed according to suggestive formulas of expression, which

[3] τύπος ἱερός, in late antique literature and art: L'Orange, *Studien zur Geschichte des spätantiken Porträts*, Oslo, 1933, pp. 91 f.

25

14. Spiral tendrils of the time of Augustus.
Detail from Ara Pacis, Rome

are associated with something higher and more essential than the individual himself. One may compare the stereotype character-masks of the antique theater, which "depict" the role played by the actor, and at the same time conceal the actor's personal features. We see men, not as lifelike individuals but in the role they play upon the stage of eternity. One's thoughts go to the late antique priests of the Eleusinian mysteries who, upon entering their office, gave up their names.

The inner meaning pierces through the natural exterior of an object and creates new formulas of expression and new patterns of composition. Instead of grouping the figures according to their natural order, they are now placed according to a pattern that allows their inner significance and their inner reciprocal relationship to be revealed. Especially characteristic of this trend, as we shall see, is the *Maiestas Domini* composition with all elements—men, architecture, etc.—placed symmetri-

26

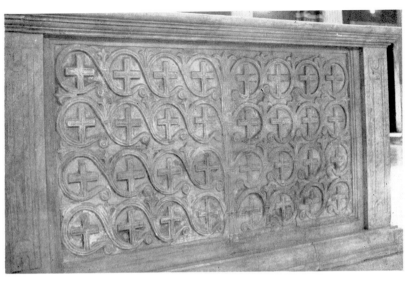

15. Early mediaeval spiral tendrils,
Santa Sabina, Rome

cally around God or emperor (pp. 101 ff.). Like the grouping of figures, their dimensions are also divorced from
their natural relations to one another: the relative size
of the figures does not correspond to their real measurements, but to their inner import and significance. Thus
the form and action, the grouping and dimensions of
the figures correspond to a reality in the realm of ideas,
a function and a dignity in an eternal unchanging hierarchy of powers and orders.

The same shift of emphasis from the external to the
internal appears at the same time in aesthetic theory. In
the classical period, beauty is defined as proportionality:
a proportionality which can be expressed in measures and
numbers and thus is based upon the proportions of the
human body (Polyclitus' Canon). This ideal of beauty
applies to all fields of classical art, in sculpture as well as
in architecture (pp. 21 ff.). A completely new aesthetic was
developed during the third century: beauty does not re-

16. Procession of figures. Detail of a relief on the Ara Pacis, Rome

side in the proportions of the body, but in the soul which penetrates and illuminates it, that is, in expression (the Enneads of Plotinus). Beauty is a function of the inner being (τὸ ἔνδον εἶδος).

Also on the ethical level we are dealing with a revaluation and transformation of the classical attitude to life, an *Umwertung aller Werte*. And again the change is marked by a turning away from the external towards the internal world. The ideal is no longer what one could call proportionality of the soul, the harmonic organization of its natural energies with acceptance also of the instinctive and sensual life—the whole state of mind which is defined in the term σωφροσύνη. The goal is now a pure spiritual existence in faith and wisdom, an overcoming of the impulsive and sensual life, the body—

indeed, the whole outer world—consequently a concentration upon the inner life which shatters the traditional organic ethic of "a sound mind in a sound body." The hero of Late Antiquity is the martyr and the ascetic—the legends of martyrdom replace the heroic myths of classical times.[4]

The philosophy of Late Antiquity teaches that the natural sensual life—all life in the "flesh"—belongs to a lower form of existence. The aim is to free one's spirit, one's *pneuma*, from the natural man. The last great unifying religion of antique paganism, Neo-Platonism, systematizes this view. The soul, untouched by the material, is a celestial being; but through "a downfall into matter" it has materialized in a body and has been cast down into this world. In our natural existence here on earth the soul is therefore chained to a lower principle

[4] E. Lucius, *Die Anfänge des Heiligenkults*, Tübingen, 1904, *passim*.

17. Procession of figures. Detail of a mosaic in Sant'Apollinare Nuovo, Ravenna, VI cent. A.D.

and left to the deceitful perceptions of the senses. The object is to liberate this heavenly being from matter and make it independent of the corporeal nature and sensuous apprehension. We must fight our way out of the chaos of feeling and imagination in which our senses ensnare us and strive for a higher reality, the eternal order behind the things of nature. Still in the middle of the third century A.D., Plotinus saw in the tangible reality of nature a beautiful reflection of the Ideas. However, at the beginning of the fourth century things of nature have lost this luster, they are now considered only a jungle of confusion where humans lose their way. One withdraws from the external and changeable world of illusions, from the things of nature, from "the body beautiful," and concentrates upon the abstractions of the inner life, upon symbols, ideas, and conceptions, upon contemplation of the unchangeable sky of a higher reality.

It is, as we have seen, precisely this withdrawal into the realm of abstraction which characterizes art at the transition from Antiquity to the Middle Ages.[5] Immediate sensory perception has lost its strength and joy. The overflowing richness of form in nature in all its tangible beauty and abundance, no longer moves the artist. The whole outer world, according to the language of the time, is a confusion in his senses, a deceitful illusion, a misty dream. Behind the fleeting world of nature, art perceives the large regular contours in an unchangeable, supernatural hierarchy of forces and ideas, of substances and beings, and attempts to capture this eternal order by new abstract means of expression, by a system of fixed formulas of types and of compositions. Such a stereotype has, however, a negative side, namely, schematization which, as we shall see, corresponds to a peculiar a priori

---

[5] For the much discussed late classical transcendentalism, the central factor of late classical art, see G. Rodenwaldt, *CAH*, xii, p. 563.

formation of concepts and a summary way of thinking both in the legislation and in the practical organization of the life of the period.

A striking parallel to that which occurs in art is the remarkable new reinterpretation and revaluation of the whole classical mythology during the Roman Empire. The god and the hero are thought of in the abstract: instead of the mythical beings in their concrete situations, one searches for the internal truth, the hidden meaning behind the figure and its action. Divinity, myth, and legend lose their substance, but receive a new content in allegory and symbol. The myth is a lie, we learn, but "a lie which depicts the truth." Like a shell the myth encloses this truth which is its new core and "interior."[6]

Everywhere there is the same negation of what is concrete, plastically delimitated and determined, the same turning towards simplifying concepts and symbolic absolutes. In an imperial triumph it is no longer the historical victor who is celebrated, the victor who conquered a specific enemy at a particular time and place; rather, the historical victor is elevated to the absolute victor, the *ubique victor*, the *victor omnium gentium*; his historical victory becomes the *victoria perpetua*—thus the emperor and his imperial victory are named on late antique coins and thus he is represented in triumphal art. On the Arch of Constantine, it is not only the representatives of the nations Constantine actually conquered who are laid at his feet, but representatives of the sum of Rome's enemies; and in a similar way the river gods depicted on the Arch no longer represent a specific geographical locality, but the totality of *orbis Romanus*.

Abstract man with eyes immersed in a transcendent world: is it not just this man whose own living self

[6] F. Cumont, *Recherches sur le symbolisme funéraire des Romains*, Paris, 1942, *passim*.

18. Portrait head, Ostia, v cent. A.D.

stands before us embodied in late antique portraits (for example, Fig. 18). In the great picture gallery of the Empire a change in the whole physiognomical typology takes place towards the end of the third century: a change that eloquently accompanies the change in mentality mentioned above. The eye is now directed towards a new goal: it looks past the things surrounding man, through time and space—indeed, through the whole tangible reality—and rests upon a point at an endless distance (compare Figs. 61 and 66). "The eye is the mirror of the soul"—and the eye we here describe has been pointed out by students of antique portraiture as the most profound physiognomical characteristic of the human image during Late Antiquity: this distant glance which gives such a distinctive expression not only to the artistic portrait but also to man himself as we see him in the spiritual life and behind the whole state and civic life of the Dominate. It looks through our elusive, changing, discordant, physical world and immerses itself in the higher absolutes, the unchangeable symmetry, in the realm of eternity.

THE GREAT CRISIS AND
ITS SOLUTION
UNDER DIOCLETIAN

I. THE REFORMS OF DIOCLETIAN

DIOCLETIAN

DIOCLETIANUS—in private life called Diocles—began his reign by administering justice in his own person: with his own hand he executed the man considered guilty of murdering the ruling emperor in the East, Numerian. On the high tribunal, before the eyes of the assembled army, he stabbed Aper, the Commander of the Praetorian Guard. Equally dramatic was his departure from the summit of power. Upon the high tribunal, again before the eyes of the assembled army, he took the purple from his shoulders and threw it about the new Caesar whom he had chosen; Diocletian was once again Diocles. The whole rule of Diocletian is characteristically framed by these two acts of state. A brief description of them may, therefore, serve as an introduction to this study of Diocletian's reforms.

In A.D. 284, the Roman armies under Emperor Numerian were marching home from a Persian campaign. The Emperor, suffering from an eye infection, was carried in a sedan-chair which concealed him from sight. He was accompanied by his father-in-law, Aper, prefect of the Praetorian Guard. One day a macabre stench emanated from the royal sedan-chair, and soon the whole army knew that it was occupied by a corpse. "Immediately all fell upon Aper who could no longer hide his treachery, and they dragged him before the banners in front of the high command in the camp. The soldiers flocked together to form a great military gathering and erected a tribunal. When the question was posed as to who, with greatest right, was to be Numerian's avenger and a good ruler of the Roman Empire, all in heaven-sent accord (*divino consensu*) conferred the title of Augustus

37

upon Diocletian, who, it was said, had already received a portent of his future imperium. This man now ascended the tribunal and was hailed Augustus. When asked how Numerian had been murdered, Diocletian pointed with his drawn sword to Aper, the Praetorian Prefect, and driving it through him said: "This is Numerian's murderer."[1]

At the imperial twenty-year jubilee in Rome, A.D. 303, Diocletian, with his extraordinary will power, had persuaded Maximian, his co-Emperor in the West, to swear by Jupiter Capitolinus that he would abdicate simultaneously with Diocletian, in accordance with the new order of succession. Thus on the very same and historic day, but with a continent between them, the eastern and the western Emperors abdicated to be succeeded by the two Caesars, each in his own part of the Empire, in this way solemnly affirming the collegiate principle of the four-man rule of the Empire which sustained the whole new order of state. The abdication of Diocletian is described by Lactantius. On May 1, 305, we read, the eastern armies, together with representatives from the whole imperial army, are deployed upon a hill near Diocletian's residence, Nicomedia in Asia Minor, on the exact spot where Diocletian had bestowed the purple upon his eastern co-Emperor, Galerius. Upon this hill was erected a column crowned by a statue of Jupiter, the god-protector of Diocletian's whole order of state. Diocletian ascends the tribunal. In tears he addresses the army: his work is completed, he wishes to relinquish his power. "And so, suddenly, he proclaims Severus and Maximinus Daza the new Caesars" alongside of the two older Caesars who are now promoted to Augusti. "He divests himself of the purple and places it around the shoulders of Maximinus Daza. *Et Diocles iterum factus est*. The abdicated Emperor now steps down from the tribunal. He drives

[1] *Script. hist. aug., Vita Car., Carin. et Num.,* 12-15.

through the city in a simple gallic carriage, he travels far away and withdraws to the land of his birth."[2]

A rather brutal rectitude and an almost pathetic sense of duty speak to us in these contrasting but equally revealing scenes. The two acts, upon assuming and upon relinquishing power, sharply profile the reign of Diocletian; they show the active man's imprint upon events, the energetic intervention in the course of history—in short, the personality which creates history. This picture becomes clearer when one studies the rule of Diocletian and the governmental acts upon which the new state developed. As far as I can see, the basic features of the picture do not change if one sees in Diocletian, as did earlier historians, the great systematizer who pressed a ready-made governmental system upon the Empire, or if one sees him as William Seston does in his great work on Diocletian,[3] and in our opinion rightly, as the vigorous man of action who reacted to the challenge of events with strong measures and defensive efforts which only gradually took the form of a new system of government.

Under this energetic regime which took without mercy the full consequences demanded by the situation and followed every line of thought to the very end, tendencies come into view which had long been latent in both the spiritual and material life of the time.

THE GREAT CRISIS

In the second half of the third century the Roman Empire went through a shattering crisis which accelerated the transition from Principate to Dominate. Terrible wars, both internal and external, threw the Empire into a chaos in which all remnants of the traditional civic and social order became more or less completely dissolved. It

---

[2] Lactantius, *De mort. pers.*, I, 19.

[3] Above, p. 7, note 10.

is necessary in this connection to sketch briefly the *disintegrated* Roman Empire which forms the background for Diocletian's appearance and the founding of the new tetrarchic form of government.

During the second half of the third century all the borders of the Empire were invaded: along the northern frontiers invasions of Franks, Alamanni, Vandals, Goths, Sarmatians; from the Black Sea incursions of Gothic vikings into the Mediterranean; pressure of the Sassanian Persians in the east; invasions of Blemmyes, Libyans, and Mauretanians in the south. At the same time incessant murder of the emperors and usurpation of power took place within the Empire; the separate provinces severed ties and became organized against one another under their provincial armies and usurpers; constant civil war broke up the old Empire. Trebellius Pollio, though with the aid of imagination, tells of thirty usurpers (*tyranni triginta*) who, during the reign of Emperor Gallienus, "from all parts of the realm stormed towards the Empire."[4] Everywhere power was in the possession of the local army which proclaimed its leaders emperors. The traditional connections between the provinces were dissolved and the unity of the Empire was shattered. We find ourselves in a strangely *de-composed* Empire, with the provinces in mutual conflict.[5]

Chaos on the economic front accompanied this confusing state of affairs. Devaluation of money, resulting from the diminution of the amount of precious metal in the coin, led to inflation and violently fluctuating prices. There was a constant increase in taxes to maintain the standing armies; there were continual requisitions of provisions, especially of farm products, for armies on the move. Financial and monetary difficulties

[4] *Script. hist. aug., Tyranni Triginta,* 1.
[5] Oertel, *op.cit.,* pp. 260 ff.

forced the state to take what it needed in kind instead of the unreliable, increasingly devaluated money brought in by normal taxation.

All this, naturally, was first of all felt by the propertied classes, who groaned under the burden of taxes, military requisitions, intolerable *munera* (pp. 4 ff.). It was not unusual for municipal officials to surrender their whole fortune in order to free themselves from the forced duties it entailed. At the same time we hear of flights from homesteads and of the refusal to work, a form of strike.[6] The literary sources give a vivid glimpse into a period of terror, murder, and confiscations. Also to be taken into consideration in this connection was the hostility of the military proletariat of the provinces, who were then in power, to the bourgeois economic and social order—indeed, against the whole culture which it represented.[7] The traditional forms in the world of art and culture were disintegrating—we will see this point again (pp. 87 ff.; 111 ff.). In religion a symbiosis of the most divergent beliefs was established simultaneously with the penetration and transformation of the traditional Greco-Roman Olympus by an invasion of influences from the provinces, especially by Eastern religions and philosophies. Unrest and alarm was everywhere. Nothing was secure.

In this chaotic situation Diocletian made his appearance upon the stage of world history. He was the new Jupiter on earth who would master chaos and fling the rebelling giants to the ground; it was in this aspect that Diocletian was celebrated by panegyrists and artists (p. 79). The divided Empire was again united, a confused humanity rearranged itself, activities were again gathered up and distributed in a community-like order. But this

[6] *Ibid.*, pp. 265 ff.

[7] M. Rostovtzeff, *The Social and Economic History of the Roman Empire*, Oxford, 1941, pp. 376 ff.

The Great Crisis and Its Solution

order was now contained within a system of absolutes, the Dominate. The transformation, outlined above, of the Principate's forms of life—a transformation which actually had begun in the early part of the second century—was only accomplished with the reforms of Diocletian after the great crisis in the second half of the third century.

THE TETRARCHIC STATE SYSTEM

During the third century A.D., the century of the soldier-emperors, it had become accepted practice for armies to proclaim the emperors; the senate with its investiture could only confirm the fact. In the divided Empire it was not sufficient, however, that only a single provincial army supported the election of an emperor, as, after the death of Numerian (pp. 37 f.), the eastern armies were responsible for the election of Diocletian. After the murder of Emperor Carinus, Numerian's father, Diocletian also became commander of the western armies and took up the legitimate position as universal ruler of the Roman Empire (A.D. 285). One would expect the Emperor at this point to repay his debt with a declaration of loyalty to the imperial army; Diocletian's first governmental declaration, on the contrary, was a proclamation of his sovereignty. All the mints of the Empire now struck coins which did not, as had been the custom, carry legends such as *fides militum* or *concordia militum*, but rather *Jupiter conservator augusti*, invoking for the Emperor a divine protection that sanctified his leadership. In his dealings with the senate he was just as sovereign as in his relationship with the army. As far as one can judge from the numismatic material, he did not find it necessary to visit Rome in order to receive the investiture of the senate;[8] at the beginning of 286 he was in Nicomedia in Asia Minor, his permanent residence.

With divine sovereignty Diocletian now built up the new governmental system which secured the integrity of the Roman Empire. The separate parts in the structure of this new system were originally created—according to Seston—as necessary security measures in a given historical situation and only gradually did they grow together into a logical structural whole. Thus when, in 285/86, Diocletian appointed Maximian co-ruler and adopted him as *filius augusti*, with the title of *nobilissimus caesar*, it was mainly in order to gain a loyal and effective ally in the western provinces of the Empire, while he himself, watched over the eastern; Maximian was to secure the western border against the threatening pressure from invasions by Frankish, Germanic, and other barbaric tribes, and at the same time pacify the peasant insurrection in Gallia, the Bagaudae rebellion. When in 286 Diocletian's protégé, Carausius, usurped imperial power in Britannia and proclaimed himself emperor, Maximian could not have a rank lower than the usurper-augustus he was to combat; Maximian, therefore, was called upon to participate in the governing of the Empire and was elevated to Augustus.[9] With this Diarchy—with one Augustus in the East and one in the West—the process of division was introduced which led into the Tetrarchy's "symmetric" state order, with four ruling emperors.

Maximian's expedition against Carausius failed and the unity of the Roman Empire was endangered. Diocletian

[8] Seston, pp. 54, 205 ff. The Senate became important to Diocletian as an expression of *consensus omnium*, that is, the acceptance of his government by the whole population of the Empire. In this sense the *Genius Senatus* is represented, for example, on the monument erected by Diocletian on the Forum Romanum (see below, p. 67, Fig. 22).

[9] Seston, pp. 59 ff., 76.

reacted again as in 285/86: in 293 he elevated Costantius Chlorus to Caesar at the side of Maximian. He was to continue the fight against the warring usurper in Britannia while Maximian guarded the Rhine border.[10] When, a short time later, Diocletian elevated Galerius to Caesar at his own side, it was again under the pressure of the historical situation.[11] As in the West, an equal danger now threatened in the East: it was in the years 290/93 that the Sassanian Empire attempted to recover the Persian lands from Rome. Galerius became Caesar in 293, three months later than Constantius.[12]

Thereby the tetrarchic Empire was completely constituted. The whole Empire was now ruled according to a constitutional system which secured it from outside attack and prevented usurpations within. There was one Augustus in the East and one in the West, and each of them had a Caesar at his side. At the death of an Augustus, the Caesar beside him promptly took his place. The Empire was thus armed against any aggression, from whatever side and against whatever part of the realm it might be directed. The legitimate Empire was also secured within against murder of the emperor and usurpation. The fundamental principle of the whole structure was found in the continually proclaimed imperial *concordia*, on which was based the delegation of power, the balance, the imperturbable suprapersonal *symmetry* of the Tetrarchy. "L'institution impériale reçut pour couronnement un édifice imprévu aux lignes symétriques."[13]

Closely linked with the new system of government was a form of succession that surely is unique in monarchical history and, at the same time, extremely characteristic of the symmetrical structure of the Tetrarchy. At the termination of a given period of reign, which perhaps

---

[10] Seston, pp. 88 f.
[11] Seston, pp. 89 f.
[12] Seston, p. 94.
[13] Seston, p. 100.

was intended to be twenty years, both Augusti were required to abdicate on the same day, and simultaneously
both Caesars advanced to Augusti while two new Caesars
were advanced to assist them. To prevent undue influence upon the new Tetrarchy from the abdicated *seniores
augusti*, they were required to remove themselves from
the imperial residences and withdraw to retirement
palaces in the provinces. Nor were these mechanics of
succession, though so well adapted to the governmental
system of the tetrarchic state, the result of a system. They
had grown out of the historical situation in order to avoid
usurpations and rivalries over the throne—as a necessity,
in consequence of life itself.

Thus the emperors' periods of reign, their succession
and abdication, their jubilees, etc., occurred in regular
cadence, or at least were planned to do so according to
the system. The biographical data in the reign of the
emperors were forced into a depersonalized, rhythmic
succession. Thus, for example, after some years had
passed, the anniversary of the ascension to the throne of
the two Caesars, their *dies imperii*, was celebrated on the
same day and likewise the place of their investiture—
again contrary to the actual fact—became one and the
same. "Pour répondre au gout de la symétrie."[14] The *dies
imperii* of the one emperor, the place of his investiture,
the anniversary of his jubilee, and the year of his abdication are assumed by the other, just as the one emperor's
portrait is substituted for the other's on coins (p. 121).
When, for example, Diocletian in November 303 celebrated his *vicennalia* in the old capital of the Empire,
Maximian was also the hero of the day, and simultaneously both of the Caesars celebrated their *decennalia*. The
event was commemorated with a monument erected behind the Rostra at Forum Romanum, a monument which

[14] Seston, p. 94.

45

can be reconstructed on the basis of the surviving fragments and a rendering of it on a relief on the Arch of
Constantine.[15] It consisted of five huge columns crowned
by statues: at the center Jupiter and, symmetrically
grouped around him, the four emperors, all of them of
exactly the same type.

A system of "double-principate"[16] was also known to
the earlier Empire, for example, the co-rule of Marcus
Aurelius and Lucius Verus. But it was not until the
Tetrarchy that the conception of a twin-Empire was developed where the two Augusti appeared as complete
equals and alike—cast from the same mold, so to speak.
In Mamertinus' speech in honor of Maximian on his
"birthday" in A.D. 291, we meet for the first time this
conception of the emperors' ideal similarity. At the pin-
nacle of the Roman Empire stood a twin-god, *numen
geminatum*.[17] The similarity of the emperors is evident
in their whole being, their physical exterior, even their
age.[18] "The immortal gods cannot divide their benefac-
tions between you; that which is given to one of you, belongs to you both."[19] Coin portraits proclaim with equal
emphasis the *similitudo* of the emperors; as said above,
this assimilation was carried so far as to enable one emperor portrait to be substituted for another and thus to
be considered current under the four different imperial
names.[20] The emperors are portrayed alike also in mon-

[15] L'Orange, "Ein tetrarchisches Ehrendenkmal auf dem Forum
Romanum," *Mitteilungen des Deutschen Archäeolog. Instituts, Röm.
Abt.*, 53, 1938, pp. 1 ff. H. Kähler, *Das Fünfsäulendenkmal für die
Tetrarchen auf dem Forum Romanum*, Cologne, 1964, pp. 5 ff.

[16] E. Kornemann, *Doppelprinzipat . . . im Imperium Romanum*,
Leipzig, 1930.

[17] E. Galletier, *Panégyriques Latins I, Mamertini genethl. Max.*, 11.

[18] *Ibid.*, 7.

[19] *Ibid.*

[20] J. Maurice, *Numismatique Constantinienne*, 1, Paris, 1911, pp. 4 f.
L'Orange, *Studien*, pp. 101 f.

umental sculpture (pp. 121 ff.), for example, in the well-known porphyry groups in Venice and in the Vatican (Figs. 19-21).[21] One and all are represented in high relief, almost as sculpture in the round projecting from porphyry columns and arranged in pairs. Each pair is of equal height, with the same dress and weapon, the same decorations and insignias, the same posture and gesture, and joined in the same expressive embrace—the image of their *concordia*. The perfect *similitudo* affects also the physiognomical type, the facial features, and above all the expressions—this is best seen in the Vatican groups where each pair represents a more or less mechanical duplication of the same figure. Also in the aforementioned tetrarchic monument at Forum Romanum and in the tetrarch-group on a relief on the Arch of Galerius in Thessalonika (Fig. 40) is the *similitudo* of the emperors articulated in their type, dress, gesture, and entire appearance.

This *similitudo* that we meet in the portraits of emperors by panegyrists, in coin portraits, and in monumental sculpture, has its own explanation, which gives an important glimpse into the theocratical ideas of the Dominate. The key to the understanding of it lies in the seemingly inconsequential fact that both Augusti celebrate their "birthday" on the same day: this birthday, *gemini natales*, is actually not their proper and personal birthday, but their joint divine birthday, calculated from the day in 287 when the two Augusti adopted the names Jovius and Herculius, after their fathers Jupiter and Hercules.[22] On this common origin the *similitudo* of the emperors is founded. The identical emperor type with its divine

[21] R. Delbrück, *Antike Porphyrwerke*, Berlin, 1932, pp. 84 f., pls. 31-34; pp. 91 f., pls. 35-37. L'Orange, *Studien*, pp. 16 ff., figs. 32-35.

[22] Seston, pp. 211 ff. E. Galletier, *op.cit.*, I, *Mamertini paneg. Max.*, 10 ff. Compare *Mamertini genethl. Max.*, 2.

19. Porphyry group of the Tetrarchy, the two Augusti, Vatican

20. Porphyry group of the Tetrarchy, the two Caesars, Vatican

21. Detail of porphyry group of Fig. 19

origin replaces the personal individuality, just as the divine birthday replaces the personal *dies natalis*. The *similitudo* in the portraying of the emperors is thus of the same nature as that in the portrayal of saints; a "sacred type," τύπος ἱερός (pp. 121 ff.) permeates all individual characteristics. It is toward this manifestation of the divine in the emperors and not toward their individual personality that the eye of Late Antiquity is directed, it seeks the eternal God-Emperor which undoubtedly was seen in the image of Diocletian. The individual personality is replaced by the type. The imperial *concordia* itself, the basis of the tetrarchic government, is built upon this *similitudo* of the emperors: *hac ipsa vestri similitudine magis magisque concordes.*[23]

[23] *Mamertini paneg. Max.*, 9.

The Reforms of Diocletian

The *concordia* of the emperors expressed itself in the complete mutual equality of the two Augusti and of the two Caesars. In the court ceremonial the two Augusti stood as divine twins, side by side, so that the adoring subjects had to lay aside the traditional form of worship directed toward the single God-Emperor; instead, a new ceremony of worship was established with double adoration (*duplicatum pietatis officium*).[24] At gatherings the emperors always appeared together. During their discussions they clasped hands.[25] They drove in the same carriage and the onlookers shouted with joy as it passed, they pointed and exclaimed: *Vides Diocletianum? Maximianum vides? Ambo sunt, pariter sunt. Quam iunctim sedent! Quam concorditer colloquuntur.*[26] As in the emperors' *similitudo*, a higher stability and regularity, a divine order, was manifest also in their *concordia*. "What century has ever seen a like *concordia* at the summit of power? Which brothers, what twins respect one another's equal rights to undivided property as You Your equal right to the Roman Empire? Through all this is revealed that though other human souls be worldly and transient, Yours are celestial and eternal (*caelestes et sempiternes*)."[27] It is therefore, Heaven which makes itself known in the mutual *similitudo* and *concordia* of the emperors, in the whole imperturbable symmetry of the tetrarchic Empire. The very dividing of the Empire into four quarters is derived from Heaven. In this godly number resides all the highest strength and joy (*Isto numinis vestro numero summa omnia nituntur et gaudent*). The panegyrist speaking these words to Constantius Chlorus, praises the anchoring of the whole universe in the cosmic number four—there are four elements, four seasons, four corners

---

[24] *Mamertini genethl. Max.*, 11. [25] *Ibid.*, 12.
[26] *Ibid.*, 11. [27] *Ibid.*, 6.

of the earth, four horses in the quadriga of the sun, four celestial lights, etc.[28]

The description of the "advent" of Diocletian and Maximian to Italy and their meeting in Mediolanum in the winter of 290-91,[29] gives an idea of what conceptions were connected with the Emperors as *dei praesentes*. The winter transforms itself into spring; the approach of the Emperors gleams over the peaks of the Alps, all Italy shines in a clearer light; not only people but also herds of animals, leaving their forests and distant pastures, swarm forth where the Emperors pass. The entire population celebrates, flames adorn all altars, wine and animals are sacrificed, there is the fragrance of incense from the altars; everywhere the people rejoice, everywhere dance and applause. "Hymns of praise and thanksgiving to the immortal Gods were sung, Jupiter was invoked at close range, not as he appeared in the ordinary conception but as visible and physically present (*conspicuus et praesens Jupiter*); Hercules was worshiped, not as a stranger, but in the very person of the Emperor."[30] The divine Empire permeates nature and the elements. "Wherever You are, even when You have retired into one and the same Palace, everywhere Your divinity is present, the whole earth and all the seas are filled with You."[31]

The emperors are, therefore, gods elevated above the Empire they govern. "Your immortal soul is greater than any power, any fortune, yes, even than the Empire"— *ipso est maior imperio.*[32] Their power is absolute, their right to form the world, set free and bind humanity, is unlimited. Independent of the senate and the army, Jovius Diocletianus can himself create emperors, i.e., appoint his co-emperors and successors who—created by him—

---

[28] E. Galletier, *op.cit.,* IV, *Incerti paneg. Constantio Caesari,* 4.
[29] *Mamertini genethl. Max.,* 6.   [30] *Ibid.,* 10.
[31] *Ibid.,* 14.   [32] *Ibid.,* 6; cf. 2.

are gods. The emperors are, as it is said in an inscription, "born of God and themselves creators of Gods."[33] In reality it is Jupiter himself, the *summus pater*[34] of all the emperors, who is present at the investiture and who adopts as a son the new Augustus or the new Caesar. The titles of Jovius and Herculius given to the Caesars of 293 and 305 on the day of their nomination were a justification of the choice; it is Jupiter himself who had chosen.[35]

The tetrarchic state rested thus, firmly and immovably, in the eternal world order. In the constitution and the administration of the state, in financial reforms, economic and social stabilization measures, in war and peace, cultural and religious politics—everywhere the Jupiter-Empire of Diocletian was present as the organizing force. The reforms carried out in all sectors of life introduced one single order willed by the gods. As Jovii and Herculei, the emperors belonged to a higher world "où ils ont trouvé une sorte d'harmonie préétablie qu'aucun d'eaux ne pouvait contester ou changer" (W. Seston). The great regularity and lawfulness of this higher and eternal world now, with the reform work of Diocletian, descended into our temporal reality, and the confusing multitude of obstinate and unruly natural forms were aligned and arranged according to the strict lines of a transcendent order and symmetry.

Let us see how the Tetrarchy organized this new order in some of the central spheres in the life of the state and the individual.

THE TETRARCHIC STATE ADMINISTRATION

A characteristic feature of the administrative reform was the splitting up of the large and organic provincial

---

[33] Seston, p. 218.   [34] Seston, pp. 217 ff.   [35] Seston, p. 231.

territories into smaller, more uniform and mutually equal parts, about one hundred in number, which were then grouped into twelve larger administrative units (*dioeceses*). Italy and Egypt also, in spite of having had their special, historically qualified status, were regulated according to the general scheme with partitioning into small provinces aggregated into dioceses.[36] In accordance with the uniform nature of the new small provinces, all the provincial governors had the same title: that of judge (*judex*). At the head of each diocese were the *vicarii* for the four Praetorian Prefects, while the prefects themselves represented the highest division of the Empire, the four prefectures corresponding to the divine tetrarchical order itself. In the governing of all these administrative units—province, diocese, prefecture—a vertical dividing line was drawn (except where defense installations were threatened with imminent danger) between the civil and the military administration. *Judices* and *vicarii*, later also the prefects, were in principle to be civil servants only. Beside them were the military commanders (*duces*).

In this checkered carving-up of the territories into new, equal, and uniform administrative units, arranged in three levels, a scheme of division was employed which was characteristic of the tetrarchical system. Here is a construction that can be compared to composition according to a geometrical coordinate system in contemporary art and architecture (pp. 71 f., Fig. 23). The complex and composite were not resolved into their natural components, but were divided more mathematically and appeared, after this division, as regular and equal parts.

---

[36] Compare the way in which Diocletian made the fortification of the *limes* uniform along all of the borders; from the Sahara to the Syrian desert, from the Rhine to the coast of Britannia, there is now a oneness as never before in the *castra* and all the defenses of the *limes* (Seston, p. 297).

Still, this administrative geometry, no less than the tetrarchic system, was not part of a predetermined plan but the result of historical circumstances. Both the dividing up of the provinces and the separation of the civil and military administration were intended to split the concentration of power and thereby prevent usurpation— the latent danger ever-present in the enormous Empire.

Simultaneously, Diocletian completed the total integration of the municipalities into the state whereby they lost the last remnants of an organic life of their own. As we have seen, the various civic functions in the cities gradually became obligatory duties or services, which were laid upon the wealthy citizens, and were increasingly organized in the interests of the state and less in that of the municipalities. The magistrates of the municipalities, their public organizations, even individuals from the propertied classes, were now placed under the authority of the provincial governors, while the latter in turn were controlled by the imperial central administration through its vicars. In this way the central administration, surmounting a hierarchy of functionaries whose authority increased as they approached the pyramid's peak, magnetically drew all activities in toward itself: toward the emperor in his *consistorium*.[37]

THE TAX REFORM OF DIOCLETIAN

During the earlier Empire the collection of state revenues, such as taxes and custom duties, were farmed out to private citizens (*publicani*), who could become rich in this business. Later city officials and council members were appointed as collectors of these state revenues. During the third century, as we have seen, an increasingly hard policy of taxation made these collectors, who rep-

[37] Seston, pp. 343 ff.

resented the wealthy citizens, personally liable for the full return of the collection.

Diocletian now introduced a new standard of value which made possible a thorough and systematic utilization of all the existing resources of value.[38] The peculiar late antique tax, called *capitatio* (head tax), created by Diocletian, instituted a new unit (*caput*) beside the traditional *iugum*, as a basis for taxation. A "head" or "person" tax (*caput*) was added to the property tax. While the traditional unit of assessment (*iugum*) was used only for land, the Diocletian *caput*, did not, as one would think, apply only to people but also to animals and land. The same word, *capitatio*, was used without differentiation for the tax to be paid for the people who work the soil and the tax levied on the soil itself and the animals it nourishes. As a fiscal quantity the *iugum* and the *caput* are equivalent even though the objects of taxation, people and land, are fundamentally different. Thus, the tax register in some districts shows that *capita* and *iuga* were added together, as both were united under the term ζυγοκέφαλα.[39]

Piganiol has assumed—and Seston follows him—that this assessment of both humans and land in *capita*, was advanced as a practical solution inspired by the historical circumstances at the time when Diocletian intervened in the chaotic conditions, which also in the fiscal area characterized the period of dissolution in the second half of the third century. Inflation increasingly necessitated the demand that taxes be collected in kind, particularly grain,

---

[38] We recall the harsh words of Lactantius about what he calls the *avaritia* of Diocletian, which burdens the people with such new taxes as the farmers cannot bear and they are forced to abandon the soil: *ut enormitate indictionum consumptis viribus colonorum desererentur agri* (De mort. pers., 7).

[39] Seston, p. 275. H. Bott, *Die Grundzüge der Diokletian. Steuerverfassung*, Darmstadt, 1928, pp. 40 ff.

but also raw material and manufactured goods. Everywhere armies were on the march and everywhere there were impending requisitions of the supplies that were to insure the army's *annona*, their store of the yearly corn supply. Diocletian's *capitatio* seems to have raised the summary taxation practiced by these military requisitions to a permanent institution. By a summary estimate of the cultivated land, cattle, and the number of working "heads" on an estate, one could evaluate its wealth and fix the size of the requisition. With the systematic utilization of all resources it became natural to use a standard of measure that could be applied to everything; a unit of measure was settled upon that represented the amount of agricultural produce equal to a *caput*, i.e., the needs of a single farm-worker.[40] Thus arose an oversimplified and generalized system, without adjustment to the changes in economic life and the shifts in the social structures in the different provinces.[41] Such a system of taxation, which lumped together the land and its inhabitants, at the same time favored the general tendency to bind the farmer and tenant farmer to his native soil.

At the beginning of his reign Diocletian has sought an immediate result by his reforms and was content for the time being with summary evaluations in order to raise the *annona*. In the tax reform of 297, estates were counted, land, animals, and humans accurately assessed, and the equivalent apportionment of *capita* was set, in accordance with the divine providence of the emperor. "Nos empereurs très prévoyants, Dioclétien, etc. . . . ont décidé . . . de publier un règlement salutaire (τύπον σωτήριον), auquel on doit se conformer pour fixer les impôts. Quelle charge a été imposée à chaque aroure, d'après la qualité de la terre, e quelle charge à chaque

[40] A. Piganiol, *RHist*, 1935, p. 1. Cf. Seston, pp. 274 ff.
[41] Kornemann, *Weltgeschichte*, p. 259.

tête de paysan, et depuis quel âge jusqu'à quel âge, il est loisible à tous de la connaître . . . Après avoir été gratifiés de si grands bienfaits, que les provinciaux s'empressent de payer leurs impôts très promptement, conformément aux règles posées par la décision divine, et qu'ils n'attendent pas l'intervention des compulsores."[42]

Of special importance from our point of view is the fact that the *capitatio* of Diocletian made persons and things equivalent so that for the purpose of taxation they could be added as ζυγοκέφαλα. A farmer paid for himself or his worker the same quantity of agricultural produce or the equivalent in goods that he pays for a determined area of his estate or a certain number of heads of his cattle. "Une côte fiscale est crée dans l'abstrait, le caput, et dans ce moule tout sera jeté, les hommes et la terre, et les animaux qui vivent de la terre."[43] Here again, we meet the peculiar attitude of Late Antiquity, which is not concerned with individuality and the nature of things but applies to everything one and the same common denominator, reduces forms to homogeneous units, and marshals them in unending rows. One may compare with this what we saw in the *spolia* architecture of Late Antiquity, where building elements of widely different function and form were made equal within the totality of the structure and made to function in one and the same way.

THE PRICE LAW

Diocletian's endeavors to stabilize the currency was an attempt, continuing that of the Emperor Aurelian, to conquer the perilous inflation that had arisen during periods of crisis in the third century when a state of

[42] A. Piganiol's translation, *op.cit.*, p. 1 (repeated Seston, p. 283), of the imperial decree dispatched by the prefect of Egypt.

[43] Seston, pp. 281, 288.

emergency led, as it had at earlier periods of the Roman Empire, to the minting of debased coins. Like Aurelian, he resumed the minting of full-value gold and silver coins, *aureus* to 1/60 pound, *argenteus* to 1/96 pound, as under Nero. The copper coinage (*follis, radiatus* and *denarius communis*), was, however, as before, not of full-value copper. The over-evaluation of the copper coins in comparison to the gold and silver was the cause of disturbances in the new monetary system. "*Valutarische Gewaltstreiche*," to use Regling's phrase, in the end completely destroyed confidence in Diocletian's financial system and led to an increasing rise of costs in the Empire.[44]

To stabilize prices, Diocletian intervened with his famous price law in A.D. 301. The law affixed a maximum tariff, which regulated all prices for goods, wages, and salaries on the basis of the *denarius* as the smallest monetary unit, the value of which was put at 1/50,000 pound gold.[45] In the preface to the price list a fundamental explanation for the establishment of such a maximum tariff is given: this encroachment upon the economic life, we read, is based on an eternal, god-willed judicial order, which was violated by the individual desire for profit. We relate here the main points contained in this preface.

Mention is made of "the furious avarice which, with no thought for mankind (*sine respectu generis humani*), hastens to its own gain and increases its property at a tempo which does not take into account years or months

[44] K. Regling, "Münzkunde" in Gercke-Norden, *Einleitung in die Altertumswissenschaft*, II, 2 (ed. 4), pp. 28 ff. Kornemann, *Weltgeschichte*, p. 263.

[45] Th. Mommsen-H. Blümner, *Edictum Diocletiani de pretiis rerum venalium*, Berlin, 1893. The original text is accompanied by an English translation by Elsa Graser, "The Edict of Diocletian" in Tenney Frank, *Economic Survey of Ancient Rome*, V, pp. 307 ff., Baltimore, 1940. Graser's publication of the tariff has also included fragments of inscriptions which came to light after the Mommsen-Blümner publication.

or days, but only hours and even minutes." The "furious avarice" and "untameable greed" (*avaritia, cupido furoris indomiti*) of the individual are in conflict with the "general welfare" (*fortunae communes; communis necessitudo*), and makes many people "enemies both of the single individual and of the universal order" (*inimici singulis et universis rebus*). This "unbridled passion for gain" (*effrenata libido rapiendi*) is mitigated neither by abundant supplies nor by fruitful years. Above all this affects the army. With "the monstrous prices that human speech is incapable of describing . . . it follows that in a single purchase a soldier is deprived of his bonus and salary and that the contributions of the whole world to support the armies fall to the abominable profit of thieves so that our soldiers seem with their own hands to offer the hopes of their service and of their completed labors to the profiteers, with the result that those who plunder the nation constantly take in more than they can use themselves."

With all this taken into consideration, the edict states, it is necessary for the state to intervene. "We (the emperors)—who are the protectors of the human race—viewing this state of affairs, find ourselves called upon to intervene with the rule of justice, so that the long-hoped-for solution which mankind itself could not supply, might be brought about, through our foresight, for the betterment of all. . . . It is our pleasure therefore, that the prices listed in the summary appended be observed in the whole of our Empire. . . . For buyers and sellers who customarily travel to foreign ports and provinces, this universal decree should be a warning so that they too know that in the time of high prices there is no opportunity of exceeding the fixed maximum prices, for example by including the location of the place or transportation . . . and so that the justice of our decree forbidding those who transport merchandise to sell anywhere at higher prices, may be evident."

"Since fear has always been regarded as the most influential preceptor in the performance of duty, it is in accordance with our will that anyone who shall have resisted the regulation set forth in this statute, shall for his daring be subject to the death penalty. . . . To the same penalty, moreover, is he subject who in the desire to buy shall have conspired against the statute with the greed of the seller. Nor are they exempt from the same penalty who, although possessing the necessities of life and business, believe that to escape this regulation, they may withdraw them from the general market. . . . We, therefore, appeal to the loyalty of all our people that a law created for the public good may be observed with willing obedience and due fear of God (*cohortamur ergo omnium devotionem ut res constituta ex commodo publico benignis obsequiis debita religione teneatur*)."

The individual desire for profit, is thus placed in contrast to "the general welfare" (*fortunae communes*), which is based upon a "universal order" (*res universae*) surpassing the individual. The divine Empire which is the realization on earth of this higher order, sets up the dominion of righteousness (*arbitram justitiam*) against lust of gain and establishes by its providence the higher order that mankind itself is not able to set up, everything for the common good (*ad comune omnium temperamentum*). The price law is based immovably upon *res universae* and must be upheld with pious devotion and fear of God (*devotio* and *religio*); he who offends this law sins against the divine—and imperial—order of life and has forfeited his life.

How abstract and detached from the realities of life the Diocletian price law was, is evident in the fact that the established maximum tariff was inflexibly the same

all over the Roman world (*totus orbis*), in all places and
at all times, in retail and wholesale. Again the eye skips
over the concrete and realistic, seeks beyond detail and
differentiation to rest upon the grand lines of the *res universae*.

DIOCLETIAN'S CULTURAL AND RELIGIOUS POLICY

Diocletian considered himself a Roman and wished to
renew the Roman state, Roman religion and morals,
Roman customs and mores, Roman civilization. In place
of *Sol Invictus* which, since Severan times and, to an even
higher degree, after Aurelian, had occupied the central
position in the religion of the Empire, there appears once
again, as we have seen, the national-Roman Jupiter, lord
of the Capitol, and Hercules, hero of the Palatine. Diocletian's special relationship with Jupiter (pp. 38 ff.) fills
him with a genuinely Roman religiosity. His *pietas* is
commemorated by his contemporaries. "How great is
Your piety for the gods," says a panegyrist to the two
Augusti. "You have showered them with altars and
statues, with temples and offerings which You embel-
lished with Your image and inscribed name, and which
You made even more holy by the example You set by
your own worship of the gods. Now, surely, men understand what power resides in the gods when they are
worshiped so fervently by You."[46] The reward for this
imperial piety is happiness for the whole Empire (*Felicitatem istam, optimi imperatores, pietate meruistis*).[47]
This happiness won by the *pietas* of the emperors, is
a new golden *saeculum* and everlasting peace. In an
inscription from the year 291, Diocletian is commemorated as "founder of the eternal peace."[48]

[46] *Mamertini genethl. Max.*, 6.   [47] *Ibid.*, 18; cf. 6.
[48] CIL, III, 5810.

The Reforms of Diocletian

Such a joy-bearing Jupiter religion was intended to unite all Romans, to promote unity in thought and feeling, and to consolidate the whole Empire.[49] With the Jupiter religion follows the ideal of Roman civilization: *disciplina legesque Romanae*. All of the inhabited world, in spite of ethnic differences, had to be made alike following the precepts of Roman discipline and law. Diocletian sought therefore, as far as possible, to widen the areas of influence of Roman law and to remove from the law of the Empire the infiltration of non-Roman, especially Greek elements.[50] Roman law became a main pillar in the romanization of the provinces. But the peculiar character of this law required Latin as the judicial language. Diocletian, therefore, sent Latin rhetors and grammarians to the Greek-speaking eastern provinces. Even in Egypt, which up to now had occupied a special position somewhat apart, Latin became the judicial language; and even upon coins the Greek inscriptions gave way to Latin. The Dominate did not concern itself with the natural, individual lives of the eastern population but sought to instill Latin as the administrative language in the whole of the Greek-speaking east. Again, this was a result of the general process of equalization and uniformity which Kornemann describes as Diocletian's "Drang nach Gleichmacherei, Vereinfachung, Mechanisierung."[51]

In the marriage laws of Diocletian we have a typical result of these endeavors towards romanization. The Emperor turned against the more lenient practice of the third century, which was consistent with the complex

[49] Kornemann, *Weltgeschichte*, pp. 248 ff.

[50] K. Stade, *Der Politiker Diokletian und die letzte grosse Christenverfolgung*, n.pl., 1926, pp. 68 ff.

[51] Kornemann, *Weltgeschichte*, pp. 270 f. Cf. R. Laqueur in *Probleme der Spätantike*, 1930, 4, pp. 1 ff. Stade, *op.cit.*, pp. 67 f.

situation in the world Empire, with a diversity of popular customs in this intimate domain of life. Laws were established for marriage contracts, and family marriage was forbidden even though such marriages had become increasingly common and were, moreover, ancient custom in many parts of the eastern provinces. The ordinance specifies in detail all blood relationships which could conceivably preclude marriage contracts—it was thus forbidden to marry one's great-grandmother. *Disciplina legesque Romanae* is constantly the directing and regulating principle.[52] "To our pious and religious disposition it seems that what in Roman law is prescribed as chaste and holy is especially admirable and should be preserved with eternal religious veneration" (*ea quae Romanis legibus caste sancteque sunt constituta venerabilia maxime videntur atque aeterna religione servanda*). In the face of violations of these laws "the discipline of our time urges us to interfere."[53] Here the battle was fought against everything felt to be dissolving the traditional Roman form of life and culture.

The uniformness of religious life in the spirit of the Jupiter religion led to persecution of self-willed religious societies. In the midst of a world of tolerant Sun- or Cosmic religiosity where Roman and Greek were mingled with and had absorbed diverse elements of the religions of Egypt, Syria, Asia Minor, and Persia, and where the Hellenistic-Oriental mystery worship, gnosis, philosophy, and astrology permeated the traditional forms of Roman worship, efforts emerged towards the end of the third century to unify and fortify the Roman world under a state church: efforts which were only fulfilled with the constitution of the Christian state. The world strove toward a *rapprochement* of state and church in a way unknown before in Antiquity, but to

[52] Stade, *op.cit.*, p. 82.   [53] *Ibid.*, p. 79.

which close parallels can be found in the contemporary Empire in the east, the Sassanian Persia.[54] Immediately before Diocletian, Aurelian had put the Syrian sun religion, in a Romanized form, at the center of the state cult. Diocletian "causes the Emperors' gods to become leaders" (βασιλέων θεοὺς ἡγεμόνας ποιούμενος)[55]—in other words, he founded a kind of celestial Jupiter monarchy. Above the chaotic, infinitely complex religious world of the third century with its amalgamation or symbiosis of a multitude of diversified religions, now arose a well-regulated Olympus with Jupiter upon the central peak; and, reflecting this celestial Olympus, the Jovian Empire on earth surmounts the State. Nothing must violate this symmetry.

Diocletian's persecution of foreign cults was, in the religious sphere, completely parallel to contemporary intervention in all sectors of economic and social life. In the Manichee-edict of March 31, 297, the Tetrarchy proceeded with the severest punishments against the religion of Mani: against the insane and wretched "who set new and unheard-of teachings up against the older religions" (*qui novellas et inauditas sectas veterioribus religionibus obponunt*). The leaders of this movement were to burn, "together with their abominable writings" (*cum abominandis scripturis*), and their sympathizers were to be executed. "For it is the greatest crime to oppose that which —determined and decided by the fathers—has its firm place and its sure course."[56]

This violent intervention against the followers of Mani preludes the Tetrarchy's persecution of the Christians, which was the most extensive and systematic ever carried out by the Roman Empire. In the year 298 the armistice

---

[54] Kornemann, *Weltgeschichte*, p. 241.

[55] Libanius, *Orationes*, 4, p. 331, ed. Förster.

[56] Stade, *op.cit.*, p. 160.

between the state and the Christian community was broken after having existed for nearly forty years.[57] The Christians had refused to sacrifice to the emperor: that is, had refused to give the obligatory proof of loyalty to the present Jupiter. The state reacted by removing all Christians from its service, in particular from the army. The first general edict against the Christians followed on February 23, 303. The Christian meeting houses were ordered destroyed and cult assemblies forbidden; the holy scriptures and liturgical books were to be surrendered and burned; all Christians were outlawed. A short time after the issuing of this edict a fire broke out in the imperial palace at Nicomedia and the blame was laid upon the Christians. This gave rise to another and more rigorous edict: the whole of the Christian clergy was to be imprisoned. "Everywhere countless numbers were locked up and in every place the prisons, which had been built long ago for murderers and grave-robbers, were filled with bishops, elders, and deacons, with readers and exorcists, so that there was no longer room left in the prisons for convicted criminals."[58] A third edict ordered that the imprisoned Christians should be forced to sacrifice and then set free. At last there came the sanguinary fourth edict which commanded all Christians—men, women, and children—to sacrifice or die. The greatest period of Christian martyrdom had begun.

The original and deepest motive for the persecutions is apparent, according to K. Stade,[59] from Galerius' later edict of tolerance. The emperors would "improve everything according to the old Roman laws and public discipline" (*iuxta leges veteres et publicam disciplinam Romanorum cuncta corrigere*), and "would see that the Christians . . . came to their senses again." The emperors'

[57] Seston, pp. 122 ff., 155.   [58] Eusebius, *Hist. eccl.*, VIII, 6, 9.
[59] Stade, *op.cit.*, pp. 162 f.

22. Tetrarchical emperor at the state sacrifice. Relief on base of column of honorary monument, Forum Romanum

intention with the persecutions was to have been "to lead all men's thoughts along the pious and right path of life" (πάντων τῶν ἀνθρώπων τὰς διανοίας πρὸς τὴν ὁσίαν καὶ ορθὴν τοῦ ζῆν ὁδὸν περιαγαγεῖν).[60] Only the Jupiter religion, however, could lead men along this path. In the year 303—contemporary with the persecution of the Christians—an imposing monument was erected at Forum Romanum which eloquently expresses this religion: the previously mentioned five-column monument dedicated on the occasion of the twentieth anniversary of the reign of the Augusti. The four Emperors, who are all identical, are grouped around the colossal Jupiter on the central column. On each of the column bases is depicted the sacrificing Emperor, an illustration of his *pietas* (Fig. 22). At the same time coins are struck showing Diocletian and Maximian at the state sacrifice,

[60] Eusebius, *op.cit.*, IX, 1, 3.

accompanied by Felicitas, the personification of the happiness of the Empire, and surrounded by the symbols of peace, prosperity, and fertility. The legend reads: *felicitas temporum*. The *pietas* of the emperor guarantees the *felicitas* of the world.

Felicitatem istam, optimi imperatores, pietate meruistis. Thus, in accordance with the monument and the coins, the panegyrist addresses the Christian-persecuting emperors. There was, however, only one *pietas*: that which conformed with *disciplina legesque Romanae* and which resided in the perpetual order of Jupiter. We sense the contours of a compact tetrarchical state religion which was to unify and equalize the spiritual life of Rome.

II. TRANSFORMATIONS IN THE ART AND ARCHITECTURE OF THE DIOCLETIAN PERIOD

W E HAVE seen how the traditional forms of organization, both in the life of the state and of the individual, changed with the transition from Principate to Dominate. The new pattern is most clearly outlined in the Diocletian state. Let us sum up the main points of the transformation as we have described it in our preceding study.

The free and organic grouping of individuals and institutions was replaced by a mechanical coordination of the elements, by row formations and symmetry; everything was aligned according to the strict ordinates of a higher axial system, an order imposed from above. There is no eye for the individual, no feeling for the differentiations of an organically developing nature, no appreciation of detail and variety, but a peculiarly distant glance following the abstract lines of the inner unity of things and seeking fixed, unchangeable conceptions which embrace them all. Here, simultaneously, is simplification and stabilization.

The new pattern of the Dominate as it was revealed in life itself, appears, as we have seen, *explicite*—in what can be seen with our own eyes and therefore with greatest perspicuity—in the contemporary art and architecture. Above (pp. 9 ff.), in a general survey of the transformation of building forms toward Late Antiquity, we have seen how a new conception of structure is developed in architecture. More specifically we will concentrate our comments upon the new solutions to problems of form which came about in the time around A.D. 300, after the tetrarchic state had overcome the great crisis of the second

69

half of the third century. We shall encounter compositions which can be described with words very like those used to characterize the constitutional organization of the tetrarchic state and its administrative system. We will first examine the imperial palace and from there pass on to the Christian basilica. Thereafter we will look at figurative art. Here, above all, two groups of monuments have left to us a body of material from the period around 300 sufficient for a study in detail of the transformation of form which took place during this critical period: the first of these groups is sculptured reliefs upon sarcophagi and public monuments; the second, portrait sculpture.

THE IMPERIAL PALACE AND THE BASILICA

In the development of the Roman imperial palace we see—in accordance with the whole basic tendency in the architectural development during the Roman Empire (pp. 13 ff.)—how a rather free disposition of the building units gives way to strictly bound axial compositions, the individual parts of which are, in a more or less heavy-handed manner, symmetrically arranged. The more open, villa-like palace architecture of earlier times becomes enclosed in fortresslike blocks.

The best preserved of all the Roman imperial palaces, Diocletian's palace in Spalato on the Dalmatian coast (Fig. 23), illustrates the new palace type of the Dominate.[1] While in earlier tradition—exemplified by the imperial palaces on the Palatine and in Hadrian's palace at Tivoli—the ground plan and the elevation may show great irregularity in that new parts grow organically out of the older, Diocletian's palace is a closed stereometric block of mathematic regularity, with a ground plan of

---

[1] G. Niemann, *Der Palast Diokletians in Spalato*, Vienna, 1910.

23. Palace of Diocletian in Spalato, reconstruction (Niemann)

rectangles arranged according to a strict coordinate system. It is fixed in each part, unchangeably stipulated on a geometric formula, thus without possibility of further growth and development. Here is the same contrast between free grouping and mechanical coordination, between organic growth from within and symmetrical stabilization imposed from above, as that which we have indicated as characteristic in all relations between the Principate and the Dominate. Let us examine Diocletian's palace at Spalato more closely.

The ground plan of the palace is approximately rectangular and in each of the four corners of the rectangle is placed a mighty tower. The side of the rectangle which faces the sea, is formed as the façade; the three other sides, facing land, are formed as fortified walls secured by towers closing off the palace from the land. Lengthwise, through the whole palace runs a main axis from a tower-flanked portal at the center of the landward side to a three-bay columned opening at the center of the side facing the sea. At a right angle to this main axis, a transversal axis cuts through the palace, running from a tower-flanked portal at the center of one length of the palace rectangle to a tower-flanked portal at the center of the other. Along these two axes, which form a cross, are built columned streets. The longitudinal axis is clearly marked out as the main axis: in this axis, provision is made in constantly rising architectural movements for the most holy suite of rooms for the imperial ceremonials (*palatium sacrum*) with columned atrium, vestibule, and throne room. The four rectangles formed by the main axes are again subdivided into rectangular units, all firmly enclosed within the coordinate system of the palace rectangle: the whole, a composition at right angles, along horizontal and vertical lines and dominated by the quadratic-rectangular framework—everything corresponding to the new pattern of composition we shall find in the pictorial art of that time (p. 90).

That the palace at Spalato is clearly symptomatic of the time is shown by Diocletian's palace in Palmyra on the Eufrates.[2] As in Spalato, the palace in Palmyra is cut by crossed axes of wide, columned streets which, as at Spalato, run between fortified gates. In Palmyra also the columned street forming the longitudinal axis marks the main axis and leads into the great columned atrium in front of the ceremonial suite of the palace. As at Spalato, the large rectangular building units into which the palace is divided are enclosed within the coordinate system of the crossed axes. The ceremonial suite again lies at the rear of the whole plan, but in Palmyra it rises majestically upon a high, built-up terrace above the steeply falling terrain upon which the other buildings are symmetrically regulated according to the main axis.

[2] Th. Wiegand, *Palmyra*, Berlin, 1932, pl. 10; cf. D. Krencker, *ibid.*, pp. 84 ff., and H. Lehner, *ibid.*, p. 160: interpretation of the complex as a palace. Newest excavation of the building by K. Michalowski and discussion by D. Schlumberger, *Mélanges Monterdi*, II (1962), pp. 79 ff. and by E. Will, in *Syria*, 40, 1963, pp. 385 ff.

Transformations in the Art and Architecture

This palace architecture of Diocletian is clearly influenced by Roman military architecture. The rectangular plan of the palace at Spalato, its fortified walls and crossed axial streets connecting the gates at the center of each side: all this belongs inseparably to the Roman fortified camp, the *castrum*. Such a fusion of *castrum* into the architecture of the imperial palace is in strict accord with the militarization of state and administration—indeed, of the whole style of life—which took place during the third century (pp. 7 f.). Where before, Greek names—Academy, Lyceum, etc.—were used to indicate the different parts of the palace, now the word *praetorium*—i.e., the headquarters of the camp commander—became the common term designating the main building in the palace precinct. It is a development toward the fortified palace of the Middle Ages, the fortress, where the palace lives on in the castle—as the word itself, *palatium*, survives in the mediaeval term *Pfalz*. Swoboda refers to a number of eastern examples of this militarization of the palace buildings during Late Antiquity and the early Middle Ages, for example, to the Byzantine Kasr Ibn Wardan in northern Syria, from the sixth century A.D., and to Arabian desert castles such as Mschatta. In Kasr Ibn Wardan the palace had become "a cubic crystal of a building enlivened only by the windows which break the wall surfaces."[3]

The nucleus of the imperial palace was a suite of rooms dedicated to the imperial ceremonials. With the increasing importance of the emperor cult in Late Antiquity, this ceremonial suite attains a more and more dominating position in the imperial palace: it becomes the holy of holies, the *palatium sacrum*, where the emperor himself

[3] K. M. Swoboda, *Römische und Romanische Paläste*, Vienna, 1919, fig. 70, p. 56. Cf. Alföldi, "Insignen," *Mitteilungen des Deutschen Archaeolog. Instituts, Röm. Abt.*, 50, 1935, p. 46.

is enthroned in his throne room like a divine image of worship.[4] In Diocletian's palace in Spalato, this *palatium sacrum* received the form which was to become the prototype for the palaces of the Dominate.[5] Let us examine it more closely.

From the land façade, as we have seen, a broad, columned street runs along the main axis of the palace and after crossing the transversal columned street, it leads into the ceremonial suite. This consists of the large columned court (*atrium*), which continues the axis of the columned street and ends with a three-bay, columned gable-pediment at the back; beneath this gable, which is a gable of glorification, the emperor appears before those gathered in the atrium (Fig. 24). Behind the gable is a circular, domed vestibule and behind this lies the throne room itself, the *triclinium*, all in the same axis. The rear of the throne room opens onto a portico at the center of the sea façade of the palace; here the emperor appeared, again in the same commanding ceremonial axis, at the middle of the sea façade where he stood with a great three-bay, columned opening framing his divine person as did the glorification gable in the atrium when he emerged from the throne room in the opposite direction.

The large, columned atrium was the gathering place for the court—even today the name court is derived from this open courtyard in the imperial palaces of Late Antiquity: court, *cour, corte, Hof*—and when, from the inner halls of the ceremonial suite, the emperor appeared under the glorification gable, those assembled in the columned court sank to their knees before the God-Emperor. The privileged, who were granted audience in the

[4] Alföldi, *op.cit.*, pp. 127 ff.

[5] Fundamental for the study of late antique imperial palace architecture are the works by E. Dyggve, cf. his *Ravennatum Palatium Sacrum*, Copenhagen, 1941, and, *Dödekult, keiserkult og basilika*, Copenhagen, 1943.

throne room, assembled first in the domed vestibule behind the glorification gable. From there they proceeded,
surrounded by the chamberlains and officials of the imperial ritual, into the throne room and waited there, in
a mysterious *silentium*, the moment when the heavy
draperies which hung down before the holy of holies in
the rear of the throne room would be drawn aside—these
curtains which in the language of the Byzantine court
poetry are called "clouds which conceal the light of
heaven." The clouds part and the sun shines forth: those
seeking audience see the God-Emperor enthroned before
them beneath his columned baldachin, the ciborium
(compare Fig. 25), surrounded by lighted torches, shining
in gold and silver, glittering with jewels and with the
godly light radiating around his head, *lux divinum verti-
cem clare orbe complectens.*[6] All fall to their knees and
hymns, shouts of praise, and acclamations resound
throughout the hall.

Around this *palatium sacrum* in the main axis of the
palace, the architectural elements are symmetrically arranged, not unlike, as we shall see, the way in which all
the figurative elements in the contemporary imperial art
are symmetrically disposed around the emperor to whom
they all are subordinated (Figs. 35 f., 48 f.). For one walk-
ing down the columned street towards the atrium, the
emperor-axis was marked by the imposing columned
gable at the rear of the atrium and by the cupola which
towers behind the gable. The mausoleum of the Jupiter-
Emperor and the Temple of Jupiter which lie directly opposite one another on each side of the atrium, are both
subject to the order of this palace axis—even the Temple
of Jupiter! Octavian, the first augustus, had already constructed in connection with his own *domus* a temple to
his patron god, namely, the Temple of Apollo on the

---

[6] *Mamertini paneg. Max.*, 3. Cf. the portrait of Theodosius, Fig. 24.

24. Emperor-image of Theodosius, Madrid (Delbrück)

Palatine; however, he had subordinated his *domus* to the temple. In Diocletian's palace the relationship has changed; it is now the imperial suite which is superior, everything is regulated according to the emperor-axis, the symmetric order of the Dominate.

In these axially dominated imperial suites even the figurative decoration is now regulated according to the emperor-axis. A splendid example of how the figurative decoration accompanies the ascending order throughout the succession of rooms in the ceremonial suite is found in the floor mosaics of the recently excavated palace in Piazza Armerina in Sicily (Fig. 26), which has been much discussed by archaeologists and historians as to date and interpretation during recent years. In our opinion the

25. Empress beneath ciborium (Delbrück)

ceremonial suites are to be dated around A.D. 300 and may have been built by Diocletian's co-augustus, Maximianus Herculeus.[7] The porticos of the atria in both the

[7] This interpretation has been approved by G. V. Gentili, the excavator of the palace. Presumably it was a retirement palace for the abdicated Maximian, thus a parallel to the retirement palace in Spalato for Maximian's imperial colleague, Diocletian: L'Orange-Dyggve, "E' un palazzo di Massimiano Erculio che gli scavi di Piazza Armerina portano alla luce?", *Symbolae Osloenses*, 29, 1952, pp. 114 ff. L'Orange, "Il palazzo di Massimiano Erculio di Piazza Armerina," *Studi in onore di Aristide Calderini e Roberto Paribeni*, III, 1956; *Idem,* "Nuovo contributo allo studio del Palazzo di Piazza Armerina," *Acta Instituti Romani Norvegiae*, Rome, 2, 1965 (in press). G. V. Gentili, *La Villa Erculia di Piazza Armerina, I mosaici figurati*, Rome, 1959. Also approved by I. Lavin, "The Hunting Mosaics of Antioch," *Dumbarton Oaks Papers*, 1963, pp. 244 ff. Objections to this interpretation of the palace have

ceremonial suites are covered with a mosaic carpet with images of wild animals—heads, protomes, beasts in rinceau —most of them belonging to the arena. In the larger of the two suites, the vestibule that forms a sort of narrow narthex between the atrium and the throne room gives us the next movement in the mosaic decoration: the wild beasts, shown here entire and in their natural surroundings, are hunted by the imperial huntsmen, captured, and transported over the sea to the arena. The enormous mosaic which measures more than 60 meters in length, shows in the dominating central scene, which is placed in the very axis of the ceremonial suite, *four men* with the typical tetrarchical vestments and insignia: thus the tetrarchical state and administration is manifest in the picture. The hunting scenes seek to comprise all the wild beasts of the east and the west, the north and the south, as the imperial games had to embrace *omnia in toto orbe animalia*, to demonstrate the universality of the Empire.

The blood bath of the amphitheater emanates from these pictures even while they convey the genuine antique idea of the heroic slaughter of animals, the triumph over "the beast," the idea of the great subduer of wild monsters, Hercules. In the closing movement of the pictorial decoration, in the very throne room itself, this Hercules idea is extolled in clear figures and symbols to the one entering. Here, in the smaller of the two ceremonial suites, we see the "labors" of Hercules presented as an accomplished fact—the slaughtered or captured animals

been made by B. Pace, *I mosaici di Piazza Armerina*, Rome, 1955; by M. Cagiano de Azevedo, "I proprietari della villa di Piazza Armerina," *Scritti di storia dell'arte in onore di Mario Salmi*, 1961, pp. 18 ff.; by G. Lugli, "Contributo alla storia edilizia della villa romana di Piazza Armerina," *Rivista dell'Istituto Naz. d'Archeologia e storia dell'arte*, Nuova Serie XI-XII, Rome, 1963, pp. 28 ff. The palace itself has collapsed, but the ground plan and the floor mosaics have been preserved. Originally also the walls and the vaults were adorned with mosaics.

and monsters, the Hydra, the Cerberus, the Nemean lion, etc., lie scattered about us. The symbolism is carried even further: we see Hercules crowned by Jupiter. The whole pictorial decoration reaches its final culmination in the central apse. Here, at the "high point" of the emperor-axis is portrayed the *gigantomachia*, the Olympians' fight against the world rebellion of the giants, a battle which Jupiter could only win with the help of Hercules. At the corresponding place in the larger ceremonial suite stood a colossal statue of Hercules.[8]

In reality it is the Emperor himself who is revealed in this progressive interpretation of the Hercules idea. The emperor himself is the heroic hunter; Hercules-emperors, as for example Commodus, could therefore take direct part in the animal slaughter of the arena. In such hunts was revealed the victorious power which invincibly strikes down all the evil "beasts" that threaten human order: the power which is constantly active in the *praesens Hercules*, Maximian (p. 52). The greatest manifestation of this power is shown in the victory over the mutinous powers of earth, the children of Gaia, who arise from the elements against the heavenly Olympus. In this mythical picture the warring emperors receive—both in figurative art and in the panegyrics[9]—their highest realization, in that the *gigantomachia*, in which Jupiter and Hercules fling the destructive powers of the earth into the depths of Tartaros, is the uniting symbol of the two imperial dynasties.

The same strict axial disposition of the room units into the same ascending order of rank toward the holy of

[8] L'Orange, "Il palazzo di Massimiano Erculio . . . ," *Studi in onore di Calderini e Paribeni*, p. 596, with illustrations.

[9] The emperors as Jupiter and Hercules in the gigantomachia: for example, *Mamertini paneg. Max.*, 4; *Mamertini genethl. Max.*, 3.

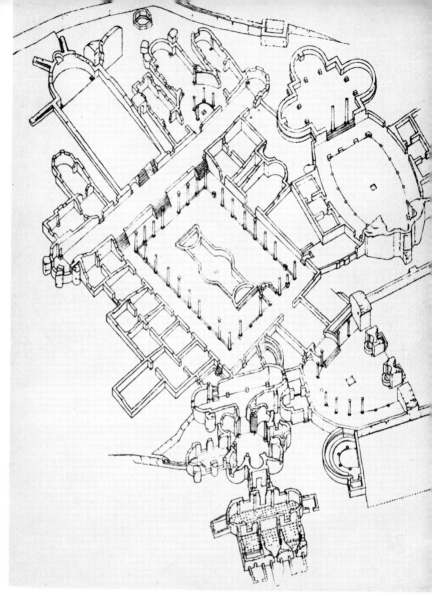

26. Palace at Piazza Armerina (Gismondi)

holies, and the same firm symmetrical grouping of the separate building parts around this axis, is repeated in the "normal-basilical" church architecture created under Constantine the Great, which in Rome is represented by

27. San Paolo fuori le mura, Rome, exterior

such monumental complexes as the Christ Church (now St. John's Church) in the Lateran, Old St. Peter's, San Paolo fuori le Mura, and Santa Maria Maggiore (Figs. 27-30) and which afterwards lives on in simplified forms in the mediaeval basilica of Rome. While previously the Christian basilica was thought to be derived from the antique market-basilica, modern scholars emphasize the differences between the market and the Christian normal-basilica. The market-basilica, which is dedicated to secular and everyday life, stretches along the side of the market as a sort of architectural addition to it, a kind of market under a roof. In the Christian basilica, on the other hand, which is dedicated to the Christian cult, the entire architecture is axially directed toward the center of the cult in the rear, toward the altar, glorified under its celestial baldachin, the ciborium: precisely in the same way in which the imperial *palatium sacrum* was oriented axially toward its cult center, the enthroned emperor

28. San Paolo fuori le mura, Rome, interior

under the ciborium. Indeed it is just these fixed architectural elements of the imperial *palatium sacrum*—first
the open atrium at the front of the palace, then the vast
covered assembly hall before the holy of holies, and further, a number of glorifying architectural forms such as
the glorification gable and the ciborium—which recur in
more or less remodeled form in the Christian normal-
basilica of Constantine.[10] The sacral architectural forms
which framed and glorified the appearance of the God-
Emperor before the people, are taken over and sublimated
in the Christian normal-basilica, which framed and glorified the presence of the celestial King in the sacraments—
the altar of the Lord.

Along the longitudinal axis we walk first through the
open, columned atrium, then through a vestibule (*narthex*), then through the covered basilica—all corresponding to the arrangement in the *palatium sacrum.* The wide

[10] E. Dyggve, *Dödekult, keiserkult og basilika,* Copenhagen, 1943;
Palatium sacrum Ravennatum, Copenhagen, 1941, *passim.*

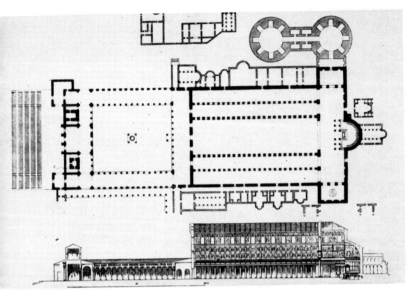

29. Old St. Peter's, Rome

and lofty nave between narrower and lower aisles in the covered basilica, runs between rows of columns, like a *via triumphalis*, towards the apse at the other side of the transept. In front of the transept this columned street passes under a triumphal arch that rests upon the axis of the complex no differently than the glorification gable rests upon the axis of the imperial palace. From the nave one looks through this columned portal, which focuses all eyes upon the "apex" of the axial line, the altar, and the ciborium in the apse. Three heavens—the triumphal arch, the apse vault, the ciborium vault—extend in glory above this altar. Both nave and transept have an open timber roof, only the triumphal arch, the apse niche and the ciborium are vaulted; therefore the eye is drawn to the altar which they frame; everything is arranged according to the altar-axis which here replaces the emperor-axis of the *palatium sacrum*.

All the architectural elements tend toward symmetrical grouping around this axis. The columns may differ as the movement glides forward through each separate row

30. Santa Maria Maggiore, Rome

of columns, but the columns opposite one another are usually alike, thus forming symmetrical pairs on either side of the axis. In each pair the columns thus usually have the same type of capital, and they increase in magnificence as they approach the holy of holies.[11] This conscious directing of all the elements from the cult center forms a precise analogy to the symmetrical arrangements in contemporary figurative art. If, in imitation of what occurs there (pp. 94 f.), one turned each of the two rows of columns framing the nave 90 degrees to each side into the plane of the triumphal arch so that they formed wings on each side of it, the columns, with their changing capitals, would form ever-changing symmetric pairs around the cult center which emerges under the triumphal arch, similar to the way in which the figures in representational

[11] F. W. Deichmann, "Säule und Ordnung in der frühchristl. Architektur," *Mitteilungen des Deutschen Archäolog. Instituts, Röm. Abt.* 55, 1940, pp. 121 ff.; *idem, Frühchristliche Kirchen in Rom,* Basel, 1948, pp. 12 ff.

84

images form varying symmetrical pairs around the central figure.

The whole decoration of the church interior, the encrustation and the ornamentation of the walls, the covering of the individual parts with gold, silver, colored glass, etc., follows the ascending line towards the apse, and in the same measure on both sides of the axis. Again, as we found in the imperial *palatium sacrum*, this applies also to the figurative decoration. The great culmination is found at the "apex" of the axis where Christ himself, like Hercules in Piazza Armerina, appears in all his might. Towards this representation of Christ the whole pictorial decoration of the basilica is directed with increasing momentum and according to the laws of axiality.

THE PICTORIAL RELIEF

As an example of the classical pictorial composition that lived on for a long time in the art of the Principate, we choose a well-known relief medallion from the period of Emperor Hadrian (A.D. 118-136), which was used two hundred years after it was made to decorate the Roman Triumphal Arch of Constantine (Fig. 31). Hadrian has just finished his hunt and, followed by his hunting companions, steps up to the statue of Apollo and pours his offering upon the flaming altar at the foot of the statue. Here, the classical tradition of form is alive not only in the magnificent plastic modeling of the bodies but also in the ideal proportioning of the figures and in the way the weight of the body has been placed on one foot while the other is unburdened, the whole figure thereby receiving its swinging curve in a freedom which, as far back as the fifth century B.C., gives to the portrayal of man in classical art its typical expression of calm, relaxed naturalness. Equally characteristic of the classical tradition of form is the arrangement of the figures: they are

31. Hadrianic medallion, Arch of Constantine, Rome

32. Circus sarcophagus, Foligno, Umbria. Second part of
    III cent. A.D.

33. Prometheus sarcophagus, National Museum, Naples.
    Second part of III cent. A.D.

34. Sarcophagus with myth of Phaethon, Giardino del Lago,
    Villa Borghese, Rome. Second part of III cent. A.D.

35. *Oratio*. Relief on the Arch of Constantine, Rome, A.D. 312-315

separated from each other in order that each body may be
seen in itself as an organic unit and a corporeally beautiful whole; at the same time they are, by their position,
movement, and gesture, placed in a certain rhythmic
mutual relationship, a certain reciprocal contact which
causes us to perceive them as an organic, living group.

In the development which takes place during the critical third century, this classical composition is shattered.
At the same time as the disintegration of the Empire and
the general social and economic disorganization (pp. 39
ff.), there takes place in art a characteristic destruction
of traditional form. One may choose examples of this
among the circus, the Prometheus and Phaethon sarcophagi of that period (Figs. 32-34). The figures lose
their corporeal beauty and no longer exist in organic
groupings. They overlap and cover one another in such
a way that they no longer appear as organic units but
rather as parts of entwined tangles of figures. The organic groups of harmonically related figures are replaced
by turbulent throngs of entwined but contrasting figures.
The contours of the figures no longer flow rhythmically,
but are formed by straight and jagged lines, somewhat
spasmodically; characteristic are the abrupt, marionette-
like movements. With distinctive exaggeration of ges-
tures, movements, and mimicry, the confrontation of the
individual figures is rich in contrast and drama. We are
faced with singularly excited and harried, peculiarly dis-

88

integrated compositions with a strangely glimmering and flickering life.[12] One may speak of anarchy of form.

Toward the end of the third century and during the first decades of the fourth, the disconnected pictorial elements are collected into a new compositional order. But, as in the contemporary tetrarchic reorganization of state and civic life, the new order in art is not, as in the classical tradition, an organic order based upon free figures in spontaneous groupings, but a *mechanical* order imposed upon objects from above, regulating their mutual relationship—an order which is based upon a higher regularity than that of nature. If we look at the two well-known reliefs on the façade of the Arch of Constantine (312-315)—namely *Oratio*, i.e., Constantine's speech on the Rostra at the Forum Romanum (Fig. 35), and *Liberalitas*, i.e., Constantine's distribution of a gift of money to the citizens of Rome (Fig. 36)—we will find this new mechanical order fully developed: the separate figures are not gathered in free, natural groups, but are

---

[12] The art of the Tetrarchy and the late third century was, on the basis of then unpublished material, analyzed and characterized in my work *Studien zur Geschichte des spätantiken Porträts*, Instituttet for sammenlignende Kulturforskning, Oslo, 1933. The sarcophagi of that period have, above all, been treated in German research, G. Rodenwaldt, F. Gerke, Fr. Matz, H. von Schoenebeck, cf. bibliography in L'Orange—von Gerkan, *Der spätantike Bildschmuck des Konstantinbogens*, Berlin, 1939, p. 207, note 4; cf. also Rodenwaldt, *op.cit.*, CAH, XII, 1939, p. 558. In the work already mentioned on the Arch of Constantine, pp. 192 ff., I have presented the material on which my analysis of the stylistic development in that work and in the present study is based.

---

36. *Liberalitas.* Relief on the Arch of Constantine, Rome, A.D. 312-315

arranged as uniform elements side by side in rows; neither these rows nor the architecture that frames them are free, but everything is strictly subordinated to and symmetrized according to the dominating figure of the Emperor at the center of the relief; the compelling regularity which row and symmetry impose upon the figures, is increased by the fact that the axes of the whole composition conform to the horizontals and verticals of the framework. The main lines in the figures and architecture represented either coincide with or are parallel to the framework—for example, the line just above the head of the figures and that just under the feet. The new compositional system is thus characterized by row formations, symmetry, and the total subordination to the ordinates of the framework: an organization of form that completely corresponds to the structure of the Dominate. At the same time that the individual figure loses its well-proportioned, organic integrity, and becomes straightened out according to the verticals of the framework the tradi-

37. Detail of *Oratio* in Fig. 35

38. Detail of a relief on the Arch of Constantine, A.D. 312-315

tional curve of the figure at ease disappears and thereby the genuine classical expression of idle, relaxed humanity.

There is a mechanical anchoring of the form down to even the smallest detail. Where a surface presents the possibility for a freer use of form—for example, in the rendering of hair and feathers, of water and stone— it is usual to repeat regularly the same form-motif. In distinct contrast to the tumultuous effervescence of hair and beard, horse's mane etc., from the end of the third century, there appears the monotonous dividing and stratifying of the locks in the reliefs on the Arch of Constantine (Fig. 37) or on contemporary Early Christian sarcophagi. We find everywhere the same mechanical partitioning of the form, for example, in the rendering of the feathers on Victory's wings and of the folds of her

39. *Adlocutio militum* of Galerius. Relief on the Arch of Galerius, Thessalonika, ca. A.D. 300

drapery (Fig. 38). Most striking in this abstract regularity is the way in which rock formations are rendered in the form of a honeycomb (Fig. 47: lower angle).

Particularly characteristic of the new type of composition is the mechanical unity achieved by symmetry which around the year 300 replaces the organic unity achieved by living group formations. In the reliefs on the Arch of Galerius in Thessalonika, from ca. A.D. 300, the endeavor is manifest to symmetrize the composition around the Emperor, or the Emperors. In the representation of the *Adlocutio Militum* of Galerius (Fig. 39), the whole pyramidal composition is topped by the head of the Emperor; his mighty body, arising powerfully above the surrounding figures, is placed in the middle of the two wings of soldiers, in rows gradually sloping downwards. In the composition one perceives the strong lines of an isosceles triangle with its apex, the Emperor's head.

In the four-emperor relief on the same arch (Fig. 40) the symmetry penetrates even deeper into the whole construction of the composition. The group of Emperors takes the dominating central position in the picture; at the center are the two augusti enthroned, each upon his heavenly vault formed by a drapery arched dome-like over a bust of a sky-god; each has his assisting caesar beside him and they are both being crowned by a small Victory hovering between the caesars and augusti. In the side-fields the figures are made symmetric around the central group, as is evident in the reclining figure in each corner—Oceanus in the left, Tellus in the right—and in the figures hastening towards the emperors—Rome on the left, Mars on the right. In spite of their difference as iconographic types, these last two gods correspond to each other symmetrically in their position, movement, attributes (trophy and helmet), as do also the figures that frame them.

We find similar symmetrical compositions on contemporary sarcophagi; for example, a sarcophagus from ca. A.D. 300, in the Terme Museum, Rome (Fig. 41). The turbulent, excited life of the departing third century is still present in the fluttering individual forms, in the sharp, jerky movements, and in the wind-blown hair and drapery forms. All the more remarkable is the unmistakable effort to bring the whole composition to rest in a symmetric order. At the center of the relief stands the main figure: the toga-clad deceased. All the other components of the relief—the two banner-bearers (*vexillarii*), the trophies—are placed symmetrically around the central figure as corresponding, objectively homo-

40. Four-Emperor relief on the Arch of Galerius, Thessalonika, ca. A.D. 300

41. Sarcophagus, Terme Museum, Rome, ca. A.D. 300

geneous pairs. The iron grip of symmetry and the uniformness of the figures within the separate symmetrical pairs
are carried through also in the details, as can be seen,
for example, in the swords of the soldiers, the *vexilla*, and
in the swords hanging on the two trophies.

A good ten years later, as seen in the reliefs on the
Arch of Constantine discussed above, the symmetric
crystallization of the composition is complete. In both
Oratio and *Liberalitas* the Emperor appears—elevated
upon the Rostra or sitting upon his high throne—as the
dominating central figure, with rows of acclaiming and
jubilant figures surrounding him symmetrically and subordinated to him. In *Liberalitas* (Fig. 36) the central
section with the Emperor enthroned above the cubic
pedestal, is framed by perfectly symmetric architectural
settings on either side. The structures are divided into
a first and a second story, and the second story is again
divided into two completely equal loggia-like rooms,
where the symmetry is extended also to the furnishings.
Indeed, even the human figures represented in the two
loggias of the two side sections—four male figures who
take part in the distributing and receiving of the imperial

94

gift—are subject to the same law of symmetry (Figs. 42, 43). On the floor in the middle, between the four active figures, stands a coffer full of money. In the part of the loggia which lies farthest to the right in the right-hand section, and in the corresponding part to the left in the left-hand section, a man wearing a paenula comes out of a hatchway from the story below and protrudes halfway into the loggia to receive the gift of money in his paenula. Opposite him in the other corner of the loggia, a high state official in the toga is sitting on a chair, holding a diptycon or a scroll. Before him a lower official, wearing a simple tunic, empties the gift of money from a tray into the paenula of the recipient. Between this official and the recipient appears still another high official, again in the toga. The whole complicated scene with roll call and accounting, distribution and receipt of the monetary gift, is repeated thus in each loggia according to exactly the same pattern, and on both sides of the enthroned emperor at the center of the relief the self-same pattern is reversed, in keeping with the laws of symmetry.[13]

The acclaiming citizens who fill the lower zone in both wings of the picture both in *Oratio* and in *Liberalitas*, as noted above, do not stand in natural groupings in free and open space, but are placed side by side against the firm plane of the ground—in *Oratio* in two parallel rows (Fig. 44), in *Liberalitas* in one single row (Fig. 36). Because the figures are thus placed side by side, not gliding behind one another in depth and disappearing into the background, they all appear with the same substantial weight and fullness, with the same degree of volume. Thus one could say that they appear as equal units. This impression is further strengthened by the avoidance, as far as possible, of rhythmic contractions or dispersions of the figures. No melodic undulating movement goes

[13] L'Orange—von Gerkan, *op.cit.*, pp. 89 ff. Pls. 5 b, 16, 17, 22.

42. Detail of *Liberalitas* in Fig. 36: loggia farthest left

through these rows of figures, only the monotonous
cadence of equal units.[14] The uniformity of the figures
is accentuated also by the arrangement of the individuals
in the row according to the same horizontal axes: their
heads, feet, etc., are on the same line. Particularly in the
two parallel rows in *Oratio* (Fig. 44) do the figures
unite, between distinct horizontal lines, to form a compact mass, and they rise like parallel walls one above another. Such solid masses of figures were to the organic
figure-groups of classical times as the collective corporations of the Dominate are to the free organizations of the
earlier Empire.

The emphasizing of horizontal dividing dominants
of this kind derives from a totally new order of form
which—as we saw it above—subordinates the whole
pictorial scenery to the coordinate system of the frame.
The horizontal and vertical lines of the frame exercise a

[14] Cf. G. Rodenwaldt, "Reihung identischer Glieder," *SBBerl*, 1933,
pp. 1036 f.

43. Detail of *Liberalitas* in Fig. 36: loggia farthest right

new compulsion upon the composition of both the architectural and figurative scenes. Thus, for example, in
Liberalitas, the framing fillets of the relief determine the
divisions into the loggia-formed enclosures. And with
similar effect the architectural elements in the *Oratio* are
made parallel with the rectangle of the frame—indeed,
the accentuated horizontal line of the upper edge of the
background architecture coincides partly with the fillet
of the relief's frame. But also the whole scene of figures
is made to conform with the vertical and horizontal lines
of the frame. It is, for example, remarkable how in the
double row of figures in both wings of *Oratio*, each row
is enclosed in a rectangle conforming to the framework;
particularly marked is the horizontal line formed by the
crowns of the heads in each rectangle. It is no coincidence
that the block joint running through the middle of the
whole relief and forming a dominating horizontal dividing line coincides with and sets off the line formed by the

97

44. Left wing of *Oratio* in Fig. 35

crowns of the heads in the lower row (Fig. 44). If one studies the single figures on the reliefs of the Arch of Constantine, as for example the hovering Victories with trophies in the spandrels of the main archway (Figs. 45-46), one may realize the power that the outer frame exercises in the whole design. The upper part of the body is straightened as vertically as possible, while the lower part of the body swings out horizontally, and the trophy in Victory's hands bends concentrically with the curved frame of the arch underneath. Also in a peculiar stair-like construction (for example, Fig. 47) the figures are made to conform to the frame. *The weaker the organic integrity of the figure, the greater the pliancy of its separate parts toward the force of the outer framework:* we have found analogous the relationship in contemporary life between individuals and community, between the

98

city and the provinces on the one side and the fixed blocks of the new state on the other. As a post-Constantinian example of this total subordination of all the figure elements under the coordinates of the framework, we reproduce here two reliefs on the base of the Theodosius Obelisk on the hippodrome in Constantinople (Figs. 48, 49).

We emphasize finally how characteristic the absence of open space around the figures is for the entire expression in these compositions. The figure is bound to the row, just as the soldier to his rank or file, and the row in turn to the narrow space before the plane of the ground. The figures are restricted to this narrow space; they can neither press forward toward the viewer nor recede into the depths of a background.[15] The only pos-

---

[15] In *Oratio* the breaking down of the natural space and the mechanical division of it into layers parallel to the background is particularly noticeable. As the locality here represented, namely the Forum Romanum, is still preserved, the artist's transformation of it can be analyzed in a very concrete way. We see in the background the buildings which frame the Forum, from right to left the Arch of Septimius-Severus, the Rostra, the Arch of Tiberius, the Basilica Julia. While in reality the Basilica Julia is placed at a right angle to the Rostra and the fronts of the two arches, in the relief it is projected into the plane of the relief and receives the same front as the other three monuments. Thus the four buildings do not enclose, as in reality, a three-dimensional space, but are arranged into one *stratum* parallel with the ground of the relief. As with the Forum architecture, so also with the crowds which fill the space enclosed by the buildings. Of course, these crowds, who are listening to Constantine's speech from the Rostra, in reality are gathered together in the large open space in front of the Rostra and push forth in depth toward the speaker. However, to avoid the natural development in depth, the artist projects the crowd into the plane and places the figures at each side of the Rostra where it divides into double rows in narrow strata parallel to the ground. In effect it is precisely the same which has occurred in *Liberalitas*. The architecture of the two wings should, in reality, be seen in perspective, parallel to each other, leading in towards the emperor and senators in an apse-like termination at the end of the room. And again, the crowds of people who throng

99

sible movement is along the axis of a plane parallel to
the ground; but in this plane any movement is prevented
by the symmetric order which keeps the figures firmly in
position, subordinated to the central figure. Thus, in a
peculiar way the figures are *immobilized*—just as in real
life individuals were firmly tied by the Dominate to their
state duties, their *munera*, the place of their employment
and property (pp. 4 f.).

Row formations of the type we are studying, accommodate and simplify the symmetrical arrangement of
the composition and strengthen the expression of subordination to the central figure. In quite a different way
than in traditional art where the figures moved more

together in the large open space before the emperor and between the
loggia-constructions, are projected into the plane and placed to both
sides of the enthroned Majesty dividing into rows parallel with the
plane of the ground. Cf. L'Orange—von Gerkan, *op.cit.*, pp. 81, 86
f., 98.

45-46. Victories with trophies in spandrels of main archway,
Arch of Constantine, A.D. 312-315

freely in space, it now becomes possible to direct all the
elements towards the emperor in the center, in order to
experience the irresistible magnetic charge emanating
from him and the higher order to which he belongs. It
is the divine Empire which is represented in this supernatural, immovable, and therefore unchangeable constellation of figures and architecture. The figures in the
symmetrical rows are often seen in profile and they are
generally directed inward towards the emperor at the
center. The emperor himself, on the other hand, is represented frontally and thus directed out of the relief; he
interrupts the narrative continuity just as the God-Emper-
or himself is placed above the life of mortals, and just as
the imperial ceremonial isolates him in a divine image
raised above the world of the living. The very essence

47. River god on Arch of Constantine, A.D. 312-315

of the *dominus* is expressed in this arrangement: his central position in the state, the dependence and subordination of all citizens on him, his superhuman nature. Here is created a compositional scheme expressing the *maiestas domini*, which was to be of fundamental importance for the official art of Late Antiquity and the Middle Ages.

Let us choose as an example of this scheme the famous silver emperor-image in Madrid, representing the Emperor Theodosius enthroned between his co-emperors, Valentinian and Arcadius (Fig. 24). It is not the laws of life and nature which are at work in the grouping of these figures and in their placement within architecture and space. A new order has replaced that of life and nature, a kind of crystallic order: the whole complex of forms is symmetrized around the supernaturally large figure of Theodosius, the groups of figures on both sides arise pyramidally towards him, and pyramidally the gable gathers the architecture around him. The whole Emperor-ideology of Late Antiquity, the sacred absolutism has become evident in this transformation and spiritualization of natural form. The Emperor is God himself on earth. He is the center in a kind of superhuman symmetry, he is the apex of the pyramid of the hierarchy of the state. The emperor-image is a devotional picture.

The church took over this compositional scheme from the state. As an example we illustrate a sarcophagus in Milan, from ca. 400 (Fig. 50). Here it is Christ who is placed at the center, raised high above his surroundings, and here it is the Apostles who are disposed in symmetric rows beneath the central figure. And again this central figure breaks through human context: while the Apostles are facing Christ, Christ is facing frontally toward the viewer like a cult statue to be worshiped. The higher static order, which in the imperial images on the Arch of Constantine are imposed upon the human world, is in the image of Christ sublimated into an expression of the transcendent beauty and regularity of the Kingdom of God. Just as the Emperor in *Liberalitas* made a donation to the people, so also Christ in our relief; but Constantine gave a gift of money to the Roman citizens, Christ gives to all humanity the *nova lex* of the Christian world order (the book-roll in Christ's left hand, presented to Peter). And as the citizens in *Liberalitas* receive the gift with one hand lifted in acclamation, so also the Apostles around Christ: but the citizens are giving thanks for a gift of money, the Apostles are rejoicing in a celestial gift of grace. While, finally, the Emperor is raised up upon a historic tribune, so Christ is elevated

48. Theodosius presiding at circus games. Relief at base of Theodosius Obelisk, Constantinople hippodrome. End of IV cent.

to the Mount of Paradise, with the jewel-adorned walls and gates of the Heavenly Jerusalem behind him. *Civitas domini*, which is reflected in the buildings of Forum Romanum surrounding Constantine, has become *civitas Dei.*

The Christian expression of supernatural transcendence in these row formations and symmetries becomes ever more manifest—with the intensification of the mystic— in the development of Late Antique and Early Christian art. We reproduce as an example the apse mosaic in Santa Maria in Domnica in Rome (Fig. 51): Christ between Archangels and Apostles in an upper zone, and the Infant Christ on Mary's lap surrounded by throngs of angels in the apse vault below (817-824).

49. Theodosius enthroned at circus games. Relief at base of Theodosius Obelisk, Constantinople hippodrome. End of IV cent.

PORTRAIT SCULPTURE

Throughout the first three centuries of the Empire the Roman portraits, in continuation of the Hellenistic portrait tradition, seek *always*—however different the stylistic currents may be—to convey personal individuality: and this individuality is *always*, still in continuation of the Hellenistic portrait tradition, "life-like," that is, endowed with a natural, animated countenance. Portrait sculpture from the first three centuries of the Empire presents, therefore, *lifelike individuals*. Around A.D. 300 a fundamental change took place in this form of portraiture.[16]

[16] Fundamental for the history of portraiture in Late Antiquity is R. Delbrück, *Spätantike Kaiserporträts*, Berlin, 1933. A good account

50. Paleochristian sarcophagus, Sant'Ambrogio in Milan. End of IV cent.

Let us take as our point of departure the peculiarly anxiety-filled, glimmeringly mobile portraits from the middle of the third century. The intention is not only to render the individual physiognomic features, but also to represent them in the movement of life. To a degree unparalleled in ancient art the whole personality is caught in a snapshot, in transitory movement, in a sudden glimpse. Thus also the realistic determination of time is introduced in portraiture. The image does not only intend to give the objective physiognomical forms, it also aims at revealing them in time, in the very movement of life, at depicting the play of features in the nervous face, the very flash of personality. Take, for example, the quivering, lifelike image in a sculpture characteristic of this period, for instance the marvelous portrait

---

of the development in the portrait of Late Antiquity is given by G. von Kaschnitz Weinberg, "Spät-römische Porträts," *Die Antike*, 2, 1926, pp. 36 ff. A broad collection of chronologically arranged material on the history of portraiture from the middle of the third to the end of the fifth century is given in my above-mentioned work, *Studien zur Geschichte des spätantiken Porträts*, Oslo, 1933.

of the Emperor Decius (Fig. 52) in Oslo (249-251). The sideways turning of the head expresses movement, and so does the entire facial composition. Notice the stress that is laid upon asymmetrical constellations of folds and wrinkles, especially striking in the muscles of the forehead and round the mouth with their violent, undulating furrows. Such asymmetries do away with all sorts of stability, firmness, and permanence of form, creating, one might say, a physiognomic situation, only fleetingly possible and bound to change every moment—that is, a constellation suggesting movement. The forehead, for instance, is furrowed by deep but sketchy traces of the chisel: not the furrows themselves as permanently existing lines, but the play of light in them when moving like shifting shadows over the forehead. This also is true for hair and beard: not a plastic chiseling of the individual locks of hair, but a pointillistic hatching and stippling of the forms, so that only at a distance and under the play of light does one get the illusion of hair. It is a technique principally reckoning with the same optic effects as did the impressionistic color decomposi-

51. Apse mosaic in Santa Maria in Domnica, Rome, A.D. 817-824

52. Portrait bust of Decius, private collection, Oslo. A.D. 249-251

53. Portrait bust of Philippus Arabs, A.D. 244-249, Vatican

tion of the last century, and in both cases the new illusionistic style springs from the older more plastic sense of form. The development follows the same line as in the nineteenth century: impressionism develops from the older realism.

This impressionism, culminating towards the middle of the third century, has produced some of the greatest achievements in ancient portraiture. A thrilling human document is the portrait of Philipus Arabs (244-249) (Fig. 53). With a great simplifying touch the artist has managed to concentrate physiognomic life in *one* characteristic sweep. The central motif is the threatening lowering of the brows, corresponding to convulsions of the forehead muscles and responding to nervous contractions of the muscles of the mouth. The psychological picture achieves an almost uncanny intensity. Behind the quivering features the very expression seems to change and move, flashing like a flickering flame over the face.

Such portraits represent, as we have said, the Roman art that dominates the period around the middle of the third century. We find here an impressionism able to capture in marble the very movement of reality, the very shifting fluctuations of psychic life. In the course of two generations, however, this art was totally transformed, its seething life had vanished in abstraction (Figs. 61, 62). The face no longer vibrates in the current stream of time; the features suddenly stiffen in an expressive Medusa-like mask. The inner life—a life beyond space and time—has been stamped in its large and immovable features.

How can one explain this radical change in the portrait form and intention in the latter part of the third century? Impressionism itself, we may answer, produced—in Antiquity as in modern times—the artistic means, rendering possible the break-through of the new form. To give an intense and spontaneous illusion of living, moving reality, form was accentuated so that it fluctuated entirely according to its expressive power, its possibility of giving life in motion. One availed oneself of a decompositional technique reducing plastic values into optical ones and dissolving reality in an illusionary glimmer. The artist thus obtained in the very service of reality, a constantly increasing liberty in relation to the exact details of it. And thereby infinite new possibilities were opened. In the last generation of the third century the overaccentuation of the expressive forms, the dissolving of plastic details, the pointillistic technique becomes ever more predominant. Expression is more and more concentrated in masklike lines. Thus by degrees arises a system of free means of expression, rendering possible a revelation of entirely new psychic contents. These new contents represent the man of Late Antiquity: the inner and spiritual human being, the "pneumatic" personality, to speak in the language of that period. An "abstract" or "expressionistic" portrait, to use the modern term, comes to life.

We select as examples two male heads from shortly before the turn of the third century (Figs. 54, 55). The conflict between the new endeavors and the traditional impressionistic cliché is evident. The abstract articulation of the eyes, the distant glance beyond time, derives from the new aim of expression. But still tradition is at work quivering in momentary life, even though about to stiffen into an abstract serenity which spreads from the eyes to the entire face. The uneasy almost pained movements which run across the surface in asymmetric flickers, are confined in a peculiar way to certain areas of the face, particularly to the muscles of the forehead; they do not emanate from an organic emotion embracing the whole. Thus the physiognomic life is shattered and

54. Portrait head from end of III cent., National Museum, Naples

55. Portrait head from end of III cent., Ny Carlsberg Glyptothek,
Copenhagen

burst, the nervous play stiffens into cramps and convulsions. One must compare the peculiar disintegrated
compositions and the strange marionette-like movements
in the contemporary art of sarcophagi (pp. 88 ff.; Figs.
32-34): a dissolving in the sphere of art which, as we
have seen, coincides with the anarchic conditions of the
spiritual and material existence of the period (pp. 39 f.).

Contemporaneous with this disintegration of traditional
organic form is a new feeling for the compact mass, the
"stereometric" form.[17] As examples we reproduce three
portrait busts from the period around A.D. 300, one from
the Latin, two from the Greek region of the Empire[18]
(Figs. 56-60). The same blocklike simplification of the
organic form asserts itself everywhere. At the same time
there is a weakening of the individualizing facial features; they no longer evolve from deep within a thoroughly articulate head structure, but reside in their own layer
on the outside of the block. As demonstrated by coin
portraits, this new portrait style first appeared in the
eastern part of the Empire;[19] it is first found on coins
struck by the mints in Nicomedia, Kyzikos, Antioch, and
Alexandria. But the style soon becomes common in all
the provinces of the Empire, even though the West
Roman and, to an even greater extent, the local Greek
portrait always preserves more of the traditional organic
form structure. This new, immobile, blocklike form
which strikes through physiognomic articulation has its
striking parallels in the contemporary cubic palace style
(pp. 70 ff.), in the massive wall formations that now
absorb the traditional décor in architecture (pp. 16 ff.),
in the compact row formations of figurative art (p. 96)
—indeed, in the whole militaristic way of life character-

[17] L'Orange, *Studien*, p. 37.   [18] *Ibid.*, figs. 51-58, 64.
[19] *Ibid.*, p. 25.

istic of the period, which makes individuals disappear into columns and squares (pp. 7 f.).

Characteristic of the development throughout the following decades is an increasingly regular and more statuesque block form as illustrated by a porphyry portrait (Fig. 61) of an emperor in the museum in Cairo.[20] The structure of the head and the features of the face are confined within large, clearly defined flat or curved planes, individual forms, such as wrinkles, furrows, locks of hair, become more and more firmly symmetrized according to the vertical axis of the face. It is thus again, as we saw in the reliefs, a sort of mechanical way of planning the modeling which replaces the organic way that had already disintegrated.[21]

The portrait in Cairo is of Eastern origin and more advanced in the new tendency than West Roman portraits. But these also follow, as has been indicated, the same line of development. A late tetrarchic portrait in the Vatican (Fig. 62) and the famous Dogmatius portrait in the Lateran (Fig. 63), dated by an inscription to the late Constantinian period (A.D. 323-337), demonstrate two steps in the advancing process of stereometric crystallization in western Roman art. The impressionistic glimmer, the fleeting asymmetries in the skin and muscular surface are smoothed out. All the creases in muscle and skin are simplified in clear, regular strokes. The eye no longer flickers, but rests immobile upon a point in the distance. In the portrait of Dogmatius we find the full stereometric simplification of the whole complex of form and the strict symmetric subordination of all the individual forms according to the central axis of the face.

[20] R. Delbrück, *Antike Porphyrwerke*, Berlin, 1932, pp. 92 f., pls. 38 f. L'Orange, *Studien*, pp. 22 ff., figs. 42, 44.

[21] L'Orange, *op.cit.*, pp. 21 f., 53 f., 56, 64 f. A. Riegl, *Spätröm. Kunstindustrie*, pp. 48 f., Vienna, 1901-1923.

56-59. Two portrait heads from ca. A.D. 300, National Museum, Athens

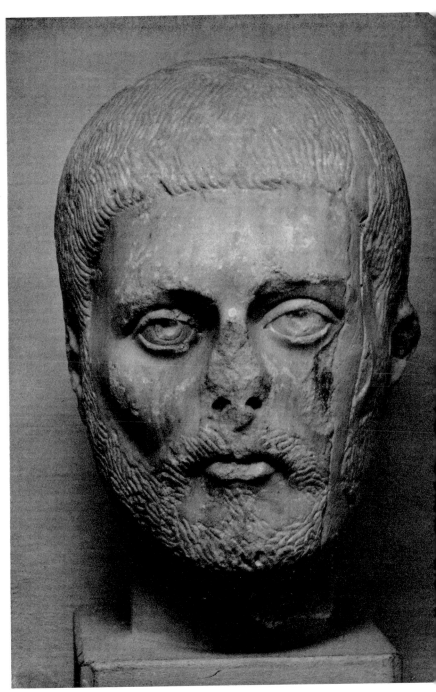

60. Portrait head from ca. A.D. 300, Museum of Bardo

61. Porphyry portrait bust of an emperor, probably Licinius,
A.D. 307-323, Museum of Cairo

62. Portrait head from the late Tetrarchy, Vatican

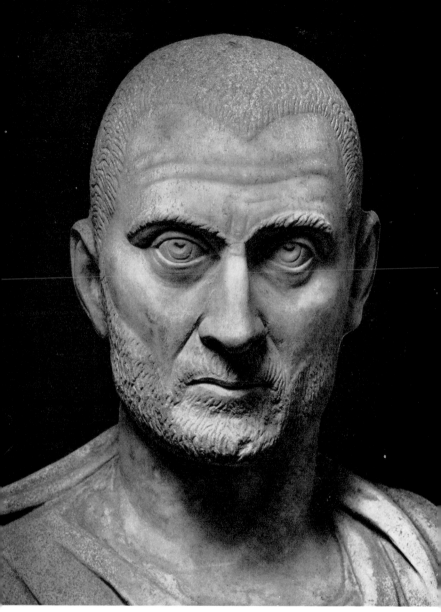

63. Head of portrait statue of Dogmatius, A.D. 323-377, Lateran, Rome

The cap of hair is outlined by mathematically regular contours with the point of its "widow's peak" in the axis, the furrows of the forehead undulate in severe parallel curves, the eyes are framed by concentric arches. Instead of the quivering life of the surface a crystallic reflection of the inner abstract life. No longer the flashing play of features, but a permanent expressive mask. In this mask the eyes in their frame of intensifying curves dominate the total expression.

As the vivid organic nature now gives way to a very firm regularity, so the individual to the type. We have seen in the portrayal of saints (pp. 24 ff.) how the natural human features yield to a higher stereotypy which characterizes the unchangeable nature of the holy and indicates their position in an eternal hierarchical order. The saints, therefore, appear identical. A similar stereotypy also asserts itself, beginning with the tetrarchic period, in the portrayal of the emperors. We have listened to the panegyrist's praise of the *similitudo* of Diocletian and Maximian (pp. 46 ff.). And we hear further how this ideal similarity rests upon their common divine essence. An unchangeable "holy type" (p. 50) permeates all earthly chance and marks the facial features of the God-Emperors.

However, it was not the emperor-image of the Tetrarchy which was to become definitive in the sacred typology of the Empire. It was Constantine's universal monarchy (from 324), heir to the Tetrarchy, which in its emperor image was to create the lasting emperor ideal. The type emerges with such portraits as the colossal head of Constantine in the Palazzo dei Conservatori in Rome, which originally surmounted the enormous statue of the enthroned emperor in his Basilica at Forum Romanum (Fig. 64). The head faces front, originally in the axis of the basilica. It is built up by clearly defined planes

64. Colossal head of Constantine, Palazzo dei Conservatori, Rome

65. Colossal bronze head of emperor, probably Constantius II,
A.D. 323-361, Palazzo dei Conservatori, Rome
66. Imperial portrait from v cent. A.D., Ny Carlsberg Glyptothek,
Copenhagen

that are outlined by geometrically regular curves, the separate elements submit to the strict symmetry around the center axis of the face; the cranium is rounded dome-like, the hair closes about the forehead and temples in a complete archivolt of locks where the center lock is the keystone; the eyes, eyelids, and eyebrows conform to the system of concentric arches and curve one above another, arcade over arcade. Every movement has subsided. The features, the whole face rests firmly within the imperturbable order of eternity.

The eyes, being supernaturally large and wide-open and framed by the accentuated concentric curves of the deepcut lids and brows, express more clearly than ever the transcendence of the ruler's personality. In this gaze he travels far beyond his physical surroundings and attains his goal in a higher sphere, in contact and identity with the governing powers. Providence in person, the irresistible controller of fate, *fatorum arbiter*, rises before us, with all the future on his knees. The imperial ideology of the time is crystallized in this face. It makes us think of those representative scenes in art or in life, where the emperor appears as judge of the world, as cosmocrator, as μοῖρα and *fatum*. His throne is set in the hub of the universe, he is the very law of cosmic motion, *rector totius orbis*, with the wheel of the zodiac in his hand. The head is an expression of the emperor's divine power, his *divina maiestas*, rather than a portrait of an individual man. We are confronted with the "holy countenance" of this power, and we experience ourselves the significance and reality of such terms as *sacer vultus, sacrum os, divinus vultus*, generally applied to the effigy of the emperors of Late Antiquity (compare Figs. 65, 66).[22]

Do we not perceive, we ask in the end, behind this image type, the solemn ritual style in the personal appearance of the emperor? Do we not receive a glimpse of the ceremonial symmetry around the emperor's immobile figure—around this glittering *caeleste miraculum* described in contemporary sources? The living emperor appears in a peculiar statuesque way, monumentally elevated over the world of mortals. Ammianus Marcellinus (16,10) has drawn a famous picture of Constantius II on his entry into Rome—a picture of the living Emperor which can be compared to the imperial portrait-type we have been studying. "He looked so stiffly ahead as if he had an iron band about his neck and he turned his face neither to the right nor to the left, he was not as a

[22] L'Orange, *Apotheosis in Ancient Portraiture*, Oslo, 1947, pp. 116 ff.

living person, but as an image." (*Nec dextra vultum, nec laeva flectebat; tamquam figmentum hominis.*) This hieratic emperor style, which, as an expression of *divina maiestas*, in the same way leaves its mark upon palace (pp. 73 ff.), image, and living reality, can furthermore be traced through Byzantium all the way down to the Holy Russian Empire. With words that in a striking way remind us of Ammianus', Bertel Gripenberg recounts his childhood impressions of Alexander III: "He stared straight ahead, and his features were as immovable as those of a statue. A man of stone, a personification of power and fate."[23]

[23] A. Boëthius has collocated these striking parallel passages. B. Gripenberg, *Det var de tiderna*, quoted from A. Boëthius in *Svenska Dagbladet*, 4.5. 1944. Cf. O. Treitinger, *Die oström. Kaiser und Reichsidee*, Jena, 1938, p. 235.

CONCLUSION

IN THIS study we have attempted to demonstrate how the disintegration of society under the Principate and the establishment of a new order under the Dominate were accompanied by a parallel break-up and reorganization in the world of art. We have, for instance, seen how the new "block-style" in art emerged contemporary with the formation of massive structures in the state and community, and how in both contexts the traditional individualization and articulation of the various elements were gradually reduced or disappeared altogether.

Such a correspondence between the structure of the state and the forms in art would be easy to comprehend if the arts were directed by the state and if the stylistic form, so to speak, were derived from the state itself as a reflection of the state system and as a servant of the state's intentions. As we have seen, however, the new language of art forms emerged *spontaneously*, as a result of a profound logical development within art itself, and not simply by mirroring the development in another sector of human activity, although it may also be true that reciprocal influences between the various activities were present and played their part in the total development. The new solutions in architecture and art were, as we have seen, at each step the result of a natural development of certain stylistic predispositions of the preceding artistic situation, as the consequence of special qualities inherent in the material itself. The similarity between the form of practical organization and that of free art was thus based upon a deeper identity than that of a simple reflection: namely, upon the need of a specific mentality for identical form in all sectors of life; in other words, both the form of practical organization and of free art were the expression of the spiritual mentality of the period.

We can, therefore, speak about autonomous courses of *evolution* and *devolution* which run parallel in both the world of art and society. Thus the disintegrated Empire and the anarchical conditions of the second half of the third century formed, as we have seen, a striking parallel to the "burst" pictures and physiognomically "decomposed" portraits in contemporary art. But just as striking is the parallel between the structure of society and of art during the reaction to the anarchy which followed under Diocletian. And again we see that identical solutions were reached, not as a reflection, but independently of each other. They emerged as a logical consequence of particular qualities inherent in each of the two spheres of human activity. The new tetrarchical order of state which grew up as the solution to the acute political situation, showed in its characteristic features—symmetry, row formations, mechanical coordination—exactly the same pattern of composition that became dominant in contemporary art. But also in art, this pattern of composition was a solution resulting from the special predispositions within the proper field of form during the previous period. It is the spontaneous reaction to the "burst" type of composition—the disjointed pictorial elements cry for a new order.

Should we summarize the basic characteristics of the structural change taking place in the transition from Principate to Dominate they would appear perhaps with greatest clarity when seen under two aspects: that of massive simplification and that of mechanical crystallization. Let us briefly sum up our investigation under these two aspects.

To the massive, all-absorbing formations in the life of

state and society correspond the distinctive compact form creations in contemporary architecture and art. Here also the individual articulations disappear into immovable blocklike solids. We have seen in portrait sculpture how the decline in the plastic differentiation of the form corresponded to a new feeling for the solid mass. The block form which here breaks through the physiognomical features has its striking parallels in the contemporary cubic palace style and the solid wall formations which now absorb the traditional decoration in architecture. And everywhere the block tends towards crystallized regularity and static repose.

In the whole of conceptual life there is a movement away from the complex towards the simple, from the mobile towards the static, from the dialectic and relative towards the dogmatic and the authoritarian, from the empirical towards theology and theosophy. There is a trend towards plain, uncomplicated absolutes which are imperturbably fixed in themselves. In this way the historical victory tends, as we have seen, to become "the eternal victory"; the historical victor to become the absolute victor, "the universal victor," "the victor over all people." When actions or things are embodied in such absolutes, their individual outlines and their adaptability to situations, everything relative, dialectical, and mobile, disappear; they all become alike and come to rest in this similarity.

In the same way figurative art moves away from the animated forms of nature towards a firm and unflexible typology, from plastic articulation to conceptual image, from body to symbol. The concrete representation of nature is forced into a simplified, idealized image and comes to rest within this image. Thus, as we have seen in the depiction of saints and emperors, the individual human features give way to a higher order of types which

67. Row of saints in Sant'Apollinare Nuovo, Ravenna

characterizes the immutable essence of the holy one. Here is a sacral stereotypy which fixes the divine essence of emperors and saints and at the same time indicates their place in an unalterable hierarchical order.

A static world of types and eternal orders: it is towards this—cutting through our diverse and changeable reality —that Late Antiquity's transcendent glance is directed. In this way art tries to capture the exalted, unchangeable regularities behind the shifting multiplicity of our world. A fixed, mechanical coordination replaces the free groupings in earlier art. In the large relief compositions the free space around the figures disappears; they lose their mobility. At the same time the figures are usually placed in rows with an infinite repetition of identical elements (Fig. 67). And this system is made even firmer by the rows of identical elements or pairs of identical elements being symmetrized around a fixed center. The greatest solidity in the static system is achieved when the main axes of the composition are made parallel to the framework, whereby all the pictorial elements are fixed within a geometrical coordinate system.

A similar placing of the contents within an immovable static order is brought about with the systematizing of belief and teaching, which during Late Antiquity totally changes the manifold religiousness and dialectical wisdom of Antiquity. The Neo-Platonism after Plotinus becomes a speculative theology which combines the various classical cults into a systematic whole and brings religious movement, with the exception of Christianity, to a standstill. The philosophical theology of "the Hellenistic Scholastic" Proclos (A.D. 410-485) marks the final point of this process. The religions and philosophical doctrines of Antiquity arise with fossilized authority in his all-embracing system which transforms the Greek world of ideas into a "hierarchy of mythologemes."[1] Also in the doctrines of Christian teaching the theological dialectic of earlier times gives way to increasingly authoritarian and immovable conceptions.[2] During the third and fourth centuries, on the basis of the theology of Clemens and Origenes, a constantly more systematic elaboration of doctrine takes place, which in the end is crystallized into the Catholic dogma. As we have seen, the characteristic Late Antique endeavor of the Christian Empire, to bring the whole religious life under the fixed norms of a "state church," is already apparent under Aurelian and the Tetrarchy.

[1] W. Windelband - A. Goedeckemeyer, *Geschichte der abendländischen Philosophie im Altertum* (Handb. d. klass. Altertumswiss., v, 1, 1, 1923), Munich, 1923, p. 295.

[2] A. von Harnack, *Grundriss der Dogmengeschichte*, pp. 150, 209, 232 f., 235. Windelband-Goedeckemeyer, *op.cit.*, pp. 301, 284 ff.

Conclusion

Thus, in all fields of human endeavor the process of *evolution* and *devolution* tends towards simplified, massive, and at the same time statically fixed forms. Is it not as if life itself, during this great, dangerous, all-encompassing metamorphosis leading from Antiquity to the Middle Ages, armors and encloses itself in these massive blocks and unbreakable rigid systems in the spheres of state, art, and religion? Thus Rome and Constantinople and behind the *limes* the whole Roman Empire, at this period literally armored and enclosed themselves within the hard shell of the most powerful fortifications of Antiquity. Is it not as if life itself, both of the spirit and of the body, sacrificed liberty and mobility to security and permanence? Who knows if the seed could have survived without this firm shell.